THE PLAY OF
WISDOM

AMS Studies in the Middle Ages, No. 14
ISSN: 0270-6261

THE PLAY OF WISDOM

Its Texts and Contexts

Edited by
Milla Cozart Riggio

AMS Press
New York

COMMITTEE ON
SCHOLARLY EDITIONS

AN APPROVED EDITION

MODERN LANGUAGE
ASSOCIATION OF AMERICA

The Center emblem means that one of a panel of textual experts serving the Center has reviewed the text and textual apparatus of the printer's copy by thorough and scrupulous sampling, and has approved them for sound and consistent editorial principles employed and maximum accuracy attained. The accuracy of the text has been guarded by careful and repeated proofreading according to standards set by the Center.

Library of Congress Cataloging-in-Publication Data

Wisdom (Morality Play). English & English (Middle English)
The Play of Wisdom: its texts and contexts / edited by Milla
Cozart Riggio
(AMS Studies in the Middle Ages: no. 14)
Text in Middle English and Modern English on Facing
Pages. Includes bibliographical references.
ISBN 0-404-61444-2
1. English Drama—Middle English. 1100-1500—Criticism,
Textual. I. Riggio, Milla Cozart.. II. Series.
PS1261.w5   1998
822'. 1—dc20   95-39740
                                                 CIP

All AMS Books are printed on acid-free paper that meets the guidelines for performance and durability of the Committee on Production Guidelines for Book Longevity of the Council on Library Resources.

AMS Press, Inc.
56 East 13th Street
New York, NY 10003-4686 U.S.A.

MANUFACTURED IN THE UNITED STATES OF AMERICA

CONTENTS

For Mildred Cozart
Who without even knowing it pointed me toward the study of Wisdom

Preface

As a child growing up in Arkansas, I heard over and over again that I was living in the only state in the union that was — or at least theoretically could be — self-sufficient. "Build a fence around this state," my family always said, "and we would have everything we need to survive." In a sense, that upbringing lies behind this edition of the play of *Wisdom*. This book is designed to be free-standing and independent. It builds on previous editions of the play, most notably the original Furnivall and Pollard EETS edition and Mark Eccles's more recent EETS edition of the Macro plays and Donald Baker, John Murphy, and Louis Hall, Jr.'s EETS edition of the Digby plays, as well as David Bevington's facsimile transcription of the Macro manuscript. But rather than referring the reader back to those fine editions, I have aimed instead to incorporate into this one volume all the information necessary to the study, analysis, or performance of this play on virtually any level. The scholarly apparatus is designed for those whose interests are in the careful reproduction of texts. The edition itself eclectically blends the two extant manuscripts of the play into one text, but it also draws road maps through the path of assimilation so that the diligent student of textual or linguistic history can sort through the divisions. The modern translation, which began as an acting text, is designed both for students and for performers. If they are successful, the introduction, notes, and glossary should also provide useful information for the scholar, the cultural critic, and the student. At a time when books are expensive to produce and difficult to keep in print, this volume attempts to bridge the gap between the different kinds of editions that often develop in separate volumes: it is intended to be scholarly and yet useful in the classroom, full of crutches for the beginning student, sufficient for actors or directors who wish to produce *Wisdom*, and rigorous enough for early drama specialists.

In the years it has taken to prepare this edition, I have incurred debts I can never begin to repay: to Roger Shoemaker for his fine direction of the Trinity Medieval Festival production of *Wisdom*, in which this project took root; to Donald Baker, Theresa Colletti, John Elliott, Jr., Gail McMurray Gibson, Alexandra Johnston, David Parry, Pamela Sheingorn, and John Woolley for turning the *Wisdom* symposium at Trinity into the launching pad for this book; to Martin Stevens who allowed me to test this text on an NEH summer seminar at Columbia University and who has been a mainstay through the subsequent years; to Steven Spector for providing important information and judiciously reading sections of the book; to Adelaide Bennet of the Princeton Index of Christian Art; to the

National Endowment for the Humanities and the ACLS for supporting grants; to Laetitia Yeandle of the Folger Library, Daniel Traister of Special Collections at the University of Pennsylvania Van Pelt-Dietrich Library, and to the staffs of the Pierpont Morgan Library in New York, the British Library in London, the Bodleian Library at Oxford University, the Cambridge University Library and the numerous college libraries at Cambridge between which I trekked in search of manuscripts and devotional miscellanies.

Martha Driver graciously searched out early printed editions of Suso for me; Michael Sargent guided me to the manuscripts of the works of Hilton, Suso, and other source documents. Michael Davis generously led me to important sources in art history. Pamela Sheingorn first introduced me to the Schützmantel Madonna, and Kathleen Scott provided illustrations. Gerhard Strasser took time from his own research to track down and arrange for photographs from a Suso manuscript in Wolfenbüttel. Meg Twycross helped locate descriptions of British coronation regalia. I also owe thanks to Richard Beadle, Father Edmund Colledge, Ian Doyle, Roger Lovatt, and my colleague in German studies Donald Hook; to the deans and clerical staff of Trinity College, especially Deans Andrew DeRocco, Borden Painter, and Jan Cohn whose tenures in office my work has spanned and who buoyed that work in numerous ways; to my editorial associate Melanie Kulig for her diligent work on the glossary, and to my student research assistants Christopher Foster, Elizabeth Wilner, and Emily Fraser; to the English Department secretary Elestine Nicholson; to John Langeland who has created extraordinary computing capabilities at Trinity College, his assistant Bob Greene, whose computer skills have enabled me to produce this text, and Mary Santomeno for her unstinting courtesy; and to the English Department administrative assistant Margaret Grasso, without whom no project of mine could ever have been realized; to Jack Hopper of AMS Press, who has been both an editor and a friend throughout this venture. And finally, there are those whose service cannot be defined: David Bevington, who was present at the beginning of the project as one of the key participants in the initial production and symposium and who, as a reader for AMS Press, has offered me criticism and editorial assistance beyond imagining. And my husband and children who for the past decade have endured the inevitable days of distraction that this book has occasioned and have in turn distracted me at crucial times.

Milla C. Riggio
Trinity College
April, 1994

INTRODUCTION

THE TEXTS

Of the English Catholic morality plays, *Wisdom* alone exists in two extant manuscripts. The exemplar is a 752-line fragment in Bodleian Library Manuscript Digby 133. The only complete text — that of the Washington, D.C., Folger Manuscript V.a. 354, usually referred to as the Macro manuscript — has almost certainly been copied from the text of which the Digby Ms. is the surviving fragment.

I. Description and Brief History

A. The Digby Text

A paper manuscript, Bodleian MS Digby 133 contains several treatises and tracts written on paper of different sizes, and four plays, also transcribed on different sized paper: *The Conversion of Saint Paul* (fols. 37r-50v), *Mary Magdalen* (fols. 95r-145r), *Candlemas Day and the Killing of the Children of Israel* (fols. 146r-157v), and the first 752 lines of *Wisdom* (fols. 158r-169v), which fill a single quarto gathering of twelve leaves measuring 8 1/2 x 6 2/3 inches, at the end of the manuscript. The watermark for *Wisdom*, the bottom half of which appears on folio 162, the top on fol. 165, and almost all of which appears on 167 and 169, is a hand with a laced wrist and a cross on the palm, surmounted by a five-point star, dated before 1506 (Heawood 294; ctd. by Baker *et al.* lxiii). The scribe, who according to Baker, Murphy, and Hall, also copied *The Killing of the Children*, writes in a somewhat more formal style in *Wisdom* than in *The Killing of the Children*, which is probably later (lxiv). The evidence of the paper, combined with other indications, suggests a date somewhere in the 1480s or early 1490s for the Digby *Wisdom*. The scribe averages thirty to thirty-three lines per page, with some tail-rhyming lines added in the right margin for a maximum of thirty-seven lines in the middle section of the play. He brackets rhyming lines throughout. The speakers' names are written in red ink in the right-hand margin, with stage directions written across the page. Dotted lines separate the speeches. On the bottom of the first four folio sheets, the numerals i, ii, iii, and iv are written.

The early history of Digby 133 is obscure; numbered gatherings indicate that some texts were removed from and added to the original manuscript compilation. Damage to the first and last folios of *Wisdom* suggests that this play probably existed outside the bound volume for some time (Baker *et al.* lxiii). The name or initials of "Myles Blomefylde" appear on three of the plays, *Mary Magdalen*, *The Conversion of Saint Paul*, and *Wisdom*, where "M.B." is written at the top of the first folio. Blomefylde (or Blomefield [1525 - 1603]) was a sixteenth-century alchemist, physician, and avid book collector born at Bury St. Edmunds who lived in Chelmsford, Essex, from the 1460s until his death (L. Stephen, ed., *Dictionary of National Biography*, v, 288 ctd. with other sources by Baker *et al.* xli). Baker, Murphy, and Hall conjecture that the Digby *Wisdom* could have passed to Myles Blomefield through the person of a William Blomfild of Bury St. Edmunds; though there is no external evidence to support this supposition, if accurate it could suggest a Bury St. Edmunds connection for the Digby play. Some Digby plays may have passed to Blomefield by way of the Chelmsford play book; John Coldeway has produced evidence that two of them were performed at Chelmsford (Coldeway 1975 103-21, ctd. by Baker *et al.* xiv-xv). There is no indication that Blomefield owned any portions of the Manuscript except for the three plays which bear his imprint, though Baker, Murphy, and Hall assume he may also have owned *The Killing of the Children* (xiii). The manuscript (or at least some portions of it) came to the Bodleian Library as part of the collection donated by Sir Kenelm Digby in the seventeenth century; three of the works in the manuscript are cited in the 1634 presentation catalogue (MS Digby 2342), but *Wisdom* is listed for the first time, identified only as "A Play" in a 1697 catalogue of materials in the Bodleian Library (Vol. 1, p. 83; ctd by Baker *et al.* x). The manuscript, now bound in a nineteenth-century Bodleian replacement for the seventeenth-century Digby binding, is available for research use at the Bodleian Library. It has been compared in detail with the Macro manuscript for this edition.

B. The Macro Text

Also paper, the Macro manuscript contains three morality plays: *The Castle of Perseverance*, *Wisdom*, and *Mankind*. At some early point the three Macro plays were bound with other manuscripts into a single volume, in which the folios were numbered in the upper right-hand corner with the numbers that are still used. The numbering indicates that *Wisdom* (fols. 98r-121r) was followed by *Mankind* (fols. 122r-134r), and, after other texts, *The Castle of Perseverance* (fols. 154r-191v). In 1820, when the Gurney family acquired the manuscript, the plays were bound into a separate volume with *Mankind* first, followed by *Wisdom* and *The Castle of Perseverance* (Bevington 1972 xvii). In 1936 the Folger Shakespeare Library purchased the manuscript, which in 1971 was unbound to facilitate the facsimile edition of David Bevington, who presented the plays in what he presumed to be the chronological order, with *The Castle of Perseverance* followed by *Wisdom* and *Mankind* (Bevington 1972). The manuscript, restricted from common use because of its delicate condition, is still in the Folger Shakespeare Library. It has been examined and freshly transcribed for this edition.

Wisdom occupies two quarto gatherings of twelve leaves each. The first of these gatherings has been numbered by the scribe in the lower right-hand corner. Some of the numbers have apparently been cropped off, but numbers ii, iii, iv, vi, viii, ix, x, xi (partly cropped), and xii remain. The scribe has a casual style, roughly hybrid secretary with some anglicana features. He averages twenty-three to twenty-five lines per page, with marginal lines in the middle section increasing the total number of lines per page to a maximum of thirty-six. In general, the format of the text follows that of Digby; lines separate the speeches, with speakers' names in the right hand-margin. Though he does not bracket rhyming lines throughout the play, the scribe does follow Digby's bracketing of consecutively rhyming lines beginning with the shift of rhyme scheme at line 325, where he also copies Digby's pattern of placing tail-rhyming lines in the right-hand margin. Unlike the Digby scribe, however, the Macro scribe brackets only those triplet rhymes which precede marginal tail-rhyming lines. He does not follow the Digby practice of bracketing rhymes consistently throughout, nor does he bracket the tail rhymes themselves.

The paper, now cropped, measures approx. 8 2/3 by 7 1/4 inches. The watermark, which appears on leaves 98 - 109, 101 - 106, 103 - 104, 110 - 121, 113 - 118, and 115 - 116, is a tall covered pot with a handle, which appears to resemble Briquet's nos. 12477, dated 1476 - 81, and 12478, dated 1481 and 1484 (Spector 1979 223). On fol. 98v is a page of sketches, centered on a man who appears to have a dragon attached to his back, with a number of dragon heads and one head of a girl scattered around the page. These sketches are not related to *Wisdom*, the text of which continues without interruption from fol. 98r to fol. 99r, indicating that the sketches were on fol. 98v before the beginning of the play was inscribed on the opposite side. The scribe may have overlooked these sketches until he had finished copying his first folio. The doodlings on fol. 98v indicate that the paper was not new. It is reasonable, therefore, to suppose that this text might have been written up to at least a decade or so after the paper was issued. Since it now appears likely that the Macro *Wisdom* is a copy of the full text of the now-fragmented Digby, this date accords with other evidence, to suggest that the Macro text was probably copied sometime during the 1480s, possibly as late as the 1490s, though it could have been as early as the 1470s. The Macro scribe's casual style and his general carelessness throughout leave the impression that this is probably not a manuscript copied in a formal scriptorium. The manuscript may have been used later in a school, since throughout there are schoolboy ciphers, doodlings, and marginal scribblings of various kinds, many in sixteenth-century hands (see Bevington 1972 xix; Gibson 1985 118-20).

The Macro manuscript has long been associated with Bury St. Edmunds. At the bottom of fol. 105 an inscription, probably in an early sixteenth-century hand, reads " . . I Richard Cake of Bury . . . ." Though unable to identify this Richard Cake in her extensive searches through local records in the Bury St. Edmunds area, Gail McMurray Gibson has corrected a misidentification of Richard Cake with "Richard Coke," and she has identified other names which appear in cipher as prominent Bury names, including Plandon (fol. 104r) and Oliver ("Robert Oliver," fols. 101r & 119v; see Gibson 1989 204n; 1985 118-20). The entire Macro manuscript was in the library of Cox Macro, an eighteenth-century citizen of Bury and son of a Bury alderman.

Despite the role the powerful monastery and city of Bury St Edmunds played in the development of East Anglian drama in the fifteenth and early sixteenth centuries, using Bury as a touchstone by which to identify individual texts has created problems. To illustrate: at the end of *Wisdom* (fol. 121r) beside a list of characters in the play appears a Latin inscription, possibly written by the scribe himself, which (with the expansion of some abbreviations) reads "*O liber si quis cui constas forte quaeretur / hyngham que monachio dices super omnia consto*" ("O book, if anyone should perhaps ask to whom you belong, say that I belong above all to Hyngham, a monk"). As the name of a place in Norfolk close to Norwich, Hengham is an East Anglian name frequently assumed by late fifteenth-century monks from the region. At least two monks named Hengham are known to have lived in the vicinity of Norwich after the 1470s, George Hengham, who was at Norwich Cathedral Priory in 1492 and who later became prior at King's Lynn, and a John Hengham, disciplined in Wymondham in 1514 (see Eccles xxviii and Beadle 12). Various city records of Norwich also list at least a half dozen Henghams. But as early as 1912 Walter K. Smart suggested that this "monk Hyngham" might be Richard Hengham, who served as abbot of the monastery at Bury from 1474 - 1479 (86). Even after Richard Beadle pointed out that the popularity of Hengham as an East Anglian name in the fifteenth century makes any such attribution difficult to verify (1984 12), this assumption was widely accepted. Because Hengham would not have called himself "monk" after he became abbot, general agreement established 1474 — a date thought to be too early for Digby 133 — as the *terminus ad quem* for the Macro text, thus creating a set of blinders that long obscured the relationship between the Digby and Macro manuscripts of *Wisdom*.

Recently, however, Richard Beadle has identified the handwriting in the inscription at the end of *Mankind* and *Wisdom* as that of the monk "Thomas Hyngham" who apparently lived at Bury St. Edmunds at least during the 1470s and who inscribed his name as owner ("constat") in a Boethius *De Consolatione Philosophiae* manuscript translated by John Walton (now owned by Martin Schoyen and catalogued as Ms 615 in the Schoyen Checklist 1992 21). This "monk Hyngham" is one of two Thomas Henghams, both monks, known to have owned books in the fifteenth century (Ker 234, 285; James 1912 1: 506; ctd. by Eccles xxxviii).

II. The Relationship Between the Digby and the Macro Texts

The Macro text follows the extant Digby fragment with close fidelity broken only by minor variations in phrases and an occasional omitted line in the Macro text. When the Macro scribe accidentally transposes two speeches, he indicates his error by marginally lettering the misplaced sections "A" and "B" (ll. 637 - 52). The two texts resemble each other closely enough for F. J. Furnivall to have assumed that the same scribe copied both, despite consistent differences in spelling conventions and handwriting styles, which Furnivall overlooked. Since Digby contains five complete lines omitted in Macro (66, 448, 496, 600, and 720), the Digby scribe obviously could not have copied the Macro text, though both could theoretically have copied a third text. Assuming that the Digby text was necessarily later than the Macro, Eccles asserted the two texts to be independent of each other (xxx). Even though Bevington provided some evidence to support his assumption that "the Digby manuscript could not have been copied from the Macro manuscript, whereas the reverse is possible," he did not pursue the argument (1972 xix). Baker, Murphy, and Hall conjectured an earlier, missing exemplar copied by both scribes (lxvi), a presumption which has been generally accepted. However, a careful examination of the manuscripts suggests that this phantom text is not necessary. The Macro *Wisdom* is almost certainly copied from Digby.

Not only is the Macro text (to be referred to as M) unusually close to that of Digby (to be referred to as D), but in a number of instances M has been influenced by scribal choices and accidents not likely to have been present in a common exemplar. To take the most obvious example: the omitted lines. Four of the five D lines omitted in M are tail-rhyming lines from the mid-section of the play. Throughout, such lines are regularly but inconsistently copied in the right-hand margin of the D text. At l. 420, for instance, after 23 straight marginal tail-rhyming lines, D begins to write tail-rhyming lines with flush left margins, rather than to the right of the text. At line 448, he once more writes a line to the right. The first tail-rhyming line omitted by M (l. 448), this line represents a change in the D pattern of transcription, which M has apparently failed to notice; and for the remaining three omitted tail-rhyming lines, the forgotten line is the only marginal line on the D page, and a careless M scribe may simply have overlooked it.

To spell this out in more specific detail: When Lucifer enters the play in line 325, the rhyme scheme changes from Wisdom's consistent pattern of ababbcbc to Lucifer's jauntier scheme of triple-rhyming lines connected by a final rhyme in the pattern aaab cccb, which varies at times to aaab aaab. At first, D consistently places the rhyming lines which recur every fourth line, usually called tail-rhymes, in the right-hand margin; beginning with l. 328 "God hath made man" D transcribes twenty-three marginal lines in succession. M follows suit, copying all but two of those lines (ll. 400 and 416) in his margin. In both ll. 400 and 416, a marginal line would have created textual awkwardness for M. D brackets rhymes throughout his text and is, thus, accustomed to a page slightly cluttered with bracketing lines. M, however, brackets only the triplet rhyming lines which precede marginal tail rhymes. That is, M brackets rhymes only to identify the position of the marginal lines with respect to the triple rhymes which precede them. In this respect, he partially follows the practice of D, as exemplified in the first of Lucifer's verse sequences:

> Owt, harow, I rore
> For envy I lore   god hath mad a man
> My place to restore
>   (Macro, 325 - 28)

In this pattern marginal line 328 is written to the right of 326, the second line in the rhyming sequence. The brackets serve to indicate that the tail rhyme follows ll. 325 - 27, despite its marginal position. M maintains this consistent D pattern for the first eighteen lines, bracketing the triple rhymes as D does. However, D — who brackets all the rhyming lines in the play — adds brackets not only to the triplets as above but also the tail-rhymes themselves, whether these lines are written in the body of the text or the margins. That is, for the lines quoted above, D would have a large bracket extending from "god hath mad e [sic] man" to the subsequent tail rhyming line "for I am he that synne beganne" (l. 332). M does not bracket the tail rhymes. Therefore, when because of a change of speaker, D has written line 400 lower than usual to avoid the name of the speaker "Lucyfer," M apparently prefers to incorporate the line into the text in its normal place following l. 399, thereby saving himself the problem of bracketing the triplet rhymes across speeches. Similarly, line 416 occurs in a sequence of rapid speaker changes. D has tucked this line between the speaker names. Apparently again preferring to avoid the confusion of brackets that carry across speeches, M also incorporates this line into his text. No other lines in this sequence require bracketing across speaker changes, and M has followed the D practice in transcribing the other twenty-one initial tail-rhyming lines.

At l. 420 D becomes more erratic. But with the instincts of a bloodhound, M zealously tracks the irregular D path. Both scribes incorporate seven tail-rhyming lines into the text between lines 420 and 444. At line 448 D resumes his habit of transcribing these lines into the margin, tucking the first marginal line ("Yowr resons be grete") below the speaker's name, "Mynde," one line lower than usual. This line is easy to overlook, especially since it occurs in the middle of an aaab aaab pattern with six successive rhyming lines ("reson," "conclusyon," "replycacyon," "informacyon," "saluacyon," and "delectacyon," ll. 445 - 47; 449 - 51), and M omits it. The next tail-rhyming line (452) is incorporated into both texts, with the two subsequent tail-rhyming lines (456, 460) written marginally in both.

After line 460 both texts leave off this practice of marginal transcription until line 496 where D transcribes the line "Ye may not mysfare" into the margin. It is the only marginal line on that page; again it occurs in a sequence of six rhyming lines, and M omits it. At line 600 the same pattern is repeated. D once more transcribes one line into the margin — the first since line 496 — and again M omits it. At 648, D writes one marginal line ("& take large yeftys") on a page and M copies him. Then at line 675, for the first and only time, M copies a tail-rhyming line in the margin which D incorporates into the text. It is the last line on his page ("þa þe pore trowth ys take ryght nought a hede") and the last line in a speech by Wyll. M apparently did not want to carry it over into the next page and so copied it into his right margin.

In the next eight lines, M follows a see-saw pattern set up by D: Line 680, "seth god was bore," is marginal; line 684 written into the text; line 688, "þis were a dysporte," marginal. The next marginal line in D is line 720, "is it not ruthe." It is the only marginal line on the page; it occurs in a sequence of six rhyming lines, and M omits it. But he follows D at line 748 in writing "þat to me attende" in the margin, the only marginal line on the page for either text and the last D marginal line. Between the end of the extant D text at line 752 and the change of rhyme scheme at Wisdom's re-entry in line 873, M scatters a total of eight marginal lines throughout his text, presumably still following the irregular pattern established by the missing portion of D.

Overall, M has followed an arbitrary and irregular pattern of Digby marginalization and intertextual transcription for 97 out of 104 tail-rhyming lines, more than ninety percent of the time. And all seven of the deviations are attributable to circumstances consistent with M's copying of D. Four of the seven M lines which deviate from the D pattern are lines which M accidentally omits, in each case because of a change in the pattern of D transcription. Three of the omitted lines are the only marginal lines on a page and the fourth tail-rhyming line omitted is the first marginal line after a break in the pattern. With regard to the remaining three deviations: M transcribes one line marginally at the end of a speech which also occurs at the end of his page that D — for whom this line occurs in the midst of the page — does not marginalize, and, to avoid an awkward pattern of bracketing, M copies two D marginal lines into his text.

It is unusual for one scribe to follow the textual format of another so closely. To assume that two copyists would have followed the same irregular pattern line by line stretches the imagination, but it is possible. However, M was also influenced by chance strokes which must be peculiar to D. One instance occurs in line 199, where D has written "vnstabyllnesse." The top part of the initial "v-" in that word has been obscured by the curve of an initial "y-" (in "yeres") from the previous line which renders the initial "v-" difficult to read; indeed, among modern editors, only Furnivall and Baker (et al.) have read it correctly. Other editors have consistently read this letter as "s," often assuming an unknown word "sustabylnesse" as an error in both D and M, presumably copied from the mythical common exemplar. However, though partially obscured, D's "v-" is still recognizable from the thin, downward stroke that closes the bottom loop of the letter, a characteristic feature of D's large (or "capital") "v," as illustrated throughout the text, for instance, in lines 207, 226, 227, 231, 273, 286, and 302. In contrast, D completes the loop in his small "s" with a thicker upward stroke, not present in this letter. Since large letters are scattered throughout both texts without reference to our modern practices of capitalization, the large "V" is as appropriate a midsentence letter as the smaller "s" would be. The copyist's difficulty is compounded by the second letter of the word, which may be either "u" or "n," though slightly closer to D's ordinary "n." Misled by the accidental overstroke which obscures the first letter, M seems to have read this initial letter as "s" and then presumed "u" where he should have read "n." He transcribes the term as "sustabullnes," an unattested word, rather than the logically correct "vnstabylnesse" of the D text, restored in this edition.

Similar scribal accidents influence M in other instances. For example, in line 378, D has altered the word "provyt" to "prove," but M copies the initial word, which still shows through the alteration. Similarly, in line 740, D has written "though," but a cross stroke through the "g" and an open top combine to make the "h" look like a "t." Reading rapidly, as he often seems to have done, M may have read this word as "thougt" and "corrected" it to "thought," his choice possibly influenced by other instances in which "thought" is transcribed for "though" in comparable East Anglian texts, as for instance in two marginal additions to the N-Town cycle plays 35 and 37 (information provided in correspondence by Spector; see endnotes at l. 740). At times, M seems carelessly to have read his own handwriting into his exemplar, as, for instance, in line 547 when, ignoring the rhyme scheme as he was occasionally wont to do (see ll. 69, 270, 706, and 722), M transcribes D "gynne" as "gyane. The first D "n" at that point does not resemble any form of D "a," but it is similar to one form of the M "a," and, perhaps unconsciously mindful of his own handwriting, M misreads this letter as "a." A similar misreading results in M's "haue" for D's "howe" in line 615, where the D "o" resembles the M "a," with the change from "w" to "u" a conventional Macro alteration; or, earlier, in line 328, the first marginal line, D has written "god hath mad e man,' leaving a small space between the last letters of "made." M has transcribed this line as "god hath mad a man."

Errors occur at times from M's accidentally or willfully altering terms because he misappropriates D's scribal conventions, as, for instance, the abbreviation over the final "-p" in "hap" (l. 511); D apparently intends the final "-p" to be doubled (probably with the addition of a final "-e") as "-pe," but since the symbol that would double the letter may also signify a missing nasal, M writes the meaningless term "hamp" instead of "happe." Similarly, though more deliberately, M chooses to alter the medial "-y-" in "fayer" (l. 69) to "-th-." M first writes "faye" and then cancels that partial word in favor of the more explicit "father." Since D distinguishes between "y" and "þ," which M does not do, this choice is another instance of M's imposing his own orthographic conventions on the text of D. But in this instance M makes his choice consciously, correcting his own ambiguous "y," which may represent either "y" or "þ," to the more explicit "-th-."

In preferring "father" to "fayer," M has apparently chosen a word to suit the meaning of the text as he reads it rather than maintaining the rhyme scheme, in which "fayer" rhymes with "repeyer" (l. 71). In other instances M overlooks the rhyme scheme; for example, in l. 706 he alters D's "mayntement" to "meyntnance," perhaps a more familiar term but one which aborts the "-ent" rhyming pattern of lines 705-07. M occasionally sacrifices rhyme to "correct" grammar, altering the person of the verb in lines 270 (D "telles," M "tell") and 722 (D "rechases," M "rechase"). This edition has restored the D readings, which in fact represent an acceptable use of the singular form of the verb to indicate the plural (see discussion of "difficult readings" below).

Most consistently difficult for M to recognize is the D lower case "i," used where M frequently prefers "y." When this letter occurs in particular combinations, as for instance "ri" in line 414 where the D "r" extends below the line, M seems to have assumed this letter to have been part of the "r," writing "mara" for the D "maria." He seems to have mistaken "i" for "n" in line 584, where he replaces D "streightly" with "strenght." At line 697, where the combination of *is* resembles *y*, M has written "dycorde" for "discorde." Again, in line 256, the D *i* causes M to mistake "thei" for "þer."

In one or two instances, M corrects his own text to follow a D reading more closely. For instance, in line 180 M begins to spell the speaker's name "Understanding" with a "wn-," his own preferred form, which he cancels in favor of the D "vndyrstondynge." He subsequently alternates between his own preference for "wn-" and the D "vn-," in instances in which his own spelling preferences are inconsistently modified by the direct influence of his exemplar. Interestingly enough, his desire to make his text look as much like Digby as possible seems to have led him to follow, though somewhat belatedly, the D marginal abbreviations for "Vndyrstondynge." D recurrently alters this term when it designates the speaker from the full name, which he often uses, first to the abbreviation "Vndyrstond" and then to "Vnderst." In almost all instances, after a short lag, M picks up the change.

On several occasions, as for instance in the case of the "singular" verbs "telles" (l. 270) and "rechases" (l. 722), M corrects what he must think of as D errors. In such cases, D has what Paul Maas would call a *"lectio difficilior"* or "difficult reading" which would indicate a prior text.

Ordinarily, when a scribe "corrects" a difficult reading, he does so by replacing an "uncommon expression" with a "common one," as for instance replacing the rare use of a singular form for a plural verb with the more normal plural (ll. 270 and 722; see Maas 13). Applying the test of *lectio difficilior* to another M change can help one understand the pattern of "trivialization" that helps textual editors to determine prior texts: In line 497, Mind vows his allegiance to Lucifer with the formula "agre me." Although "me" in this context is a recognized, though rare, use of the oblique case "me" as subject of the verb "agre" (see 497n), M apparently does not recognize the difficult reading; he changes the term to the similar word "we," in the process altering the dramatic fealty ceremony which is central to the play at this point, but gaining a more recognizable rhetorical structure. The difficult reading in this, as in other cases, points to D as prior to M.

Occasionally, a scribal error in D causes an alteration in M. For instance, after line 396, D erroneously draws a line indicating a change of speaker where there is none. D cancels the line under the text by lightly marking through it with a series of perpendicular strokes, but leaves it extending uncancelled into the right margin. M copies the line at the bottom of folio 106r and then repeats the name of the speaker, "Lucyfer," at the top of the next page. It is the only time he has repeated a speaker's name when a speech continues from one page to the next. In line 725 D has mistakenly attributed a speech to "Mynde." M almost but does not quite repeat this error; he first writes the speaker's name as "Mynde," then cancels that word and correctly abbreviates "Wnd."

In other instances, M copies D errors without correcting them, as, for instance, when both scribes write "hestys" for "hettys" in line 716; and "For for" rather than "But for" at line 268 where D has placed two dots between the words, one of which is copied by M. At line 175, both scribes have "euer" where previous editors have expected "neuer" (see textual footnotes and endnotes for more information on this term). And when D apparently omits a line after line 579, the second and last of what should be a pattern of triple rhyming lines, M dutifully follows suit. At times, as at lines 16sd, 324sd, 692sd, and 724sd, M wholly or partially follows the precise line divisions of D's stage directions.

So zealous is M to incorporate into his text details of the D format that at times the two texts could appear to a quick perusal almost to be photocopies of each other. Why, then, has this argument been so long in the making? The answer, obviously, lies largely in the assumption that D is a later transcription than M and so cannot be the exemplar. It is true that D contains linguistic features that, initially at least, give it a more modern appearance than M. But when examined carefully, even this evidence yields its ground. The "modern" appearance of D essentially derives from a limited set of consistent scribal conventions, which may have more to do with regional dialectical choices than with date. Setting these aside, D is in some important respects more conservative linguistically than M.

To cite some of the conventions which give D a superficially more modern look than M: for example, M prefers the East Anglian "x-" in "xall" and "xulde" where D writes "schal" and "shuld(e)" or, in one occurence, "scolde;" M uses the more Northern form "sch-" in place of OE "sc-" where D uses "sh-," as in M "schadow," D "shadow" (l. 166). Most consistently, D prefers "-i-" or "-e-" where M uses "-y-" in almost any position: for instance, M "dysgysyde" (692 sd), "dysyer" (ll. 87, 254), and "laboryde" (l. 427) in place of D "disgysed," "desire," and "labored." This preference frequently results in more modern grammatical suffixes in D: "-ed" appears in D beside "-yd," along with an occasional "-n" for past participles, in contrast to M "-yde;" D uses "-es" for plurals of nouns where M often has "-ys," a form also used in D; and an occasional present participial ending of "ing," not present in M, alongside "-aunde" or "-ande" and "-ynge," contributes to D's more "modern" look. M often prefers "-ow-" where D has "-ou-."

The effects of these conventions can be seen in a set of sample lines:

Thus alle the soules that in this lyve be
  Stondyng in grace be lyke to this.
    A quinque prudentes your wittes fyve
    Kepe you clene and ye shalle neuer deface.
        (Digby, ll. 170-73)

Thus all þe sowlys þat in þys lyff be
  Stondynge in grace be lyke to thys.
    A quinque prudentes yowr wyttys fyve
    Kepe yow clene and 3e xall neuer deface.
        (Macro, ll. 170-73)

In this sample, endings like the plural "-es" ("soules," "wittes" rather than "sowlys" and "wyttys," ll. 170, 172), "-is" rather than "-ys" ("this" rather than "thys," l. 179), and the preference for "-ou" rather than "-ow" ("soules," "you," instead of "sowlys," "yow," ll. 170, 173) make Digby appear more modern. This appearance has reinforced arguments based largely on the assumption that D must be a text of the 1490s and that M, partly because of the supposed association with Abbot Richard Hengham of Bury, cannot be later than the mid-1470s.

However, during the last quarter of the fifteenth century the transition to modern linguistic forms, though more meaningful than the inconsistent paleographical variations of English scribal hands, nevertheless varied considerably even within a given region. As a result it is difficult to use spelling choices or grammatical forms to differentiate manuscripts by one or two decades. The difference in D and M spelling conventions could in this environment easily reflect a more cosmopolitan, less provincial hand in D rather than a later transcription, especially when considered in connection with some clearly conservative features of D.

Since copyists generally mediate between their own natural repertoire of spelling preferences and the choices made in the manuscript from which they are copying, one must be able to compare two or more texts by a given scribe in order to determine any genuine pattern of scribal choices. Fortunately, Richard Beadle has demonstrated that the scribe who copied the Macro *Wisdom* also transcribed the bulk of *Mankind* (1984 1-13). By comparing these texts, one can determine something about the spelling habits and preferences of the scribe.

Isolating some specific linguistic features, Beadle notes a consistent pattern of conservative choices in *Wisdom* which leads him to conclude that the *Wisdom* text was probably a decade or so earlier than *Mankind*. Though Beadle's conclusion is a logical one, his evidence takes on a very different coloration when traced back to its probable origins in D. There we find a pattern which suggests that the apparent conservatism of *Wisdom* over *Mankind* could easily have resulted from the scribe's copying of Digby forms rather than from an earlier and, thus, more conservative transcription.

To illustrate the point, Beadle selected three specific differences on which to focus: (1) *h-* vs. *þ-* / *th-* in the third person pronoun ("her" or "hem" vs. "their" or "them"); (2) intervocalic *-d-* vs. *-th-* in words like "father" ("fadyr"); (3) initial consonant *y-* vs. *g-* in various forms of the verb "to give" (e.g., "geve" vs. "yeve"). In each of these three cases, in *Wisdom* the scribe prefers the conservative *h-*, intervocalic *-d-*, and *y-*, whereas in *Mankind* he uses the more modern forms. Charting these forms as Beadle first describes their use in *Mankind* and then tracking them in both D and the first 752 lines of M, one finds the following:

1. *h-* vs. *þ-* / *th-* in pronouns "their" and "them": In *Mankind* the scribe overwhelmingly prefers the latter (presumably more "modern") form, using the *h-* only 3 out of 29 times, according to Beadle's count. In *Wisdom*, however, though the numbers are more evenly divided, the same scribe uses *h-* more frequently than *þ-* / *th-*, 13 times to 9 as Beadle counts. My overall count (15 to 7 in favor of *h-* over *th-* in the M *Wisdom*) differs slightly from that of Beadle, but this is inconsequential. What matters is that the apparently anachronistic forms in the M *Wisdom* closely follow the pattern of D. These letters appear in both M and D 22 times with the following results: both D and M use *h-* in "her(e)" and "hem" a total of 15 times in lines 3, 56, 293, 295, 331, 588, 599, 634, 635, 701, 710, 711, 743, 749, and 752sd; both D and M use *þ-* / *th-* 4 times, in lines 48, 68, 346, and 438. In only two instances do the two scribes use different forms, and in both cases, at lines 664 and 746, D has the conservative *h-* form where M has *þ-* / *th-*.

2. Intervocalic *-d-* vs. *-th-*: Beadle notes 18 occurrences in *Wisdom*, with *-d-* appearing 14 times to 4 instances of *-th-*, whereas he counts 28 instances in *Mankind*, with *-th-* used 21 times to 7 instances of *-d-*. Once more, my numbers do not tally precisely, but they are close, and again the D and M texts appear to follow each other, as illustrated in occurrences of terms for "father," "hither and thither," and "together" (all 5 occurrences of the term for "mother" appear in M after D ends, making comparison impossible):

A. *father* — M has "fadyr" 4 times (ll. 122, 279, 744, and 989); in the 3 which also occur in D (122, 279, 744), the D scribe also uses -*d*-, though the vowels differ. M uses -*th*- twice (285 and 1096). In the only line in both texts, l. 285, the D scribe uses the more conservative -*d*-.

B. *hither / thither* — M and D read "hedyr & thedyr" in 1ine 199.

C. *together* — M and D use -*d*- in all four occurrences, lines 8, 197, 495, and 728, though again the vowels sometimes differ.

3. Initial consonant *y*- vs. *g*- in various forms of the verb "give:" in *Mankind* only the *g*- form is used; Beadle cites 11 instances. In contrast, in *Wisdom* M and D both clearly prefer *y*-. Specifically, M and D have *y*- in ll. 73, 78, 82, 226, 411, 504, 576, 579, 704, and 730. M reads *g*- only 4 times, in ll. 479, 550, 689, and 999. D likewise reads *g*- in lines 550 and 689 but retains *y*- in 479 and, of course, the extant D fragment does not contain line 999. In line 647, M has "yeff" where D reads "geve." This represents the single instance in which M has used a more conservative form than D, and this instance is itself a little problematic. To begin with, this *y*- form appears in other very late East Anglian texts, so it is difficult to pin the term down to a particular date. Moreover, it occurs in a stanza in which M is not paying careful attention to his text. He has transposed a stanza out of order so that this line, for instance, appears as l. 639 rather than l. 647. And, finally, the M *y*- in this line appears to be hastily made with the downward stroke on the left rather than the right side and without its usual curve. It appears, in fact, as if the scribe had first re-written *l*, the letter immediately preceding, and then quickly altered that *l* into a *y*. The letter he is copying from D is also slightly difficult to read since it is intersected by a capital I from the line above and a curved abbreviation from the line below.

Charting these forms in a modified version of the diagram used by Benskin and Laing to identify and compare scribal repertoires (78) produces the following results:

ITEM TO COMPARE	conservative / usage	modern usage	Macro *Mankind*	*Wisdom*	Digby *Wisdom*
their,	*h-*	*þ- / th-*	*þer, þem, them* (*(her, hem)*)*	*her(e), hem* *þer, þem, them*	*her, hem them* (*(ther)*) (*(them)*)
intervocalic *-d-* vs. *-th-*	*-d-*	*-th-*	*-th-* (*(-d-)*)	*-d-, -th-*	*-d-* (*(-th-)*)
forms of *give*	*y-***	*g-*	*g-* only	*yeve, yewe, yeff* *gyff, geve*	*yeve,* *geve*

*(( )) Represents a rare form
**Though conservative, this form occurred in late East Anglian texts.

What this chart indicates is that the scribe who copied the M *Wisdom* and most of *Mankind* shows a preference in *Mankind* for certain "modern" forms, in particular for *th-* rather than *h-* in the third person pronoun, for *-th-* rather than *-d-* as an intervocalic consonant in words like "father" and "together," and for *g-* rather than *y-* in various forms of the verb "give." When he copied *Wisdom*, his own customary practice was influenced by his exemplar, the Digby manuscript, which consistently recorded the more "conservative" forms *h-, -d-,* and *y-*. In all but four instances in which these forms occur in the first 752 lines of the play, M follows D. In three of those four instances, D has the more conservative reading. And in the one instance where M is more conservative, he chooses a form, "yeve," which in any case occurs in late East Anglian manuscripts. This word appears in a stanza that has been reversed in the manuscript; M is copying a D *g-* which is slightly difficult to read, and his own *y* appears to be formed from a hastily corrected *I*.

Since we are dealing with relatively few occurrences in only two-thirds of the play, this evidence alone cannot prove the case for M's copying D. However, when combined with the physical evidence of the two manuscripts, it does reinforce what must finally be seen as a compelling case. D and M resemble each other so closely that if there were a common exemplar, we would scarcely need to see it. We know what its dialect was, how its lines were arranged, what its marginal lines were, the shape of its brackets, what its textual errors were and even where chance strokes have intersected its letters to create potentially confusing readings. It seems likely that we have that text — or 752 lines of that text — in our hands.

III. Copytext

This edition aims to present an eclectic text rather than a faithful transcription of either the Digby or the Macro manuscript of the play. Almost by default, the copytext for *Wisdom* is the complete text from the Macro manuscript (Folger V.a.354). Though almost certainly copied from the full text that now remains as the 752 line fragment in Bodleian manuscript Digby 133, which often provides superior readings and which contains 5 lines not in M, the M text contains spelling and orthographic features which, to maintain consistency, must be carried throughout the play. In order to present a document with as much linguistic integrity as is consistent with the eclecticism of this edition, M will be regarded as the authoritative text for all the accidentals; that is, when both M and D record the same word with variant spellings or grammatical markers, M will be chosen in any instance in which the M form is either a historically verifiable or logically derived variant of the word in question. Conversely, because it is almost certainly prior to M and because it is in many respects a more carefully transcribed text, D will be regarded as authoritative when it differs in matters of substance from M. The five missing lines have conventionally been restored from D. And this edition further restores the D text in instances when D provides neutrally equivalent or superior readings. The test for inclusion of D lines, words, and phrases has in almost every instance been a test of meaning, rather than form. With the sole exception of using "wyth" rather than M's preferred "wyt" to expand the contraction "w^t," I have resisted the temptation to use D readings simply because they appear to be more modern than M, which because of scribal choices they frequently do. For instance, in ll. 289, 812, 817, and 839 Macro transcribes "thys," an obsolete form of "thus," where Digby has "thus." For linguistic consistency, this edition retains the M form. In most cases, when a D reading has been accepted, the spelling conventions of D have been retained, though in instances in which word order only has been corrected through a D reading, as in l. 455, the M spellings have been retained. All D variant readings are identified in textual footnotes. Words in the text taken from D are identified in the glossary by an asterisk (*), with M readings given both in textual footnotes and parenthetically in the glossary. Such changes are not marked in the text. For the most part, with the notable exceptions of such terms as "[n]euer" (l. 175), transcriptions regarded as errors by previous editors which are common to both M and D have been retained in the text, with possible emendations provided in footnotes and alternate readings both in endnotes and in the glossary.

For the first 752 lines, textual footnotes primarily record and briefly gloss significant differences between the M and D texts (see "Editorial Principles" for more detail). For these 752 lines, previous editors' readings are for the most part not cited. In one or two instances in which Mark Eccles in his EETS edition of *The Macro Plays* emended the text to provide what are now regarded as standard readings, Eccles's emendations (which often follow the earlier Furnivall and Pollard EETS edition) are cited in the footnotes as a guide to the reader or director of the play familiar with the Eccles text. After line 752sd, this edition follows the Macro text, emending only in the case of obvious error. From l. 753 on, the textual footnotes record all instances in which Eccles' edition of *The Macro Plays* and Bevington's facsimile transcription of the Macro text differ from the text in this volume. The format for collating such editorial differences is the same as that employed in the first 752 lines for recording significant differences between the M and the D texts (see "Editorial Principles" for more detail). Such citations are provided primarily to place the portion of the play for which there is no D equivalent in the context of the most recent editorial choices. No attempt has been made to collate all variant readings from previous editions.

IV. Modern Text

The modern text, in this edition printed opposite to the early text, was initially created as an acting script for the Trinity College Medieval Festival production of *Wisdom* in 1984. As far as possible, this text literally translates the early text into modern English. Particular care has been taken, for instance, to preserve the longer Latinate lines and liturgical rhymes of Wisdom's verse patterns, which govern the language of all characters who are on the stage in the framing sections of the play, 11. 1 - 325 and 872 - 1162. All characters on the stage with Wisdom use his verse form, structured in eight-line stanza patterns (not marked in the manuscript) with lines ranging from an occasional eight to a rare sixteen syllables per line, with an average line typically containing nine to twelve syllables. To a large extent the stately rhythm of these sections of the play depends upon the formality of phrasing, the polysyllabic terms, and the peculiarly "liturgical" nature of the rhymes, which often involve nothing more than the repetition of a Latin or French-derived suffix, such as "-tion. These so-called *Wisdom* sections of the play provide the theological basis for the argument on which the drama of repentance and redemption depends. At the same time, however, drawing upon the language of biblical books like Ecclesiasticus, Proverbs, and the Song of Songs, as well as fourteenth- and fifteenth-century documents belonging to the tradition of late medieval lay piety, the opening and closing sections of the play dramatize a contemplative love affair between Christ and his consort, the human soul. Thus, while the style is formal and the theological argumentation important, the language of Christ and Anima is also sensuously affective. With an eye to the theatricality of these portions of the play, which had been called virtually unplayable, the modernization attempts to retain both the formal qualities and the sensuality of the original text in terms which might be easily understandable by a modern listener. To give an example of the kinds of changes one might expect throughout, consider the opening poetic stanza of the play:

The medieval text reads as follows:

Wysdom

Yff 3e wyll wet þe propyrte
    Ande þe resun of my nayme imperyall,
I am clepyde of hem þat in erthe be
    Euerlastynge Wysdom, to my nobley egalle,
    Wyche name acordyt best in especyall
And most to me ys convenyent.
    Allthow eche persone of þe trynyte be wysdom eternall
And all thre on euerlastynge wysdome togedyr present,
               (ll. 1 - 8)

This is rendered into modern English, thus:

Wisdom

If you wish to know the special property
    And the meaning of my name imperial
I am called by those whom on earth you see
    Everlasting Wisdom, to my nobility full equal,
    Which name accords best in terms most special
And is for me most fitting.
    Although each person of the Trinity is Wisdom eternal
And all three are together present in Wisdom everlasting,

Terms which remain current in modern English, such as "Yff," "3e," and "þe" (l. 1) are simply modernized as "if," "you," and "the." Other terms, such as "clepyd" (l. 3), are given in their modern meaning, in this case, "are called." In a few instances, terms which retain the same form in modern English require some explication or at least some small modification, as, for instance, "propyrte" (l. 1), which signifies the philosophically defining — or special — property of an object or a term. For such a term the clarifying adjective is built into the translation. In all the cases cited so far, the rhyme scheme of the modern text and that of the medieval text remain the same. At times, however, effective modernization has demanded slightly more elaborate alteration of the medieval text, as, for instance, changes in phrasing in lines 3 and 4, to avoid awkwardness in the modernized lines, or in the final rhyming lines of the stanza (ll. 6, 8), where the original text rhymes "convenyent" with "present." The modern term "convenient" does not convey the meaning of the medieval term, which is more accurately rendered by another modern word, such as "fitting." This choice in I. 6 necessitates a change in the word order of I. 8, in order to preserve the rhyme scheme of the stanza. The original rhyme of "convenyent" with "present" is changed so that in the translation "fitting" rhymes with "everlasting." In such cases, the final confirmation of the modernized text came in the testing laboratory of the theatre.

In the mid-section of the play, II. 325 - 871, when Lucifer's verse form (aaab cccb) with its triplet rhymes, tail-rhyming lines, and shorter lines dominates the play (with the three Mights adopting Lucifer's verse form even when he is not on stage), similar principles of modernization have been observed. Initially, it was feared that preserving the original syntax and phrasing would create a stilted translation in portions of the play that demand the quick action and colloquial response of bawdy comedy. However, at the insistence of Roger Shoemaker, who directed the Trinity production of *Wisdom*, the temptation to render the language of Lucifer and the Mights into a racier and more colloquial modern idiom was resisted in favor of greater allegiance to the text. And, when staging the play, trusting the text proved to have been a fortunate choice; Lucifer's language and the comic interaction of the Mights play very well on stage as written in the late fifteenth century, presenting comedy which is understandably modern, reducing (or perhaps raising) itself literally to the level of slapstick in the fight sequence (II. 761 - 80) and yet maintaining the measured rhythm that characterizes this stately play.

There are, to be sure, some instances in which textual modifications were necessary for clarity or for linguistic smoothness, as, for instance, in I. 579 when the verb "mase," meaning "makes," has been changed to the modern English noun "maze" in order to preserve the rhyme and render intelligible the idea of disdaining the kind of intuitive, non-logical thought that is called "oncunnynge," i.e., a kind of "[redeeming] ignorance," "intuition," or, as translated, "simplicity" of thought. Again, in I. 731 the phrase "an euyll entyrecte," meaning "an indirect evil" has been changed to "an evil twisted into a spin" to imply the crookedness of the indirect path of evil, while preserving the rhyme with "thin" and "win" of the preceding lines. Such modifications should be easily apparent to the reader who has the original text at hand in this edition. However, if there is any doubt about whether the modern text is a literal transcription or an adaptation of the medieval, the reader is referred to the glossary where terms are defined with an eye to both their theological and their sociological significance and to the endnotes where more literal translations are often printed. Latin quotations are printed as transcribed in the medieval text and are modernized in the modern text, with translations in the endnotes. Stage directions are similarly printed as written in the old text; unlike Latin quotations, the stage directions are translated in the modern text. Stage directions are also appropriately added to the modern text only, clearly visible across the page from the old text. The modern text is offered partially as a gloss upon the medieval text for the reader, but it was created and still primarily remains an acting script.

CONTEXTS

The term "context" is deceptively simple. One speaks of studying literature "in context" or of taking a statement "out of context" as we might talk of putting a piece into or taking it out of a jigsaw puzzle. But determining "context" means choosing from a range of possibilities, historical or formal in nature. By placing an object, a statement, or a work of art in one context rather than another, we frame that work by surrounding it with information of a particular kind (Goffman 1974). The frame itself determines meaning. To take an obvious analogy from nature: an apple may be nothing more than a piece of fruit; in the context of Christian mythology, it symbolizes the temptation and fall of humanity; in a Norman Rockwell illustration it may signify a teacher's desk; or it may be the centerpiece for a medieval play about the gulling of the devil (*The Blessed Apple Tree*). The object itself does not change but the context we choose determines its significance.

And so it is with the play of *Wisdom*, extant in two manuscripts, probably written in late fifteenth-century East Anglia. The meaning of the play depends on how we frame the drama. When production records exist, they constitute one set of contextualizing documents; performance history at least gets a play mentally off the page and onto the stage. But no performance records exist for any of the Macro plays. Without such records, we must place the drama in other frames. By asking contextual questions, one may, for instance, inquire about the social and political implications of religious allegory: could the play have been staged by an aristocratic or wealthy family as a visible symbol of status and power, much like later masques? Could it have been staged in a religious house? Was it potentially subversive? To what extent is its religious imagery — its metaphors (Christian life as a royal marriage), symbols (ermine robes), and fixed visual emblems (God as a king) — shaped by social concepts? And what meanings can a medieval allegorical play have for us as twentieth-century viewers and readers? Such questions as these, which highlight cultural functions as well as dramatic forms, have guided this analysis of *Wisdom*, dictating not what contexts to choose so much as how to evaluate those contexts. *Genre*, for instance, could be simply a description of dramatic form, just as a study of *sources* might well be limited to examining the extent to which one text relies on another. But as presented here, *sources* and *genre* reflect facets of social and political history equally as much as dramatic form or intertextuality.

I. SOURCES IN CONTEXT:

"The Religion Of þe Hert" —
Piety, Femininity, and Moral Drama

A dramatized sermon, not a play: the repeated charge of undramatic "sermonizing" has been levelled at the play of *Wisdom* largely because of its incorporation of sources taken from the late medieval literature of lay contemplation, much of which appropriated documents initially composed by and for cloistered contemplatives. The first sixty-five lines of the play, for instance, have been directly quoted from the English translation of the *Orologium Sapientiae* or *Clock of Wisdom*, a fourteenth-century Latin dialogue between Sapientia and the human soul most likely written in the 1330s by Heinrich Suso, a Dominican who lived first in Constance and then in Ulm. The *Orologium* was in part a Latin translation of an earlier German work of Suso's called *Das Büchlein der Ewigen Weisheit* (*The Little Book of Eternal Wisdom*), a highly popular mystical text, now extant in 100 complete and 80 fragmentary manuscripts (Künzle 28 - 54). Written by a Dominican who stringently worshipped the name of Jesus, Suso's *Orologium* was probably known in England at least by 1375 and was translated into English possibly as early as 1390 in an anonymous work popularly titled *The Treatise of the Seven Points of True Love and Everlasting Wisdom* (Lovatt 48). Appearing repeatedly throughout the fifteenth century in anthologies designed for lay men and women, complete texts of these *seven points* are now extant in at least eight manuscripts, with points four and/or five extant in another five; ten of these manuscripts have been examined for this edition. In 1491 Caxton printed the English version as *The Treatise of the Seven Points of True Love* in a volume entitled *The Book of Divers Ghostly Matters* (STC 3305; the only complete copy is in CUL; the incomplete Pierpont Morgan Library PML704 is one of five known copies). In 1880 K. Horstmann published Ms Douce 114 in *Anglia* under the title "*Orologium Sapientiae* or *The Seven Points of Trewe Wisdom.*"

Wisdom also incorporates portions of Walter Hilton's *Scala Perfectionis* or *Scale of Perfection*, an instruction manual for those desiring to achieve perfection through contemplation of God written in two books by an English Augustinian canon, probably between 1380 and 1396, the year Hilton is assumed to have died (D. Knowles and J. Russell-

Smith in *Dictionnaire de Spiritualité* . . .; ctd. by Lovatt 49). The play also makes recurrent allusions to Hilton's *Vita Mixta* or *Epistle on the Mixed Life*, a document purporting to reconcile the contemplative and the active lives for those with contemplative inclinations living outside the cloisters, also composed before 1396. Other primary sources include treatises formerly ascribed to St. Bernard of Clairvaux, *Meditationes Piisimae de Cognitione Humanae Conditionis* and *Tractatus de Interiori Domo*, a portion of the pseudo-Bonaventuran *Soliloquium de Quatuor Mentalibus Exercitiis* taken from Hugo of St. Victor's *De Arrha Animae*, and the anonymous *Novem Virtutes* or *Nine Points Pleasing to God*, formerly attributed to Richard Rolle (see Smart, *passim*; Sargent 1984 145 - 47).

In addition to the sources cited above, *Wisdom* quotes, paraphrases, or alludes to a range of shorter English texts (ctd. in notes), including at least one English *Charter of Heaven* (see, for instance, CUL Ms. Ff.5.45 fol. 986), and quotes Latin biblical verses, taken especially from Ecclesiasticus (or the Wisdom of Joshua ben Sirach), Cantica Canticorum Salamonis (Song of Solomon), Sapientia (The Wisdom of Solomon), Proverbs, Isaiah, and Paul's letters to the Corinthians. Some of these biblical passages are quoted by Suso and Hilton; others are not. But collectively they speak to the power and beauty of *Sapientia*, the goddess of wisdom, to the soul's yearning love of God in whose image the soul was created, and to the healing power of Christ's Passion. By providing scriptural foundations for the metaphor of the soul's marriage to Christ, the biblical passages reinforce the quasi-mystical theology of the play. In coming to terms with *Wisdom* one must assess the apparent contradictions between this mystical ideal, which appears at points to affirm the cloistered contemplative life, and Christ's endorsement of public Christian charity. Placed within the context of late medieval piety, particularly as practiced by aristocratic women, this contradition disappears. *Wisdom* establishes a model of piety which ultimately begs the distinctions between what were called "religiose," i.e., cloistered, and "oþer devowte," i.e., lay contemplatives (see, for instance, Corpus Christi Ms. 268; qtd. in Doyle 1: 213), though its trappings are essentially feminine in nature and aristocratic in style, this ideal of piety engages its audience — men and women, clerical and lay persons — both as onlookers and participants, as worshippers of the beauty of God portrayed in the play and as players in the drama of the soul.

A. Contemplation and Charity:
The Ideals of the Play

Like the other Macro plays, the play of *Wisdom* stresses human insufficiency and the need for personal penitence, through which the sorrowing human soul may re-discover her likeness to God. But *Wisdom* differs from *The Castle of Perseverance* and *Mankind* in its focus upon contemplation and its apparent idealization of the contemplative life (see ll. 393 - 510). One of the "clene sowlys" (l. 45), Anima is the lover of God, her mind strengthened, her soul made perfect and herself mated in wisdom to Christ (ll. 54 - 55). Her love affair with Christ evokes the metaphors of contemplative marriage which constituted the substance of late medieval mystical unions with God. In this same vein, Anima's faculties, or Mights (Mind, Will, and Understanding), are treated as cloistered contemplatives. Lucifer first addresses the Mights as "fonnyde fathers" (l. 393). Then he apparently attempts to entice Mind to leave the cloisters in order to "be in þe worlde" (l. 442), to abandon the "contemplatyff lyff" (l. 417) for the "comyn" (l. 443). He similarly lures Understanding to "se and beholde þe worlde abowte" (l. 464) and Will to "lewe yowr nyse chastyte and take a wyff" (l. 476), to lead a "comun lyff" (l. 472), to take pleasure "in met, in ale, in wyn . . . in ryches, in clothynge fyne" (ll. 473 - 74). As part of his argument, Lucifer invokes Christ as an example of one whose life encompassed both the contemplative and the "comun," i.e., the public, active life seen by Lucifer only in terms of excess and indulgence:

> Sumtyme wyth synners he had conversacyon
> Sumtyme wyth holy also comunycacyon
> Sumtyme he laboryde, preyde; sumtyme, tribulacyon.
> (ll. 425 - 27).

In short, Lucifer associates the Mights with "harde lywynge and goynge wyth dyscyplyne dew," with chastity, prayer, and vows of silence, all attributes of the cloisters. Urging Mind and Understanding to go out into the world and Will to take a wife, he addresses the Mights, in Bevington's terms, "as holy men" (1963 44).

Urging the Mights to abandon what clearly seems to be cloistered lives, Lucifer pushes them toward the "vita mixta þat Gode here began" (l. 428), thus parodying the argument of Walter Hilton's *Epistle on the*

Mixed Life, a document written to enable those with public responsibilities, including powerful clerics such as abbots or bishops, to reconcile their administrative duties with a private commitment to contemplation. By proposing to "schew . . . perfyghtnes" to be "sen," to prove "wertu . . . wykkydnes" and "under colors all thynge perverse" (ll. 377 - 79), Lucifer consciously inverts the moral perspective established by Christ as Wisdom. By establishing Lucifer as a negative gauge of the play's values, *Wisdom* appears to attack the idea of the *vita mixta* and to affirm the cloistered life (for a supporting argument, see Smart 78 - 86, 90).

The contemplative ideal upheld in this section of the play finds echoes in Lucifer's earlier invocation of "perfyghtnes" (l. 377) and Wisdom's final exhortation to the audience to seek "perfeccyon" (l. 1163) as the goal of wisdom. Within the contemplative frame "the gift of perfection," as Walter Hilton calls it, can be achieved only through the "gostly burning love in Jesu" found by withdrawing from the world into a focused, all-encompassing, and highly disciplined contemplation of God (Hilton 2: 226 - 28; qtd. by Knowles 109). Without such withdrawal, the Christian may live a good life but cannot fully attain spiritual perfection.

Building on the thematic centrality of contemplation, one might concur with Smart that the play was written to oppose abuses, including apostasy, which were weakening monastic life in the late fifteenth century. Some have, in fact, agreed with Smart's assumption that the play itself was written for performance within a monastery, perhaps at Bury St. Edmonds (see, for instance, Gibson 1985). Indeed, the 1984 Trinity Medieval Festival Production of the play was fictionally set as a performance before the English King in the abbot's Palace of the abbey of Bury St. Edmonds, a location that might have included the kind of disparate audience for whom the play is most suited. Certainly, the dramatist seems to have presumed that his natural audience would include clerics at whom Lucifer could satirically point his finger. Using as theatrical pointers the demonstrative pronoun "þes" (l. 488) and adverb "ther" (l. 490), Lucifer adopts Wisdom's verse form rather than his own to single out "prechors" in the audience:

> Ya, ser, by Sent Powle,
>> But trust not *þes* prechors, for þey be not goode.
>> For þey flatter & lye as þey wore woode.
>> *Ther* ys a wolffe in a lombys skyn! (487 - 90; italics mine)

At the same time, the aristocratic themes and the costuming, dancing, and song seem designed for a partly secular audience. And, as scholars like J. J. Molloy, Alexandra F. Johnston, and Donald Baker have pointed out, the monastic ideal is not consistently upheld within the play (see, for instance, Molloy 186 - 87; Johnston 95 - 96; Baker 1986 80 - 81). Most obviously, in his sermon on the nine points of charity, Christ elevates "pyte and compassyon off þi neybur" above rigorous religious discipline (ll. 997 - 1064; quotation 1029 - 30). Considered overall, the *Novem Virtutes* is the only major source for the play which — despite its occasional attribution to Richard Rolle — does not initially confirm the contemplative emphasis of the drama. Delivering this sermon to the audience while Anima and the Mights change costume offstage (ll. 997 - 1064), Christ seemingly steps out of character, directly quoting not only God (see ll. 997, 1005, 1013, 1021, 1029, 1037, 1053, and 1057) but at one point himself — "Cryst seth in þis wyse" (l. 1031) — to establish an ideal of public charity as an alternative to at least extreme forms of discipline required for cloistered contemplation: fasting "forty yer" (l. 1032), laboring "wyth grett dylygens / Wpon thy nakyde feet and bare / Tyll þe blode folwude for peyn and vyolens" (ll. 1041 - 43).

The emphasis on public acts of charity in these nine points seems initially at odds with the contemplative focus of portions of the play, raising questions about the nature of the play and about the kinds of places in which it might be played. The very contradiction, however, is in some measure the key to the play, which on balance was not likely to have been performed in a monastery, though it is conceivable that it could have been performed in the chamber of a priory or the great hall of an abbot's palace. Certainly, the most likely venue for *Wisdom*, with its elaborately aristocratic costumes and its masked dances as well as its references to the presence of food and drink as props ("Now go we to þe wyne," l. 868), would be the banquet hall of a great house, whether a secular or religious residence. And within households wealthy enough for a play like *Wisdom* to have been presented, the contradiction between the ideals of contemplation and public charity did not exist. As Kate Mertes has pointed out, in a century that depended upon the patronage and protection of large houses to keep order, acts of public charity combined with severe piety to provide models of "good lordship," establishing symbols of the power and authority which were maintained partly through household discipline, enforced at times through attendance at religious services:

[A]cts of charity were almost a social duty of the aristocracy, as were attendance at mass and the initiation of other religious services. Certainly chroniclers cite such pietistic practices as synonyms of good lordship; and we would be hard-pressed to discover a noble who never gave alms or endowed a chantry.

(Mertes 146)

Both charitable acts, which sprinkled personal wealth and influence throughout a community, and daily household masses, which demanded the presence of a chaplain, signified station. In this context, religious discipline could, as Mertes implies, serve Caesar as well as God. One of the characteristic features of the fifteenth century was the extent to which piety cohabited with power, particularly in wealthy households. Far from contradicting the ethos of its age, a play like *Wisdom* finds its place at the end of a century in which in England, as elsewhere, quasi-monastic lifestyles had a strong currency among lay contemplatives, particularly among powerful women.

B. Piety and Power:
Devotional Miscellanies of the Fifteenth Century

Treatises, dialogues, and poems, many of which were written in the fourteenth century as manuals for cloistered contemplatives but which were adapted to lay use throughout the fifteenth century, introduced a special rhetoric of devotion through which the actual life of the cloisters was re-written as a metaphorical model for lay men and women. This rhetoric was reiterated throughout the fifteenth century in miscellanies that anthologized dialogues such as Suso's *Seven Points of True Love and Everlasting Wisdom* with treatises on religion or poems on death that graphically described the physical horrors of worm-eaten flesh as a way of stressing the need for the redemption of the presumably immortal soul. These lay manuals stressed personal, individual devotion of the kind which characterized late medieval piety. Correspondingly, they depended heavily on appeals both to the private conscience and to the discipline of the mind as well as the body. By developing the Augustinian notion of "inner" sight, such devotional miscellanies prepared lay men and women through what in at least one manuscript was called *the religion of the hert* to create a contemplative cell in their individual consciences, and, thus, to separate the "inner," contemplative life from the active, "outer life" required by positions of public power and authority.

The dynamic of "inner" cloistering and "outer" activity governs the allegory of Anima and her Mights in the play of *Wisdom*. The Mights, or inner faculties of Anima, are being treated as contemplatives — cloistered men who are asked by Lucifer to "go in the worlde" (l. 501), with Mind exhorted to give up his "syngler deuocyons" (l. 451), Understanding to "se & beholde þe worlde abowte" (l. 464) and Will to "lewe yowr nyse chastyte & take a wyff" (l. 476) — while Anima herself is not in any similar way cloistered. In this sense, the play itself reiterates the internal/external dichotomy of the lay contemplative who keeps an internal cloister of the self while living in the world. Mind, Will, and Understanding as the internal faculties reside within the soul; they are the contemplatives, while Anima herself as a representative of humanity lives a life encumbered with the public responsibilities of charity, the very responsibilities which Christ exhorts the audience (whom Anima represents) to perform while Anima herself is making her confession after her recognition of sin (ll. 997 - 1064).

In the opposition between the internal and the external played out in the allegory of Anima and her Mights, the play itself enacts the drama of internal cloistering and external public activity that was idealized in the miscellanies. In one popular poem, for instance, a 470-couplet exhortation to virtue called *the Desert of Religion*, the lives of hermits — who are pictured in illustrations of the poem in British Library Mss. Stowe 39 and Additional 37049 — become a model to help Christians build a *castell of the hert*. The highest ideal of such a model is contemplation, leading to perfection (the life of the Mights as portrayed in ll. 393 - 510 of *Wisdom*) though the quasi-contemplatives who subscribed to this form of ascetic religious discipline were not themselves cloistered. The anonymous transcriber of British Library Harley Ms. 2406 *Abbey of the Holy Ghost* explains this idea:

My dere Brother & Sister! I see welle that many men
wold be in Religion, but þei mow no3t for pouert; or for
awe, or for drede of kyn; or for þe bond of wedlock;
þerfor I make here a bok of Religion of þe Hert; þat is of
þe Abbey of þe Holy Gost.

(fol. 61; qtd. in Riggio 1989 239)

Filled with excerpts from Richard Rolle, Hilton, and others, including *The Seven Points of True Virtue*, such miscellanies exhort their readers or hearers, both men and women, though often perhaps primarily women, to follow a model of piety grounded in contemplation. Through meditations, which often focus on death, particularly on Christ's Passion, the fifteenth-century lay contemplatives targeted by such manuscripts aspired to a goal of perfection, often imagined as a ladder, scale, or tree of love. Typically, couplets urge both men and women to remember *"Cristes Passion devotely"* (Brit. Lib. Ms. Addit. 37049, fol. 28) and to desire death as an access route to God's "higher" love. (Despite the scribe's mention of poverty, many of those who subscribed to this form of devotion were far from poor.)

Such miscellanies, which abounded in the fifteenth century, represent a virtually unstudied chapter in the history not only of lay piety but also of female literacy, of women as potential listeners, readers, and patrons. The English translator of Suso's *Orologium Sapientiae* complains that "this short lyve shal ratherer have and ende of ony man, þan he may eithyr stodyen or redyn hem" (Corpus Christi Ms. fol. 55v; see also Doyle 1: 213). Texts recur from manuscript to manuscript in a way that makes these miscellanies seem much like modern anthologies, repeating, though in different combinations, the same literary works. As represented by Ms. Rawlinson 894, for instance, such volumes might include *The Twelve profits of tribulation* by Adam the Carthusian; *The Boke of the Craft of Dying*, six chapters attributed to Richard Rolle; *A tretise of gostly batayle*; *Treatise of the active & contemplative Life* — i.e., the *Vita Mixta* described as a "devout boke compyled by mayster Walter Hylton to a devout man in temperal estate how he sholde rule hym"; several chapters "in what maner mene or women of simple cunnyng mow þinke or praise in hir begynnyng"; a treatise on "a good contemplacion for a prest or he go to masse"; *A Tretise of the love of God*, eight chapters attributed to Walter Hilton; *The Blyssed meditacions of the holy doctor Seynt Bernarde* (one of the most important source documents for *Wisdom*); the *Consilia Isidori*, a *contemptus mundi* piece; some instructions in holy living addressed, as it seems, to a non-cleric showing "that man shall sumtyme have more devotion whan he hath . . . outeward werkis," and *a litill tretise agence fflessly affeccions and all unprifty loves.*

Not all of the texts are specifically contemplative, though most deal with the theme of religious discipline understood partly as a way of preparing for death. And the texts are variously directed to religious and secular male and female readers. Most of the English miscellanies are unillustrated, but three illustrated manuscripts (the Brit. Lib. Stowe 39, Addit. 37049, and Cotton Faustina B vi, pt. ii) include drawings of two "cartoon" poems, one showing death calling a bishop, a knight, and a king and another depicting the intercession of the Virgin for the soul of a dying man. Our habit of editing texts such as *The Abbey of the Holy Ghost* or *The Desert of Religion* separately without reference to the collected volumes has to a large extent obscured the way these miscellanies transmit and modify contemplative documents and even of their influence on the development of other literary forms, as, for instance, household drama like *Wisdom* (for a major exception to this practice, see Ian Doyle's recent publication of *The Vernon Manuscript*).

Many such books, including Corpus Christi College Ms. 268, were transcribed for women, some cloistered and some not, often by household chaplains. Even in the fourteenth century, women were primary patrons or recipients of such documents. The first book of Hilton's *Scala Perfectionis* was written to a cloistered woman. And during the fifteenth century, when such books were appropriated for lay use, women remained prominent among patrons. Some tracts are to a woman only, as in the case of Brit. Lib. Ms. Royal 17C, with its directions that a "Doughtir, take heide of this, loke that thi conscience and thi fame acorde both togethir" (fol. xviii), or *a lytil tretise agenes fleischly affeccyones and all unthrifte lustes*, which is addressed "to women all only," though also useful, says the scribe, for men. Targeting feminine readers often led scribes to use modern sounding gender-specific terms, for example designating readers as "he or sche." In *A tretis of viii chapitres necessarie for men þat ʒiven hem to perfection*, a tract attributed to Walter Hilton, the title, with its designation of "men," is a misleading remnant corrected by fifteenth century scribes who end with a prayer to "save us and alle cristen men and women." The image of love and the metaphor of marriage and spousal affection serve as a basis for devotional exercises throughout these volumes, in which the devout Christian is portrayed as the lover of God, seeking perfection through contemplative marriage. For instance, *A tretise of viii chapitres* begins "the first tokyn of leve is that the lover submytte fully." Or Christ himself is portrayed as the lover: "Jhesus my luf, my ioy, my reste / þi perfite luf close in my breste . . ." (Brit. Lib. Ms. Addit. 37049 fol. 24). Sometimes distinctions are drawn between those within and those outside of the cloisters. The scribe of Corpus Christi 268, for instance, explains to this patron, whom he addresses as "my dere lady" that he would omit "manye maters . . . towchynge . . . religiose persones [which] were lytel edificacione [for you] & oþer devowte persones þat dysrene þis drawynge out in englische" (qtd. in Doyle 1: 213). More often, however, the distinction between the cloistered and the lay reader (or hearer) is blurred by scribes who address their books to "religiose and oþer devowt persones" (CUL Ms. Ff.45, fol. 2; see also Riggio 1989 238-42).

Such miscellanies were often read aloud as entertainment, probably, as Ian Doyle conjectures, in installments, perhaps in the place of romances. One author, probably William Nasington, a secular priest and ecclesiastical lawyer of York, specifies such a purpose in his prologues to the *Speculum Vitae*, a 440-folio poem of didactic couplets, adapted from and embellishing a fourteenth-century treatise on the Lord's prayer. Nasington exhorts his hearers, whom he calls "gode men and wommen," to keep each other awake as he reads: "and whyl I speke kepe folk fro slepe" (CUL Ll.18) and he "warnes yow folk" that he

> wil make no veyn spekyng
> Of dedes of armes ne of amourys
> As don mynstreles and oþer gestoures
> That make spekyng in meny a place,
> Of octavian and isambrace
> And of many oþer gestes
> And namely whan þei come to festes.
>   (CUL Ms. Ll.1.18; see also Doyle 1: 76-77)

Nasington offers his poem as an alternative to the "gestes" of minstrels sung "namely whan þei come to festes." In the company of such "festive entertainment," the play of *Wisdom* truly shines. It presents a similar theme, exhorting its viewers to a stringent concept of piety which, though it finally upholds conservative traditions of power and authority, ironically allows lay persons to live "in the werld" only by denying the validity of that world. Speaking of Germany what was also true of England, John Dahmus has pointed out that "The [fifteenth-century] layman was being refused first-class citizenship in the kingdom of heaven unless he became, in effect, a monk" (62; qtd. in Riggio 1986 15). The point here is that in addition to elevating fifteenth-century lay persons to a preferred status in the kingdom of heaven, this quasi-monastic ideal of piety also implicity guaranteed its practitioners a continuing place as prominent subjects, if not citizens, in the kingdom of man.

What is striking about this tradition of piety is both the ease with which it found its niche amongst the trappings of aristocratic splendor and the role of women in its promulgation. Writing of Cicely, Duchess of York and mother of Edward IV and Richard III, C. A. J. Armstrong pointed out that:

> The contribution of women to the contemplative piety of the later Middle Ages can scarcely be rated too high. When all is said, the figure of St. Catherine of Siena can be regarded with much justification as forming something of a water-shed in the history of mediaeval devoutness. The fifteenth century witnessed a general diffusion of a spirit characterized by an ardent humility, yet tender and intimate in its approach to the Godhead. . . . . As ever in the history of types of thought, a new affection produced a special emphasis inside the traditional form, and thus arose a new phase which might be held to characterize an age . . . . Throughout Europe the "Devotio Moderna" was greatly encouraged and promoted by women, and England, if unacquainted with the more organized forms of this school as they flourished in the Netherlands, was perhaps the principal hearth of mysticism, and the especial home of that devotion to the Holy Name of Jesus so typical of the movement as a whole.
>
> (Armstrong 135 - 36)

One of the chief proponents of the "devotion to the Holy Name of Jesus" was Henrich Suso, the Dominican author of the *Orologium Sapientiae*, a primary source document of *Wisdom*. And it was texts like the English translation of Suso that provided the blueprints for devotions that were both private and exemplary. As recorded in a household ordinance probably written between 1485 and 1495, perhaps as a model for other noble women, Cicely of York's daily regimen is — as it was meant to be — instructive. The Duchess spent her morning in worship, privately reciting matins and hearing a low mass before breakfast. After breakfast, she assisted in the household services in the chapel with the office of the day and two low masses. At dinner, which she took immediately after, she listened to works such as Hilton's *Contemplative and Active Life* or Bonaventura's *Life of Christ* read aloud. Then following afternoon audiences and rest, she turned to prayer and contemplation. To this point, Cicely's routine, though devout and strict, was fairly conventional for the female head of a large conservative household. But the Duchess's afternoon meditations took on a strongly contemplative cast as "now at her private devotions she would follow in the path of the mystics whose work she dwelt upon so affectionately" (Armstrong 142). As described by Armstrong "in the secrecy of this inner life the Duchess of York was completely merged in the humble seeker of divine mercy, just as the character of the mystic had co-existed all the while in the great lady who presided over the secular duties of the day" (142).

The image of Cicely, the queen mother of two kings, seeking the mercy of God through mystical union with Christ, is not unlike the portrait of Anima, the consort of the king, kneeling for favor in *Wisdom*. And among the authors Cicely chose for her dinner entertainment were at least two, Walter Hilton and Bonaventura, who served as sources for the play. On one level, through its sources, the play enacts an ideal of piety which a woman like Cicely of York lived out and which, in practice, was at once ascetic and ambitious. In her lifestyle Cicely was able to bring the inner searching for perfection through contemplation of God together with her role as a powerful public woman helping to maintain religious discipline within her household through the activities of the chapel while granting public suits and controlling household ceremonies. Ceremony was itself a part of the public posture which allied piety with power and aristocratic splendor. In the reburial in 1476 of Cicely's husband Richard, Duke of York, at Fotheringay, the figure of Christ sitting on a gilded rainbow nimbus on a black "cloth of majesty" both lent sanction to and took authority from the shields of France and England which were quartered in the corners of the image. For a family "intensely pre-occupied with the sacred character of kingship," it was essential to validate the claim of York to both the English and French crowns; the visual reference to the majesty of Christ furthered such a claim (Armstrong 140).

Similarly, though more extreme, the piety of Margaret Beaufort, the mother of Henry VII, exemplifies the pattern of the aristocratic and powerful lay contemplative in the late fifteenth century. Beaufort's ambitions resulted in the house arrest for treason of this woman who had been married to the brother of Henry VI, for attempting to secure the crown for her son. During Henry's reign Beaufort's entertainments set the style for Tudor splendor. Beaufort herself had an active public life; she helped to adjudicate legal cases; she founded Corpus Christi College at Cambridge and served as the guardian to several landed young orphans. But her own regimen, as described by her chaplain John Fisher in *A Mornynge Remembraunce*, was even stricter than that of the Duchess of York. She often said sixty-three aves, kneeling at each one, along with "matynes of our Lady . . . also matyns of the days. And after that dayly herde iiii or v masses vpon her knees, soo contynuynge in her prayers & devocions vnto the hour of dyner," though she apparently often fasted. She wore "shertes & gyrdles of heere" (Fisher 294 - 95; qtd. in Riggio 1989). And when she was not entertaining she held herself to a strictly disciplined ritual of self-restraint.

Margaret Beaufort's regimen once more echoes the blend of aristocratic elegance and pious self-denial characteristic of late medieval English piety and dramatized in *Wisdom*. There was a strong feminine influence on that piety, which was connected with the devotional miscellanies and contemplative treatises that serve as the sources for much of *Wisdom*. As a patron of early British publishing, Margaret Beaufort favored devotional books of the kind that fed such household piety. At her request, Wynkyn de Worde published an edition of Walter Hilton's *Scale of Perfection* with the *Epistle on the Mixed Life* silently appended as Book III of Hilton's two-volume guide to contemplation. Clearly, Hilton's "mixed" or "medled" life of contemplation and activity served Beaufort well. And though the play itself equivocates about the *vita mixta* as a model, it does implicitly set before its audiences an ideal of piety which blends public acts of charity with private asceticism and self-denial, draping humble obedience and respect for superiors in luxurious robes.

The apparent contradiction between the asceticism of the play's themes and the luxury of its trappings is reconciled in the image of peace and plenty that is projected through "every human soul" Anima, who combines in her own person the ascetic renunciation and the aristocratic beauty which actual women like Margaret Beaufort and Cicely of York acted out. To understand the dynamics of this image, one must consider the general and recurrent ways in which images that imply social acceptability and expensively purchased style can be used effectively as a lure to piety. Despite the widespread importance of what has come to be called "liberation theology," i.e., religion pressed into the service of revolution and resistance, often the most fundamentally religious sectors of a society are among the most conservative, tying issues of piety to strict, often racially or ethnically tinged models of behavior. Themes and mottoes like "cleanliness is godliness" can, for instance, mask a high level of intolerance for those whose patterns of behavior challenge an established concept of social (as well as ethical and religious) acceptability and order. To be effective, such imagery often engages its viewers in sympathetic identification with those whose social superiority conveys power and who, in fact, possess the very wealth which the strict religious code negates.

Clearly, most members of any fifteenth-century audience would not be wearing the rich clothing of Anima, the queen who was set before them as an embodiment of their own souls in *Wisdom*, and whose rich cloth of gold, miniver-lined cloak, regal "side" (e.g., long) tassels, and golden headband ally her visually with the queen of England as well as the queen of heaven (see 16n; also see Riggio 1986 9 - 10). The play effectively asks Christians to accept the rigid mental discipline of the "religion of the hert." Those in the fifteenth century who answered this call claimed to have cloistered corners of their internal lives, to have in effect constructed an "abbey of the holy ghost" within themselves which allowed them to live in the world but practice in privacy the strict religious discipline of the cloisters. Ascending the lower rungs of Hilton's ladder or *scale of perfection*, they espoused values that appear to negate worldly gain and to disparage rich food and drink as well as wealth. But, like modern fundamentalist Christians who deny the value of all earthly possessions but aspire to own a mansion in a heaven in which the streets are paved with gold, those who identified with Anima could claim a gilded crown (in heaven) along with the hairshirts they wore on earth as a reward for their Christian virtue and good behavior. What one claims to give up on earth, one lays in store for heaven. And the images of that reward betray an ideal that links religion with established order. If the wages of sin are death, then the wages of religion, from this perspective, are a place on — or near — the throne.

C. When Everyman is a Woman and Wisdom is a Man:
Source as a Guide to the Implications of Gender

The play of *Wisdom* differs from the other Macro plays in several respects, but none more startling than the portrayal of the "every*man*" character as an aristocratic woman, the queen of heaven and consort of Christ. In the process of establishing the gender identity of the human soul as feminine, the play performs a delicate operation on what might be called the genitalia of its most important source document. In the *Orologium Sapientiae*, Heinrich Suso's Sapientia speaks "nowe as manne, now as he þat is spowse of his chirche & nowe as sche that is spowse & wyfe of euerye chosene sowle" (Ms. Corpus Christi 268 fol. 56). That is to say, in Suso's dialogue Wisdom, though always identified with Christ, is sometimes manifested as the beautiful biblical goddess Sapientia, the spouse of Suso's masculine soul, and sometimes as the masculine Christ of the cross, spouse of the Church and saviour of humanity. Thus, both Suso's Sapientia and the disciple with whom s/he talks are effectively androgynous, encompassing in their androgyny the masculine and feminine aspects of human nature. By disburdening Anima of her masculinity and Christ of his femininity, *Wisdom* collapses the gender identities of the two characters in favor of a paradigm that associates power and authority solely with the masculine Christ while relegating the feminine Anima to a position of devoted subjection, incapable even of affirming her own nature. Whereas all the male characters of the play, Christ, Lucifer, and the three Mights, have expository monologues in which they identify their own "propyrte" or nature (see, for instance, ll. 1 - 14; 181 - 276), Anima simply asks Christ as Wisdom to explain her nature to her: "Wat ys a sowll, wyll 3e declare" (l. 102).

As Caroline Bynum has made clear, a feminine Christ was not unusual in the later Middle Ages. Identified with his mother in her guise as protector and comforter of humanity, the feminine Christ helps to blur gender lines in a period that struggled to reconcile its need for a God of mercy and compassion with a firmly fixed paradigm of masculinity. The identification of Christ with the female goddess of Wisdom, which was but one of the manifestations of the maternal Christ, merges two distinct biblical wisdom traditions. Sapientia is personified as a woman in a number of biblical texts. Ecclesiasticus (or the Wisdom of Joshua ben Sirach) 1.9-10 identifies Sapientia as an original creation of God:

Ipse creavit illam in Spiritu Sancto,
et vidit, et dinumeravit, et mensus est.
Et effudit illam super omnia opera sua,
et super omnem carnem, secundum datum suum,
et praebuit illam diligentibus se.

(The Lord himself created wisdom in the holy spirit; he saw *her* and apportioned *her*. He poured *her* out upon all his works, and *she* dwells with all flesh according to his gift, and he supplied *her* to those who love him; italics mine.)

Sapientia has her origins in the fear of God, but she is persistently an understanding and loving goddess, most frequently pictured with a book or a scroll. Ecclesiasticus 24.32 - 33 identifies her with the covenant of Moses: *Haec omnia liber vitae / et testamentum Altissimi, et agnitio veritatis / Legem mandavit Moyses in praeceptis justitiarum.* ("All this is the book of the covenant and the testament of the Most High God, the law which Moses commanded us.") Other biblical books, including Proverbs, the Wisdom of Solomon, and Psalms, describe Sapientia as an object of human desire, giving her specific attributes that appear periodically in her iconography. She is, for instance, at times identified with the Virgin, as in the Van Eyck Ghent Altarpiece (1432; see Riggio 1986 plate 7) where the *Virgo Sapientissima* appears holding a book.

As the enthroned Virgin of Wisdom exemplifies, the attributes of Sapientia do at times include regal authority, in the manifestation of which Sapientia was not always a woman. King Solomon, too, epitomized Wisdom, and more importantly Christ as the second person of the Trinity was persistently associated with Wisdom, an attribution which, though not established in the Bible, does have biblical justification. Isaiah 11.2, 1, 3 prophesies that:

> . . . *Et requiescet super eum spiritus Domini [virga de radice Jesse] . . . et replebit eum spiritus timoris Domini.*

> (. . . the Spirit of wisdom and understanding shall rest upon [a shoot from the stump of Jesse] . . . and his delight shall be in the fear of the Lord.)

n Luke 11.49 Christ is called *sapientia Dei*, "the Wisdom of God," and, most obviously, the Gospel of John furthers the association between God and Wisdom by identifying God as the *logos*, the divine made incarnate, of course, in the birth of Christ. Typological associations between Christ as king and the wise King Solomon further reinforce the notion of Christ as Eternal Wisdom, a personification that parallels and is at times fused with the female Sapientia, reflected especially in the *Virgo Sapientissima* or Virgin of Wisdom, who is herself often enthroned, and echoed in the role of the Virgin acting as the "throne of Wisdom," or seat of Christ, and Solomon enthroned on the "throne of Solomon." (The Trinity production of the play exploited this implicitly androgynous connection between Christ and the female Sapientia by seating Christ on a throne of Solomon, marked by its six steps with two lions at the ends of each step.)

As the tradition develops, Christ takes on features attributed biblically to the feminine Sapientia. Suso's dialogue attributes these qualities to the feminine Christ. To begin with the attributes quoted on the scroll of the *Virgo Sapientissima* in the Van Eyck Ghent Altarpiece:

> *Haec speciosior sole, et super omnem dispositionem stellarum . . . . Candor est enim lucis aeternae,/ et speculum macula Dei majestatis,/ et imago bonitatis illius.*
> Wisdom of Solomon 7.29, 26

> (She is more beautiful than the sun and above all the disposition of the stars . . . . For she is the light of the eternal and a spotless mirror of the majesty of God.)

n Suso's dialogue, the masculine soul speaks these lines of his beloved, the feminine Sapientia:

> *Sapiencia speciosior est sole a super omnia dispositionem stellars . . . et ymago bonitatissime.* That is to seyne wysdom is fayere þan ys þe sonne & in comparison of hire to lyght. She is fonndyn passyng abovyn alle þe disposicion of sterrys. She is for sothe þe brythnesse of evirlastyng lyght & the mirror withoutyn weme of goddys mageste & ymage of hys goodnesse.
> (Corpus Christi Ms. 268 fol. 56)

The feminine beauty of the woman who for both Joshua ben Sirach (author of Ecclesiasticus) and Henry Suso is more beautiful than the sun, who excels every constellation, superior even to light, is claimed in the play by Christ, in a passage that has a startlingly narcissistic ring:

> *Sapiencia specialior est sole*
> I am founden lyghte wythowt comparyson,
> Off sterrys aboue all þe sysposicyon,
>   Forsothe of lyght þe very bryghtnes,
> Merowre of þe dyvyne domynacyon
>   And þe image of hys goodnes.   (ll. 27 - 32)

Or, again, the Wisdom of Solomon describes Sapientia as an object of desire, courted as a bride:

> *Hanc amavi, et exquisivi a juventute mea,*
> *et quaesivi sponsam mihi eum assumere.* (8.2)

> (I loved and sought her from my youth, and I
> desired to take her for my bride.)

In the English translation of the *Orologium Sapientiae*, the soul similarly desires Sapientia:

> She is that I have levyd & I have vtturly sowt fro myne
> 3owthe & desyryd to have to myn spowse, and I am
> made a lovere of hyr forme and schap.
>   (Corpus Christi Ms. 268, fol. 56)

In *Wisdom*, the feminine Anima speaks these lines to Christ:

> Fro my yougthe thys haue I sowte
>   To haue to my spowse most specyally.
>   (18 - 19)

To the biblical goddess Sapientia is attributed long life and great riches as properties of her own:

> *Longitudo dierum in dextera ejus,*
> *et in sinistra illlius divitiae et gloria.* Proverbs 3.16

(Long life is in her right hand; in her left hand are riches and honor.)

The *Seven Points of True Wisdom* follows suit:

> The lengthe of 3erys is in hir ryth syde and in hir lefte syde rychesse & ioye.
>
> (Corpus Christi Ms. 268 fol 56)

In the play Christ predictably claims these attributes as his:

> The lengthe of þe yerys in my ryght syde be
> And in my left syde ryches, joy and prosperyte.
> (36 - 37)

In a process of gender transformation, the feminine Sapientia has become the masculine Christ; the "sche þis I haue louede and . . . vtturlye sowhte . . . for to haue to my spowse" has become the "he" of Anima's professed love for Christ. Christ claims for himself the "lengthe of þe yerys" and the "ryches, ioy, and prosperyte" which Suso, following Proverbs, attributes to the Goddess Sapientia. The only trace in the play of the feminine Sapientia occurs at the end of Christ's opening monologue where, again quoting Suso, he identifies himself as the "wyfe of eche chosen sowle" (l. 16). In Suso's dialogue, Christ is feminine when the spouse of the masculine soul, and masculine when the spouse of the feminine Ecclesia. But in the play the soul, personified as Anima, is a woman, the mate of the masculine Emperor Christ as Wisdom. In making this shift, the dramatist altered the gender identify of Christ but kept the line in which he identifies himself as the "wyfe" of the soul, a hint of gender ambivalence discussed in the notes (see 16n).

The gender simplification by which the androgynous Sapientia becomes the masculine Christ is, from one point of view, characteristic of the English adaptation of Suso. From the beginning, Suso's *Orologium* entered English in excerpted, edited, and simplified versions. The original Latin text details elaborate devotional rituals, such as carving Christ's initials into Suso's chest, which are ignored in the *Seven Points of True . . . Wisdom*. The playwright's levelling of the complex, dual identity of Christ as both man and woman is in keeping with that general impulse to simplify this devotional treatise for a pragmatic and probably lay English audience. And then, of course, there is the distinction between written and visual media: a written dialogue may preserve a change of gender more easily than a play which depends upon visual representation, a point which might be illustrated by reference to the miniatures which illustrate various Suso manuscripts. Despite Sapientia's dual identity as a man and a woman in the text of Suso's dialogues, pictorial illustrations habitually depict a consistently gendered Wisdom. Illustrations of the Latin *Orologium Sapientiae*, for instance, tend to portray Sapientia consistently as a woman, offering the book of wisdom to frequently male listeners. In contrast, illustrations of Suso's German *Vita* consistently portray Wisdom, or *Weisheit*, as a man, though the illustrations of various manuscripts of the *Vita* do hint at least at a process of evolution that parallels the English re-gendering of Wisdom (see Riggio 1989).

As noted earlier, the *Orologium* was in part a translation of an earlier German work of Suso's called *Das Büchlein der Ewigen Weisheit* or the *Little Book of Eternal Wisdom*. Suso continued the motif of the dialogue between an alternatingly masculine/feminine Sapientia in his spiritual autobiography or *Vita*, written at the request of his spiritual goddaughter, which he included with the *Büchlein* in a large manuscript, called the *Exemplar* at the end of his life. Six manuscripts of the *Vita*, conveniently spanning a period from c. 1360 to the late fifteenth century, are extant. To these may be added early printed editions of Suso's German works. Examined, these texts show a definite pattern of evolution in the visual representation of Christ enthroned as Wisdom. These manuscripts and early printed volumes all contain eleven or twelve illustrations, which with the exception of one plate (sometimes omitted) recur in the same places in each text, but which evolve pictorially from the fourteenth to the sixteenth century.

As in the Latin *Orologium*, so, too, in the *Vita* Wisdom speaks to a disciple; here, too, the voice of Christ, whose name Suso professes to worship, takes on both masculine and feminine characteristics. In chapter three, for instance, the disciple describes his "marriage" to Lady Wisdom, whose radiant beauty has won his heart. But the heart's beloved alternates between the feminine Wisdom addressing her lover and the masculine Christ addressing his bride. Despite some ambivalence and imitative echoes that only slightly blur gender lines, for the most part the illustrations stabilize the masculine identity, portraying Christ as a king.

However, figure 9, the one illustration in which Christ is enthroned in a posture that specifically recalls — or foreshadows — the Wisdom of the English play, does bear a diminishing imprint of the feminine Sapientia, evoked as the *schützmantel madonna*, who is in her own right a complex, potentially bi-gendered figure. From at least the twelfth century on, the Virgin Mary portrayed as the *schützmantel madonna* or *Virgin of the Sheltering Mantle* was figured as a protector, nurturing her "children" beneath her outspread cloak in a widely repeated image that probably originated not in feminine nurture but in the imperial authority of the Roman Emperor, as portrayed, for instance, in conjunction with Jupiter on Roman coins (Solway 363).

Seated on the throne, clad in ermine, crowned with an imperial crown, and holding an orb and a sceptre, the enthroned Wisdom of the later Suso German manuscripts has a powerful male presence, which is exaggerated until finally a 1516 printed edition of this work portrays Wisdom as Christ looking very much like the "ancient of days" (see Riggio 1989 figure 1). A hint of the nurturing mantle is figured only in the protection which Christ's slightly distended mantle, recalling the sheltering Virgin, gives the disciple, his spiritual goddaughter, and others who worship his name.

Earlier illustrations tell a different tale. In what is probably the second oldest manuscript, for instance, Christ's sheltering mantle creates a room, with the fox fur or vair lining of the mantle taking on the appearance of a tiled wall above a tiled floor in which the worshippers of Christ's name kneel (Ms. 710 fol. 96). The mantle itself iconographically invokes the *schützmantel madonna*. And if there were any doubt about the origins of the nurturing posture, the earliest extant manuscript, Ms. Strasbourg 2929, would dispel it. There where one expects to find Christ as Eternal Wisdom is instead the madonna herself in a posture identical in main features both to those of the sheltering madonna in the Parisian Lib. Bibl. Geneviéve Ms. of 1029, which probably served as the model, and of Christ in the subsequent Strasbourg illustration. The early status of the Strasbourg manuscript, which Suso himself could possibly have seen or, as Edmund Colledge and J. C. Marler argue, even drawn, may reinforce the argument put forth by Colledge and Marler that Suso himself preferred the feminine Wisdom for figure 9, a point which is not central to an understanding of the English play. What is more significant is that the stage directions of *Wisdom* dictate costuming and position for Christ which are essentially identical to those of the later Suso manuscripts. Despite some slender

evidence that one or two of the German illustrations of Suso's *Vita* may
have been known in England, possibly brought in with the Carthusians in
the fifteenth century, the issue here is not whether the play copied the
German illustrations of Suso as it appropriated the English translation of
his Latin text;   the more important question is what to make of the
evolution from the early feminine Wisdom, nurturing humanity under a
spreading mantle, to the hoary and majestic king of the later Suso
manuscripts and of the English play.

Though portrayed as a king, Christ as Wisdom does embrace both
masculine and feminine characteristics. He is, for instance, the emanation
of perfect light and reflection of God's goodness associated biblically with
the goddess Sapientia. And, within a fairly rigid paradigm of male and
female behavior, he embodies the authority of the masculine emperor and
the weeping compassion of the nurturing mother. For all her feminine
beauty, Anima as the Soul serves as the model for male as well as female
viewers. Despite the femininity of the personification, the soul is
consistently referred to in the play as "he," even by Anima herself. When
Anima returns in the second half of the play, she has been crowned as a
"kynge" (l. 1124). And, perhaps most significantly, her three masculine
Mights act out the passive Anima's latent vainglorious desires. The
beautiful woman, entirely removed from the stage, remains an object of
desire while the more energetic but also more vulgar men play out the
comedy of sin, though, finally, of course, it is the woman who is disfigured
by the sinful experience. Only in her foulness do the Mights experience
their own debasement and only through her confession and penance do
they recover their own initial stature.

The complex process by which spectators are being asked to identify
with Anima as the representative of themselves even as they
simultaneously adore her as an aristocratic woman whose beauty places
her beyond their reach is akin to a medieval psychology of contemplative
worship, or what Wendy Wright calls "contemplative seeing." Associated
with devotional images in the late middle ages, this process involves
seeing an image both as a representative of oneself and an object of
adoration. Within this frame of reference one first contemplates the
symbol;   then one internalizes it so as to live out the experience oneself
and then in a third stage sees the image again as "an exterior guide that
informs the individual in a new way" (Wright;   for quotation and a fuller
discussion see Riggio 1989 243 - 44). The process involves both the

engagement of empathic identification (Anima as the soul of every human creature) and the distance of worship or adoration (Anima in her likeness both to the Virgin Mary and to the English queen). Like portraits of the Virgin Mary, who worshippers see as both the mother of God and a human woman receiving the benefits of God's grace, the dramatized image of Anima can be both "the icon to be venerated" and "humanity receiving the fruits of veneration" (Wright; qtd. in Riggio 1989 244).

The play dramatizes the love between Wisdom as Christ and Anima, the human soul, in a metaphor of marriage that naturally stresses the personal bond between God and humanity. Moreover, the soul is dressed as a queen as well as a virgin wife. The links to the Virgin as a redemptive maiden are clear, and the Trinity College production exploited them. By personifying the soul as a wife, however, the play further insinuates the need for subjection to authority. For all his "feminine" compassion, Christ maintains the majesty of the crowned emperor. It is true that he speaks of his humility; he talks of his Passion and, in the Trinity production which counterpointed the flow of the play with quickly drawn iconographical portraits, he briefly assumed the posture of the crucified Christ (see ll. 1100 - 07). But he maintains authority over the woman who worships him, even as she, in her aristocratic turn, controls those of her "affinity," or household. By representing humanity as a woman, the play insinuates the special need for subjection to authority which is associated with the obedient woman who learns to "know her place." All humans are like women in their obedience to God. However powerful within the frame of their own reference, all are "feminine" in their subjection to God's discipline. But by portraying Anima as a royal woman, the play also insinuates a hierarchy of authority that — within the frame of God's omnipotence — recognizes and accepts true aristocracy among humans. The contemplative tradition with which its sources link *Wisdom* similarly found one base of power within the structures of the wealthy household which oversaw the patronage of those within its affinity, but which was also asked repeatedly — and particularly under the reign of Henry VII — to recognize the limits of that authority beneath the power of the crown that authorized it.

II. GENRE IN CONTEXT:

Moral Plays and Household Masques
or
A Morality by any other Name

> *Theatre is an art form; it is also a social*
> *institution. By favoring a certain style of representation*
> *and a particular etiquette of reception, the institutional*
> *setting of a performance informs and focuses the meaning of*
> *a dramatic text and facilitates the dissemination of that*
> *meaning through the collective activity of the audience.*
> (Michael Bristol 3)

In the thirty years since David Bevington charged that "the form of the morality has not been analyzed because it has not been recognized as artistically significant" (1962 2), so-called "morality plays" have earned a place among the respectable genres of drama. The change in attitude results as much from recent performances of morality plays as from scholarship, but performance itself has yet to be taken seriously as a component of genre. Morality plays have been defined as plays that dramatize the psychomachia, as plays that portray an individual journey toward wholeness, as dramas of sin and repentance. But however defined, the generic identity of plays which, adapting a term from eighteenth-century French criticism, we call "moralities" has been determined largely by similarities of plot, character type, image, and theme — all factors that elevate the play*text* above the theatrically realized *play*.

Not that the textual similarities are insignificant. Far from it. The recurrence of what amounts to one "moral" plot, not only repeated throughout the Macro manuscript but common also to other fifteenth- and sixteenth-century plays drawn from varied performance genres, does call attention to the way in which dramatic themes inevitably reflect the culture from which they spring. What is at stake in this common plot is nothing less than the human "soul," but the way in which the plays define the contest for the soul derives as much from the politics as the theology of the period. The fifteenth century, in which the English crown was batted back and forth among feuding cousins, saw an unprecedented growth in the size and influence of large private households and a complex relationship between the king and the aristocratic families on whom peacekeeping in the realm largely devolved. In this context, the anti-modern, anti-acquisitive stances of "morality plays," best represented by the three plays of the Macro manuscript, take on particular coloration that initially links these plays together but ultimately distinguishes them from each other.

While the textual similarities help us initially to group plays like the Macro plays effectively together and in so doing to understand the contextual dynamics of what amounts to the common morality plot, defining genre with reference to likely performance conditions rather than plot, theme, and character ultimately helps to distinguish *Wisdom* from the other two Macro plays. Modern revivals of medieval plays have shown that the same play in a new environment becomes in some degree a new play. If one airlifted a fifteenth-century production into the twentieth century, changes in audience, in language, in the significance of costuming and the meaning of culturally conditioned symbols would alter not only the production but also the play itself. As we learned from staging *Wisdom* twice at Trinity College in 1984, once in a dining hall and once on an outdoor scaffold, even moving an indoor drama out of doors changes the play, elevating stage pictures or broad comedy over the subtleties of a complex textual argument and turning a dinner masque into a less successful outdoor spectacle. If changing the location, staging, and audience thus affects a play, how much more significant are distinctions in basic dramatic rhythm, audience interaction, and probable theatrical venue in determining genre.

Despite their similar plots, themes, images, and character types, even the three Macro plays differ markedly when one considers the staging demands of the plays. *Mankind* requires a small, probably professional troupe with one primary actor who may double in the roles of Mercy and Tityvillus and five additional actors; *The Castle of Perseverance* is a spectacular outdoor play, requiring a cast of thirty-five with minimal doubling possibilities, large staging scaffolds (including a raised castle), and playing to a varied audience apparently milling around in a large playing area; *Wisdom* is probably a dinner play, requiring six small boys, five "prudent virgins," at least twelve dancers, including six women, and six actors in roles that cannot be doubled, elaborate in its costuming but with minimal stage settings, also designed for a mixed audience, probably under the auspices of the ecclesiastical or secular household which presents the play. Such distinctions, which help to determine the character of any play, are crucial for *Wisdom*, a play that may be identified as a member of the extended family of English masques and disguisings that developed in and along with wealthy English households during the late fifteenth century.

A. The Plots, Characters, and Themes of the Macro "Moralities": Social Value in a Religious Text

Defining the "morality play" in 1975, Robert Potter recognized what he called different "theatrical guises" among the moralities. But he submerged those differences beneath the textual similarities that led him to identify morality drama as a "single . . . kind of play":

> The medieval morality plays, which flourished in England at the same time as the Corpus Christi cycles, took many theatrical guises, from the cosmic pageantry and spectacle of *The Castle of Perseverance* (1405 - 25) and *Wisdom* (1450 - 1500) to the barnyard scurrilities of *Mankind* (1465 - 70), from the topical satire of *Hickscorner* (1513) to the universality of *Everyman* (1495). But they seem to have been a single and very specific kind of play about the human predicament.

> A concept — what it means to be human — is represented on the stage by a central dramatic figure or series of figures. Subsidiary characters, defined by their function, stand at the service of the plot which is ritualized, dialectical, and inevitable: man exists, therefore he falls, nevertheless he is saved. This pattern, repeated in every morality play, should enable us not only to understand the form but also to fix its place in the unity of medieval religious drama.
> (Potter 1975 6 - 7)

Though Potter would no longer subscribe to the idea of a "unity of medieval drama," his description of a "single . . . kind of [morality] play" remains basic to our understanding of a large number of fifteenth-, sixteenth-, and even seventeenth-century European plays. In England alone the list of "moralities" couples fifteenth- and early sixteenth-century religious allegories, particularly the three plays of the Macro manuscript, the fragmentary *Pride of Life*, *Everyman*, *Mundus et Infans*, and *Youth* together with a wide array of political allegories, such as Skelton's *Magnificence*, the Catholic *Respublica* designed for courtly production in the first year of Queen Mary's reign, and an even larger number of often farcical popular interludes which teach their moral lessons "mixed full of pleasant mirth" (*Marriage Between Wit and Wisdom*). Bernard Spivack lists a total of fifty-seven such plays (484 - 93). Following both Bevington and Potter's lead, we can extend this generic category to Marlowe, Shakespeare, Jonson, and beyond (Bevington 1962 141 - 264 and Potter 1975 123 - 70).

A genre that links a play like *Wisdom* with Tudor farces like *Ralph Roister Doister* is almost too broad to be meaningful, but without question, the plots, character types, and themes of the Macro plays resemble each other. Typically, a personified representative of humanity (Humanum Genus, Mankind, Anima) is trapped between "good," defined in terms of Christian redemption, and "evil," defined primarily as greed, sensuality, and the pride that accompanies petty acquisition. The key element of this plot is the seduction of the central character and his/her fall from Christian grace into sin, with a final, crucial moment of repentance leading to salvation and a restoration of grace. This three-part "morality" structure, beginning and ending in a state of grace, with a comically excessive world of sin sandwiched between, presumes a universal moral code. But, as often happens when the "universal" is framed within a particular culture, the value system of the drama emerges as much from the social as from the religious fabric of society. Theology and sociology merge into one cultural whole.

Indeed, the term "grace" itself illustrates the dual nature of language which links the political world to religious, especially Catholic, value structures. As an honorific the term "[your/his] grace" historically has designated both religious dignitaries, particularly archbishops, and secular lords, especially in the fifteenth and sixteenth centuries the king or queen, as when Latimer preached a sermon before Edward VI "wyth in his Graces Palaice" in 1549 or when decades earlier Elizabeth Stonor brought the Duchess of Suffolk "to the king's good grace and the Queen's" (Stonor ii 14; qtd. in Kingsford 27). As a mark of patronage "grace" can designate royal favor; to live within the "king's grace" is to attain favor at court. Theologically "grace" is the quality conferred by God that allows for human redemption. In plays in which worldly values directly oppose religious ideals, one might expect the redemptive grace of God to be set in opposition to grace represented as royal favor. In *The Castle of Perseverance* such an opposition is implicit to the adversarial relationship between the chief villain, portrayed as a petty feudal overlord called King Mundus (or World) and the imperial God who, in his role as universal monarch, saves humanity. As used in *Wisdom* grace also has contrastive meanings: idealized as a gift from God, which makes redemption possible, and castigated as the favor of a corrupted worldly patron (see Glossary).

Though in *Wisdom*, the grace of God is not pitted against the "king's grace" as in *The Castle*, the opposition between God's grace and the grace of worldly favor is central to *Wisdom*. In this play Christ is the only king, whose favor and redemptive grace outweigh the "euell grace" (l. 550) or bad luck and the "harde . . . grace" (l. 723) or adverse court judgments that result from choosing a vulgar, lesser lord whose patronage may confer temporary wealth but lacks the genuine aristocracy, both of value and of style, which comes with the grace of God.

On the surface, it seems as if such a contrast simply pits piety against worldliness, setting divine goodness in opposition to corruption. And this is surely the most obvious theme of all these plays. But there is a subtler social dynamic at work in plays which identify religious virtue with obedient acceptance of established order. In creating the opposition between good and evil as epitomized in Christian grace and sin, all three Macro plays embody absolute, unified authority in an idealized patriarch who rules over a harmonious kingdom or "state" of grace: God the "*pater sedens in trono*" (l. 3561sd) in *The Castle of Perseverance*, Mercy the "father gostly" (l. 765) in *Mankind*, and "imperyall" Christ the "soueren auctoure" (l. 99) and "wery (i.e., true) patrone" (l. 15) in *Wisdom*. In a ritual emphasizing authority and control, God, Mercy, and Wisdom conclude each play with a benedictory statement. In all three plays the metaphors for divine power are significantly cast in terms of social order; salvation is a function of divine patronage ("patrocynye," *Mankind* l. 904) or imperial power ("All þe statys of þe werld is at myn renoun," *The Castle of Perseverance* l. 3615). Wisdom, as an imperial king, identifies the soul as Christ's "plesant see" or feudal seat (l. 132). And in two of these plays, *The Castle of Perseverance* and *Wisdom*, virtue is invested in a kind of bluestockinged elegance which embodies "true" aristocratic value — God as the guarantor of right, i.e. established, rule and upholder of social hierarchy.

The portrayal of God as a king is conventional, and one might argue that since such portrayals occur throughout the centuries of Christianity, no culturally specific conclusions may be drawn from such a portrait in any one given century. To counter this argument, one must basically ask what the portrayal of God as Emperor (*The Castle of Perseverance*) or Christ as King (*Wisdom*) has to do with the fifteenth century that distinguishes it from, say, the ninth century or even the eighteenth? The broad answer, which lies beyond the scope of this analysis, would take us through an evolving relationship between concepts of right rule, notions of monarchy, and assumptions about divinity throughout the history of European Christianity. The short, manageable answer, focusing on the fifteenth century, emerges from the intricate interaction between epistemology, theology, and political theory embedded partially in the link between knowledge of God and knowledge of self and in the contrastive imagery of divine kingship and worldly lordship in the Macro plays. In this interaction lies a subtle affirmation of a portion of the very world which the plays purport to deny.

Crucial to this issue is not only the conjunction between aristocratic women, like Cicely of York and Margaret Beaufort, and the lay piety of the fifteenth century discussed in "Sources in Context" above, but also the broad link between the British monarchy and ecclesiastical authorities during the fifteenth century. Despite the varying allegiances to the houses of York or Lancaster by large religious houses, such as the Abbey of Bury St. Edmonds, the English monarch was allied both conceptually and practically with the large religious establishments of England. The mythology of kingship owed much to theology. By intertwining an Italian concept of royal dignity with the ideal of the king's perpetual life as a *corpus mysticum*, the English in particular strengthened the mystique of perpetuity for the king. Such a notion was also occasionally extended to abbots, as, for instance, in a case under Edward IV in 1482 in which an abbot is identified as having a "mystical body . . . which never dies" (Kantorowicz 406).

Not only was the theoretical role of kingship persistently though variously defined with reference to theology, but the British king continued to exert a powerful influence over the Catholic Church throughout the fifteenth century. Emissaries to the Council of Constance, for instance, represented English royal policy far more than was comfortable for papal purposes. And throughout the century, both the Lancasters and the Yorks maintained strong ties with various religious houses. Under the tutelage of his mother Margaret Beaufort, herself a lay ascetic, Henry VII was renowned for his piety, which in no way lessened the ruthlessness with which he attempted to establish his monarchical authority over commons and nobles alike. The essentially conservative alliance between church and state, which invests value nostalgically in longstanding hierarchy while condemning the recent acquisition of wealth and upstart social pretension, underlies the polar opposition between good and evil in the Macro plays.

The opposition within the plays is binary and simple: divine wholeness is set against worldly fragmentation. Whatever is single, whole, and harmonious is identified with the Kingdom of God; opposing the unified kingdom of God is the fragmented world of sin, in which seductive agents of evil lure the human protagonist into sins of worldly acquisition and personal pleasure. In the staging plan which accompanies the Macro text of *The Castle of Perseverance*, the World, the Flesh, and the Devil all appear on separate scaffolds, which represent their seats of feudal power; these comically self-defining characters parody the role of overlords, whose followers personify the seven Deadly Sins (see Riggio 1981). Each boasts of a false sense of power and introduces his agents: conventionally, Pride, Wrath, and Envy serve the Devil; Lechery, Gluttony, and Sloth attend upon Flesh. But the prime mover of evil is a personified "Sir Couetyse," or Covetousness, an agent of the World with a staging scaffold of his own. In *Mankind*, Tityvillus, a comic devil who also defines his own nature, is flanked by the vice figure Mischief and the buffoons Nought, Newgyse, and Nowadays who represent demonic pride as inextricably linked with covetousness, i.e., with the desire for new fashion and acquisition of wealth characterized as the "new gyse and þe new jett" (l. 103). These vulgar, modish, worldly fashions and styles of behavior negate true beauty as well as virtue. In both cases, the patriarchal power of God the father or God the king overrules and negates the vulgar pretensions of upstart, newly enriched social intruders.

In contrast to the plethora of comic agents in the two previous plays, *Wisdom* pits good against a single evil force. But though *Wisdom*'s Lucifer gains power from his singleness, he echoes the theme not only of worldly acquisition but also of fragmentation established in the earlier plays, making clear the relationship between the anti-acquisitive stance of the drama and its affirmation of established hierarchy. By elevating the devil above the world as the prime mover of evil, *Wisdom* might, for instance, be expected to focus on pride, the sin that Lucifer claims as his own:

> I xall now stere hys mynde
> To þat syne made me a fende:
> Pryde, wyche ys ageyn kynde
> And of all synnys hede.
>   (ll. 527 - 30)

However, as in *Mankind* where a devil Titivillus seduces Mankind into a love of worldly wealth, so, too, in *Wisdom* pride is more a sin of the world than of the spirit. Lucifer wears a "gallant's" disguise to woo the faculties of Anima, named Mind, Will, and Understanding, with the suggestion to "Be in þe worlde," to "beholde þe worlde," and to "lede a comun lyff" (ll. 464, 472). He wins Mynde to worldly power ("lordeschyppe," l. 630), Wndyrstondynge to riches earned from corrupting the law (ll. 637 - 45), and Wyll to the spendthrifty pleasures of "onclennes" and "lust" (ll. 650, 652). Under his influence, the unity of God's kingdom, symbolized by monophonic chanting, long aristocratic or clerical clothing, and liturgical processions, gives way to the fragmentation of three-part music, short modish clothes, and bawdy masked dances — all emblems of fragmented worldliness.

The implicit locus of the drama in *Wisdom*, as in the other Macro plays, is the world of social acquisition. Despite the angry bickering which takes place in the world of sin, especially in *Wisdom* and *Mankind*, the plays do not dwell on the powerful sins of the spirit, or on the kinds of overreaching pride that characterize later English tragic heroes; instead, the covetousness of earthly goods and petty power dominates each play. In keeping with their anti-acquisitive stance, the plays emphasize the worldly acting out of petty, though deadly, vices, attacking greed and the lust for social power along with sensual pleasures. In *Wisdom*, even though Lucifer identifies pride as the sin which led him to destruction, he offers as a seductive lure the trivial pleasures of possession, ownership, and small-scale social influence, rather than the Satanic drive for spiritual mastery which one might expect to associate with this sin. The sinners in *Wisdom*, as in the other Macro plays, could earn a place only in the upper circles of Dante's hell.

Such acquisitive instincts feed the anti-modern themes of all three plays, which on the surface at least appear conventionally to idealize a lost past, a golden age of harmony and social cohesion disrupted by the acquisitiveness of an English society aping the manners, styles, and values of a cosmopolitan European world, centered in France and portrayed as increasingly corrupt, in which self-interest and monetary gain replace older values of service and respect for place. In keeping with the general triviality of evil, these plays appropriate low mimetic forms in their satire of fifteenth century "modernity." As part of its conservative religious and social stance, each play satirizes modish, French-influenced, short clothing styles and the vulgar *nouveau riche* behavior which they personify, for instance, in *Mankind* as Newgyse and Nowadays and which is reflected in the new "jakett" which Mankind dons in his pursuit of idle pleasure (l. 672). New and vulgar fashions are satirized in the coin-bedecked symbolical garments given to Humanum Genus in a ceremony of fealty to King World in *The Castle of Perseverance* (see ll. 584-776).

These same abuses are shown in the gallant's disguise assumed by Lucifer and the "dysgysynge" garments worn by Mind, Will, and Understanding in *Wisdom*, a play in which the exploits of the renamed Mights satirize social abuses which were themselves the subject of law at the end of the fifteenth century, particularly under the reign of Henry VII (see, for instance, ll. 629 - 744; 805 - 11; 849 - 57). The two Mights who represent aspects of human reason, Mind and Understanding, are re-named "Meyntnance" and "Periury," and sin is committed in the form of petty social crimes, particularly abuses of the courts — bribing juries, winning suits by default through the legal ploy of simultaneous indictments in different shires, forfeiture through false manipulation of the law — and the practice of "livery and maintenance," against which ordinances were passed from the late fourteenth century through the 1530s (Mertes 126), but which, as Bevington pointed out as early as 1963 in his analysis of topical satire in *Wisdom*, was particularly associated with the reigns of Richard III and Henry VII (Bevington 1963 41-51). Such abuses were characteristic of the latter half of the fifteenth century when forfeiture of land through the courts was a particularly popular practice, made easy by charges of treason attending upon the Wars of the Roses. The penalty of attainder, for instance, as a way of forcing forfeiture of property through a charge of treason, which often followed action in the common law courts, was imposed for the first time by act of Parliament in the fifteenth century (Lander 1970 93). One of the strategies of Mind (Meyntnance) in *Wisdom* is to force forfeiture by false charges unless he receives "mede" (a reward, l. 806).

What one sees is that the abuses satirized in *Wisdom* are, in fact, precisely those abuses which were castigated by law in the latter half of the fifteenth century, just as *The Castle of Perseverance* similarly satirizes illegal practices associated with patronage, in particular with trusteeship of property (see Riggio 1981). In *Wisdom* "divine" authority is enforced by eliminating social abuses that came under the jurisdiction of the crown. In this way, the play clearly, if subtly, allies the monarchy of God with the central authority of the king. This much of the argument is clear and fairly simple. But though the satire of the earlier *Castle of Perseverance* tends to link fealty only with the corrupted world, this is not the end of the story for *Wisdom* in which patronage with its concomitant provision of livery and expectation of fealty can be either virtuous or sinful.

To understand exactly how and where the line is drawn in *Wisdom* between good patronage and bad is not easy. The difficulty has fed a standing debate about the possible provenance of the play and about its handling of one of its central themes, the idealization of what appears at times to be monastic contemplation. Certainly, the play portrays its central characters as contemplatives in at least one section of the play and, by having Lucifer attack what was called the *vita mixta*, the mixed or "medled" life of activity and contemplation, the play appears to satirize even the intermixture of the active and the contemplative lives. Critics have taken sides (see Smart; Molloy; Bevington 1984; Gibson 1984; Johnston; Riggio 1984); even the Trinity College production was "set" in the abbot's palace at the Abbey of Bury St. Edmonds — a setting which attractively focused the conjunction between ecclesiastical authority and secular sovereignty in the play but which is not very likely for a play in which six women appear as dancers.

In a sense, the play is having it both ways: idealizing contemplation and the contemplative life but with options for public activity and gifts of charity. Such a dual thrust both toward and away from contemplation is possible in the drama only because the practices of lay piety in the fifteenth century clearly created a quasi-monastic option for lay ascetics. In its *contemptus mundi* stance, *Wisdom* implicitly, if somewhat vaguely, separates the portions of the world which it will condemn and those which it will not, and the line extends beyond the office of the monarch himself. Though it images divinity in the trappings of kingship, the play affirms more than the simple authority of the king. Through the implied value of its costuming, the play reinforces the alliances between ecclesiastical authority, lay piety, and secular power which developed during the fifteenth century, in which devotional half-portraits, narrative paintings, and books of hours became regular companions of individual exercises of piety (see Ringbom). Indeed, the heart of the Lollard attack on images lay in its opposition to the rich trappings of wealth and privilege in which devotional images, much like *Wisdom*, literally clothed the Holy Family. As one Lollard concluded:

> Though images made truly that represent verily the poverty and the passion of Jesus Christ and other saints are lawful . . . nevertheless false images that represent worldly glory and pride of the world as if Christ and other saints had lived thus and deserved bliss by glory and pomp of the world, are false books and worthy to be amended or burnt.
>
> (Compston 743; qtd. in Aston 163)

In this respect, *Wisdom* differs from its Macro companions. Though *Mankind* uses a patriarchal metaphor that links God's fatherhood with his royal power, the costuming of this probably professional play is simple. As in the other Macro plays, newfangled clothing signifies sin, but unlike the other plays, *Mankind* does not invest divine goodness in the castles or costumes of the rich and powerful. Moreover, whereas *The Castle of Perseverance* does locate God's protective power visually in a stage castle guarded by elegant ladies, royal attire itself signifies the worldly corruption of King Mundus. In contrast, the costume directions of *Wisdom* specifically link Christ and Anima, his consort, with the English king and Queen.

Fyrst entreth **Wysdome** in a ryche purpull clothe of golde
wyth a mantyll of the same ermynnyde wythin, hawynge
abowt hys neke a ryall hood furred wyth ermyn, wpon hys
hede a cheweler wyth browys, a berde of golde of Sypres
curlyde, a ryche imperyall crown þerwpon sett wyth
precyus stonys and perlys. In hys leyfte honde a balle of
golde wyth a cros þerwppon and in his ryght honde a
regall scheptur, thus seyenge:
(0sd)

Here entrethe **Anima** as a mayde in a wyght clothe of
golde gytely purfyled wyth menyver, a mantyll of blake
þerwppeon, a cheueler lyke to **Wysdom** wyth a ryche
chappetelot lasyde behynde hangynge down wyth ii
knottys of golde & syde tasselys, knelynge down to
Wysdom thus seyng:
(16sd)

Christ's ermine robe, a fur restricted in the late fifteenth-century
sumptuary laws to the royal family, his imperial crown, ball of gold, and
regal sceptre link him not only with portraits of Christ in majesty but also
with portraits of Edward IV, Henry VI, and Henry VII. Similarly, Anima's
clothing is precisely that worn by the English queen on a penitential ride
she was to take on the eve of her coronation, as described in the *Liber
Regalis* (see 16n and Riggio 1984 for fuller discussion). A member of a
late fifteenth century audience watching the play could not escape the
connection, though Anima's role as a royal queen is conflated with her
identity as the human soul and with iconic associations with the Virgin
Mary (see Riggio 1989).

When Anima kneels before Christ, she collapses within her person
several prescribed postures of obedience, all of which iterate each other
in the hierarchies of authority that link the family with the secular state and
the state with the kingdom of God. Since obedience in one structure is a
parallel to and a model for obedience in the others, the stage portrait of
the kneeling Anima signifies multiple connections between obedience and
authority. In a period in which a woman could be indicted for petty treason
for striking her husband, a "good" wife could (at least metaphorically) be

expected to kneel before the authority of her spouse; the subject kneels to offer fealty to the king; and the child of God must kneel before Christ in order to gain the grace essential for redemption. As drawn on the stage, the portrait of the kneeling Anima more specifically resembles paintings of the Coronation of the Virgin, whose kneeling posture is a gesture of fealty to Christ who is at once her father, her son, her spouse, and her king. But though images of the Virgin as well as the English queen are evoked in the portrayal of Anima, she is, in actuality, any human soul suing for favor, and she herself is in return identified as Christ's feudal "see" (l. 132). In this context, her role as an aristocratic woman positions the viewing audience, which presumably identifies with her, in a very different place from the audience that sees its own soul in the plain garments and naked simplicity of *The Castle of Perseverance*'s Humanum Genus.

In *The Castle*, aristocratic grace and beauty reside in the seven remedial virtues who inhabit the large, centrally positioned castle that safeguards the virtue of Humanum Genus and who fight, in courtly fashion, by throwing roses — a form of combat characteristic of the "chauteau d'amour" tradition. But Humanum Genus himself remains an ordinary subject both of God's divine kingdom and of the vulgar kingdom of the World. And the adversaries of the courtly ladies who guard the Castle are vulgar personifications of the seven deadly sins, who fight buffoon-fashion with vulgar weapons. The opposition between divinity and evil is also the opposition between the protective custody of a well-guarded castle and the squalid, vulgar threats of newly enriched, upstart pretenders. Though indoor masques did use elaborate staging devices, this particular configuration would suit the outdoor arena of performance much better than the wealthy dining room. Outdoors, with an audience presumably drawn from a wide range of social estates, the dignity and beauty of *The Castle*'s elegant ladies do make the link between the power of courtly beauty and divine goodness. The protection of a "castle" against the threats of a hostile surrounding countryside would without question resonate socially as well as allegorically for a fifteenth century audience, many of whom must perforce depend on the protection of a "good lord" against the dangers of marauders in an unprotected countryside. But while the subject who learns this lesson aspires to the protection of such beautiful and elegant women, he does not envision himself as one of them. He sees himself instead as the humble, classless *Humanum genus*, the human person who depends on the beautiful, aristocratic female virtues and on their protective castle for his security but who sees his own worldly ambitions castigated not only thematically but also visually in the strutting of King Mundus and the vaunting of his servant Sir Covetousness.

In contrast, *Wisdom* carries the metaphor of royalty further. Anima, the human soul and representative of every member of the audience, is herself the royal consort of Christ, dressed as a queen and, in lines 289 and 1064sd, called a "kynge." The play further insinuates a hierarchy of patronage through costuming. Whereas Christ and Anima are clothed in royal garments, Anima's handmaidens, "v vyrgynes" are dressed similarly "in white kertyllys & mantelys wyth cheuelers & chappelettys" (l. 164sd). And Anima's faculties, or Mights (Mind, Will, and Understanding) are "crested in her sute," i.e. liveried as her retainers, a distinction not conferred on Humanum Genus by the aristocratic virtues of *The Castle of Perseverance*. In *Wisdom*, the male Mights are "all iii in wyght cloth of golde, chevelered, as is Anima" (l. 324sd). These costumes reflect the regal clothing of the patrons Christ and Anima, bringing the representation of humanity within the aristocratic allegory of the play. Moreover, such long clothing signifies as well the alliance between the crown and the ecclesiastical hierarchy, since long clothing (idealized as virtuous and associated with the past) was identified with ecclesiastical garb as well as with luxurious secular robes throughout the fifteenth century. (To make this point, the Trinity production clothed the Mights in white costumes with black overcloaks, a costume that echoed Anima's black-over-white garments while also resembling the Dominican attire of one of the play's source authors, Henry Suso.)

A significant portion of the audience of *Wisdom* would surely identify, if only in fantasy, with these elegantly costumed representatives of the Soul, even while sharing with the audience of *The Castle* a bitter hatred directed at those who would obtrude into the world of established power by purchasing or attaining wealth and property. In short, a play like *Wisdom*, with its intricate allegory and elegant costuming, would cater more directly to the restricted guest list of a great house (whether secular or ecclesiastical), than to the more eclectic outside crowd of a spectacle like *The Castle of Perseverance*. Even the servants who might enter a dining hall to watch a household play would, of course, identify with liveried retainers who personify Anima's senses and her faculties. In this play, unlike the other two Macro plays, Everyhuman Anima moves within the realm of truly aristocratic privilege, though her role as a woman identifies her position as a gracious subject rather than a co-equal in the realm of power.

In the terminology of social historians such as Walter Ullmann, *Wisdom*, like the other Macro plays, portrays its representative human as "subject" or *sub/ditus* — i.e., one who, as a natural inferior, owes allegiance to an authority whose power is ordained perpetually by a "determined theocratic-descending form of government" — rather than the emergent "citizen" who can claim rights and privileges which no authority can contravene (Ullman 102 - 04). Such a concept has epistemological as well as sociological implications. In an exchange with Anima close to the beginning of the play Christ defines wisdom as knowledge of the self when that self is in tune with both divine and social hierarchy. Asking Wisdom to teach her the "scolys of yowr dyvynyte" (l. 86), Anima is told that she should know herself:

> By knowynge of yowrsylff 3e may haue felynge
> Wat Gode ys in yowr sowle sensyble.
> The more knowynge of yowrselff passyble
> þe more veryly 3e xall God knowe.
>   (95 - 98)

Self-knowledge is the key to wisdom only when the self is intuitively tuned to the divine. Such knowledge, presumed to exist *a priori*, was in the late middle ages identified with *sapientia*, in distinction from *scientia experimentalis*, which led to curious inquiry about the natural world. This second form of knowledge, depending primarily upon empirical observation and the processing of sense data, was, of course, at the basis of the developing interest in the natural sciences which occurred during the late middle ages (see Ullman 112). It is precisely this concept which is negated by Wisdom, who tells Anima that wisdom will lead her to eschew "cunnynge to excellent" (l. 87), i.e., the logical processes of reasoning which derive from or lead to curiosity, in favor of the obedient conformity of will which serves as the keystone of loving and fearing God:

Dysyer not to sauour in cunnynge to excellent,
But drede & conforme yowr wyll to me.
For yt ys þe heelfull dyscyplyne þat in Wysdam may be.
    The drede of God þat ys begynnynge
    The wedys of synne yt makyt to flee
    And swete wertuus herbys in þe sowll sprynge.
        (89 - 94)

Christ defines wisdom as the intuitive, contemplative love of God grounded in fear and sustained by obedience that undergirds the epistemology, theology, and — not incidentally — the social doctrine of this play. Though the theme is grounded in an apparent *contemptus mundi* stance, which values the love of God over the love of the world with its corrupting wealth and its vanity of possession, the exhortation to obedience and the link between wisdom and the love and fear of God can serve secular as well as divine authority. Note, for instance, the similarity between Christ's exhortation to Anima to "drede & conforme yowr wyll to me" and an ordinance of George, Duke of Clarence, and brother of King Edward IV who in 1469 ordered that one of his chaplains should "be redy to saye matyns and masse" regularly to his household "sith that alle wisdom, grace, and goodnesse, procedeth of veray love, drede, and feythfulle service of God, withoute whose helpe and socoure no good governaunce ne politque rule may be hadde" (Society of Antiquaries *Collection of Ordinances*, 1790; qtd. in Mertes 159). One of the side effects, as it were, of the love, fear, and "feythfulle service of God" is "good [household] governaunce" and "politique rule," which lead to "wisdom, grace, and goodnesse."

The point to be derived from Clarence's ordinance should be obvious: a stance of obedience, whether to God or king, which stresses the inadequacy of the individual in the face of the power and magnitude of the ruler, divine or secular, provides at least a paradigm for support of established authority. In *Wisdom*, Christ reinforces this paradigm in his encouragement of Anima's self-knowing dependence upon his love and goodness. In contrast, Lucifer, a lone, Iago-like sophist of "false" reason, opposes the Augustinian notion of wisdom as intuitive self-knowledge which Christ teaches Anima. In its place, Lucifer presents his own form of reason, which adheres in cunning, loveless logic. He knows, it appears, almost as much as Christ, at least about humanity:

> I am as wyly now as than,
> þe knowynge þat I hade yet I can.
> I know all compleccyons of a man,
> 　　　Werto he ys most dysposyde.
> 　　　　(341 - 44)

By giving a false credit, to use Ullman's terms, to the *civis* — or "citizen" — of the secular world and negating the world-denying *fidelis christianus*, Lucifer parodies the kinds of reasoning which were associated with Thomistic, rather than Augustinian, theology (see Ullman 123). Whereas Thomas had created a "veritable dualism of things" in which the subject of God can become a citizen without loss of faith, Lucifer creates an insoluble opposition between the two. The result, in the ethos of the play itself is to undermine both the world which Lucifer presents and the forms of logical reasoning by which he offers it to the three Mights, that is, to affirm those very values which Lucifer negates: "sapientia" or intuitive self-knowledge over logical reasoning, and disdain for the world as Lucifer defines it in favor of allegiance to godliness.

In both these stances, the play favors Augustinianism. If doing so is intrinsically conservative, it is nevertheless a kind of radical conservatism that itself characterized the fifteenth century, in which an increased reliance on the individual in the process of salvation was accompanied by a return to Augustinian epistemology and, more importantly, Augustinian concepts of the conscience as a guide to virtue and the wholeness of the self. As increased forms of private piety attest, the fifteenth century was a period in which "the direct link between the individual and divinity, without the mediatory role of ecclesiastical officers, became the pivotal point of man's religious life" (Ullman 145) or in which "people required a more intimate and personal relationship with God" (Mertes 139). As keys to redemption, all three of the Macro plays stress the theme of individual penitence and private piety, though in different ways and to a different extent each portrays God's mercy as essential to salvation for the penitent sinner. In both *The Castle of Perseverance* and *Mankind* Mercy is personified, in the one as the central character representing good and in the other as a daughter of God. In *The Castle of Perseverance*, it is Humanum Genus's dying plea for mercy that empowers God's younger daughters, Mercy and Peace, to argue for the salvation of his soul.

Wisdom, too, places much of the burden for salvation on the individual. In its use of the literature of lay piety, *Wisdom* places in one sense more weight on individual devotion than the other two plays. Married to Christ, Anima has her own version of the contemplative devotion; her mystical marriage links her through her own existence as a soul with God himself. And yet, at the crucial moment of redemption, *Wisdom* once more breaks from the other two Macro plays. Like Humanum Genus, Anima cries for "mercy" at a key moment of repentance, and Christ explains the importance of God's mercy in the process of redemption. But at her moment of penitence, after crying out for mercy, Anima waits for a transformation that does not take place:

> Than wyth yow thre þe Soule dothe crye,
> "Mercy, Gode!" Why change I nowte?
> (ll. 949 - 50)

This moment stands in refutation of the idea that the individual plea for mercy is sufficient as an agent for redemption in the other two plays: Christ explains to Anima that her plea alone will not save her; it is but a prelude to her formal confession and her absolution in the form of a "Charter of Pardon" from her "modyr Holy Chyrche" (ll. 982 - 86). Throughout, *Wisdom* is centered more on the sacraments of the Christian church than its companion Macro plays. Christ defines the sacraments to Anima as part of her initial education; he explains their role in redemption and, now, at this crucial moment Anima must leave the stage — partly of course to change her costume but ostensibly to make the confession to her "modyr . . . Chyrch" that will gain her the absolution she desires. Such a final reliance on the power of the institution is in keeping with the costuming of the play in its final positioning of the audience within, rather than outside, the established structures of religious authority, which in this play at least are allied with the powerfully conserving authority of the monarch.

Where does all this leave us in regard to the performance genre of a play like *Wisdom*? The answer to that question is crucial to the potential theatrical success of this long misunderstood play, which is separated in important ways from its Macro companions. Though, apart from the stage "plan" that accompanies the Macro text of *The Castle of Perseverance*, there is no evidence of original production conditions of any of the Macro plays, modern performances have highlighted distinctions which one can overlook in the mere reading of texts. By doubling the central characters of Mercy and Tityvillus in *Mankind*, for instance, the University of Toronto Medieval drama society known as the *Poculi Ludique Societas* (or *P. L. S.*) demonstrated that this play could have been performed by a travelling professional troupe with one major actor, six total players, and limited costumes and props — in contrast to the outdoor pageantry, processions, elaborate staging structures, and numerous actors required for *The Castle of Perseverance*. Each of these plays is a gem of its own kind: the former a racy, quickly-paced 914-line professional play, the latter a beautifully elaborate, though lengthy 3649-line outdoor drama, which in the University of Toronto's 1979 *P. L. S.* production, directed by David Parry, held its rapt audiences through a three-act, five-hour performance.

Wisdom is different. Compared to its Macro companions, *Wisdom* provides relatively little bawdy comedy. It depends instead on lengthy theological argument, formal liturgical processions, and masked dances. All of the Macro plays dramatize Catholic theological doctrines of sin and repentance, but *Wisdom* alone quotes extensively from contemporary mystical and theological treatises, widely circulated in the fifteenth century in England in manuals for use by pious lay men and women (see section on "Sources in Context" for more detail). And *Wisdom* alone incorporates four liturgical chants and processions and three masked dances, which, like the theological arguments, appear to stop the flow of the drama. Thus, judged by its "sister" plays, *Wisdom* has seemed static, lacking in dramatic motion — in Peter Happé's terms "emblematic" rather than "dramatic." It does not lend itself to professional production; it does not play well outdoors, and even in indoor productions it demands a specific kind of venue. Defining its genre, then, is in large part a measure of determining where one can effectively stage this play. An ugly duckling among the livelier and more scatological Macro morality plays, *Wisdom* emerges as a stately swan when placed among the entertainments of large ascetically inclined late fifteenth-century households. Failure to recognize the masque below the "morality" kept *Wisdom* off the stage throughout much of the twentieth century.

B. *Wisdom: Twentieth Century Stage History*

Beginning with William Poel's revival of *Everyman* in 1901, plays which, adapting a term from French eighteenth-century criticism, are ordinarily called "moralities," slowly made their way onto the modern stage. After founding the English Drama League in 1905, Nugent Monck staged "moralities" like the early sixteenth-century *Youth* and *Mundus et Infans*. The sixteenth-century moral interludes *Hick Scorner* and *Nice Wanton* were among the plays to be revived in the first half of the twentieth century. Tyrone Guthrie staged Sir David Lindsay's *Satire of the Three Estates* (1540) for the Edinburgh Festival in 1948. Of the Macro Plays, *Wisdom* alone had not been revived before the sixties; *Mankind* was first staged in 1910 and *The Castle of Perseverance* in 1939 (see Potter 1975 231 - 34). Heeding calls such as Bevington's, in 1965 John Leyerle encouraged his University of Toronto graduate students to stage medieval plays. From his class was ultimately formed the group whose Latin name *Poculi Ludique Societas (P. L. S.)* perpetually commemorates its origins in *Professor Leyerle's Seminar*. For more than twenty-five years the *P. L. S.* has staged plays and hosted drama festivals at the University of Toronto; comparable British efforts were headed up by Peter Meredith and Jane Oakshott, among others.

Despite the medieval revivals of the sixties and seventies, as late as January, 1979, medievalist John Gardner could firmly assert that "we can sooner coat the moon with aluminum than mount authentic productions of the Macro plays" (see Kelly x). Six months later the *P. L. S.* staged *The Castle of Perseverance* in a spectacular five-hour production in King's College Circle at the University of Toronto; shortly after, the same group took *Mankind* on tour. And *Wisdom* was at last staged: at the University of Colorado in 1977; at Winchester Cathedral by John Marshall in 1981; at the Medieval Festival held at Trinity College in 1984; and finally in the first *P. L. S.* production at the University of Toronto and Kalamazoo, Michigan, in 1991.

After centuries of neglect in which they were unstaged and almost unread, relegated to the archives of Catholic social history by Protestant scholars and regarded as mere "curiosities" by the Romantics and the Victorians, the Macro "morality" plays had arrived on the modern scene (see Potter 1975 192 - 221; Bevington 1991 97). This revival was driven both by archival research and modern theatrical developments. The discovery and publication of dramatic records by projects such as that of the Malone Society or the *Records of Early English Drama*, housed at the University of Toronto and linked through general editor Alexandra Johnston to the *P. L. S.*, created standards of "authenticity" in medieval production that were linked almost entirely to historical re-creation. At the same time, medieval plays — and particularly the allegorical abstractions of so-called morality drama — cohabited well with contemporary experimental staging, gestic acting, and the search for ritual origins (see Riggio 1989 31 - 34). In 1901 Poel still had to fight a Victorian prohibition against the playing of God on the stage; in 1909 the blasphemy laws prevented Nugent Monck from staging scenes from the N-Town cycle plays (see Potter 1975 1 - 5; 232). But by 1948 Tyrone Guthrie could see in Lindsay's moral drama the "opportunity to put into practice some of the theories which, through the years, I had been longing to test." Guthrie was particularly interested in plays that required venues other than a proscenium stage and that disobeyed the rules of dramatic realism, or, in his Brechtian terminology, "dramatic illusion" (306; qtd. by Potter 233). In a contemporary theatre aiming to renew what Antonin Artaud called the "l'acceptions religieuse et mystique" ("the religious and mystical significance," 68) of drama, morality plays began to rub shoulders with the work of contemporary playwrights whose didactic, presentational plays similarly discard the surface illusions of realism — dramatists as different as, say, Brecht, Richard Foreman, Caryll Churchill, or Robert Wilson.

Like all such allegorical or presentational drama, from *Everyman* to the plays of Shaw, Anouilh, Brecht, or Wilson, *Wisdom* is grounded in symbols that point to or personify ideas and dramatize moral debates, asking its viewers partly to look through its characters to the abstractions they embody: *wisdom, mind, will, understanding*. Such personified abstractions reflect a didactic point of view and argue for a coherent religious, political or intellectual stance: for Catholic theology in *Wisdom*; for Shaw's rational socialism or Brecht's nostalgic Marxism. But a coherent intellectual position alone does not create drama. Neither sound doctrine nor good ideas will insure a good play. To be successful presentational drama must engage the viewer in the human dimensions of the allegorized struggle. Such drama can either reinforce or challenge religious or political orthodoxy. But always it maintains a crucial tension between dramatic development and personified abstraction. When that tension collapses, the play fails.

That is the kind of failure which has often been attributed to *Wisdom*, too frequently seen as a moral sermon draped in the disguising garments of pageantry. As a member of this large and hybrid morality family, the play of *Wisdom* has not fared well, even among its friends. As long as *Wisdom* with its lengthy theological arguments and recurrent liturgical chants was treated simply as a "morality play," it remained the ugly stepsister of its livelier companions in the Macro manuscript. Comparing it to *The Castle of Perseverance* and *Mankind*, critics and editors alike have frequently consigned this Macro play to dramatic limbo. Reviewing John Marshall's production in Winchester Cathedral in 1981, Peter Happé characterizes *Wisdom* as an "emblematic rather than dramatic" play that reflects "a strangely limited concept of drama" (107). As a play "too intent on teaching moral virtues to have much concern with dramatic virtues," *Wisdom* is, according to its earlier editor Mark Eccles, "a good show" full of pageantry and spectacle but not a good play (1969 xxxvi). But the distinction between "emblematic" and "dramatic" movement or between the "pageantry and spectacle" of performance and the "play," associated entirely with the written text, misrepresents the drama.

Despite Juliet's famous aphorism, names can affect the scent of the rose; perhaps naming does not change the absolute smell of the flower, but the name we give something does at least determine what we expect it to be. An odiferous herb, which may be potent in the kitchen, would smell peculiar indeed in a rose garden. The tainted scent that clings to *Wisdom* has more to do with our labels than with the play itself. It is time to re-name this rose. As a "morality play," *Wisdom* must answer to the charges that it is a bad play because it is different from the other Macro "moralities." But by considering Potter's "theatrical guise" as basic to dramatic form, we change the angle of judgment on a play like *Wisdom*.

C. *Wisdom* and the Masque

At the same time that it has been characterized as a duller, more sermon-like play than its Macro companions, *Wisdom* also appears to be more aristocratic than either of the other two. At first glance, *Wisdom* and *The Castle of Perseverance* have in common a courtly emphasis lacking in the bawdy, probably professional *Mankind*. Both *The Castle* and *Wisdom* portray God not only as a patriarchal figure but also as a king — a characterization not shared, for instance, by Mercy in *Mankind*. *The*

Castle of Perseverance, furthermore, casts the remedial virtues as lovely ladies who take their refuge in a castle, one of the primary devices of courtly entertainment. These ladies fight the vices by throwing flowers at them, in an obvious echo of staged tournament-like battles between courtly ladies and courtiers (Fifield 1975).

Despite these similarities, *Wisdom* overall sounds a more aristocratic note (for a fuller discussion, summarized below, see section A above). Not only is Christ costumed as an *imperyall* king, wearing an *imperyall* crown and clothing (ermine-lined cloth of gold robe and mantle) restricted by English sumptuary laws to the British royal family, but the central "everyhuman" character is, surprisingly, a courtly woman dressed as his royal wife, rather than a naked child or de-classed man. Despite the characterization of God as a king in *The Castle of Perseverance*, kingly attire and feudal livery in that play symbolize worldly corruption. The ceremony of allegiance to King World has the trappings of a formal feudal exchange, as a primary symbol of sin, in contrast to the allegiance to God which is cast in different terms. In *Wisdom* the trappings of social patronage allegorically represent both good and evil: the fight for the soul is a struggle for lordship over a "plesant see" (l. 132), belonging first to Wisdom and then briefly inhabited by Lucifer. The Mights who serve Anima are "crestyde in [her] sute" (l. 324sd) before their fall into sin, which is marked conventionally by a change of clothing. As sinners, these characters wear the livery of Lucifer rather than Anima — their corruption portrayed as a change of fealty. Similarly, the renamed sinful Mights each control a retinue of dancers "dysgysyde in" or wearing "þe sute" of their patron (692sd, 724sd, and 752sd). Each of these costume changes represents a fall not only from grace into sin but also from aristocratic elegance into showy vulgarity. Throughout *Wisdom* aristocratic imagery — and specifically the visual imagery of kingship and of royal patronage — provide the primary metaphor for moral virtue.

More important than its costumes or its themes, however, in determining the genre of *Wisdom* is its basic dramatic rhythm, and it is this rhythm that most directly connects the play with the tradition of early masques and courtly disguisings. What Mark Eccles assumed to be the "overdone" use of "monologue" together with the play's dependence on liturgical procession and the three masked dances which appear in the interlude of sin: all these features create the "static" quality often attributed to the play. Seen in a different light, however, these static qualities provide the basis for a stately and formal rhythm — Happé's "emblematic" movement — which sets this play apart from the other Macro plays, even as they are distinguished from each other.

The kind of stasis that characterizes *Wisdom*, grounded in expository debate and centered on the essentially choreographed action of procession and dance, does in fact form the basis for the allegorical debates and mimed action of the masque and, before it, the courtly disguising. The term "masque" does not appear to have been used in England to describe a dramatic spectacle before 1512, when in his Chronicles Hall borrowed the term from Italian. Thereafter, it appears intermittently as a name for formal court masquerades, usually masked allegories ending in a dance, with men and sometimes women choosing their dancing partners from the audience. The sixteenth-century masque, which culminated a century later in the elaborate spectacles of Ben Jonson and Inigo Jones, featured masked actors and dancers performing sometimes slight allegorical drama in an elaborate and often expensively staged spectacle.

The fifteenth-century forerunner of the masque was called a disguising. By the beginning of the sixteenth century the disguising was essentially an indoor form of presentational drama, associated with wealth and privilege, as in John Lydgate's *Mumming at Hertford*, for instance. The disguising contained many of the features of the masque: masked characters, lavish settings, ritualized allegory dramatized through music, dance and disguise, and often presented as banquet entertainments. Such drama frequently represented human vice in animal form. At times, members of a wealthy family or royal household performed in such entertainments, in which key elements included exposition, allegory, and spectacle. Richard II is known to have participated in at least one mumming, for instance. Whereas masked drama probably began as an occasion for gift-giving, both the masque and the disguising characteristically center on a moral argument.

Certain elements of the masque resemble key aspects of morality plays as we have described them. Both depend heavily on visual representations of metaphor for their success; both center on the presentation of a personified moral argument or ceremonial allegory. Both contrast the harmony, dignity, and beauty of genuine aristocracy (associated with God in the morality play and with the court in the masque) to a vulgar world of gaudy social pretension or bestial vice. Both involve the audience — the morality play by implicating it in the world of sin, the masque by involving the audience in the moral debate of the drama but also by inviting participation in the festivities. Moreover, characters in both masques and moralities participate in and comment on the dramatized action, a form of characterization which may derive ultimately from the use in earlier mimed allegory of a formal presenter who introduced the action of mute mummers. Certainly, both the masque and the morality play similarly use characters as expositors.

Conventionally, however, characters in Macro plays participate in the drama, at the same time that they comment on their own roles in that drama. In this sense, they stand both inside and outside the fiction of the play in a way that is not specifically associated with the masque or disguising. Each major character ordinarily serves as his or — in *The Castle of Perseverance* — her own expositor, explaining to the audience the character's nature and the theological or dramatic significance of the personification. In expository addresses, each broadens the frame to include at least the present audience, and, by allusion, the rest of Christian humanity. To give an example: *Wisdom* opens with a sixteen-line prologue spoken by Christ, in which he explains the "propyrte / Ande þe resun" of his "nayme imperyall" (ll. 1 - 2). He ends this speech by saying "Thus Wysdom began," and thus formally distancing himself from his role. And, in a closing exhortation inaccurately attributed in other editions to Anima, Wisdom directly addresses the audience again: "Now ye mut euery soule renewe / In grace and vycys to eschew" (ll. 1159 - 60).

Other characters also define their own natures and their potential for good and evil. In the *Castle of Perseverance*, the newborn infant Humanum Genus, who "þis nyth was . . . of my modyr born" (l. 276), describes his own birth and defines his vulnerable infant innocence. Such self-definition makes sense only within the conventions that allow a newly born infant to speak intelligently. Other characters who define their own nature in *The Castle of Perseverance* include Lady Lechery and the seven remedial virtues, all portrayed as women. In *Wisdom*, however, this convention is somewhat altered; five of the six speaking characters — all masculine — do serve as their own expositors, but the central figure, Anima, the only female character of the play, does not do so. Instead, she asks Christ naive, uninformed questions about her own nature:

I þat represent þe sowll of man.
    Wat ys a sowll, wyll ȝe declare?
      (ll. 101 - 02)

In contrast to Anima's schooling by Christ, the three masculine "Mights" who represent her faculties of Mind, Will, and Understanding do define and explicate their own characters, in lengthy expositions in the state of grace (ll. 183 - 276) and shorter, more comic self-vaunting boasts in the world of sin (ll. 639 - 52). In both cases these speeches are introduced as a ritual of self-definition; in the first instance, Wisdom asks the Mights to "declare . . . yowr syngnyfycacyon and yowr propyrte" (ll. 181 - 82); in the second instance when they speak in their newly acquired identities as sinners, Understanding commands that "eche man tell hys concycyons howe" (l. 626).

Similarly, the characters representing evil all define their own natures in expository speeches addressed directly to the audience. In *The Castle of Perseverance* and *Mankind*, such speeches tend to be broadly comic, showing evil as an object of ridicule as well as a force with which to be reckoned. For instance, in *The Castle* Belyal describes himself as "deuyl dowty" who "champes" and "chafe[s]" and "chocke[s] on my chynne" (ll. 197 - 98) while World calls himself a "lykynge lord" who "trotte[s] and tremble[s]" (ll. 461, 457). In *Mankind* Tityvillus boasts of having persuaded Mankind to "schyte lesynges" (l. 568). In *Wisdom*, however, Lucifer is a powerful character who repeats and answers Christ's warnings to Anima's mights point-by-point in a way that reveals him to be the precise antithesis of Wisdom — i.e., one who knows a great deal but whose knowledge does not add up to true wisdom. He maintains his knowledge of human nature and the cunning of his former angelic self, but lacks the elements of love, grace, and mercy that constitute Wisdom. In keeping with this balance of opposites, there is correspondingly somewhat less bawdy humor in *Wisdom*; though in his disguise as "gallant," Lucifer exhibits pleasure-loving gaity, he basically persuades the Mights with his quasi-theological arguments rather than his bawdiness. He does not make scatological jokes, as farting and shitting are not comic themes in the play. Though the central interlude of sin does contain its share of satire and broad, slapstick humor in the interplay of the renamed Mind, Will, and Understanding, the comedy in general is not as vulgar as in the other plays, particularly the professional play *Mankind*.

As the convention of direct character address would suggest, the audience of the morality is implicated in the action of the play, particularly in the world of sin. By portraying actions which mirror vices of the audience, morality plays point an accusing finger at their viewers as part of the dramatic web designed to stimulate piety and promote repentance in the audience as well as in the play. The audience is expected to identify with the sinner(s) who represent humanity, an identification partly stimulated by laughing at faults one recognizes as one's own and partly resulting from characters telling the audience it belongs in the world of sin: Anima's black mantle of sin implicates "Euery sowll here, þis ys no nay," says Wisdom (l. 152).

Beyond these generic similarities, *Wisdom* bears a more specific resemblance to the masque or courtly disguising. Though in their presentation of allegorical combat, masques and disguisings resemble courtly tournaments, they are quintessentially indoor entertainments, staged in large chambers and often in dining halls as banquet performances. And it is at this point that potential (or probable) theatrical setting becomes a factor in determining genre. *Wisdom*, too, is an indoor interlude. Such exhortations as "go we to þe wyne" (l. 868) and the plan to lay on a big meal (ll. 813 - 27) give value to banquet tables with their food and, especially, drink as dramatic props and suggest this to be an appropriate dinner play.

Though its text is more elaborate and the dialogue probably more integrated into the action of the play than one would expect from a masque or disguising, *Wisdom* does depend heavily upon expository speeches, theological debate, and choreographed action. *Wisdom* does not, it is true, feature the elaborate "pageants" — models of the world, allegorical castles or ships — which sometimes characterize the visual allegory of the masque or disguising. Like other dramatic interludes of the late fifteenth and early sixteenth century, as, for instance, those of Henry Medwall, *Wisdom* is a play in which characters speak their own lines and interact through dialogue to carry out the dramatic action directly. The expositors are, in short, also characters in the drama. But the elaborate cast of *Wisdom* features more non-speaking than speaking parts, with six major speaking actors (none of whose roles can be doubled) and at least seventeen, probably twenty-three and possibly twenty-nine singers, dancers, and children: five singing prudent virgins, who could be played by male choir members or members of a household chapel; minimally six women dancers, who cannot be played by men, and more probably twelve and possibly eighteen dancers, of whom six must be women; and six small boys. As in the masque, which was often a very expensive form of entertainment, the costumes of *Wisdom* are both numerous and elaborate.

D. Date, Place, and Time: Summarizing The Range of Probabilities

Wisdom is an East Anglian play, probably written at or near the Abbey of Bury St. Edmonds. Though we cannot rule out any date between 1470 and 1500 for its composition, the available evidence points to the 1480s, or at earliest the late 1470s, as the most likely date of the extant manuscripts, which could have been copied as late as the 1490s. Earlier assumptions that the play was written between 1465 and 1475 were based partly on an erroneous identification of the "Monk Hyngham" who signed both the *Wisdom* and *Mankind* manuscripts with Richard Hengham who became Abbot of Bury St. Edmonds in 1474, a date previously thought to constitute a *terminus ad quem* for the transcription of the Macro text. Richard Beadle's identification of the Monk Hengham of the manuscripts with Thomas Hengham, known to be at Bury in the 1470s, pushes the probable date forward by at least a decade. The likelihood that the Macro text has been copied from the Digby positions the extant manuscripts somewhat awkwardly between two chronological poles created by Thomas Hengham's residence at Bury in the 1470s at one end and the probability argued by Baker, Murphy, and Hall in their edition of *The Digby Plays* that the scribe of the Digby *Wisdom* copied the Digby *Killing of the Children*, a manuscript dated in the hand of the main scribe as "Anno Domini 1512." Even if one grants the argument that the main scribe of the Digby *Killing of the Children* also copied *Wisdom* — and the evidence is not conclusive —, the Digby editors assume *Wisdom* to be significantly earlier than *The Killing of the Children*; they postulate a date for the Digby *Wisdom* as early as 1490 (see Baker et al lxv). The evidence given in section one of this introduction suggests that despite the initial impression that the Digby *Wisdom* is later than the *Macro*, a comparison of linguistic features shows that the Digby scribe, though less provincially East Anglian in his transcription than the Macro, is in some important respects more conservative linguistically than the Macro scribe (see "The Relationship Between the Digby and Macro Texts," above).

Thus, it is altogether possible that the Digby text was written and copied in the 1480s.

That date accords well with evidence based on the style and thematic content of the play, which belongs generically to the period of transition between the *disguising* and the more formal *masque*. In its recurrent use of the term *disguising* and its focus on the allegory of costuming, *Wisdom* identifies itself with this dramatic form, which as Suzanne Westfall has pointed out, "would never appear in the church, inn-yard, or city street" (Westfall 32). It is a genre that belongs quintessentially to households. In terms of staging, *Wisdom* requires at least forty-one costumes for a complex cast of six actors (none of whom could easily be doubled), seven singing "prudent virgins" (roles easily sung by chapel boys), and at least twelve dancers, six of whom must be women; it intermingles drama, antic masque dances, liturgical chants and processions; it requires at least three minstrels, playing "trumpes" (l. 692sd), a "bagpype" (l. 724sd), and a "hornepype" (l. 752sd). Just as Westfall has argued, such a complex production well suits the auspices of a noble or ecclesiastical household large enough to maintain a household chapel: "more than perhaps any other genre the disguising encouraged Chapels to experiments with allegory" and "the script of *Wisdom* reflects the aesthetics of household performance" (Westfall 32, 53). With its devotional emphasis the play seems particularly suitable for a household of the late fifteenth century. Its source authors, especially Walter Hilton and Henry Suso, wrote devotional treatises like *Scala Perfectionis* or the *Orologium Sapientiae*, which were circulated in English miscellanies and printed in early volumes patronized by such aristocratic women as Margaret Beaufort, mother of Henry VII (see "Sources in Context" above). The play is a dramatic counterpart to such devotional texts, which were presumably read aloud in such households as part of the regimen of piety which helped to establish standards of "good lordship" in the late fifteenth century. Moreover, the play focuses on the vice of "maintenance," which was rampant particularly in the 1470s and against which both Richard III (1483 - 85) and Henry VII (1485 - 1509) instituted legislation upon assuming the throne.

Of households which might have produced such a play as *Wisdom*, Milton Gatch has pointed to that of John Morton, the Bishop of Ely and patron both of Thomas More and of Henry Medwall, whose allegorical moral interlude *Nature* is a slightly classicized counterpart to a play like *Wisdom* (Gatch 358 - 60). Certainly, the play invokes the name of "St.

Audrey of Ely" (l. 832), and the Bishop had a home in Holborn, a place which twice figures in the satire of law (ll. 721, 731) in *Wisdom*. Other, probably more likely candidates might include, as Alexandra Johnston has conjectured, the Howards, Dukes of Norfolk who had a seat at Stoke-by-Nayland or the family of John de la Pole, Duke of Suffolk, who had a household at Wingfield in the general area of the Abbey at Edmondsbury (Johnston 1986 101; see Westfall 221-22 for information on John Howard, First Duke of Norfolk).

These are some possible homes for the play of *Wisdom* among the great families whose names and histories are written large. It is, of course, not certain that such a family was responsible for the production, much less the writing, of this play. But the circumstances of artistic production at the end of the fifteenth century, with royal households for the first time under the latter York and early Tudor reigns containing troupes of players within themselves, do suggest a wealthy aristocratic household — either secular or ecclesiastical — of the late 1400s as the most likely locus of origin for this play.

APPENDIX: STRUCTURAL SYMMETRIES OF *WISDOM*

I. OVERALL FRAME

	STATE OF GRACE	WORLD OF SIN
ritual movement	processionals	masque dances
music	plainsong (monophonic & diaphonic)	three-part songs (tertial harmonies)
clothing	long, elegant robes, signifying aristocratic sovereignty	short, modish OR foul
ruler	Christ as Wisdom	Lucifer as Anti-Wisdom

II. COSTUME: ARRAY AND DISGUISE

STATE OF GRACE

	— *signification*	— *actual costume*
Wisdom	sovereign array symbolizing majesty	purple cloth of gold ermine-lined royal hood and mantle gold wig; emblems of state
Anima	royal array sybmbolizing aristocratic beauty & purity	white cloth of gold, lined with miniver gold wig, chappelet with two long tassles and two gold knots (or buttons)
	disguise signifying original sin	black mantle over white robe
five Wits	array	long, white robes
Mights	array #1 signifying for both Wits & Mights their fealty to Anima	long, white robes, gold wigs, Both Wits & Mights liveried and crested in the suit of Anima.

WORLD OF SIN

Lucifer	array disguise	black devil's costume modish clothes of gallant
Might	array #2	short, modish clothes probably animal imagery to indicate sin & bestiality; masks for dancing
Anima six little devils		"fouler than a fiend" costume indicating sin devil's costumes

III. ATTRIBUTES OF MIND, WILL, AND UNDERSTANDING

MIND	The "true figure" of God	
	Virtue:	Faith (the power of God the Father)
	Sin:	Pride (the "Devil's" man)
	New Name:	Maintenance
	Tempted by:	Suggestion
	Redeemed by:	Confession
	Satire of:	Lordship (linked to noble family)
	Emblem:	Lions rampant, color red
	Minstrel:	trumpets
UNDERSTANDING	(No imagery of likeness or figure of God)	
	Virtue:	Hope (associated with Christ)
		Also linked with Charity in opening section
	Sin:	Covetousness (the "World's" sin)
	New Name:	Perjury
	Tempted by:	Delight (also called Delectation)
	Redeemed by:	Contrition
	Satire of:	Law courts (sources of wealth, bribing jurors)
	Emblem:	Two-faced hoods, jurors robes
	Minstrel:	bagpipe
WILL	The "likeness" and "figure" of God	
	Virtue:	Charity (love of the Holy Spirit)
	Sin:	Lechery (the "Flesh's" sin)
	New Name:	Lechery (also called Gentle Fornication and Sensuality)
	Tempted by:	Consent
	Redeemed by:	Satisfaction
	Satire of:	Riotous living, lavish spending
	Emblem:	Gallant's clothing; pig
	Minstrel:	hornpipe

IV. DANCERS: Liveried retainers of the three Mights

First Dancers, liveried to Mind (Maintenance): Costumed in "royal" red (also the Devil's color), with lions rampant as symbols of perverted lordship, holding "warders," crude symbols of authority, inversion of Wisdom's sceptre. Minstrel: Trumpets, the instrument of battle and judgment

Second Dancers, liveried to Understanding (Perjury): Costumed in juror's robes (though short) and hoods, with hats of "maintenance" and two-faced masks, symbolic of hypocrisy. Minstrel: Bagpipe, associated with vulgarity, acquisition.

Third Dancers, liveried to Will (Lechery): Six women, three dressed as men. Costumed as gallants and matrons, with emblems of lechery. Minstrel: hornpipes, sweet-sounding but actually "foul."

THE PLAY OF
WISDOM

Editorial Principles

The guiding principle in determining the text to be printed has been the authority of the manuscripts. The only complete manuscript of the play, the Macro manuscript (Folger Ms. V.a. 354, designated as M), has served as copytext. However, since M was almost certainly copied from the Bodleian Library Ms. Digby 133 (designated as D), D readings have been used to supply missing words and lines, to correct errors, and to provide more authentic readings in the first 752 lines of M. After D ends, M has been closely followed with a few minor emendations (see 2 below). Folio numbers are given for M only, identified in the margin by *v* for verso and *r* for recto, thus: *f.98r*. Specific editorial procedures include:

1. Textual authority: As the prior text, D is regarded as authoritative for all matters of substance, with M the authoritative text for accidentals. This means that in any instance in which the meaning, of a line or phrase in D differs from M, D will be regarded as the authority. D words, lines, and phrases have been incorporated when the D reading is substantially superior to or equivalent to that of M. M will be adopted only when the M reading is obviously superior to that of D. Conversely and partly in order to insure as linguistically consistent a document as possible within the eclectic format of this edition, M is regarded as authoritative for all recognizable variants (dialectical or grammatical) of the same word. Thus, for grammatical endings, distinctions in spelling, and orthographic choices M is presumed to provide the authoritative text, except in the few instances in which M makes changes that negate the rhyme scheme which D carefully preserves or in cases in which the M form is neither a historically verifiable nor logically derived variant of the D term.

2. Emendations: Since this is an eclectic text, which grants textual authority to D as well as M, all D readings are incorporated silently into the text but, for the convenience of the reader who wishes to distinguish D from M, are noted in textual footnotes and asterisked in the glossary; significant D variants not incorporated into the text are also indicated in textual footnotes (but not cited in the glossary). Differences in spelling have been noted only when they appear to be significant, i.e. when the variant spelling of the same term is not immediately apparent or when the grammatical differences have occasioned some confusion about the forms. All emendations for which there is no textual authority from either

M or D are marked by italics in the text and the endnotes; they are marked by square brackets in the glossary. Such italics, which pertain to single letters, pairs of letters, or single words only, are not to be confused with the italics used throughout the text to distinguish Latin quotations.

3. Transcriptions of footnotes for D and M variants: In footnotes, when the textual reading is taken from M, it is listed without identification inside a square bracket, so: *37 ioy]*. *D form (e.g. ioye)* to the right of this bracket indicates a D variant of the printed M reading; *from D* indicates that word, phrase, or line has been supplied from D; if an M variant for words or phrases taken from D exists, it is listed as — *M form. Line no. speaker]* refers to speaker's name above listed line; *sd* = stage directions. Abbreviations are not regularly noted in textual footnotes, but they are recorded for the speaker prefix designating *Wndyrstondyng*'s name. Similarly, "a" or "ad" as contracted forms of *and* and *at* are expanded silently in the text but are footnoted. Ordinarily, variants in other printed editions are not collated for the first 752 lines. This principle is violated only in the few cases of emendations recorded by Eccles which readers may now regard as standard but which are not replicated in this edition; these are listed for convenience sake in the footnotes.

4. Latin quotations within the text: All Latin lines and phrases are transcribed faithfully in the old text, printed in italics to distinguish them. They are rendered in modern Latin in the modernization and translated in the endnotes, where the source of each Latin phrase is provided.

5. Transcriptions of footnotes for ll. 753 - 1163: After the D text ends at l. 752sd, emendations and variants from the Bevington facsimile edition (designated as B) and the Eccles EETS edition (designated as E) are specified in textual footnotes; with a few minor exceptions, indicated by italics as emendations, they are not incorporated into the text. B expands the M abbreviation which this text transcribes *cyon* as *cion*; E expands abbreviations for *&*. These distinctions are not recorded in footnotes, though E's writing out of numbers — *thre* for *iii* — is noted (in keeping with the principles of this edition, M iij and similar numbers are transcribed iii, etc.; see no. 12). Readings from other editions are not collated.

6. Punctuation and word division: These have been silently emended to modern usage, except for instance for a term like *in dede*, which was

written as a phrase until 1600 and which is treated as a two-word phrase in this text (see l. 455).

7. Speaker prefixes: Speakers' names appear in the right margin above the text with a line drawn from the left margin to the name, to indicate the change of speaker. Names are centered and spelling standardized in this text. Variants are indicated in textual footnotes; variants of D are given only in relationship to M variants. In two instances (before ll. 17 and 1154) speakers' names have been inadvertently omitted in the manuscript(s). I have provided these names in square brackets.

8. Capitalization: Capitalization has been standardized to modern practice. Speakers' names are capitalized and standardized as are names in stage directions; in the body of the text proper names are capitalized when they appear in a form of direct address or clearly refer to a person or place. Because of the way in which the text plays with the personifications of mind, will, and understanding, in some instances it is not clear whether the term refers to the concept or the character. I have judged these as best I could. The first word in each line has been capitalized. Conversely, capital letters which appear at random in the text where we would use a small letter have been silently emended to lower case letters in keeping with modern usage. Such capitalization (or lowercasing of random uppercase letters) is noted in footnotes only in the case of *I, i* (see 12 below). All terms in the glossary, including personifications, are recorded in lowercase form except for proper names used in idioms. Ordinary proper names, not included in the glossary, are explained in endnotes.

9. Stray marks and cancelled text: Words, partial words, and letters written erroneously in the text and cancelled have been noted in textual footnotes, as have dots between words. Such cancellations and punctuation have been noted for D only in relationship to markings in M. Stray marks that seem clearly to have been written by the M scribe are also recorded in footnotes, but later doodlings in the manuscript are ignored.

10. Transcription of the text — poetry or dialogue: The scribes of both D and M maintain a flush left margin, with no indication of poetic stanza form, except for tail rhyme lines in the midsection of the play, which are sometimes written to the right of the text. At those points triplet rhyming

lines in the body of the text are bracketed in both M and D. D further brackets all rhyming lines in the play. No brackets of rhymes have been incorporated into this edition. I have indented lines to show the stanza patterns and have cited the lines written in the right margin in textual notes. But I have followed the manuscripts in blocking the text as dramatic dialogue rather than stanzas of poetry.

11. Numbers and the & sign: These have been transcribed according to manuscript usage, with the exception of the word *forty* at l. 1032, which for clarity I have written out. Eccles transcriptions of numerals have been footnoted only for ll. 753 - 1163.

12. Transcription of specific letters in this edition, with particular attention to *i* and *I / j*: M writes both *þ* and *y* as *y*; D distinguishes between them, as does this edition. Initial *ff* is printed as *F*; manuscript distinctions between *u* and *v* are maintained. Throughout the yogh is transcribed as *3*. The most complex question relating to the transcription of specific letters pertains to *I* and *i* and requires some historical justification. Modern *J/j* developed as a transcription of certain sounds that evolved from some Latin *I/i* words. No systematic distinction between *i* and *j* in these words appears to have existed before the seventeenth century, when the capital *J* entered English orthography. Initially, the letter which we now regard as *j* developed as a way of avoiding confusion caused by the small *i*, which was often confused for other letters or portions of other letters (an error M makes several times in his transcription of D). To distinguish this letter, scribes during the later middle ages extended the *i* above or, particularly, below the line. The *i* that descended below the line eventually developed a curved tail; it was dotted like the *i*, and ultimately became modern *j*. By modern editors it is often treated as if it were an uppercase *I*, and in footnotes this edition so records this letter when it exists in words spelled in modern English with an *i*. But this same letter increasingly designates *j* in those words which are now consistently spelled with a *j*. Probably written close to the turn of the sixteenth century, the *Wisdom* texts represent an interesting stage in the evolution of *j*. Both M and D frequently use *I* descending below the line (and, thus, resembling *j*). In instances when M's *I* indicates *I* or *J / j*, I have transcribed it with the modern equivalent, capitalized according to modern usage. Thus, for instance, the name of Jesus has been transcribed as the appropriate variant of *Jhesus*. When *I* is used where we would expect *i*, I have followed the standard practice with other letters and silently emended it to

i; when *i* is used where we would expect *j*, I have transcribed it as *i*, capitalized according to modern usage (as in *Ierusalem*, l. 164, 165; since this is an accidental, the M text is treated as authoritative in this instance). Thus, the text contains both *J-* and *I-* words where we would use *J*. Because variations in this letter illustrate some early development of the letter *j*, I have indicated all D and M variants for *I* / *j* / *i* in textual footnotes.

13. Abbreviations: English and Latin abbreviations and contractions are silently expanded, while flourishes and penstrokes that do not affect spelling, such as a straight stroke over *ght*, a stroke crossing *ll*, or final flourish on *n*, are ignored. English Expansions reflect the scribe's own spelling habits when he writes out a word in full. The single exception is *ẃ*; M writes this word out only three times — twice as *wyt* (ll. 215, 975) and once as *wyth* (l. 863). The few instances do not warrant expanding as *wyt*, and, following the practice of D which is closer to modern English, it has been expanded as *wyth*. For Latin abbreviations, see the Bevington facsimile. Other English abbreviations in M, silently expanded and not noted in textual footnotes, are as follows:

a vowel or a vowel plus *p* or *m/n* with a straight stroke over the letter(s) = *m/n* added after vowel or doubling the consonant w. optional *-e*
a final flourish looping back over *a* = *an*
c followed by a downward loop curving back under *c* = *con*, *com*, *-con* final flourish looping back over *on* = *-cyon* (see ll. 478, 961, 1068, 1152 for confirmation of the expansion; the M scribe never spells this suffix *-cion*, as does the D scribe).
o with a small c-shaped half-circle superscripted on the right = *our*
p with a straight stroke through the leg of the letter = *par* / *per*
p ending in a curved stroke looping to the left through the leg = *pro*
p with a small c-shaped half-circle superscripted on the right = *pre*
q with a stroke curving through the leg of the letter, first to the right and then to the left = *quod*, used as English slang
r final flourish looping back over the letter = *re*
s with a stroke curving through the letter first to the right and then to the left = *syr* / *ser* (no textual evidence to indicate preference)
terminal s final flourish curving right at the top and crossing back through the letter = *ys*
u final flourish looping back over *u* = *un*
w with a stroke resembling a small z superscripted to the right = *wr*

w with a small *t* superscripted to the right = *wyth* (modern *with*) (but see
      note 12 above)

x = *Crist* (designating Christ)

y (not distinguished from þ) with *an* superscripted to the right = þ*an*

y (not distinguished from þ) with *i* superscripted to the right = þ*i*

y with *t* superscripted to the right = either *yt* or þ*at*

y with *u* superscripted to the right = þ*ou* or þ*u*; the scribal practice of both
      M and D favor expanding to þ*u*

Fyrst entreth **Wysdome** *in a ryche purpull clothe of golde wyth a*   f. 98r
mantyll of the same ermynnyde wythin, hawynge abowt hys neke a ryall
hood furred wyth ermyn, wpon hys hede a cheweler wyth browys, a berde
of golde of Sypres curlyde, a ryche imperyall crown þerwpon sett wyth
precyus stonys and perlys. In hys leyfte honde a balle of golde wyth a
cros þerwppon and in his ryght honde a regall scheptur, thus seyenge:

Wysdom

Yff 3e wyll wet þe propyrte
    Ande þe resun of my nayme imperyall,
I am clepyde of hem þat in erthe be
    Euerlastynge Wysdom, to my nobley egalle,
    Wyche name acordyt best in especyall   5
And most to me ys convenyent.
    Allthow eche persone of þe trynyte be wysdom eternall
And all thre on euerlastynge wysdome togedyr present,
Neuerþeles, for as moche as wysdom ys propyrly
    Applyede to þe sune by resune,   10
And also yt fallyt to hym specyally
    Bycause of hys hye generacyon,
    Therfor þe belowyde sone hathe þis sygnyficacyon:
Custummaly wysdom — now Gode, now man,
    Spows of þe chyrche & wery patrone,   15
Wyffe of eche chose sowle. Thus Wysdom begane.

0 sd entreth] from D — M enteryde; wyth a mantyll of the; ryall hood furred; of Sypres; and
per (in perlys); his (last occurrence)] all from D — cropped in M;   precyus] D has canc.
precyus, w. ryche written above   0 speaker] M & D — all speakers names written in right
margin; spelling standardized throughout this text   0 speaker] Wysdom omitted in D
1 3e] throughout the text, notes, and glossary the yogh will be represented by 3
3 of] in erthe canc. before   4 nobley] from D — M noble   8 on] M & D point before   11
to] yt fa canc. before; hym] point in the loop above m   12 hye] D highest
13 sygnyficacyon] point in the loop above n   14 now . . . now] point before each
Custummaly] D Custumably   15 wery] var. of D verray

First **Wisdom** *enters in a rich purple cloth of gold robe with a mantle of the same material lined with ermine, about his neck a royal hood furred with ermine, upon his head a wig with bangs, a beard of curled Cypress gold, wearing a rich imperial crown set with precious stones and pearls, in his left hand a gold orb with a cross on it and in his right hand a royal sceptre, saying thus:*

Wisdom

If you wish to know the special property
    And the meaning of my name imperial,
I am called by those whom on earth you see
    Everlasting Wisdom, to my nobility full equal,
    Which name accords best in terms most special   5
    And is for me most fitting.
    Although each person of the Trinity is Wisdom eternal
    And all three are together present in Wisdom everlasting,
Nevertheless, since Wisdom is properly
    Attributed to the Son with good reason,   10
And since it also falls to him especially
    Because of his high birth and royal generation,
    Therefore, the beloved son has this signification:
Customarily Wisdom — now God, now man,
    Spouse of the Church and true patron,   15
Wife of each chosen soul. Thus Wisdom began.

Here entrethe **Anima** *as a mayde in a wyght clothe of golde gytely purfyled wyth menyver, a mantyll of blake þerwppeon, a cheueler lyke to* **Wysdom** *wyth a ryche chappetelot lasyde behynde hangynge down wyth ii knottys of golde & syde tasselys, knelynge down to* **Wysdom** *thus seyng:*

Anima

Hanc amaui et exquisiui.   f. 99r
    Fro my yougthe thys haue I sowte
To haue to my spowse most specyally.
    For a louer of yowr schappe am I wrowte.   20
    Aboue all hele & bewty þat euer was sowght
I haue louyde Wysdom as for my lyght,
    For all goodnes wyth hym he broughte.
In Wysdom I was made all bewty bryghte.
Off yowr name þe hye felycyte   25
    No creature knowyt full exposycyon.

Wysdom

Sapiencia specialior est sole.
    I am foundon lyghte wythowt comparyson,
    Off sterrys aboue all þe dysposicyon,
Forsothe of lyght þe very bryghtnes,   30
    Merowre of þe dyvyne domynacyon
And þe image of hys goodnes.
Wysdom ys better þan all worldly precyosnes,
    And all þat may dysyryde be
Ys not in comparyschon to my lyknes.   35
    The lengthe of þe yerys in my ryght syde be
    Ande in my lefte syde ryches, ioy, & prosperyte.
Lo, þis ys þe worthynes of my name.

---

folio 98v] filled with sketches unrelated to play; not used for text   16sd gytely] from D — M gyedly;   menyver] menver w. y over n canc. before;   er (in cheueler); wn (in down); eyng (in seyng)] all from D — cropped in M   chappetelot] D/ chapetelet; poss. error for chapp(e)let; see ll. 164sd, 1064sd;   ij] M & D ij; I and j (identical in M & D) will be transcribed as I or i as appropriate and J or j as appropriate, capitalized according to modern usage in text; i will always be transcribed as I or i, capitalized according to modern usage; M & D i and I/j will be noted when they differ from text; capitalization of other letters (standardized to modern practice) will be unnoted;   knelynge] ke canc. before   17 speaker] Anima missing in D & partly obscured in M; written Ana w. abbrev. over na throughout, unless otherwise noted   18 yougthe] from D — M thowte   23 he] from D, w. b canc. after — M ys, w. n or u canc. after   24 In] from D M I; see 133, 613, 1064sd   27 speaker] M & D Wysdam — standard D spelling   31 domynacyon] point in the loop before n   33 worldly] wordy, w. ink spot before d, canc. before — D wordly   36 lengthe] g inserted above word   ryght] ryth canc. before

*Here **Anima** enters as a maiden, in a white cloth of gold handsomely
bordered with miniver, a mantle of black over it, a wig like that of
Wisdom, with a rich coronet laced at the back, from which hang long
tassels with two knots or buttons of gold. She kneels down to **Wisdom**,
saying thus:*

Anima

Hanc amavi et exquisivi.
    From my youth this have I sought
To have as my spouse most specially.
    For a lover of your shape was I wrought.   20
    Above all health and beauty that ever was sought
I have loved Wisdom as my light,
    For all goodness with him he brought.
In Wisdom I was made all beauty bright.
Of your name the high felicity   25
    No creature knows the full exposition.

Wisdom

Sapientia specialior est sole.
    I was created light without comparison,
    Above the pattern of each constellation,
In truth, of light the model of brightness,   30
    Mirror of the divine domination
And the image of his goodness.
Wisdom is better than all worldly richness,
    And all that may desired be
Cannot be compared to my likeness.   35
    The length of the years in my right side be
    And in my left side riches, joy, and prosperity.
Lo, this is the worthiness of my name.

Anima

A soueren Wysdom, yff yowr benygnyte
Wolde speke of loue, þat wer a game.   *40*

Wysdom

Off my loue to speke, yt ys myrable.   f. 99v
    Beholde now, Sowll, wyth joyfull mynde,
How louely I am, how amyable,
    To be halsyde & kyssyde of mankynde.
To all clene sowlys I am full hende,   *45*
    And euer present wer þat þey be;
    I loue my lovers wythowtyn ende
That þer loue haue stedfast in me.
The prerogatyff of my loue ys so grett
    þat wo tastyt þerof þe lest droppe sure   *50*
All lustys & lykyngys worldly xall lett;
    They xall seme to hym fylthe and ordure.
    They þat of þe hewy burthen of synne hathe cure
My loue dyschargethe & puryfyethe clene;
    It strengtheth þe mynde, þe sowll makyt pure,   *55*
And yewyt wysdom to hem þat perfyghte bene.
Wo takyt me to spowse may veryly wene,
    Yff aboue all thynge 3e loue me specyally,
That rest & tranqwyllyte he xall sene
    And dey in sekyrnes of joy perpetuall.   *60*
The hye worthynes of my loue
    Angell nor man can tell playnly.
Yt may be felt in experyens from aboue,
    But not spoke ne tolde as yt ys veryly.
    The godly loue no creature can specyfye.   *65*
What wrech is that louyth not this love
    þat louyt hys louers euer so tendyrly
That hys syght from them neuer can remowe?

Anima

O worthy spowse and soueren fayre,
    O swet amyke, owr ioy, owr blys!   *70*

---

41 speaker] Wysdom on previous folio; spelled as such throughout text   47 my] D the
49-61] 12 line stanza   50 tastyt] D tast   52 to] D tyll   55 strengtheth] M & D;
in M strenth w. g above nt, canc. before   57 wo] D who   58 specyally] D specially --
both lose rhyme   61 hye] D hey; worthynes] D loue of my subpuncted to indicate
cancellation before   63 in experyens from] word order and word in from D (in experience
from) — M from experyens   66, 68] repeat rhyme of 61, 63   66 line from D   wrech] D
wreth, prob. error for wrech   69 fayre] from D — M father w. faye canc. before

Anima

Ah, Sovereign Wisdom, if your benignity
Would speak of love, that were a game.   40

Wisdom

To speak of my love, it is a miracle.
   Behold now, Soul, with joyful mind,
How lovely I am, how amiable,
   To be embraced and kissed by humankind.
   To all clean souls I gently bend,   45
Ever present wherever they be;
   I love my lovers without end
   Who place their steadfast love in me.
The prerogative of my love is so great
   That whoso tastes thereof the least drop sure   50
All lusts and worldly desires shall abate;
   They shall seem to them filth and manure.
   They that of the heavy burden of sin need a cure
My love cleanses from sin and purifies straight;
   It strengthens the mind, the soul makes pure,   55
And gives wisdom to those that are perfect.
You who take me as a spouse may surely expect,
   If above all things you love me as special,
That rest and tranquillity you shall collect
   And die in certainty of joy perpetual.   60
The high worthiness of my love
   Neither angel nor man can tell plainly.
It may be felt in experience from above,
   But not spoken or told as it is truly.
   The love of God no creature can specify.   65
What wretch is there who loves not this Love
   That loves its lovers so tenderly
That his sight from them he never can remove?

Anima

O worthy spouse and sovereign fair,
   O sweet beloved, our joy, our bliss!   70

To yowr loue wo dothe repeyer,
  All felycyte yn þat creature ys.
  Wat may I yeue yow ageyn for þis,
O creator, louer of yowr creature?
  Though be owr freelte we do amys,   75
  Yowr grett mercy euer sparyth reddure.
A soueren Wysdom, *sanctus sanctorum,*
  Wat may I yeue to yowr most plesaunce?

Wysdom

Fili, prebe michi cor tuum.
  I aske not ellys of all þi substance.   80
  Thy clene hert, þi meke obeysance:
Yeue me þat & I am contente.

Anima

  A soueren joy, my hertys affyance,
The fervowre of my loue to yow I present;
That mekyt my herte yowr loue so ferwent.   85
  Teche me þe scolys of yowr dyvynyte.

Wysdom

Dysyer not to sauour in cunnyngys to excellent,
  But drede & conforme yowr wyll to me,
  For yt ys þe heelfull dyscyplyne þat in Wysdam may be —
The drede of God, þat ys begynnynge.   90
  The wedys of synne yt makyt to flee
And swete wertuus herbys in þe sowll sprynge.

Anima

O, endles Wysdom, how may I haue knowynge   f.100v
  Off þi godhede incomprehensyble?

Wysdom

By knowynge of yowrsylff 3e may haue felynge   95
  Wat Gode ys in yowr sowle sensyble.
  The more knowynge of yowrselff passyble,
þe more veryly 3e xall God knowe.

---

71 to] D tyll; wo] D who   78 may I] D I may I; plesaunce] pl canc. before   83 my] D
myn   84 present] D represente   87 cunnynges] from D, w. abbr. expanded to ys — M
cunnynge   93 speaker] Anima on previous folio

To your love whoever does repair,
    All felicity in that creature is.
    What may I give you in return for this,
  O creator, lover of your creature?
    Though through our frailty we do amiss,   75
  Your great mercy ever spares us forfeiture.
Ah, sovereign Wisdom, *sanctus sanctorum*,
    What may I give for your greatest pleasaunce?

Wisdom

Fili, praebe mihi cor tuum.
    I ask not else of all your substance.   80
    Your clean heart, your meek obedience:
  Give me that and I am content.

Anima

    Ah, sovereign joy, my heart's affiance,
  The fervor of my love to you I present;
That makes my heart meek, your love so fervent.   85
    Teach me the schools of your divinity.

Wisdom

Desire not to savor cunning skills too excellent,
    But fear and conform your will to me,
    For this is the healthful discipline that in Wisdom may be —
The fear of God, that is the beginning.   90
    The weeds of sin it causes to flee
And sweet virtuous herbs in the soul to spring.

Anima

Oh, endless Wisdom, how may I have knowing
    Of your Godhead incomprehensible?

Wisdom

By knowing yourself you may have feeling   95
    What God is in your soul corporal.
    The more you know in yourself what is sensible,
  The more truly you shall know God.

Anima

O soueren auctoure most credyble,
 Yowr lessun I attende as I owe.   100
I þat represent here þe sowll of man,
 Wat ys a sowll, wyll 3e declare?

Wysdom

Yt ys þe ymage of Gode þat all began,
 And not only ymage but hys lyknes 3e are.
 Off all creaturys þe fayrest 3e ware   105
Into þe tyme of Adamys offence.

Anima

Lorde, sythe we thy sowlys þat nowt wer þer,
 Wy of þe fyrst man bye we þe vyolence?

Wysdom

For euery creature þat hath ben — or xall —
 Was in natur of þe fyrst man Adame,   110
Off hym takynge þe fylthe of synne orygynall,
 For of hym all creaturys cam.
 Than by hym of reson 3e haue blame
And be made þe brondys of helle.
 Wen 3e be bore fyrst of yowr dame,   115
3e may in no wyse in hewyn dwell,
For 3e be dysvyguryde be hys synne   f.101r
 Ande dammyde to derknes from Godys syghte.

Anima

How dothe grace þan ageyn begynne?
 Wat reformythe þe sowll to hys fyrste lyght? 120

Wysdom

Wysdam þat was Gode & man ryght
Made a full sethe to þe fadyr of hewyn.
 By þe dredfull dethe to hym was dyght,
Off wyche dethe spronge þe sacramentys sevyn,
Wyche sacramentys all synne wasche awey. 125

---

103 <u>began</u>] D <u>bygan</u> 113 <u>hym</u>] point in the loop above <u>m</u> 114 <u>And</u>] point after

Anima

Oh, sovereign author most credible,
Your lesson I attend as I should.   100
I, that represent here the soul of man,
    Ask, what is a soul, will you declare?

Wisdom

It is the image of God that all began,
    And not only his image but his likeness you share.
    Of all creatures the fairest you were   105
Until the time of Adam's offense.

Anima

Lord, since we, your souls, were not yet there,
Why from the first man inherited we the violence?

Wisdom

Because every creature that has been — or shall —
    Has the nature of the first man Adam,   110
From him taking the filth of sin original,
    For from him all creatures came.
    Then from him with good cause you inherit blame
And are made the brands of hell.
    When you are first born out of your dame,   115
    You may in no wise in heaven dwell,
For you are disfigured by his sin
    And damned to darkness out of his sight.

Anima

How does grace then again begin?
    What restores the soul to its first light?   120

Wisdom

Wisdom that was God and man in one
Paid the full price to the Father of heaven.
    Through the dreadful death prepared for him alone,
    From which death sprang the sacraments seven,
Which sacraments wash all sin away.   125

Fyrst, baptem clensythe synne orygynall
And reformyt þe sowll in feythe verray
 To þe gloryus lyknes of Gode eternall
 Ande makyt yt as fayer and as celestyall
As yt neuer dyffowlyde had be.   130
 Ande ys Crystys own specyall,
Hys restynge place, hys plesant see.

Anima

In a sowll watt thyngys be
 By wyche he hathe hys very knowynge?

Wysdom

Tweyn partyes: þe on is the sensualyte   135
 Wyche ys clepyde þe flechly felynge.
 The v owtewarde wyttys to hym be serwynge.
Wan þey be not rewlyde ordynatly,
 The sensualyte þan — wythowte lesynge —
Ys made þe ymage of synne then of hys foly.   140
That other parte, þat ys clepyde resone,   f.101v
 Ande þat ys þe ymage of Gode propyrly,
For by þat þe sowll of Gode hathe cognycyon,
 And be þat hym serwyt & louevyt duly.
 Be þe neyther parte of reson he knowyt dyscretly   145
All erthely thyngys how þey xall be vsyde,
 Wat suffysyth to hys myghtys bodely,
 Ande wat nedyt not to be refusyde.
Thes tweyn do sygnyfye
 Yowr dysgysynge & yowr aray: 150
Blake & wyght, fowll & fayer, vereyly,
 Euery sowll here — þis ys no nay —
 Blake by sterynge of synne þat cummyth all day,
Wyche felynge cummythe of sensualyte
 Ande wyght by knowenge of reson veray   155
Off þe blyssyde infenyt deyte.
Thus a sowll ys bothe fowlle & fayer:
 Fowll as a best be felynge of synne,
Fayer as a angell, of hewyn þe ayer
 By knowynge of Gode by hys reson wythin.   160

---

126 baptem] from D — M bapten 130 had] point after 133 In] from D — M I; see
ll. 24, 613, 1064sd 135 on is the] from D — M on 137 v] M & D point after; D point
before 141 That] from D — M The 143 sowll] point after cognycyon] g added above
word 156 infenyt] D infinite 159 as a] D as; ayer] D hayr

First, baptism cleanses sin original
And restores the soul to true faith, yea,
 To the glorious likeness of God eternal
 And makes it as fair and as celestial
As if it had never defiled had been.   130
 It is Christ's own special,
His resting place, his pleasant den.

Anima

In a soul what things may there be
 By which he may of himself have a true knowing?

Wisdom

Two parts: The one is the sensuality   135
 Which is called fleshly feeling.
 The five outward wits are to him serving.
 When they are not ruled obediently,
  Sensuality, then — this is no lying —
Is made the image of sin by his own folly.   140
The other part, that is called reason,
 And that is the image of God properly,
For by that the Soul has cognition of God,
 And by that serves and loves him duly.
  By the lower part of reason he knows with discerning 145
All earthly things how they shall be used,
 What suffices to his body's yearning,
 What needs not to be refused.
These two do signify
 Your disguise and your array: 150
Black and white, foul and fair, truly,
 Every soul here — this is no nay —
 Black by the stirring of sin that comes all day,
 Which feeling comes from sensuality,
  And white by knowing from right reason, yea, 155
Of the blessed infinite deity.
Thus, a soul is both foul and fair:
 Foul as a beast by desiring sin,
Fair as an angel, of heaven the heir
 By knowing God through his reason within.   160

Anima

Than may I sey thus & begynne
Wyth v prudent vyrgyns of my reme —
Thow be þe v wyttys of my sowll wythinne.
Nigra sum sed formosa filia Jerusalem.

Her entreth v vyrgynes in white kertyllys & mantelys wyth cheuelers &   f.102r
chappelettys and synge:

*Nigra sum sed formosa, filia Ierusalem, sicut tabernacula cedar & sicut
pelles Salomonis.*

Anima

The doughters of Ierusalem me not lake   165
    For þis dyrke schadow I bere of humanyte,
That as þe tabernacull of Cedar wythowt yt ys blake
    And wythine as þe skyn of Salamone full of bewty.
    Quod fusca sum, nolite considerare me
Quia decolaravit me sol Jovis.   170

Wysdom

Thus all þe sowlys þat in þis lyff be
    Stondynge in grace by lyke to thys.
A, *quinque prudentes* — yowr wyttys fyve —
    Kepe yow clene, & 3e xall neuer deface;
Ye Godys ymage *n*euer xall ryve,   175
    For þe clene sowll is Godys restynge place.
    Thre myghtys euery cresten sowll has,
Wyche bethe applyede to þe trynyte.

---

162 v] M & D point after; D point before   163 v] M & D point after; D point before   164
sed] D &   164 sd entreth] from D — M enteryd;   in white] from D — M wyth, abbr.
cheulers] elers from D   chappelettys] D chapelyttys;   Ierusalem] M & D ierusalem   sicut]
cut from D   salomonis] line filler after in M, not in D   165 Ierusalem] M ierusalem — D
Jerusalem   168 full] o canc. before   172 by] D be; see also ll. 287, 304, 1094   175
[n]euer] both D & M read euer; Mss. readings are defensible, but emendation is preferable
   176 is] from D

Anima
Then may I say thus and begin
With five prudent virgins of my realm —
Those are the five wits of my soul within.
Nigra sum sed formose, filia Jerusalem.

Here five virgins enter in white outer skirts and mantles with wigs and chaplets, singing:

Nigra sum sed formosa, filia Jerusalem, sicut tabernacula cedar et sicut pelles Salomonis.

Anima
The daughters of Jerusalem find in me no lack   165
    Because I bear this dark shadow of humanity,
That, as the tabernacle of cedar, without it is black
    And within as the skin of Solomon, full of beauty.
    Quod fusca sum, nolite considerare me
Quia decolaravit me sol Jovis.   170

Wisdom
Thus all the souls that in this life be
Standing in grace are like unto this.
Ah, *quinque prudentes* — your wits five —
    Keep clean, and you shall never yourself deface;
God's image you shall never rive,   175
    For the clean soul is God's resting place.
    Three powers ever the Christian soul has,
Which are allied to the Trinity.

Mynde
All thre here, lo, byfor yowr face:
Mynde,

Wyll
Wyll,

Wndyrstondynge
    Ande Vndyrstondynge, we thre.   180

Wysdom
3e thre declare þan thys,
    Yowr syngnyfycacyon & yowr propyrte.

Mynde
I am Mynde þat in þe sowle ys   f.102v
    The veray fygure of þe deyte.
    Wen in myselff I haue mynde & se   185
The benefyttys of Gode & hys worthynes,
    How holl I was mayde, how fayere, how fre,
    How gloryus, how jentyll to hys lyknes,
Thys insyght bryngyt to my mynde
    Wat grates I ough to God ageyn   190
þat thus hathe ordenyde wythowt ende
    Me in hys blys euer for to regne.
    Than myn insuffycyens ys to me peyn.
That I haue not werof to yelde my dett.
    Thynkynge myselff creature most veyn,   195
    Than for sorow my bren I knett.
Wen in my mynde I brynge togedyr
    þe yerys & dayes of my synfullnes,
The vnstabylnesse of my mynde hedyr & thedyr,
    My oreble fallyngys & freellnes,   200
    Myselff ryght nought than I confes;
For by myselff I may not ryse
    Wythowt specyall grace of Godys goodnes.

180] Vndyrstondynge] wns canc. before — D vnderstondyng   181 speaker] Wysdam;
canc. m, abbrev. over a   183 speaker] Mende — D Mende; M & D on previous folio
188 how jentyll] D & how gentyll   190 ough to god] from D — M ought   191 wythowt]
D wyth outen   192 euer] point before   199 vnstabylnesse] from D — M sustabullnes
     200 My oreble] D Myn horrible   fallyngys] from D, w. abbr. expanded to -ys — M
fallynge

[Enter Mind, Will & Understanding]

Mind
All three here, lo, before your face:
Mind,

Will
 Will,

Understanding
And Understanding, we three.   180

Wisdom
You three declare then this,
 Your signification and your property.

Mind
I am Mind, that in the Soul is
 The true figure of the deity.
 When I look into my own mind and see   185
The benefits of God and his worthiness,
 How whole I was made, how fair, how free,
How glorious, how noble in his likeness,
This insight brings to my mind
 What gratitude I owe to God again   190
That thus has ordained without end
 Me in his bliss forever to reign.
 Then my insufficiency is to me pain
That I have nought wherewith to repay my debt.
 Thinking myself a creature most vain,   195
Then for sorrow my brows I knit.
When in my mind I bring together
 The years and days of my sinfulness,
The instability of my mind hither and thither,
 My horrible failings and frailness,   200
 Myself right nought then I confess;
For by myself I may not rise
 Without the special grace of God's goodness.

Thus mynde makyt me myself to dyspyse.
I seke & fynde nowere comforte   205
    But only in Gode, my creature;
Than onto hym I do resorte
    Ande say, "Haue mynde of me, my sauowr."
    Thus, mynde to Mynde bryngyth þat fawowre.   f.103r
Thus, by mynde of me Gode I kan know.   210
    Goode mynde, of Gode yt ys þe fygure
Ande thys mynde to haue all crysten ow.

Wyll
And I of þe soull am þe Wyll,
    Off þe godhede lyknes & fygure.
Wyt goode wyll no man may spyll,   215
    Nor wythowt goode wyll of blys be sure.
    Wat soule wyll gret mede recure,
He must grett wyll haue in thought or dede,
    Wertuusly sett wyth consyens pure,
For in wyll only stondyt mannys dede.   220
Wyll for dede oft ys take;
    Therfor, þe wyll must weell be dysposyde.
Than þer begynnyt all grace to wake
    Yff yt wyth synne be not anosyde.
    Therfor, þe wyll must be wyll apposyde,   225
Or þat yt to þe mevyngys yewe consent.
    The lybrary of reson must be wnclosyde,
Ande aftyr hys domys to take entent.
Owr wyll in Gode must be only sett
    And for Gode to do wylfully;   230
Wan gode wyll resythe, Gode ys in ws knett,
    Ande he performyt þe dede veryly.
    Off hym cummyth all wyll sett perfyghtly,
For of owrselff we haue ryght nought   f.103v
    But syne, wrechydnes, & foly.   235
He ys begynner & gronde of wyll & thought.

---

204 myself] D — M meselff   208 Haue] M haue, w. point before   214 fygure] D a
fygure   215 Wyt] D w¹, usual abbr.; M uses abbr. in all but 3 instances, twice expanding
as Wyt (see also l. 975) and once as Wyth (l. 863);   216 wythowt] D wythouten   218 in
thought or dede] dede & canc. before, w. or canc. above &; or above line before dede   220
only stondyt] word order from D (onely standyth) — M stondyt only   224 yt wyth synne]
word order from D (it wyth synne) — M wyth synne yt   225 wyll (2nd)] D wele; also see
l. 319 226 mevyngys] from D — M mevynge;   consent] from D — M cosent   230
wylfully] from D — M wysly   232 dede] point before

Thus mind makes me myself despise.
I seek and find nowhere comfort   205
    But only in God, my creator;
Then unto him I do resort
    And say, "Keep me in mind, my savior."
    Thus, mind to Mind brings that favor.
    Thus, by my own mind God I can know in thought.   210
    Good Mind of God is the figure
And to have that mind all Christians ought.

Will

And I of the Soul am the Will,
    Of the godhead likeness and a figure.
With good will no man may damn his soul to hell,   215
    Nor without good will of bliss be sure.
    That soul which great reward would procure,
    He must great will have in thought or deed,
    Virtuously set with conscience pure,
For in will only stands man's deed.   220
Will for deed is often taken;
    Therefore, the will must be well disposed.
Then all grace begins there to awaken
    If with sin it is not out-nosed.
    Therefore, the will must be well opposed,   225
    Before to its promptings it give consent.
    The library of reason must be unclosed,
And to follow those judgments fix your intent.
Our will in God only must be set
    And for God to act willingly;   230
When good Will in us rises, God in us is knit,
    And he performs the deed verily.
    From him comes all power of the will set firmly,
    For of ourselves we have right nought
    But sin, wretchedness, and folly.   235
He is the beginner and ground of will and thought.

Than þis goode wyll seyde before
   Ys behoueable to yche creature,
Iff he cast hym to restore
     The soule þat he hath take of cure,   240
     Wyche of God ys þe fygure,
  As longe as þe fygure ys kept fayer
     Ande ordenyde euer to endure
  In blys, of wyche ys he þe veray hayer.

Wndyrstondynge

The iii^{de} parte of þe soule ys Wndyrstondynge,   245
   For by wndyrstondynge I beholde wat Gode ys:
In hymselff begynnyng wythowt begynnynge
     Ande ende wythowt ende þat xall neuer mys.
     Incomprehensyble in hymselff he ys;
   Hys werkys in me I kan not comprehende.   250
     How xulde I holly hym, þan, þat wrought all þis?
  Thus, by knowynge of me, to knowynge of Gode I assende.
I know in angelys he ys desyderable,
   For hym to beholde thei dysyer souerenly;
In hys seyntys most dylectable,   255
     For in hymm thei joy assyduly.
     In creaturys hys werkys ben most wondyrly,
  For all this ys made by hys myght,
     By his wysdom gouernyde most souerenly,   f.104r
  And be hys benygnyte inspyryt all soullys wyth lyght.   260
Off all creaturys he ys lowyde souereyn,
   For he ys Gode of yche creature,
And þey be hys peple þat euer xall reynge,
     In wom he dwellyt as in hys tempull sure.
     Wan I of thys knowynge make reporture   265
  Ande se þe loue he hathe for me wrought,
     Yt bryngyt me to loue þat prynce most pure,
  For for loue þat lorde made man of nought.
Thys ys þat loue wyche ys clepyde charyte,
   For Gode ys charyte, as awtors telles,   270

238 behoueable] D behouefull   240 he hath] D hath   243 euer to] from D — M euer for
to   244 ys he] D is   245 iii] M & D iij   247 begynnynge (2nd)] D begynnyg 248
wythowt] D wythouten   254 thei] from D — M þe   256 thei] from D — M þer   257
wondyrly] D wonderfully   258 this] from D   259 his] from D   260 be] from D;
inspyryt] D inspired   264 as in] in from D — M as   265 of] from D   268 For for] point
between words 4,34 — D : between; made man] from D — M made a man; see l. 328
270 telles] from D — M tell; M "corrects" person of verb and loses rhyme

Then this good Will described before
    Is necessary to each creature,
If he casts forth himself to restore
    The soul he has taken unto his cure,   240
    Which of God is the figure,
  As long as the figure is kept fair
    And ordained ever to endure
In bliss, of which he is the very heir.

Understanding

The third part of the soul is Understanding,   245
    For by understanding I behold what God is:
In himself beginning without beginning
    And end without end that never shall cease.
    Incomprehensible in himself he is;
  His works in me I cannot comprehend.   250
    How should I reverence him, then, that wrought all this?
  Thus, by knowing myself to knowing God I ascend.
I know to angels he is desirable,
    For to behold him they desire mightily;
In his saints most delectable,   255
    For in him they joy assiduously.
    In creatures his works show most wonderfully,
  For all this is made by his might,
    By his wisdom governed most sovereignly,
And by his benignity all souls inspired with light.   260
Of all creatures he is the most loved sovereign,
    For he is God of each creature,
And they are his people that ever shall reign,
    In whom he dwells as in his temple pure.
    When this knowledge I comprehend for sure   265
  And see the love he has for me wrought,
    It brings me to love that prince most pure,
  For out of love the Lord made man of nought.
This is the love which is called charity,
    For God is charity, as each author tells,   270

Ande woo ys in charyte, in Gode dwellyt he,
　Ande Gode, þat ys charyte, in hym dwellys.
Thus, wndyrstondynge of Gode compellys
To cum to charyte — than haue hys lyknes, lo!
　Blyssyde ys þat sowll þat þis speche spellys:　　　　　　275
Et qui creauit me requieuit in tabernaculo meo.

Wysdom

Lo, thes iii myghtys in on soule be:
　Mynde, Wyll, & Wndyrstondynge.
By Mynde, of Gode þe fadyr knowyng haue ye;
　By Wndyrstondynge, of Gode þe sone ye haue knowynge; 280
　By Wyll, wyche turnyt into loue brennynge,
Gode, þe holy gost, þat clepyde ys lowe;
　Not iii godys but on Gode in beynge.
Thus, eche clene soule ys symylytude of Gode abowe.
By Mynde, feythe in þe father haue we;　　　　　　　　285
　Hoppe in owr lorde Jhesu, by Wnydyrstondynge;
Ande be Wyll, in þe Holy Gost, charyte.
　Lo, thes iii pryncypall wertus of yow iii sprynge.
　Thys, þe clene soule stondyth as a kynge;　　　　f.104v
Ande abowe all þis 3e haue free wyll.　　　　　　　　290
　Off þat beware befor all thynge,
For yff þat perverte, all þis dothe spyll.
Ye haue iii enemyes; of hem beware:
　The Worlde, þe Flesche, & þe Fende.
Yowr fywe wyttys from hem 3e spare,　　　　　　　　295
　That þe sensualyte þey brynge not to mynde.
　No thynge xulde offende Gode in no kynde,
Ande yff þer do, se þat þe nether parte of resone
　In no wys þerto lende;
Than þe ouerparte xall haue fre domynacyon.　　　　　300
Wan suggestyon to þe Mynde doth apere,
　Wndyrstondynge, delyght not 3e þerin.
Consent not, Wyll, yll lessons to lere,
　Ande than suche steryngys by no syn.

---

277 speaker] Wysdom: M Wydom, w. m cropped — D Wysdam; on] D o, a variant
of on, (number) used before consonants; point in the loop above n   277 iii] M & D iij
280 sone point before 281 into from D (in to) — M in   287 be, var. of by] both M & D;
for by meaning be, see ll. 172, 304, 1094   289 thys] var. of D thus; see also ll. 812, 817,
839   293 enemyes] from D — M enmyes   296 to mynde] from D — M yow byhynde
298 þer] D ther, or poss. thei   301-08] D & M rhyme scheme (ababcbcb) is irregular;
302 3e] D the   304 by] a var. of D be; see also ll. 172, 287, 1094

And whoever is in charity, in God dwells he,
    And God, that is charity, in him dwells.
    Thus, the understanding of God compels
    Us to come to charity — then we have his likeness, lo!
    Blessed is the soul that on this speech dwells: 275
Et creavit me requievit in tabernaculo meo.

Wisdom

Lo, these three mights in one soul be:
    Mind, Will, and Understanding.
Through Mind, knowledge of God the Father have ye;
    Through Understanding, of God the son you have knowing;
    Through Will, which turns into love burning,   281
    God, the Holy Ghost, that is called love;
    Not three gods but one God in being.
    Thus, each clean soul is a similitude of God above.
By Mind, faith in the Father have we;   285
    Hope in our Lord Jesu, by Understanding;
And by Will, in the Holy Ghost, charity.
    Lo, these three principal virtues from you three spring.
    Thus, the clean soul stands like a king;
    And above all this you have free will.   290
    Of that beware before each thing,
For if that pervert, all this does spill.
You have three enemies; of them beware:
    The World, the Flesh, and the Fiend.
Your five wits from them you must spare,   295
    So that they do not bring sensuality to mind.
    In no thing should the wits offend God in any kind,
    And if they do, see that the lower part of reason
    In no wise thereto tend;
Then the higher part shall have free dominion.   300
When suggestion to the Mind does appear,
    Understanding, delight not yourself therein.
Consent not, Will, ill lessons to hear,
    And then such promptings will be no sin.

Thei do but purge þe soule wer ys suche contrauersye.   305
   Thus in me, Wysdom, yowr werkys begynne.
Fyght, & 3e xall haue þe crown of glory;
   That ys euerlastyng ioy, to be parteners þerinne.

Anima

Soueren Lorde, I am bownde to the.   f.105r
   Wan I was nought, þu made me thus gloryus;   310
Wan I perysschede thorow synne, þu sauyde me;
   Wen I was in grett perell, þu kept me, Crystus.
   Wen I erryde, þu reducyde me, Jhesus.
   Wen I was ignorant, þu tawt me truthe;
   Wen I synnyde, þu corecte me thus;   315
   Wen I was hewy, þu comfortede me by ruthe.
Wen I stonde in grace, þu holdyste me þat tyde.
   Wen I fall, þu reysyst me myghtyly;
Wen I go wyll, þu art my gyde;
   Wen I cum, þu reseywyste me most louyngly.   320
   Thu hast anoyntyde me wyth þe oyll of mercy;
Thy benefyttys, Lorde, be innumerable.
   Werfor, Lawde, endeles to þe I crye,
Recomendynge me to thi endles powre durable.

Here in þe goynge owt, þe v wyttys synge "tota pulcra es & cetera," they goyng befor, **Anima** *next, & her folowynge* **Wysdom**, *& aftyr hym* **Mynde**, **Wyll**, *&* **Wndyrstondynge**, *all iii in wyght cloth of golde, chevelered & crestyde in on sute.*

And aftyr þe songe entreth **Lucyfer** *in a dewyllys aray wythowt, & wythin as a prowde galonte, seynge thus on thys wyse:*

305] Thei] from D — M The   308 ys euerlastynge] word order from D (is euerlastyng) — euer ys lastynge;   þerinne] M þer Inne — D ther Inne   309—speaker] on previous folio   310-20 þu] in all instances D thu — M þ^u 311 me] from D   between 315/16] este written in margin, perhaps in later hand   316 me] from D; comfortede] D conforted   319] wyll] D wele; also see l. 225.   320 louyngly] from D — M louynly   321 thu] both D & M;   me] from D   324 thi] from D — M þu   324 sd goyng] oyng from D; hym] point in loop above m;   Wyll] yll from D; iii] M & D iij;   golde] point after;   chevelered] from D -- M thevelerdye;   crestyde] es from D;   in on sute] on from D;   dewyllys] D deuely;   aray] a from D;   wythowt] M : after;   wyse] se from D

They do but purge the soul wherein lies such controversy.   305
   Thus in me, Wisdom, your works begin.
Fight, and you shall have the crown of glory;
   That is everlasting joy, to be partners therein.

Anima

Sovereign Lord, I am bound to thee.
   When I was nought, you made me glorious;   310
When I perished through sin, you saved me.
   When I was in great peril, you preserved me, Christus;
   When I erred, you straightened my path, Jesus.
   When I was ignorant, you taught me truth;
   When I sinned, you corrected me thus;   315
   When I was sad, you comforted me with ruth.
When I stand in grace, you hold me by your side;
   When I fall, you raise me mightily;
When I go astray, you are my guide;
   When I come, you receive me most lovingly.   320
   You have anointed me with the oil of mercy;
Your benefits, Lord, are innumerable.
   Wherefore, Lord, endlessly to thee I cry,
Entrusting myself to your endless power immutable.

*Here, in going out, the five wits sing "Tota pulcra es," etc., they going before, **Anima** next, and following her **Wisdom**, and after him **Mind**, **Will**, and **Understanding**, all three in white cloth of gold, wigged and wearing Anima's livery.*

*And after the song, **Lucifer** enters wearing a devil's suit on the outside, dressed underneath as a proud gallant, saying thus:*

Lucyfer

Owt, harow, I rore!	325

For envy I lore.
My place to restore,
    God hath mad man.

All cum þey not thore,	f.105v
Woode & þey wore.	330

I xall tempte hem so sorre,
    For I am he þat syn begane.
I was a angell of lyghte;
Lucyfeer, I hyght,

Presumynge in Godys syght.	335

    Werfor I am lowest in hell.
In reformynge of my place ys dyght
Man, whan I haue in most dyspyght,
Euer castynge me wyth hem for to fyght,

In þat hewynly place that he xulde not dwell.	340

I am as wyly now as than;
þe knowynge þat I hade yet I can.
I know all compleccyons of man,
    Werto he ys most dysposyde,

Ande þerin I tempte hym ay whan.	345

I marre hys myndys to þer wan,
That whoo ys hym þat God hym began.
    Many a holy man wyth me ys mosyde.
Of Gode, man ys þe fygure,

Hys symylytude, hys pyctowre,	350

Gloryosest of ony creature
    þat euer was wrought,
Wyche I wyll dysvygure
Be my fals coniecture.

Yff he tende my reporture,	355

    I xall brynge hym to nought.
In þe soule ben iii partyes, iwys:
Mynde, Wyll, Wndyrstondynge of blys —
Fygure of þe godhede, I know well thys.

And þe flesche of man þat ys so changeable,	360

325] rhyme scheme changes to Lucifer's aaab cccb (or, as here, aaab aaab)   328 mad man] word sequence from D (mad e man) — M mad a man; see l. 268   328, 332, 336, 340, 344, 348, 352, 356, 360] M & D tail rhymes written to right of text   333 was angell] word sequence from D — M was a aungell   334 Lucfeer] D Lucifer   338 whan] M & D obsolete form of whom; in] from D   339 for to] from D — M to   340 that] from D   343 man] from D — M a man   345 hym] from D   346 þer] D ther, or possibly thei   347 whoo] D wo   348 a] D an   350 man] point before   357 iii] M & D iij; iwys] I wys M & D   358 wyll] M & D points before and after

Lucifer

Out, harrow, I roar! 325
For envy all sore.
My lost place to restore,
    God has made man.
If they should not come to that shore,
They would be mad forevermore. 330
I shall tempt them so sore,
    For I am he that sin began.
I was an angel of light;
Lucifer, my name, was bright,
Before presuming in God's sight, 335
    For which I am the lowest in hell.
To fill my place on that site
God made man, whom I hold most in despite,
Ever resolving against him to fight,
    So that in that heavenly place he shall not dwell. 340
I am as wily now as then;
The knowledge I had is still in my ken.
I know all complexions of men,
    What things they will most easily believe,
And therein I tempt them whenever I can. 345
I mar man's mind to make it wan,
Till he is sorry that God his life began.
    Many a holy man I know how to deceive.
Of God, man is the figure,
His similitude, his picture, 350
Most glorious of any creature
    That ever was wrought,
Which I will disfigure
By my false conjecture.
If he heed my overture, 355
    I shall bring him to nought.
In the Soul are three parts, iwis:
Mind, Will, Understanding of bliss —
Figure of the godhead, I well know this.
    And the flesh of man that is so changeable, 360

That wyll I tempte, as I gees.
Thow þat I perwert, synne non ys
But yff þe Soule consent to þis,
      For in þe Wyll of þe Soule ben the dedys dampnabyll.
To þe Mynde of þe Soule I xall mak suggestyun,   365 f.106r
Ande brynge hys Wndyrstondynge to dylectacyon,
So þat hys Wyll make confyrmacyon.
      Than am I sekyr inowe
That dede xall sew of damnacyon;
Than of þe Sowll þe dewll hath domynacyon.   370
I wyll go make this examynacyon,
      To all þe dewllys of helle I make a wow!
But for to tempte man in my lyknes,
Yt wolde brynge hym to grett feerfullnes.
I wyll change me into bryghtnes   375
      & so hym to begyle.
Sen I xall schew hym perfyghtnes,
And wertu prove yt wykkydnes.
Thus, wndyr colors, all thynge perverse.
      I xall neuer rest tyll the sowle I defyle.   380

Her **Lycyfer** *dewoydyth & cummyth in ageyn as a goodly galont.*

Mynde
My mynde is euer on Jhesu,
That enduyde ws wyth wertu;
Hys doctryne to sue,
      Euer I purpos.

Wndyrstondynge
My wndyrstondynge ys in trew,   385
That wyth feyth ws dyd renew.
Hys laws to pursew
      Ys swetter to me þan the sawowre of þe rose.

363 to þis] D vn to mys; Soule] sour canc. before; 364] word order from D ben the
dedys damnable 364, 368, 372, 376, 380, 384, 388] M & D written to right of text 368
inowe] D I now — M I nowe w. I cropped in margin 369 dede] from D — M dethe 371
this] from D — M hys 372 helle] elle from D 373 But for] from D — M For for
375 bryghtnes] -s from D; M bryghtne — D brightnesse 376 begyle] le from D 377
sen] var. of D syn 378 prove] from D; in D provyt altered to prove w. e over yt — M
provyt 380 the] from D — cropped in M 385 My] D Myn 388 the] from D

That will I tempt, as I guess.
Though if I pervert that, still no sin there is
Unless the Soul consent to do amiss,
    For in the Will of the Soul are the deeds damnable.
To the Mind of the Soul I shall make suggestion,   365
And bring his Understanding to delectation,
So that his Will make confirmation.
    Then am I certain to show how
That deed shall lead to damnation;
Then of the Soul the devil has domination.   370
I will go make this examination,
    To all the devils of hell I make a vow!
But, should I tempt man in my likeness,
It would bring him to great fearfulness.
I will change myself into brightness   375
    And so him beguile.
I shall show him that perfection is sinfulness
And prove virtue to be wickedness.
Thus, under colors, turn all to perverseness.
    I shall never rest till the soul I defile.   380

*Here **Lucifer** goes out and comes in again as a well-dressed dandy.
[Mind, Will, and Understanding enter but do not see Lucifer.]*

Mind
My mind is ever on Jesu,
That endowed us with virtue;
His doctrine to pursue,
    Ever I propose.

Understanding
My understanding is true,   385
That with faith did us renew.
His laws to pursue
    Is sweeter to me than the savor of the rose.

Wyll

And my wyll ys hys wyll, veraly,
That made ws hys creaturys so specyally,   390
Yeldynge vnto hym laude & glory
  For hys goodnes.

Lucyfer

Ye fonnyde fathers, founders of foly,
Vt quid hic statis tota die ociosi?
Ʒe wyll perisshe or Ʒe yt aspye.   395
  The dewyll hath acumberyde yow expres.
Mynde, Mynde, ser, haue mynde of thys.   f.106v

Mynde

He ys not ydyll þat wyth Gode ys.

Lucyfer

No, ser, I prowe well yis.
  Lo, thys ys my suggestyun: 400
All thynge hat dew tymes —
Prayer, fastynge, labour — all thes;
Wan tyme ys not kept, þat dede ys amys.
  Be more pleynerly to yowr informacyon.
Here ys a man þat lywyt wordly,   405
Hathe wyff, chylderne, & serwantys besy,
And other chargys þat I not specyfye.
  Ys yt leeffull to þis man
To lewe hys labour wsyde truly?
Hys chargys perysche, þat Gode gaff duly,   410
And yewe hym to preyer & es of body?
  Woso do thus wyth God ys not, than.
Martha plesyde Gode grettly thore.

Mynde

Ye, but Maria plesyde hymm moche more.

389 ys hys] hys hys w. first h canc.   391 vnto] from D — M on   395 p[er]isshe] D
pisshe, prob. error for perisshe, w. abbr. for per omitted — M pyse   397 M repeats name
of lucyfer as speaker — D has line indicating change of speaker drawn but cancelled;
mynde of] from D — M in mynde   399 yis] from D — M thys   400 Lo] from D; D line
written to right of text   401 thynge] from D — M thnge   403 amys] D mys
404, 408, 412] D & M written to right of text   405 wordly] D wardly   408 Ys yt] word order
from D (Is it) — M Yt ys   410 perysche] D parisch   411 hym] point after
413 Martha] from D — M Mertha   414 Maria] from D — M Mara

Will

And my will is his will, verily,
That made us his creatures so specially,   390
Yielding unto him laud and glory
    For his goodness.

                    [Lucifer approaches the mights]

Lucifer

You foolish fathers, founders of folly,
Ut quid hic statis tota die ociosi?
You will perish before you see glory.   395
    The devil has burdened you for certain, iwis.
Mind, Mind, sir, take note of this.

Mind

He is not idle that with God is.

Lucifer

No, sir, I shall well prove this.
    Lo, this is my suggestion: 400
All things have due times —
Prayer, fasting, labor — all this;
When the time is not kept, that deed is amiss.
    Be more accurate in your information.
Here is a man that lives worldly,   405
Has wife, children, and servants busy,
And other charges I will not specify.
    Is it lawful for this man
To leave the job that belongs to him truly?
To let his charges perish, that God gave duly,   410
And give himself to prayer and ease of body?
    Whoso does this is not with God, then.
Martha pleased God much therefore.

Mind

Yea, but Mary pleased him much more.

Lucyfer

Yet þe lest hade blys for euermore.   415
    Ys not that anow?

Mynde

Contemplatyff lyff ys sett befor.

Lucyfer

I may not belewe þat in my lore.
For God hymselff wan he was man borre,
    Wat lyff lede he? Answer þu now.   420
Was he euer in contemplacyon?

Mynde

I suppos not, by my relacyon.

Lucyfer

And all hys lyff was informacyon   f.107r
    Ande example to man.
Sumtyme wyth synners he had conversacyon;   425

Sumtyme wyth holy also comunycacyon;
Sumtyme he laboryde, preyde; sumtyme, tribulacyon.
    Thys was *vita mixta* þat Gode here began,
Ande þat lyff xulde ye here sewe.

Mynde

I can belewe that ye say is trewe.   430

Lucyfer

Contemplatyff lyff for to sewe,
    Yt ys grett drede & se cause why:
They must fast, wake, & prey euer new,
Wse harde lywynge & goynge wyth dyscyplyne dew,
Kepe sylence, wepe, & surphettys eschewe,   435
    Ande yff þey fayll of thys, þey offende Gode hyghly.
Wan þey haue wastyde by feyntnes,
Than febyll þer wyttys & fallyn to fondnes,
Sum into dyspeyer & sum into madnes,
    Wet yt well, God ys not plesyde wyth thys.   440

415 þe] stroke before, resembles the inverted apostrophe which ordinarily signifies an omitted
-er   416 that] from D — M þis;   anow] var. of D lnow; D line written to right of text 422
speaker] lucyfer, on previous folio   427 preyde] M point before and after -- D point after
430 I can beleve that ye say is trewe] from D — M I kan not belewe thys ys trewe;   I, w.
Contemp canc. before   434 lywynge] D levyngys, w. abbr. expanded to -ys

Lucifer
Yet the least had bliss forevermore.   415
   Is that not enough to know?

Mind
The contemplative life is to be preferred.

Lucifer
I may not believe it; that is absurd.
For God himself, Mary's son, upon my word,
     What life led he? Answer you so.   420
Was he ever in contemplation?

Mind
I suppose not, by my information.

Lucifer
And all his life was explanation
     And example to man.
Sometimes with sinners he held conversation;   425
Sometimes with holy men he had communication;
Sometimes he labored, prayed; sometimes, tribulation.
     This was **vita mixta** that God here began,
And that life should you here pursue.

Mind
I can believe what you say is true.   430

Lucifer
Contemplative life to pursue
     Is very frightening; you can surely see why:
They must fast, watch, and pray ever new,
Live hard lives, and follow discipline due,
Keep silence, weep, and surfeit eschew,   435
     And if they fail in this, they offend God highly.
When they have wasted away to faintness,
Their wits grow feeble and fall into foolishness,
Some into despair and some into madness,
     Know it well, God is not pleased with this.   440

Lewe, lewe, suche syngler besynes.
Be in þe worlde; vse thyngys necesse.
The comyn ys best expres.
      Who clymyt hye, hys fall gret ys.

Mynde
Truly, me seme 3e haue reson.   445

Lucyfer
Aplye yow then to þis conclusyun.

Mynde
I kan make no replicacyon;   f.107v
      Your resons be grete.
I kan not forgett þis informacyon.

Lucyfer
Thynke þerwppon; yt ys yowr saluacyon.   450
Now, & Wndyrstondynge wolde haue delectacyon,
      All syngler deuocyons he wolde lett.
Yowr v wyttys abrode lett sprede.
Se how comly to man ys precyus wede;
Wat worschype yt ys to be manfull in dede.   455
      þat bryngeth in domynacyon.
Off þe symple what profyght yt to tak hede?
Beholde how ryches dystroyt nede.
It makyt man fayer, hym wele for to fede.
      & of lust & lykynge commyth generacyon.   460
Wndyrstondynge, tender ye þis informacyon?

Wndyrstondynge
In thys I fele a manere of dylectacyon.

Lucyfer
A ha, ser! Then þer make a pawsacyon.
      Se & beholde þe worlde abowte.

442 vse] wse canc. before   447 speaker] Mynde on previous folio   448] line from D —
written to right of text; first marginal line since l. 416   449 informacyon] M Informacyon —
D information   453 v] point after— D points before and after   454 comly] from D — M
comunly   455 yt ys] D it   456 bryngeth] from D — M bryght   456] M & D written to
right of text   459 wele] from D (added above line) — M werkys   462 a manere] from
D — M in manere   463 ha] points before and after

Leave, leave such obsessive display.
Be in the world; use things everyday.
The common is best in every way.
>Whoever climbs high, his fall great is.

Mind
Truly, it seems to me you have reason. 445

Lucifer
Apply yourself then to this solution.

Mind
I can in no way deny your conclusion;
>Your reasons are great.
I cannot forget this information.

Lucifer
Think on this; it is your salvation. 450
Now, if Understanding would delight in recreation,
>All singleminded devotions he would forget.
Let your five wits stretch out and feed.
See how comely to man is precious weed;
What privilege it is to dress well, indeed! 455
>That gives you domination.
Of simple things, what profits it to take heed?
Behold how riches destroy need.
They make a man wealthy, himself well to feed.
>And of lust and pleasure comes procreation. 460
Understanding, do you like this information?

Understanding
In this I feel great delectation.

Lucifer
Aha, sir! Then you should pause at that station.
>See and behold the world about.

Lytyll thynge suffysyt to saluacyon.   465
All maner synnys dystroyt contryscyon.
They þat dyspeyer, mercy haue grett compunccyon.
     Gode plesyde best wyth goode wyll no dowte.
Therfor, Wyll, I rede yow inclyne.
Lewe yowr stodyes, þow ben dywyn,   470
Yowr prayers, yowr penance — of ipocryttys þe syne —
     Ande lede a comun lyff.
What synne is in met? In hale? In wyn?
Wat synne ys in ryches? In clothynge fyne?
All thynge Gode ordenyde to man to inclyne.   475 f.108r
     Lewe yowr nyse chastyte & take a wyff.
Better ys fayer frut þan fowll pollucyon.
What seyth Sensualite to þis conclusyon?

Wyll

As þe fyue wyttys gyff informacyon,
     Yt semyth yowr resons be goode.   480

Lucyfer

The wyll of þe soule hathe fre domynacyon.
Dyspute not to moche in þis wyth reson.
Yet þe nethyr parte to þis taketh sum instruccyon,
     And so xulde þe ouerparte, but he were woode.

Wyll

Me seme, as 3e sey, in body & soule,   485
     Man may be in þe worlde & be ryght goode.

Lucyfer

Ya, ser, by Sent Powle!
     But trust not þes prechors, for þey be not goode.
     For þey flatter & lye, as þey wore woode.
Ther ys a wolffe in a lombys skyn.   490

Wyll

     Ya, I woll no more row ageyn þe floode;
I woll sett my soule on a mery pynne.

---

469 wyll] written above well, canc.; point after wyll   471 ipocryttys] M & D Ipocryttys
473 is] from D   479 As] from D — M At   481 speaker] lucyfere — D lucifer w. smudge
to right of word   483 instruccyon] M instrucccyon, w. middle c canc.   485-92] reverts to
Wisdom's poetic stanza   487 Ya] from D   by] D be   490 lombys] M bo canc. before —
D lombe   492 on] from D

Little things suffice for salvation; 465
All manner of sin destroys contrition;
For those that despair, mercy has great compunction.
    God is pleased best with good will, no doubt.
Therefore, Will, I advise you my way to incline.
Leave your studies, those that are divine, 470
Your prayers, your penance — of hypocrites the sign —
    And lead a common life.
What sin is in meat? In ale? In wine?
What sin is in riches? In clothing fine?
All things God ordained to man to incline. 475
    Leave your prim chastity and take a wife.
Better is fair fruit than foul pollution.
What says Sensuality to this conclusion?

Will

As the five wits give information,
    Your reasons make me glad. 480

Lucifer

The Will of the Soul has free domination.
Dispute not too much in this with reason.
Yet the lower part from this takes some instruction,
    And so should the higher part, unless he were mad.

Will

It seems to me, as you say, in body and soul, 485
    Man may be in the world and be right good.

Lucifer

Yea, sir, by Saint Paul!
    But trust not these preachers, for they are not good.
    They flatter and lie, in an insane mood.
There is a wolf in a lambskin. 490

Will

    Yea, I will no more row against the flood;
I will set my soul in a merry spin.

Lucyfer

Be my trowthe, than do ye wyslye.
Gode lowyt a clene sowll & a mery.
Acorde yow iii togedyr by,   495
     And ye may not mysfare.

Mynde

To þis suggestyon agre me.

Wndyrstondynge

Delyght þerin I haue truly.   f.108v

Wyll

And I consent þerto frelye.

Lucyfer

     A ha, ser! All mery þan and awey care.   500
Go in þe worlde, se þat abowte.
Geet goode frely, cast no dowte.
To þe ryche ye se men lowly lought.
     Yewe to yowr body þat ys nede,
And euer be mery. Let reuell rowte!   505

Mynde

Ya, ellys I beschrew my snowte.

Wndyrstondynge

And yff I care, cache me þe gowte.

Wyll

     And yff I spare, þe dewyll me spede.

Lucyfer

     Go yowr wey than & do wysly.
Change þat syde aray.   510a

---

493 than] var. of D that   495 iii] M & D iij   496 line from D — written to right of text;
only marginal line on D folio 497 me] from D — M we   498 speaker] Wndyrstondynge on
previous folio; þerin] M per In — D ther In   500 ha] from D; and] from D   507 speaker]
wnderstondynge w. er, ng abbrev.) — D vnderstand   507 me] from D — M i   510
Change . . . aray] Stanza structure and rhyme suggest that this is the first half of a line;
Mynde completes line.

Lucifer

By my troth, that you do wisely.
God loves a clean soul and a merry.
In one accord you three should together be,   495
     And you will not ill fare.

Mind

To this suggestion I agree.

Understanding

Delight therein I have truly.

Will

And I consent thereto freely.

Lucifer

     Aha, sir! All merry then and banish care.   500
Go in the world, see riches all about.
Get goods freely, have no doubt.
To the rich you see men lowly brought.
     Give your body all its need,
And ever be merry. Let it all hang out!   505

Mind

Yea, else I beshrew my snout.

Understanding

And if I care, let me catch the gout.

Will

     And if I hold back, may the devil me speed.

Lucifer

Go your way then and do wisely.
Change that long, old-fashioned array.

Mynde
  I yt dyfye.   510b

Wndyrstondynge
We woll be fresche, and it happe, *La plu joly*.
  Farwell, penance.

Mynde
To worschyppys I wyll my mynde aplye.

Wndyrstondynge
My wndyrstondynge in worschyppys & glory.

Wyll
And I in lustys of lechery,   515
    As was sumtyme gyse of Frawnce.
        Wyth "Wy, wyppe,
        Farwell," quod I, "þe dewyll ys wppe"!
                                                            Exiant

Lucyfer
Off my dysyere now haue I summe.   f.109r
Wer onys brought into custume,   520
Then farwell, consyens, he wer clumme.
    I xulde haue all my wyll.
Resone I haue made bothe deff & dumme;
Grace ys owt & put arome.
Wethyr I wyll haue, he xall cum,   525
    So at þe last I xall hym spyll.
I xall now stere hys mynde
To þat syne made me a fende:
Pryde, wyche ys ageyn kynde,
    And of all synnys hede.   530
So to couetyse he xall wende,
For þat enduryth to þe last ende.
And on to lechery, and I may hymm rende,
    Than am I seker þe soule ys dede.

---

510 I yt defye] second half of l. 510; rhyme suggests line break at this point
511, 514 speaker] wnderstondynge w. er, ng abbrev.) — D vnderstand   511 and it happe]
from D; happe written as hap w. the usual D abbr. for an omitted m, n, or doubled p
(sometimes, as here, indicating pe) superscripted above ap; M mistakenly copies as hamp
514 My] D Myn   517-18] line break from D — with why whyppe / Farewell quod I the
dewyll is vp — M transcribes as one line   Exiant] from D   519 speaker] lucyfer on
previous folio   523 deff] from D — M dethe   530 all] from D

Mind

             I it defy.   510

Understanding

We will be fresh, and as it chance, *La plus joli.*
    Farewell, penance.

Mind

To worldly renown I will my mind apply.

Understanding

My understanding in fame and glory.

Will

And I in lusts of lechery,   515
    As was once the style in France.
       With "Why, whip,
       Farewell," quoth I, "The devil is up"!
                      Exeunt [*Mind, Will, & Understanding*]

Lucifer

Of my desire now have I some.
Now if this were brought into custom,   520
Then farewell, conscience, he would be mum.
    I should have all my will.
Reason I have made both deaf and dumb;
Grace has been put out to roam.
Where I would have him, he shall come,   525
    So at the last I shall him kill.
I shall now stir his mind
To the sin that made me a fiend:
Unnatural pride, which destroys humankind,
    And of all sins is the head.   530
So to covetousness he shall wend,
For that endures to the last end.
And if unto lechery I can him send,
    Then am I certain the soul is dead.

That soule God made incomparable,   535
To hys lyknes most amyable,
I xall make yt most reprouable,
          Ewyn lyke to a fende of hell.
At hys deth I xall apere informable,
Schewynge hym all hys synnys abhomynable,   540
Prewynge hys soule damnable.
          So wyth dyspeyer I xall hym qwell.
Wyll clennes ys mankyn,
Verely þe soule God ys wythin.
Ande wen yt ys in dedly synne,   545
          Yt is werely þe deuelys place.   f.109v
Thus by colours and false gynne
Many a soule to hell I wynn.
Wyde to go I may not blyne,
          Wyth þis fals boy — God gyff hym euell grace.   550

Her he takyt a shrewed boy wyth hym & goth hys wey cryenge.

Mynde
Lo, me here in new aray.
Wyppe, wyrre, care awey.
          Farwell, perfeccyon.
Me semyt myselff most lykly ay.
It ys but honest — no pryde, no nay.   555
I wyll be freshest, by my fay,
          For þat acordyt wyth my complexccyon.

Wndyrstondynge
Ande haue here one as fresche as yow,
All mery, mery & glade now.
I haue get goode, Gode wott how.   560
          For ioy I sprynge, I sckyppe.

543 Wyll] D Whyll   546 is] from D   547 and false gynne] from D — M gyane   548 to
hell] D to hevyn, w. light strokes under to, as if to alter word to fro   550 euell] D ille
550 sd shrewed] from D — M screwde w. boy canc. before   551 new] M a new — D newe
551-52] M & D rhyme scheme irregular, w. only 2 rhyming lines rather than 3. Line may be
missing.   553 perfeccyon] point appears in the loop above n   554 lykly] from D —
M lyghtly   558 speaker] M wndyrstondynge, w. -yr abbr. — D vnderstondyng; M & D return
to full names   one] from D — M me   559 mery mery] & canc. between
561 ioy] D loye

God made that soul incomparable, 535
To his likeness most amiable,
I shall make it most reprehensible,
    Even like a fiend of hell.
At his death my testimony will be invincible,
Showing him all his sins abominable, 540
Proving his soul to be damnable.
    So with despair I shall him quell.
While humankind is clean and whole,
Verily, God is within the soul.
And when deadly sin takes its toll, 545
    It is the devil's place.
Thus, by colors and false gin
Many a soul to hell I win;
I won't stop until I lure him into sin,
    With this false boy — God give him ill grace. 550

Here he takes a mischievous boy with him and goes his way, crying.
[Note: The boy may be the one crying.]
[Enter Mind, newly costumed in finery]

Mind

Lo, I am here in new array.
Dance about, whirr, put care away.
    Farewell, perfection.
I seem to myself most handsome each day.
It is but honest — no pride, no nay. 555
I will be fresh, by my fay,
    For that suits my complexion.

[Enter Understanding, similarly costumed]

Understanding

And here is one as fresh as you,
All merry, merry, and glad now.
I have great wealth, God knows how. 560
    For joy I spring, I skip.

Goode makyt on mery, to Gode avowe.
Farewell consyens! I know not yow.
I am at eas hade I inowe.
          Truthe on syde I lett hym slyppe.   565

Wyll

Lo, here on as iolye as 3e.
I am so lykynge, me seme I fle.
I haue atastyde lust. Farwell, chastyte.
          My hert ys euermore lyght.
I am full of felycyte.   570
My delyght ys all in bewte.
þer ys no joy but þat in me.
          A woman me semyth a hewynly syght.

Mynde

Ande thes ben my syngler solace: f.110r
Kynde, fortune, & grace.   575
Kynde, nobley of kynrede me yewyn hase,
          Ande þat makyt me soleyn.
Fortune in worldys worschyppe me doth lace;
Grace yewyt curryus eloquens & þat mase
          That all oncunnynge I dysdeyn.   580

Wnderstondynge

And my ioy ys especyall
To hurde wppe ryches for fer to fall;
To se yt, to handyll yt, to tell yt all,
          And streightly to spare.
To be holde ryche & reyall   585
I bost; I avawnt wer I xall.
Ryches makyt a man equall
          To hem sumtyme hys souereyngys wer.

---

564 at] from D — M a contracted form of at;   I inowe] D I Inowe — M I now   565 on] point
appears in the loop above n   566 iolye] D Iolye   569 my] D myn   570 full of] M repeats
phrase   572] M written to right of text; only marginal line on folio; one of the two M
marginal lines without a corresponding D marginal line; not a tail-rhyme line; perhaps initially
omitted and inserted as an afterthought; ll. 570-71 bracketed to indicate position of marginal
line; only brackets on page   573 a] D an   574 speaker] Mynde on previous folio   576
nobley] from D — M nobyll; see also l. 4;   yewyn] D yovyn   578-79 M & D rhyme
scheme irregular, w. only 2 rhyming lines rather than 3. Line may be missing.   581
speaker] wndyrston, ending cropped — D vnderstondyng   581 ioy] D loye   584
streightly] from D; line written to right w. plesyng vnto love canc. before — M strenght   588
hys] to canc. before

Wealth makes me merry, to God I vow.
Farewell, conscience, I know not you.
I am at ease enough for now.
      Truth on the side, I let him slip.   565

[*Enter Will, newly costumed*]

Will

Lo, here is one as jolly as ye.
I am so horny I could fly like a bee.
I have tasted lust. Farewell, chastity.
      My heart is continually light.
I am full of felicity.   570
My delight all is in beauty.
There is no joy but that to me.
      A woman seems to me a heavenly sight.

Mind

And these are my special solace:
Kindred, fortune, and worldly grace.   575
Kindred offers a rich family to embrace,
      And that makes me sovereign.
Fortune in the world's good opinion insures my place;
Grace gives subtle eloquence, language embroidered with lace,
      So that all simplicity I disdain.   580

Understanding

And my joy is special.
To horde up riches for fear of a fall,
To see, it handle it, to count it all —
      And all expense tightly to spare.
To be thought rich and royal   585
I boast; I vaunt where I will.
Riches make a man equal
      To those who were once his superiors there.

Wyll

To me ys ioy most laudable
Fresche dysgysynge to seme amyable,   590
Spekynge wordys delectable
   Perteynynge onto loue.
It ys ioy of joys inestymable
To halse, to kys þe affyable.
A louer ys son perceyvable   595
   Be þe smylynge on me wan yt doth remove.

Mynde

To avaynte thus, me semyth no schame,
For galontys now be in most fame.
Curtely personys men hem proclame.
   Moche we be sett bye.   600

Wnderstondynge   f.110v

The ryche couetyse, wo dare blame
Off govell & symony, thow he bere þe name?
To be fals men report yt game.
   Yt ys clepyde wysdom. "Ware þat," quod Ser Wyly.

Wyll   605

Ande of lechory to make avawnte,
Men fors yt no more þan drynke atawnt.
Thes thyngys be now so conversant,
   We seme yt no schame.

Mynde

Curyous aray I wyll euer hante.

Wndyrstondynge

Ande I falsnes to be passante.   610

---

589 ioy] D joye   laudable] from D — M delectable   593 ioy] D joye
596 wan] D whan   600] line from D written to right of text; only marginal line on folio
601 speaker] wndyrstondyng w. ng abbr., e cropped — D vnderstond;
couetyse] D covetouse   wo] D who   683 report] D reportith
604 ser wyly] D Wyly   610 speaker] wndyrstond — D vnderstond

Will

To me it is joy most laudable
In a fresh disguising to seem amiable,   590
Speaking words delectable
     Pertaining unto love.
It is joy of joys inestimable
To embrace, to kiss the affable.
A lover is soon perceivable   595
     By the foolish smile he cannot remove.

Mind

To strut thus, it seems to me no shame,
For dandies now earn the most fame.
Courtly persons men them proclaim.
     All men regard us highly.   600

Understanding

The covetous rich, who dare blame
For their usury and simony, though they bear the name?
To be false, men report it as a game.
     It is called wisdom. "Look out for that," quoth Sir Wily.

Will

And of lechery to make a boast,   605
Men regard it no more than drinking a toast.
These things are now so familiar to most,
     It seems to us no shame.

Mind

Fancy attire I will ever use.

Understanding

And falseness I will always choose.   610

Wyll
Ande I in lust my flesche to daunte.
No man dypsyse thes; they be but game.

Mynde
In reioys of thes, now let ws synge.

Wndyrstondynge
Ande yff I spar, ewell joy me wrynge.

Wyll
"Haue at," quod I. Lo, howe I sprynge.   615
Lust makyth me wondyr wylde.

Mynde
A tenowr to yow bothe I brynge.

Wndyrstondynge
And I a mene for ony kynge.

Wyll
And but a trebull I owtwrynge,
The deuell hym spede þat myrthe exyled.   620
Et cantent

Mynde
How be þis, trow ye nowe?

Wndyrstondynge
At þe best, to God avowe!

Wyll
As mery as þe byrde on bow,
I take no thought.

Mynde   f.111r
The welfare of þis worlde ys in ws, I avowe.   625

---

613 In] from D — M I; see ll. 24, 133, 1064sd   614, 618, 622 speaker] wndyrstond — D
vnderstond   615 howe] from D; o resembles M a — M haue   620 hym] point appears
in the loop above   625 speaker] Mynde, on previous folio   avowe] from D — M ma
vowe

Will
And my flesh I will lustfully abuse.
    No men despise these; they are but game.

Mind
To celebrate this, now let us sing out.

Understanding
And if I hold back, may wretched mirth wring me out.

Will
"Have at it," say I. Lo, how I spring about.   615
    Lust makes me wander wild.

Mind
A tenor to you both I bring out.

Understanding
And I a middle part ready for any king to shout.

Will
And unless a treble I clearly ring out,
    The devil aid him that mirth exiled.   620
                                   They sing

Mind
How is this, believe you now?

Understanding
The very best, to God a vow!

Will
As merry as the bird on bow,
    I take no thought.

Mind
The welfare of this world is in us, I vow.   625

Wndyrstondynge

Lett eche man tell hys condycyons howe.

Wyll

Begynne ye ande haue at yow,
  For I am aschamyde of ryght nought.

Mynde

Thys ys a cause of my worschyppe:
I serue myghty lordeschyppe   630
Ande am in grett tenderschyppe.
  Therfor, moche folke me dredys.
Men sew to my frendeschyppe
For meyntnance of her schendeschyppe.
I support hem by lordeschyppe,   635
  For to get goode, þis a grett spede ys.

Wndyrstondynge

And I vse jerowry,
Enbrace questys of periury,
Choppe & chonge wyth symonye,
  & take large yeftys.   640
By þe cause neuer so try
I preue yt fals — I swere; I lye —
Wyth a quest of myn affye.
  The redy wey þis now to thryfte ys.

Wyll

And wat trow 3e be me?   645
More þan I take, spende I threys iii.
Sumtyme I yeff, sumtyme þey me,
  Ande am euer fresche & gay.
Few placys now þer be
But onclennes ye xall þer see.   650
It ys holde but a nysyte —
  Lust ys now comun as þe way.

---

626 speaker] wndyrstond — D vnderstond (both w. tails indicating -ing; also l. 637 629
ys a] D is — M partial letter canc. before ys 637 speaker] wndyrstond A, w. point before
and 2 points after, to indicate misplaced lines (for abbr. see l. 626) 637-44] M stanzas in
ll. 637-52 reversed 640 M & D written to right of text; only marginal line on this folio
641 By þe cause] D Be the case 645 speaker] Wyll B, w. B partially cropped, w. point
before to indicate misplaced lines 645-52] reversed stanza, written as 637-643 645 And]
M A contracted form of D and; see l. 733 646 iii] M & D iij 648 only marginal line on
folio M & D 650 ye] from D, written above the line — M we 652 þe] D thei or ther

Understanding

Let each man describe his circumstances how.

Will

You begin and have at it now,
    For I am ashamed of nought.

Mind

This is the cause of my worship:
I serve mighty Lordship   630
And I am great in kinship.
    Therefore, many folk fear me today.
Men flock to my friendship
For maintenance of their sinship.
I support them by lordship,   635
    For to get goods, this is the best way.

Understanding

And I bribe the jury,
Establish panels of perjury,
Buy and sell with simony
    And take many a large gift.   640
Be the case ever so true to try,
I prove it false — I swear; I lie —
With a jury I am able to buy.
    This is the ready way to thrift.

Will

And what do you believe of me?   645
More than I take, I spend thrice three.
Sometimes I give, sometimes they me,
    And ever I am fresh and gay.
Few places now there chance to be
Where uncleanness you will not see.   650
It is held a nicety —
    Lust is now as common as the day.

Mynde   f.111v
Law procedyth not for meyntnance.

Wndyrstondynge
Trowthe recurythe not for habundance.

Wyll
And lust ys in so grett vsance;   655
    We fors yt nought.

Mynde
In vs þe worlde hathe most affyance.

Wndyrstondynge
Non thre be in so grett aqweynttance.

Wyll
Few þer be outhe of owr allyance.
    Wyll þe worlde ys thus, take we no thought.   660

Mynde
Thought? Nay, þerageyn stryve I.

Wndyrstondynge
We haue þat nedyt vs; so thryve I.

Wyll
And yff þat I care, neuer wyve I.
    Let them care þat hathe for to sewe.

Mynde
Wo lordschyppe xall sew must yt bye.   665

Wndyrstondynge
Wo wyll haue law must haue monye.

Wyll
Ther pouert ys þe malewrye.
    Thow ryght be, he xall neuer renewe.

653 speaker] <u>Mynde</u> on previous folio   654, 658, 662 speaker] <u>wndyrstond</u> — D
<u>vnderstond</u> (both w. abbr. for <u>ing</u>)   659 <u>outhe</u>] D <u>out</u>   660 <u>wyll</u>] D <u>while</u>   661 <u>ageyn</u>] D
<u>geyne</u>   663 <u>yff</u>] D <u>gyve</u>   665 <u>yt</u>] point before   666 speaker] <u>wndyrstond</u> — D <u>vnderst</u>

Mind

Law does not proceed against maintenance.

Understanding

Truth does not argue against abundance.

Will

And lust appears with every glance; 655
    We forbid it nought.

Mind

On us the world places most reliance.

Understanding

There are no others with such a great circle of acquaintance.

Will

Few there are out of our alliance.
    While the world is thus, we won't pause for thought. 660

Mind

Thought? Nay, against that strive I.

Understanding

We have what we need; so thrive I.

Will

And for ought that I care, never wive I.
    Let them care that have to sue.

Mind

He who would earn lordship must it buy. 665

Understanding

Whoso will have law must with money it try.

Will

Their poverty will make them sigh.
    Though in the right, the poor will not win, it's true.

Mynde
Wronge ys born wpe boldly,
Thow all þe worlde know yt opynly;   670
Mayntnance ys now so myghty,
        And all is for mede.

Wndyrstondynge
The law ys so coloryde falsly
By sleyttys & by periury;
Brybys be so gredy   675
        þat to þe pore trowth ys take ryght nought a hede.

Wyll
Wo gett or loose, ye be ay wynnande.   f.112r
Mayntnance & Periury now stande.
Ther wer neuer so moche reynande
        Seth Gode was bore.   680

Mynde
Ande Lechery was neuer more vsande
Off lernyde & lewyde in þis lande.

Wyndyrstondynge
So we thre be now in hande.

Wyll
        Ya, & most vsyde euerywere.

Mynde
Now wyll we thre do make a dance   685
Off thow þat longe to owr retenance,
Cummynge in by contenance.
        þis were a dysporte.

Wyndyrstondynge
Therto I geve acordance
Off thow þat ben of myn affyance.   690

---

672 is] from D (ls)   673, 683, 689 speaker] wndyrst, w. loop over t to indicate abbrev. —
D vnderst   676] M written to right of text; only marginal line on folio;   to] from D;   trowth]
M & D point before;   nought a] D non   677 speaker] Wyll on previous folio;   loose] D
lese   679 ther] M — D there; E emends to thei   680] M & D written to right of text
684] va w. point after in left margin — D va without point in left margin   688] M & D written
to right of text   689 l] from D — M i

Mind
Wrong is born up boldly,
Though all the world know it openly; 670
Maintenance is now so mighty,
    And all is for meed.

Understanding
The law is colored so falsely
By tricks and by perjury;
Bribes are so greedy 675
    That to the poor truth no one takes heed.

Will
Who wins or loses, you are always earning.
Maintenance and Perjury are now standing.
There was never so much arraigning
    Since Mary did Jesus bear. 680

Mind
And lechery was never more in demand
Among the learned and ignorant in this land.

Understanding
So we three are now in hand.

Will
    Yea, and most popular everywhere.

Mind
Now we three will make a dance for you 685
With those that belong to our retinue,
Hiding behind masks their faces true.
    This will be sport.

Understanding
Thereto I give my consent to you
From those who owe me obedience due. 690

Wyll

Let se, bytyme, ye, Meyntnance.
Clepe in fyrst yowr resorte.

*Her entur vi dysgysyde in þe sute of **Mynde** wyth rede berdys &*
lyouns rampaunt on here crestys & yche a warder in hys honde;
her mynstrall, trumpes. Eche answerys for hys name.

Mynde

Let se cum in Indignacyon & Sturdynes,
Males, also, & Hastynes,
Wreche & Dyscorde expres,   695
          And þe vii^te am I, Mayntennance.
VII ys a numbyr of discorde & inperfyghtnes.
Lo, her ys a yomandrye wyth loweday to dres.
Ande þe deule hade swore yt, þey wolde ber wp falsnes   f.112v
          And maynten yt at þe best. Þis ys þe deullys dance.   700
Ande here menstrellys be convenyent,
For trumpys xulde blow to þe jugemente.
Off batell, also yt ys on instrumente,
          Yevynge comfort to fyght.
Therfor, þey be expedyente   705
To þes meny of Mayntement.
Blow; lett see Madam Regent.
          Ande daunce, ye laddys; yowr hertys ben lyght.
Lo, þat other spare, thes meny wyll spende.

Wndyrstondynge

Ya, wo ys hym xall hem offende?   710

Wyll

Wo wyll not to hem condescende,
          He xall haue threttys.

Mynde

They spyll þat law wolde amende.

691 ye] þe or ye — D ye   692 sd lyouns] s from D; mynstrall] D menstra[ll]
693 in Indignacyon] M & D In Indignacyon, abbr. for last syllable expanded in M to -yon, in
D to -ion   696 vii^te] M & D vij^te   697 discorde] from D — M dycorde   703 ys]
inserted above line; instrumente] Instrumente — D instrument   706 Mayntement from D
— M meyntnance   708 ben] abbr. in M — D ben   709 spare point after   710 speaker]
M wndyrst — D vnderst, with abbr.   710 ya, wo] D ye who

Will

Let's see, right now, Maintenance, your crew.
    Call in your consort.

Here enter six disguised in the suit of Mind, with red beards
and lions rampant on their crests, and each with a warder in his
hand; their minstrels, trumpets. Each answers to his name.

Mind

Let's see, come in Indignation and Sturdiness,
Malice, also, and Rashness,
Wretchedness and Discord in fancy dress,   695
    And the seventh am I, Maintenance.
Seven is a number of discord and imperfectness.
Lo, here is a crowd with a love trial to address.
If the devil had sworn it, they would bear up falseness
    And maintain it as the best. This is the devil's dance.   700
And their minstrels are convenient,
For trumpets should blow at the judgment.
Of battle, this is the instrument,
    Encouraging the fight.
Therefore, they are expedient   705
To this troupe serving Maintainnment.
Blow; let's see Madame Regent.
    And dance, you lads; your hearts are light.
Lo, what the others save, this troupe will spend.

Understanding

Yea, who is he that shall them offend?   710

Will

Whoever will not to them bend,
    They threaten with their commands.

Mind

They break what the law would mend.

Wndyrstondynge
Yit Mayntnance no man dare reprehende.

Wyll
Thes meny thre synnys comprehende: 715
    Pryde, Invy, & Wrathe in hys hestys.

Wndyrstondynge
Now wyll I than begyn my traces.
Jorowr in on hoode beer to facys;
Fayer speche & falsehede in on space ys.
    Is it not ruthe?   720
    The Quest of Holborn cum into þis placys;
Ageyn þe ryght euer þey rechases.
Off wom þey holde not, harde hys grace ys.
    Many a tyme haue dammyde truthe.

Here entrethe vi jorours in a sute gownyde wyth hodys   f.113r
abowt her nekys, hattys of meyntenance þervpon, vyseryde
dyuersly; here mynstrell a bagpyp.

Wndyrstondynge
Let se, fyrst, Wronge & Sleyght;   725
Dobullnes & Falsehed, schew yowr myght.
Now Raveyn & Discheyit,
    Now holde yow here togydyr.
Thys menys consyens ys so streytt
That þey report as "mede" yewyt beyght.   730
Here ys þe Quest of Holborn, an euyll endyrecte.
    They daunce all this londe hydyr & thedyr,
      And I, Periury, yowr fownder.
      Now dance on, ws, all the worlde doth on ws wondyr.
Lo, here ys a menye loue wellfare.   735

714 speaker] M wndyrst — D vnderst, w. abbr.   716 invy] M & D Invy w. points before and
after   hestys] M & D; E emends to hettys   717 speaker] M wndyrst — D vnderstond, with
tail loop indicating -ing   718 beer] D berith   720] line from D, written to right of text; only
marginal line on folio   722 rechases] from D — M rechase; M "corrects" person of verb and
loses rhyme; see l. 270   724 dammyde] D dampnyd   724sd þervpon] point in the loop
above n;   bagpyp] M ba- on one line, (g cut off); pyp on line below, e prob. cropped — D
bag- w. ending cropped   725 speaker] Wndyrstondynge — Mynde canc. to right of Wndyr
— D Mynde (an error)   726 falsehed] from D — M falsenes   727 Discheyit] D dysceyte
— D Mynde (an error)   726 falsehed] from D — M falsenes   727 Discheyit] D dysceyte
730 That þey] D that   732 They] y written above line;   this] from D — M þe   733-34]
these lines do not fit the usual rhyme scheme   733 And] M A a contracted form of D and;
see l. 645   734 all] M & D point after;   doth] M point after

Understanding
Yet Maintenance no man dare reprehend.

Will
This troup three sins comprehend: 715
        Pride, Envy, and Wrath all making demands.
                        [*Exeunt dancers*]
Understanding
Now will I then begin my paces.
Jurors in one hood wear two faces;
Fair speech and falsehood crowd in tight places.
        Is it not ruth?   720
Let the Quest of Holborn come into these spaces;
Against the right ever this jury faces.
Whom they rule against, hard his case is.
        Many a time they have condemned the truth.

Here enter six jurors identically robed, in gowns with hoods about their
necks, wearing hats of livery, visored diversely; their minstrel a bagpipe.

Understanding
Let's see, first, Wrong and Slight;   725
Doubleness and Falsehood, show your might.
Now, Rapine and Deceit,
        Now come in here together.
This troupe's conscience is so thin
What they call "reward" is just bait to help them win.   730
Here is the Quest of Holborn, an evil twisted into a spin.
        They dance all this land hither and thither,
        And I, Perjury, your founder.
        Now dance on. All the world looks on us with wonder.
Lo, here is a troupe that loves its own welfare.   735

Mynde

Ye, þey spende þat tru men spare.

Wyll

Haue þey a brybe, þey haue no care
Wo hath wronge or ryght.

Mynde

They fors not to swere & starre.

Wyll

Though all be false, les & mare.   740

Wndyrstondynge

Wyche wey to þe woode wyll þe hare?
They knowe, & þey at rest sett, als tyghte.
Some seme hem wyse
For the fadyr of vs, Covetyse.

Wyll

Now Meyntnance and Periury   745
Hathe schewyde þe trace of þer cumpeny.
Ye xall se a sprynge of Lechery
þat to me attende.
Here forme ys of þe stewys clene rebaldry.   f.113v
They wene sey sothe wen þat þey lye.   750
Off þe comyn þey synge eche wyke by & by.
They may sey wyth tenker, I trow, "lat amende."

*Here entre vi women in sut [iii] dysgysyde as galontys & iii
as matrones wyth wondyrfull vysurs conregent; here mynstrell
a hornepype.*

737 haue þey] word order from D (haue thei) — M þey haue   740 Though] from D (though)
— M thouht   741 speaker] M wndyrst — D vndyrst   746 schewyde] small partial stroke
before;   þer] D here   748] M & D — only marginal line on folio
750 wene] from D — M veyn   752sd entre] from D — M entreth;   vi] M & D vij;   [iii]
dysgysyde] M & D dysgysyde, number omitted, but iii as matrones indicates the need for a
number before dysgysyde;   iii] M & D iij;   752sd D ends; from this point on in the absence
of D, Eccles' deviations from M will be indicated in notes by "E [followed by the Eccles form]";
when different from this text Bevington transcriptions will be indicated by "B [+ form]."

Mind

Yea, they spend what true men spare.

Will

If they get a bribe, they do not care
    Who has right or wrong.

Mind

They do not hesitate to swear and stare.

Will

Though everyone there is false, both rich and poor.   740

Understanding

Which way to the woods goes the hare?
    They know, and they wait at rest, sitting tight.
        Some seem to them wise
        For the father of us, Coveteise.

                    [*Exeunt dancers*]

Will

Now Maintenance and Perjury   745
Have showed the paces of their company.
You shall see the band of Lechery
    That on me attend.
Here is the form of the stew's clean ribaldry.
They think they're telling the truth when they lie.   750
Of vulgarity they sing, each week by and by.
    They may say with the tinker, I believe, "let it amend."

*Here enter six women wearing the livery of Lechery, [three] disguised
as gallants and three disguised as women with splendid visors denoting
regal livery, accompanied by a hornpipe player as their minstrel.*

Wyll

Cum, slepers, Rekleshede & Idyllnes,
All in all, Surfet & Gredynes,
For þe flesche, Spousebreche & Mastres,   755
    Wyth jentyll Fornycacyon.
Yowr mynstrell a hornepype mete
þat fowll ys in hymselff but to þe erys swete.
Thre fortherers of loue: "Hem schrew I!" quod Bete.
    Thys dance of þis damesellys ys thorow þis regyn.   760

Mynde

Ye may not endure wythowt my meyntenance.

Wndyrstondynge

That ys bought wyth a brybe of owr substance.

Wyll

Whom breydest þu vs of þin aqueyntance?
    I sett þe at nought.

Mynde

On þat worde I woll tak vengeaunce.   765
Wer vycys be gederyde, euer ys sum myschance.
Hurle hens thes harlottys! Here gyse ys of France.
    þey xall abey bytterly, by Hym þat all wrought.

Wndyrstondynge

Ill spede þe, ande þu spare.
þi long body bare   770
To bett I not spare.
    Haue the ageyn!

Wyll

Holde me not! Let me go! Ware!   f.114r
I dynge, I dasche! Þer, go ther!
Dompe deuys, can ye not dare?   775
    I tell yow, owtwarde, on & tweyn!   *Exient*

---

755 breche] & mast canc. before   759 schrew] scre canc. before   762, 769 speaker] wnd
763 Whom] E Whow   þu] B & E expand þᵘ as þou and so throughout; þᵘ is recorded in
the OED as a form of þou; but M writes this word as thu; see l. 873   766 gederyde] gat
canc. before   768 bytterly] point after   772 line written to right   773 speaker] Wyll on
previous folio   776 owtwarde] right stroke on first w is very light — E outwarde

Will

Come, sleepers, Recklesshead and Idleness,
All together, Surfeit and Greediness,
For the flesh, Spousebreach and Mistress, 755
    With gentle Fornication.
Your minstrel is a hornpipe meet
That is foul in himself but to the ears sweet.
Three furtherers of love: "I beshrew them!" quoth Bet. 759
    The dance of these damsels spreads throughout this region.

                                       [Dancers complete dance]

Mind

You may not endure without my maintenance.

Understanding

That is bought with a bribe from our substance.

Will

To whom do you jerk us off among your acquaintance?
    I value you at nought.

Mind

On that word I will take vengeance. 765
Where vices are gathered, there is always some mischance.
Hurl hence these harlots! Their disguise is from France.
    They shall buy it bitterly, by Him that all wrought.

Understanding

More harm to you, if you spare.
Your long body bare 770
To beat I'll not spare.
    Have at thee again!

Will

Hold me not! Let me go! Beware!
I bang, I bash! There, go there!
Dumb dancers, don't you know how to dare? 775
    I tell you, get out, on and twain!

                                        Exeunt [dancers]

Mynde

Now I schrew yow thus dansaunde.

Wndyrstondynge

Ye, & ewyll be þu thryvande.

Wyll

No more let vs be stryvande.
  Nowe all at on.   780

Mynde

Here was a meny onthryvande.

Wndyrstondynge

To þe deull be þey drywande.

Wyll

He þat ys yll wywande,
  Wo hys hym, by þe bon!

Mynde

Leue then þis dalyance,   785
Ande set we a ordenance
Off better chevesaunce
  How we may thryve.

Wndyrstondynge

At Westmyster, wythowt varyance,
þe nex terme xall me sore avawnce   790
For retornys, for enbraces, for recordaunce.
  Lyghtlyer to get goode kan no man on lyue.

Mynde

Ande at þe parvyse I wyll be,
At Powlys betwyn ii ande iii,
Wyth a menye folowynge me: 795
  Entret, Jugepartynge, & To-Supporte.

778, 782, 789 speaker] Wndyrst 788] Line written to right 790 me sore avawnce] my
sowrnance canc. before sore, w. me written above my 794 At] Ms. A, contracted form of
At; ii, iii] Ms. ij, iij — E to, thre 796 juge] point before

Mind
Now I curse you thus for your dancing.

Understanding
Yeah, and may you in evil be thriving.

Will
No more let us be striving.
    Now all for one. 780

Mind
Here was a troupe unthriving.

Understanding
To the devil let them be driving.

Will
He that is ill-wiving,
    Woeful is he, by God's bone!

Mind
Leave then this dalliance, 785
And set we an ordinance
Of better chevisance
    How we may thrive.

Understanding
At Westminster, without variance,
The next term I shall surely advance 790
For writ returns, for briberies, for falsely testifying by chance.
    I prosper more easily than any man alive.

Mind
And at the church door I will be,
At Paul's between two and three,
With a crowd of supporters following me: 795
    Intervention, Judge-bribing, and Illegal Support.

Wyll

Ande euer þe latter, þe leuer me.
Wen I com lat to þe cyte,
I walke all lanys & weys to my affynyte.
        & I spede not þer, to þe stews I resort.   800

Mynde   f.114v

Ther gettys þu nouhte, but spendys.

Wyll

Yis, sumtyme I take amendys
Off hem þat nought offendys.
        I engrose vpe here purs.

Mynde

And I arest þer no drede ys,   805
Preve forfett þer no mede ys,
Ande tak to me þat nede ys.
        I reke not thow þey curs.

Wndyrstondynge

Thow þey curs, nether þe wers I fare.
Thys day I endyght them I herde of neuer are.   810
Tomorow I wyll aqwyt them, yff nede were.
        Thys I lede my lyff

Wyll

Ye, but of vs iii I haue lest care.
Met & drynke & ease, I aske no mare,
Ande a praty wenche, to se here bare.   815
        I reke but lytyll be sche mayde or wyffe.

Mynde

Thys on a soper
I wyll be seen rycher,
Set a noble wyth goode chere
        Redyly to spende.   820

797] l. 802 written and canc. above 797   801 nouhte] obs. spelling for noughte;
speaker] mynde on previous folio   802 amendys] M reads amende; amendys taken from
line written and canc. above 797   804 eng[r]ose] Ms. engose prob. error for engrose
808 curs] cr canc. before   809 speaker] Wndyrst   810 n[e]ther] Ms. reading could be
uther — E never   812 Thys] var. of thus; see ll. 289, 817   813 iii] Ms. iij — E thre
820] line written to right of text

Will

And the later it gets, the better for me.
When I come late to the city,
I walk all the lanes and ways to meet those allied to me.
    If I don't make it there, to the stews I resort.   800

Mind

There you gain nothing, where everyone spends.

Will

Yes, sometimes I force others to make amends,
Exacting from one or another who in no way offends.
    I suck up their purse.

Mind

And I arrest where no suspicion is,   805
Secure a forfeit where no money is,
And take to myself whenever the need is.
    I care not for their curse.

Understanding

Though they curse, none the worse I fare.
Today I indict those I never heard of elsewhere.   810
Tomorrow I would acquit them, if the need were there.
    Thus I lead my life.

Will

Yea, but of us three I have the least care.
Meat and drink and ease, I ask no more,
Except a pretty wench, to see her bare.   815
    I care little if she be maid or wife.

Mind

Yet at a supper
I will appear to be richer,
And lay out a noble with good cheer
    Readily to spend.   820

Wndyrstondynge

And I, tweyn, be þis feer
To moque at a goode dyner,
I hoope of a goode yer,
     For euer I trost Gode wyll send.

Wyll

And best we haue wyne,   825
Ande a cosyn of myn,
Wyth ws for to dyne.
     III nobles wyll I spende frely.

Mynde

We xall acorde well & fyne.   f.115r

Wndyrstondynge

Nay, I wyll not passe schylyngys nyne.   830

Wyll

No, þu was neuer but a swyn.
     I woll be holdyn jentyll, by Sent Audre of Ely,
And now in my mynde I haue
My cosyn Jenet N, so Gode me save.
Sche mornyth wyth a chorle, a very knaue,   835
     And neuer kan be mery.
I pley me þer wen I lyst rawe.
Than þe chorle wyll here dysprawe
How myght make hym thys to lawe?
     I wolde onys haue hym in þe wyrry.   840

Mynde

For thys I kan a remedye;
I xall rebuk hym thus so dyspytuusly
þat of hys lyff he xall wery
     & qwak for very fere.

824, 828] lines written to right of text   821 speaker] wndyrstond; And] A altered to And, -nd
inserted above I   825 And] Ms. A contacted form of and; see also ll. 645, 733 & 1071 —
E And   828 III] Ms. iij — E thre   829 speaker] mynde on previus folio   830 speaker]
wndyrst;   830 nyne] Ms nyne ix   836, 840] written to right of text   839 How] E Who;
syntax is difficult   840 hy[m]] m cut off   843 wery] right stroke of w is very faint — B very
844] written to right of text

Understanding
And I, too, with this group that joins me here
To carouse mockingly at a good dinner,
I hope for a good year,
   For ever I trust God will send.

Will
And best we have wine,   825
And a cousin of mine,
With us for to dine.
   Three nobles will I spend freely.

Mind
We shall get along well and fine.

Understanding
Nay, I will not pass shillings nine.   830

Will
No, you were never anything but a swine.
   I will appear to be refined, by Saint Audrey of Ely.
And now in my mind I have
My cousin Jenny N_____, so God me save.
She frets with a churlish husband, a very knave, 835
   And never can be merry.
I play there when I'm in a poetic mood.
Thus, this punk slanders me well and good.
How can I get the law to act against this dude?
   I would have him by the throat in a hurry. 840

Mind
For this I know a remedy;
I shall rebuke him so mercilessly
That of his life he shall grow weary
   And shake for fear.

Ande yff he wyll not leve þerby,   845
On hys bodye he xall abye
Tyll he leue þat jelousy.
      Nay, suche chorlys I kan ler*e*.

Wndyrstondynge

Nay, I kan better hym qwytte;
Arest hym fyrst to pes for fyght;   850
Than in another schere hym endyght.
      He ne xall wete by wom ne howe.
Haue hym in þe Marschalsi seyn aryght;
Than to þe Amralte, for þey wyll byght;
A *preuenire facias* than haue as tyght,   855
      And þu xall hurle hym so at he xall haue inow.

Wyll

Wat & þes wrongys be espyede?

Wndyrstondynge

Wyth þe crose & þe pyll I xall wrye yt   f.115v
That þer xall neuer man dyscrey yt,
      þat may me appeyere.   860

Mynde

Ther ys no craft but we may trye yt.

Wndyrstondynge

Mede stoppyt be yt neuer so allyede.

Wyll

Wyth yow tweyn wo ys replyede,
      He may sey he hathe a schrewde seyer.

Mynde

Thow woldyst haue wondyr of sleyghtys þat be.   865

848] written to eight of text   848 lere] last e cut off   849 speaker] wndyrstondg,
w. n abbrev. over g   852 howe] wow canc. before   855 preuenire] prob. error for
praemunire   858 speaker] wndyrst on previous folio   862 speaker] wndyrst   862
stoppyt] sp canc. before

And if he will not leave off quickly,   845
On his body the price he'll pay
Till he gives up that jealousy.
  Nay, such punks I can teach to hear.

Understanding
Nay, I can better him requite;
Arrest him first for disturbing the peace by threatening to fight;   850
Then in another county him indict,
 He shall never know by whom or how.
Have him judged in the Marchalsea on some excuse;
Then to the Admiralty, for they will bitterly accuse;
With a **praemunire facias** you can him easily abuse,   855
 And harass him so that he shall have enow.

Will
What if these wrongs be spied?

Understanding
With the head and tail of a coin I shall hide it.
Thus, no one shall ever descry it
 So that it will to my discredit appear.   860

Mind
There is no trick but we may try it.

Understanding
Money blocks the law no matter how it is allied.

Will
He to whom you two have replied
 May say that he has a shrewd sayer.

Mind
You'd be amazed at the tricks there be.   865

Wndyrstondynge
Thys make sume ryche, & summe neuer the.

Wyll
þey must nedys grett goodys gett þe.
          Now go we to þe wyne.

Mynde
In trewe, I grante. Haue at wyth þe.

Wndyrstondynge
Ande for a peny or ii, I wyll not fle.   870

Wyll
Mery, mery, all mery þan be we.
          Who þat ws tarythe, curs haue he — & myn.

Wysdom
O thu, Mynde, remembyr the.
          Turne þi weys, þu gost amyse.
Se what þi ende ys, þu myght not fle.   875
          Dethe to euery creature certen ys.
          They þat lyue well, þey xall haue blys;
Thay þat endyn yll, þey goo to hell.
          I am Wysdom sent to tell yow thys;
Se in what stat þu doyst indwell.   880

Mynde
To my mynde yt cummyth from farre
          That dowtles man xall dey,
Ande thes weys we go, we erre.   f.116r
          Wndyrstondynge, wat do ye sey?

Wndyrstondynge
          I sey, man, holde forthe þi wey.   885
The lyff we lede ys sekyr ynowe.
          I wyll no wndyrstondynge xall lett my pley.
Wyll, frende, how seyest thowe?

866, 870 speaker] wndyrst, w. tail indicating -ing   873] verse pattern returns to original
stanza form;   thu] B & E thou   878 yll] point after   879 am] an canc. before   881-
892] twelve-line stanza   885 speaker] wndyrstonde   888 thowe] e unclear in Ms

Understanding

This makes some rich, while some never prosper from a fee.

Will

Then great wealth must be your destiny.
   Now let's go to the wine.

Mind

In truth, I agree. I'll go at it with thee.

Understanding

And for a penny or two, I will not flee.   870

Will

Merry, merry, all merry then are we.
   Whoever gets in our way, let him have your curse — and mine.

[*Enter Wisdom*]

Wisdom

O Mind, remember yourself and take heed of me.
   Mend your ways, you have gone amiss.
See what your end is, you may not flee.   875
   Death will claim every person as his.
   They that live well, they shall have bliss;
They that end ill, they go to hell.
   I am Wisdom sent to tell you this;
See the condition in which you dwell.   880

Mind

To my mind it comes from afar
   That without doubt man shall die,
And these ways that we go, we err.
   Understanding, what do you say?

Understanding

I say, man, stick to your way.   885
The life we lead is secure anyhow.
   I won't let understanding hinder my play.
Will, my friend, what do you say now?

Wyll

I wyll not thynke þeron, to Gode avowe.
   We be yit but tender of age.   890
Schulde we leve þis lyue? Ya whowe!
   We may amende wen we be sage.

Wysdom

Thus many on vnabylythe hym to grace.
   They wyll not loke but slumber & wynke.
þey take not drede before þer face,   895
   Howe horryble þer synnys stynke.
   Wen þey be on þe pyttys brynke,
Than xall þey trymbull & qwake for drede.
   Yit, Mynde, I sey, yow bethynke
In what perell ye be now. Take hede.   900
Se howe ye haue dyvyguryde yowr Soule.
   Beholde yowrself. Loke veryly in mynde.

*Here **Anima** apperythe in þe most horrybull wyse, fowlere þan a fende.*

Mynde

Out! I tremble for drede, by Sent Powle.
   Thys ys fowler þan ony fende.

Wysdom

   Wy art þu creature so onkynde,   905
Thus to defoule Godys own place?
   þat was made so gloryus wythowt ende
Thu hast made þe deullys rechace.
As many dedly synnys as ye haue vsyde,   f.116v
   So many deullys in yowr soule be.   910
Beholde wat ys þerin reclusyde.
   Alas, man, of þi soule haue pyte.

*Here rennyt owt from wndyr þe horrybyll mantyll of þe **Soull**, vi*
small boys in þe lyknes of dewyllys & so retorne ageyn.

---

893 hym] point appears in loop above m   901 dyvyguryde] obs. form of disfigured — E
dysvyguryde   908 thu] B & E thou   909 as] point before   912 sd horrybyll] soull canc.
before   vi] Ms. vj — E vii

Will

I will not think about that, to God I vow.
　　We are yet tender of age.　　　　　　　　890
Should we leave this life? Yahoo!
　　We may make amends when we are sage.

Wisdom

Thus many a one is disabled for grace.
　　They will not see clearly but slumber and wink.
They fear not what they see right before their face,　　895
　　How horribly their sins stink.
　　When they are on the pit's brink,
Then shall they tremble and quake for dread.
　　Yet, Mind, I say, reflect and think
In what peril you are now. Take heed.　　　　900
See how you have disfigured your Soul.
　　Behold yourself. Look truly into your mind.

*Here **Anima** appears in the most horrible costume, fouler than a fiend.*

Mind

Alas! I tremble for fear, by Saint Paul.
　　This is fouler than any fiend.

Wisdom

Why are you a creature so unkind,　　　　　905
Thus to defile God's own seat?
　　That which was made glorious without end
You have made into the devil's retreat.
As many deadly sins as you have used,
　　So many devils in your soul be.　　　　　910
Behold what is therein enclosed.
　　Alas, man, on your soul have pity.

*Here six small boys dressed like devils run out from under the mantle
of the **Soul**. Then they run back under again.*

Wysdom

What haue I do? Why lowyste þu not me?
Why cherysyste þi enmye? Why hatyst þu þi frende?
  Myght I haue don ony more for þe?   915
But loue may brynge drede to mynde.
þu hast made the a bronde of hell
  Whom I made þe ymage of lyght.
Yff þe deull myght, he wolde þe qwell,
  But þat mercy expellyt hys myght.   920
  Wy doyst þu, Soule, me all dyspyght?
Why yewyst þu myn enmy þat I haue wrought?
  Why werkyst þu hys consell? By myn settys lyght,
  Why hatyst þu vertu? Why louyst þat ys nought?

Mynde

A, Lorde, now I brynge to mynde   925
  My horryble synnys & myn offens,
I se how I haue defowlyde þe noble kynde
  þat was lyke to þe by intellygens.
  Wndyrstondynge, I sew to your presens
Owr lyff wyche þat ys most synfull.   930
  Sek yow remedye; do yowr dylygens
To clense þe soull wyche ys þis fowll.

Wndyrstondynge

Be yow, Mynde, I haue very knowenge   f.117r
  That grettly Gode we haue offendyde.
Endles peyn worthy be owr dysyrynge,   935
  Wyche be owrselff neuer may be amendyde
  Wythowt Gode, in whom all ys comprehendyde.
Therfor to hym let vs resort.
  He lefte vp them þat be descendyde.
He ys resurreccyon & lywe; to hem, Wyll, resort.   940

Wyll

My wyll was full yowe to syne,
  By wyche þe soule ys so abhomynable.

---

924 hatyst] has canc. before   929 wndyrstondynge] st canc. after wn; sew] E schew
933 speaker] wndyrstod, w. n abbrev. over od; Wyll canc. before; on prev. folio
935 dysyrynge] E dysyrvynge 935 worthy] stroke after resembling an i — E worthyi

Wisdom

What have I done? Why do you not love me?
Why cherish your enemy? Why hate your friend?
   Could I have done any more for thee?   915
But love may bring fear to mind.
You have made yourself a brand of hell
   Whom I made the image of light.
If the devil could, he would you quell,
   Except that mercy expels his might.   920
   Why, O Soul, do you hold me in such spite?
Why give my enemy what I have wrought?
   Why follow his counsel? By my seat's light,
Why hate virtue? Why love that which is nought?

Mind

Ah, Lord, now that I bring to mind   925
   My horrible sins and my offense,
I see how I have defiled the noble kind
   That resembled you in intelligence.
   Understanding, I show to your presence
Our life which is most sinful.   930
   Seek the remedy; use your diligence
To cleanse the soul which is thus foul.

Understanding

Through you, Mind, I have true knowing
   That God we have greatly offended.
Endless pain is the recompense of our desiring,   935
   Which by ourselves may never be amended
   Without God, in whom all is comprehended.
Therefore to him let us resort.
   He lifts up those that have descended.
He is resurrection and life; to him, Will, resort.   940

Will

My will was very eager to sin,
   Because of which the Soul is so abominable.

I wyll retorne to Gode & new begynne
    And in hym gronde my wyll stable,
        þat of hys mercy he wyll me able   945
    To haue þe yiffte of hys specyall grace.
        How hys seke Soule may be recurable
    At þe jugment before hys face.

Anima

Than wyth yow iii þe Soule dothe crye,
    "Mercy, Gode!" — Why change I nowte?   950
I þat thus horryble in synne lye,
    Sythe Mynde, Wyll, & Wndyrstondynge be brought
    To haue knowynge þey ill wrought.
        What ys þat xall make me clene?
        Put yt, Lorde, into my thowte.   955
    Thi olde mercy, let me remene.

Wysdom

Thow þe soule mynde take
    Ande wndyrstondynge of hys synnys all wey,
Beynge in wyll, yt forsake,
    Yit thes do not only synnys awey.   960 f.117v
        But very contrycyon — who þat haue may;
þat ys purger & clenser of synne.
    A tere of þe ey wyth sorow veray,
þat rubbyt & waschyt þe Soule wythin.
All þe penance þat may be wrought   965
    Ne all þe preyer þat seyde be kan
Wythowt sorowe of hert relesyt nought.
    That in especyall reformyth man
    Ande makyt hym as clene as when he begane.
    Go seke þis medsyne, Soull. Þat beseke   970
        Wyth veray feythe, & be ye sekyr than
The vengeaunce of Gode ys made full meke.
By Wndyrstondynge, haue very contrycyon;
    Wyth Mynde, of yowr synne confessyon make;
Wyt Wyll yeldynge du satysfaccyon.   975
        þan yowr Soule be clene, I wndyrtake.

---

946 of hys specyall] Ms. repeats phrase   947 hys point before   949 iii] Ms. iiI — E thre
953 ill] Ill   963 veray] wery canc. before   964 wythin] wyth In   975 Wyt] word written
out in text; see also l. 215 — E Wyth

I will return to God and newly begin
 And in him ground my will stable,
 So that through his mercy he will me enable   945
To have the gift of his special grace.
 Thus this sick Soul may be curable
At the judgment before his face.

  Anima

Then with you three the Soul does cry,
 "Mercy, God!" — Why change I not?   950
I that thus horrible in sin lie,
 Since Mind, Will, and Understanding have been brought
 To know that they have ill wrought.
 What is that shall make me clean?
  Put it, Lord, into my thought.   955
Your former mercy let me regain.

  Wisdom

Though you, the Soul, have recalled Mind,
 Shown Understanding his sins all the way,
And through the power of Will forsaken that grind,
 Yet these alone do not put sin away.   960
 But true contrition — whoever has that may
Know that is the purger and cleanser of sin.
 A tear of the eye, with true sorrow, I say,
Such a tear scrubs and washes the Soul within.
Not all the regret you may personally feel   965
 Nor all the prayers that you say can
Without sorrow of heart release the seal.
 That sorrow of heart in particular reforms man
 And makes him as clean as when he began.
Go seek this medicine, Soul. That seek   970
 With true faith, and you may be certain then
The vengeance of God well grow very meek.
Through Understanding, gain true contrition;
 With Mind, of your sin confession make;
With Will yielding due satisfaction.   975
 Then your Soul will be clean, I undertake.

Anima

I wepe for sorow, Lorde. I begyn awake,
I that þis longe hath slumberyde in syne.

Wysdom

Lo, how contrycyon avoydyth þe deullys blake!
                              Hic recedunt demonos

Dedly synne ys non yow wythin,   980
For Gode ye haue offendyde hyg*h*ly,
    Ande yowr modyr, holy chyrche so mylde.
þerfor Gode ye must aske mercy.
    By holy chyrch to be reconsylyde,
        Trustynge verely ye xall neuer be revylyde   985
    Yff ye haue yowr charter of pardon by confessyon.
        Now haue ye foryeffnes þat were fylyde.   f.118r
Go prey yowr modyr chyrche of her proteccyon.

Anima

O Fadyr of mercy ande of *comfort*,
    Wyth wepynge ey & hert contryte   990
To owr modyr holy chyrche, I wyll resort,
    My lyff pleyn schewenge to here syght.
    Wyth Mynde, Vndyrstondynge, & Wyll ryght,
Wyche of my Sowll þe partyes be,
    To þe domys of þe chyrche we xall vs dyght,   995
Wyth veray contricyon thus compleynnyng we.

Here þey go owt, & in þe goynge þe **Soule** *syngyth in þe most
lame[n]tabull wyse, wyth drawte notys as yt ys songyn in þe Passyon
Wyk[e]:*

*Magna velud mare contricio, contricio tua: quis consoleter tui?
Plorans plorauit in nocte, & lacrime eius in maxillis eius.*

980sd] Written in margin beside 979-80, perhaps implying action during Wisdom's speech
980 wythin] wyth In   981 hyg[h]ly] Ms. hygly — E hyghly   989 comfort] rhyme demands
this term, from E — Ms. mercy   996 co[m]pleynnyng] E compleynnyng — Ms.
copleyynnyng omitted abbr. for m   996sd lame[n]tabull] E lamentabull — M lametabull
omitted abbr. for n   wyke] e cropped

Anima

I weep for sorrow, Lord. I begin to awake,
I that this long have slumbered in sin.

Wisdom

Lo, how contrition drives out the devils black!
Here the demons leave.
Deadly sin is no longer within, 980
For you have offended God highly,
    And your mother, Holy Church so mild.
Therefore of God you must ask mercy.
    By Holy Church to be reconciled,
    Trusting verily you shall never be reviled 985
If you have your charter of pardon by confession.
    Now you have forgiveness that were defiled.
Go pray to your mother church for her protection.

Anima

O father of mercy and of comfort,
    With weeping eye and heart contrite 990
To our mother, Holy Church, I will resort,
    My life plainly showing to her sight.
    With Mind, Understanding, and Will right,
Which of my Soul the parts be,
    To the judgments of the church we shall us plight, 995
With true contrition thus lamenting we.

*Here they go out, and in going the **Soul** sings in the most mournful manner, drawing out the notes as is sung in Passion Week:*

Magna velud mare contricio, contricio tua: quis consoletur tui? Plorans ploravit in nocte, et lacrime eius in maxillis eius.

Wysdom

Thus seth Gode mankynde tyll
   The ix poyntys ples hym all other before:
"Gyff a peny in thy lyve wyth goode wyll
      To þe pore, & þat plesythe Gode more   1000
     þat mowyntenys into golde tramposyde wore
   Ande aftyr thy dethe for the dysposyde.
   Ande all þe goodys þu hast in store
   Xulde not profyght so moche wan þi body ys closyde."

The secunde poynt, Gode sethe thus: 1005
   "Wepe on tere for my loue hertyly,
Or for þe passyon of me, Jhesus,
   Ande þat plesyt me more specyally
   Than yff þu wepte for þi frendys or goodys worldly
   As moche water as þe se conteynys."   1010 f.118v
    Lo, contrycyon ys a soueren remedy,
      That dystroythe synnys, þat relessyt peynys.

The iii^{de}, Gode sethe: "Suffyr pacyenly for my loue
   Off þi neybure a worde of repreve,
Ande þat to mercy mor dothe me move   1015
   Than þu dyscyplynyde þi body wyth peynys grewe
   Wyth as many roddys as myght grow or þrywe
In þe space of days jornye."
    Lo, who suffyryth most for Gode ys most lewe:
   Slandyr, repreve, only aduersyte.   1020

The iiii^{te}, Gode sethe: "Wake on owyr for þe loue of me,
   And þat to me ys more plesaunce
Than yff þu sent xii kyngys free
    To my sepulkyr wyth grett puysschaunce
   For my dethe to take vengeaunce."   1025
   Lo, wakynge ys a holy thynge.
    þer yt ys hade wyth goode vsance,
   Many gracys of yt doth sprynge.

1001 þat] a rare variant of þan — E þan   1013, 1021] paragraph sign in left margin
1013 iii^{de}] Ms. iii1de — E thyrde   1014 repreve] reprove w. abbr. for pro canc. before
1017 or] on w. n canc., r inserted above;   [b]rywe] E þrywe — Ms. prywe   1018 days]
E a days   1020 only] E ony   1021 iiii^{te}] Ms. iiij^{te} — E fourte   1022 Gode] point after
1023 xii] Ms. xij — E twelve

Wisdom
Thus says God to mankind still
    The nine points that please him all others before:
"Give a penny in your life with good will
      To the poor, and that pleases God more   1000
      Than if mountains into gold transformed were
  And after your death for you were disposed.
    And all the goods you have in store
  Should not profit you so much when the body is enclosed."

The second point, God says thus: 1005
    "Weep one tear for my love devoutly,
Or for the crucifixion of me, Jesus,
    And that pleases me more especially
    Than if you wept for your friends or goods worldly
  As much water as the sea contains."   1010
    Lo, contrition is a sovereign remedy
  That destroys sins and eases pains.

The third, God says: "Suffer patiently for my love
    From your neighbor a word of reproof,
And that to mercy more does me move   1015
    Than if you disciplined your body with pains grave
    With as many sticks as might grow or thrive
  In the space of a day's journey."
    Lo, who suffers most for God most earns his love:
  Suffering slander, reproof, or any adversity.   1020

The fourth, God says: "Watch one hour for the love of me,
    And that to me gives more pleasaunce
Than if you sent twelve kings of great nobility
    To my sepulchre with great puissance
    For my death to take vengeance."   1025
  Lo, being watchful is a holy thing.
    Where it is held with good usance,
  Many graces from it do spring.

The v^{te}, Gode sethe: "Haue pyte & compassyon
  Off þi neybur wyche ys seke & nedy,   1030
And þat to me ys more dylectacyon
    Than þu fastyde xl^{ty} yer by & by
    Thre days in þe weke as streytly
  As þu cowdys in water & brede."
    Lo, pyte Gode plesyth grettly,   1035
Ande yt ys a vertu soueren, as clerkys rede.

The vi^{te}, Gode seth on þis wyse:
  "Refreyn thy speche for my reuerens;
Lett not thy tonge thy evyncrysten dyspyse,   f.119r
    Ande þan plesyst more myn excellens   1040
    Than yff þu laberyde wyth grett dylygens
  Wpon thy nakyde feet & bare
    Tyll þe blode folwude for peyn & vyolens,
Ande aftyr eche stepe yt sene were."

The vii^{te}, Cryst seth in þis maner: 1045
  "Thy neybur to ewyll ne sterre not thu,
But all thynge torne into wertu chere,
    And than more plesyst me now
    Than yf a thowsende tymys þu renne thorow
  A busche of thornys þat scharpe were   1050
    Tyll þi nakyde body were all rought
Ande evyn rent to þe bonys bare."

The viii^{te}, Gode sethe þis man tyll:
  "Oftyn pray & aske of me,
Ande þat plesythe me more onto my wyll   1055
    Than yf my modyr and all sentys preyde for þe."

1029, 1037, 1045, 1053] paragraph sign in left margin   1029 v^{te}] E fyfte   1032 xl^{ty}] E forty   1037 vi^{te}] Ms. vj^{te} — E sixte   1040 þan] obs. var. of þat — E þat; pleyst] E plesyst þou   1045 vii^{te}] Ms. vij^{te} — E sevente   1046 thu] E thou   1048 And] Ms. Ad contracted form of And — E And   1051 rought] E rough; rhyme favors emendation   1053 vii^{te}] Ms. viij^{te} — E eyghte   1053-56] four-line stanza; four lines may be missing

The fifth, God says: "Have pity and compassion
   Of my neighbor who is sick and needy,   1030
And that to me is more delectation
   Than if you fasted forty years continuously
   Three days each week as straitly
As you could with water and bread."
   Lo, pity pleases God greatly,   1035
And it is a sovereign virtue, as clerics have said.

The sixth, God says in this wise:
   "Restrain your speech for my reverence;
Let not your tongue your fellow-Christians despise,
   And that pleases more my eminence   1040
   Than if you labored with great diligence
Upon your feet, naked and bare
   Till the blood flowed for pain and violence,
So that after each step it seen were."

The seventh, Christ says in this manner: 1045
   "Your neighbor to evil do not stir anyhow,
But all things turn into virtue dear,
   And then you please me more now
   Than if a thousand times you run through
A bush of sharp thorns that inflict care   1050
   Till your naked body were all rough
And even rent to the bones bare."

The eighth, God says this to man still:
   "Often pray and seek for me,
And that pleases me more unto my will   1055
   Than if my mother and all the saints prayed for thee."

The ix^{te}, Gode sethe: "Lowe me souerenly,
   Ande þat to me more plesant ys
Than yf þu went wpon a pyler of tre
    þat wer sett full of scharpe prykkys   1060
    So þat þu cut þi flesche into þe smale partys."
 Lo, Gode ys plesyde more wyth þe dedys of charyte
   Than all þe peynys man may suffer, iwys.
Remembyr thes poyntys, man, in þi felycite.

*Here entrethe **Anima**, wyth þe v wyttys goynge before, **Mynde** on þe on
syde & **Wndyrstondynge** on þe other syde & **Wyll** folowyng, all in here
fyrst clothynge, her chapplettys & crestys, & all hauyng on crownys,
syngynge in here commynge in:*   f.119v

*Quid retribuam Domino pro omnibus que retribuit mihi Calicem salutaris
accipiam & nomen domini inuocabo.*

Anima

O meke Jhesu, to þe I crye,   1065
   O swet Jhesu, my delectacyon,
O Jhesu, þe sune of Vyrgyne Marye,
   Full of mercy & compassyon.
   My soule ys waschede be thy Passyon
Fro þe synnys cummynge by sensualyte.   1070
   A, be the I haue a new resurreccyon.
The lyght of grace I fele in me.
In tweyn myghtys of my soule I the offendyde:
   The on by my inwarde wyttys, thow ben gostly,
þe other by my outwarde wyttys comprehendyde.   1075
   Tho be þe v wyttys bodyly,
   Wyth þe wyche tweyn myghtys, "Mercy," I crye.
My modyr, Holy Chyrche, hath yowe me grace,
   Whom ye fyrst toke to yowr mercy,
Yet of myselff I may not satysfye my trespas.   1080
Magna est misercordia tua.
   Wyth full feyth of foryewenes to þe, Lorde, I come.

1057 paragraph sign in left margin; ix^{te}] E nynte   1063 iwys] I wys   1064sd hauyng] last
word on folio 119r; v] E Fyve; &] E et   in] M I w. a partial light long stroke after it; archaic
contraction for in — E in   1064 sd invocabo] Inuocabo   1073 tweyn] te canc. before
1076 v] point after   1081-84] four-line stanza

The ninth, God says: "Love me sovereignly,
   And that to me more pleasure imparts
Than if you climbed upon a pillar made from a tree
     That was set full of sharp darts   1060
     So that you cut your flesh into small parts."
   Lo, God is pleased more with deeds of charity
     Than all the pains man may suffer from fleshly smarts.
   Remember these points, man, in your felicity.

*Here enters **Anima**, with the **five wits** preceding her, **Mind** on one side
and **Understanding** on the other side and **Will** following behind, all in
their first clothing, their chaplets and crests, and all having on crowns,
singing as they come in:*

*Quid retribuam Domino pro omnibus que retribuit mihi? Calicem
salutaris accipiam et nomen Domini invocabo.*

Anima

O meek Jesus, to you I cry,   1065
   O sweet Jesus, my delectation,
O Jesus, son of the Virgin Mary,
     Full of mercy and compassion.
     My soul is washed clean by your Passion
   Of the sins deriving from sensuality.   1070
     Ah, through you I have a new resurrection.
   The light of grace I feel in me.
In the twin mights of the soul I offended:
     The one by my inward wits, those which are ghostly,
The other by my outward wits comprehended.   1075
     Those are the five wits bodily,
     With the which twin mights, "Mercy," I cry.
   My mother, Holy Church, has given me grace,
     I whom you first took to your mercy,
   Yet of myself I may not satisfy my trespass.   1080
Magna est misericordia tua.
     With full faith in forgiveness to you, Lord, I come.

Wysdom

Vulnerasti cor meum, soror, mea sponsa,
In vno ictu oculorum tuorum.
Ye haue wondyde my hert, syster, spowse dere,   1085
  In þe tweyn syghtys of yowr ey
By þe recognycyon ye haue clere,
  Ande by þe hye lowe ye haue godly.
  It perrysschyt my hert to here yow crye.
Now ye haue forsake synne & be contryte   1090
  Ye were neuer so leve to me, verelye.   f.120r
Now be ye reformyde to yowr bewtys bryght.
Ande ther yowr v wyttys offendyde has,
  Ande to mak asythe by impotent,
My v wyttys, þat neuer dyde trespas,   1095
  Hathe made asythe to þe father suffycyent.
  Wyth my syght I se þe people vyolent;
I herde hem vengeaunce onto me call;
  I *sm*elte þe stenche of caren here present;
I tastyde þe drynke mengylde wyth gall.   1100
By towchynge I felte peyns smerte.
  My handys sprede abrode to halse þe swyre;
My fete naylyde to abyde wyth þe, swet herte;
  My hert clowyn for þi loue most dere;
  Myn hede bowhede down to kys þe here;   1105
My body full of holys as a dovehows.
  In thys ye be reformyde, Soule, my plesynge,
And now ye be þe very temple of Jhesus.
Fyrst, ye were reformyde by baptyme of ygnorans
  Ande clensyde from þe synnys orygynall,   1110
Ande now ye be reformyde by þe sakyrment of penance
  Ande clensyde from þe synnys actuall.
  Now ye be fayrest, Crystys own specyall.
Dysfygure yow now neuer to þe lyknes of þe fende.
  Now ye haue receyuyde þe crownnys victoryall   1115
To regne in blys wythowtyn ende.

1094 by] var. of be; see ll. 172, 287, 304 — E be   impotent] Impotent   1099 [sm]elte]
Ms. felte — B selte; M f and s are very similar — E smelte; sense of line supports smelte
1100 mengylde] I canc. before y   1102 þe] E þi   1107 plesynge] E plesere; rhyme
scheme supports emendation   1114 yow] stray mark before

Wisdom

Vulnerasti cor meum, soror, mea sponsa,
In uno ictu oculorum tuorum.

You have wounded my heart, sister, spouse dear,   1085
 In the twin sights of your eye
By the recognition you have clear,
  And by the high love you have godly.
  It breaks my heart to hear you cry.
 Now you have forsaken sin and are contrite   1090
  You were never so dear to me, verily.
 Now are you reformed to your beauty bright.
And whereas each of your five wits offended has,
 And to make reparation all are impotent,
My five wits, that never did trespass,   1095
  Have made recompense to the father sufficient.
  With my sight I see people violent;
 I heard them vengeance unto me call;
  I smelled the stench of carrion here present;
 I tasted the drink mingled with gall.   1100
Through the sense of touch I felt pains smart.
  My hand spread abroad to embrace your neck here;
My feet nailed to abide with you, sweet heart;
  My heart cloven for your love most dear;
  My head bowed down to kiss you here;   1105
 My body full of holes as a dovehouse.
  In this you are restored, Soul, my pleasure,
 And now you are the very temple of Jesus.
First, you were rescued by baptism from ignorance
  And cleansed from sins original,   1110
And now you are restored by the sacrament of penance
  And cleansed from sins actual.
  Now you are the fairest, Christ's own special.
 Never disfigure yourself to the likeness of the fiend.
  Now you have received the crowns triumphal   1115
 To reign in bliss without end.

Mynde

Haue mynde, Soule, wat Gode hath do,
    Reformyde yow in feyth, veryly.   _{f.120v}
Nolite confirmare huic seculo,
    Sed reformamini in nouitate spiritus sensus vestri.   1120
    Conforme yow not to þis pompyus glory,
But reforme in gostly felynge.
    Ye þat were dammyde by synne endelesly,
Mercy hathe reformyde yow ande crownyde as a kynge.

Wndyrstondynge

Take Vndyrstondynge, Soule, now ye   1125
    Wyth contynuall hope in Godys behest.
Renouamini spiritu mentys vestre
    Et induite nouum hominem, qui secundum deum creatus est.
    Ye be reformyde in felynge, not only as a best,
But also in þe ouerparte of yowr reasun,   1130
    Be wyche ye haue lyknes of Gode mest
Ande of þat mercyfull very congnycyon.

Wyll

Now þe Soule yn charyte reformyde ys;
    Wyth charyte ys Gode, verely.
Exspoliantem veterem hominem cum actibus suis,   1135
    [Et induite nouum, qui renouatur in agnitionem Dei].
    Spoyll yow of yowr olde synnys & foly,
Ande be renuyde in Gode knowynge ageyn,
    That enduyde wyth grace so specyally,
Conseruynge in peyn, euer in blys for to reyn.   1140

Anima

Then wyth yow thre I may sey thus
    Of owr Lorde, soueren person Jhesus:
Suauis est dominus vniuersis :
    Et miseraciones eius super omnia oper eius.
    O thu hye Soueren Wysdam, my ioy, Cristus,   1145
_{f.121r}
    Hewyn, erthe, & eche creature
    Yelde yow reuerens for grace pleyntuus
Ye yeff to man euer to induyr.

1119 confirmare] E conformari   1128 induite] Induite   1129 only] inserted above line
1134 Wyth] E Wyche   1136] line omitted in M; taken from Walter Hilton; see notes; lines
from this point on differ by one number from E and B   1137 Gode] E Godys
1141 thus] E this   1143-44] M transcribes on one line — E, following F, two lines; stanza
pattern supports two lines; last line on folio   1144 oper] E opera   1145 thu] E, following
F, thou   1148 induyr] Induyr

Mind

Keep in mind, Soul, what God had to do,
　To reform you in faith, verily.
Nolite conformari huic seculo,
　　Sed reformamini in novitate spiritus sensus vestri.　　1120
　　Conform you not to this pompous glory,
　But reform yourself in spiritual feeling.
　　You that were damned by sin endlessly,
　Mercy has restored and crowned you as a king.

Understanding

Gain understanding, Soul, now that will help you see　　1125
　Continual hope from God's behest.
Renovamini spiritu mentis vestrae
　　Et induite novum hominem, qui secundum Deum creatus est.
　　You are restored in feeling, not only as a beast,
　But also in the higher part of your reason,　　1130
　　Through which your likeness to God is greatest
　And from that merciful true cognition.

Will

Now the Soul through charity restored is;
　God is with charity, verily.
Exspoliantem veterem hominem cum actibus suis,　　1135
　　[Et induite novum, qui renovatur in agnitione Dei].
　　Strip yourself of your old sins and folly,
　And be renewed in the knowledge of God again,
　　That knowledge which endued you with grace so specially,
　Preserving you through suffering, ever in bliss to reign.　　1140

Anima

Then with you three I may say this
　Of our Lord and sovereign person, Jesus:
Suavis est Dominus universis,
　　Et miseraciones eius super omnia opera eius.
　　O high Sovereign Wisdom, my joy, Christus,　　1145
　Heaven, earth, and each creature
　　Offer you reverence for the grace plenteous
　You give to man, ever to endure.

Now wyth sent Powle we may sey thus,
　　þat be reformyde thorow feythe in Jhesum,　　　　　1150
We haue peas & acorde betwyx Gode & ws:
　　Iustificati ex fide pacem habemus ad Deum:
　　Now to Salamonys conclusyon I com:
Timor Domini inicium sapiencie.

　　　　　[Wysdom]
　　Vobis qui timetis Deum.　　　　　　　　　　　1155
　　　　Orietur sol Justicie.
The tru son of ryghtusnes,
　　Wyche þat ys on lorde Jhesu,
Xall sprynge in hem þat drede hys meknes.
　　Nowe ye mut euery soule renewe　　　　　　　1160
　　In grace, & vycys to eschew,
Ande so to ende wyth perfeccyon.
　　That þe doctryne of Wysdom we may sew.
Sapiencia patris, grawnt þat for hys Passyon.　Amen

　　　Wysdom
　　　Anima, v wyttys
　　　Mynde
　　　Wndyrstondynge
　　　Lucyfer

1150 Jhesum] le canc. before E lhesum　　1155 speaker] M has drawn a line across the page, as if to designate a change of speaker; the speaker's name has been omitted. Wysdom is the most likely choice. Markings which may constitute a large, ornate W are in the right margin immediately below the line marking the change of speaker.　　1158 on] E Owr　　1164 Passyon] point appears in the loop above the n, the final word of the text.

Now with Saint Paul we may say thus,
    We that be reformed through faith in Jesum,   1150
We that have peace and accord between God and us:
    Justificati ex fide pacem habemus ad Deum.
    Now to Solomon's conclusion I come:
    Timor Domini initium sapientiae.

    [Wisdom]
    Vobis qui timetis Deum;   1155
    Orietur sol justitiae.
The true son of righteousness,
    Who is one lord Jesu,
Shall spring in them that fear his meekness.
    Now must every soul itself renew   1160
    In grace, and vices must eschew,
And so end with perfection.
    That is the doctrine of Wisdom we may pursue.
Sapientia Patris, grant that for his Passion. Amen

    Wisdom
    Anima, Five Wits
    Mind
    Understanding
    Lucifer

NOTES

These notes contain textual annotations, information on sources and analogues, and interpretive comments. Previous editions have been cited where relevant. All stage directions are noted as "sd" with reference to the preceding line. All speakers' names are numbered by the line following the name. A list of abbreviations for the notes precedes the bibliography.

0 sd: Eccles divides the play into five separate scenes, of which this is Scene I. Neither M nor D provides textual authorization for the scenes. Wisdom, as Christ, wears the garb of an emperor, with the conventional emblems of office: a sceptre representing sovereignty, an orb with a cross signifying the link between imperial power and God's authority over the world, and an imperial crown, all regalia traditional to portraits of Christ in Majesty, as, for instance, in the Hubert and Jan Van Eyck Altarpiece, Vijd Chapel, St. Bavo's Cathedral, Ghent. (See Milla Riggio 1986 color plate 7). English kings wore the same regalia. See color plates 2, 3, & 4 (Riggio 1986) for portraits of Edward IV and Henry VI, dressed in ermine with an ermine hood, holding a sceptre and an orb. The visual representation of Christ enthroned as Wisdom which most closely resembles these stage descriptions appears in illustrated mss. of Heinrich Suso's German works, particularly his *Vita*, of which eight illustrated copies are extant. Variations of the same illustrations appear at the same places in the text of each of the eight mss. Only one of the illustrations in each ms. shows Christ *enthroned* as Wisdom, though other illustrations feature Christ crowned as Wisdom in various postures. See Riggio 1986 color plate 1 for one of the eight extant mss. illustrations of Christ enthroned as Wisdom (Codex Guelf, 78.5, Aug. fol 97R 1473, in the Herzog August Bibliothek, Wolffenbüttel). No English copy of the Suso illustration depicting an *enthroned* Wisdom has as yet turned up, but there is one probable English copy of a Suso illustration depicting Christ as Wisdom, leaning from a nimbus to speak with Suso, the disciple. This may be found in Brit. Mus. Addit. MS 37049, fol. 43v.

entreth: from D; M *enteryde*. One of two stage directions in which M uses the past tense where D has the present. Apparently the M scribe thinks of himself as recording a past event, perhaps a production or perhaps because he is copying D. See also I. 164sd.

purpull clothe of golde: Usually a silk or wool fabric woven with gold thread, wires, or strips, cloth of gold was probably used more frequently in court revels than in other forms of drama (See Twycross 1983 35). In mystery plays, for instance, God's costume was often made of fabrics like leather (see Ingram 25, 93). Cloth of gold was often used as backdrop as well as costume material in entertainments presented to royalty; in a pageant prepared for Queen Elizabeth I at Norwich in 1578 the stage was "very richly apparelled with cloth of Golde" and Mercury was costumed in blue satin "lined with cloth of gold." Because of a sudden rainstorm, the city lost precious fabrics including "cloth of gold" (Churchyard 276, 303, 317). Purple was consistently the color identified with royal dress; cloth of gold and purple silk, which had been restricted to those with the rank of lord or better in 1463, were further restricted to the royal family by sumptuary laws in 1483 (see Baldwin 103, 115).

ermynnyde . . . ryall hood furred wyth ermyn: Ermine, a black-flecked white fur, traditionally a fabric associated with royalty. During the reign of Henry IV, English kings began wearing an ermine cape; throughout the fifteenth century ermine was restricted by a variety of sumptuary laws to those of aristocratic rank (see Baldwin 49, 50, 75, 79-81, 88, 103, 109, 124, 125).

cheweler wyth browys: Apparently a wig with attached eyebrows. David Parry has conjectured that the "browys" might suggest a mask (Unpublished paper presented at *The Wisdom Symposium*, Trinity College, April 1984).   And David Klausner, in his 1991 Toronto production, presented a masked Christ. As itemized in extant prop lists, wigs — called "cheuelers" (with variant spellings) or "heare" — were regularly worn in mystery plays by God the Father, Christ, angels, and apostles, sometimes by Lucifer. Some wigs were gilded, as, for instance, "Item ii Cheverels gyld for Jhe & petur," from the 1490 Smiths' Accounts (Ingram 74). The Coventry Smiths accounts for 1564 record payment for "iii cheverels and a berde" (Ingram 227). An undated Coventry drapers' account also lists "iii chefferellys & a berde of hree" (Ingram 474). The Grocers Guild Records of Norwich record a "face and heare for ye Father," in 1564 (Galloway 53). (Also see Galloway 37 and Johnston and Rogerson 55, 78, 80.)

berde of golde of sypres curlyde: A curled beard made of clcth of gold imported from Cyprus.

balle: *MED* cites this line as its only example of "balle" meaning orb.

1-8. The verse pattern here is an eight-line stanza (ababbcbc), which is identified throughout the play as Wisdom's verse. When Wisdom is on stage, all characters use this verse form as an indication of their fealty to him. The lines in this pattern tend to be ten to twelve-syllabled and may contain as many as fourteen syllables, in contrast to the frequency of shorter lines in Lucifer's section of the play. The rhymes are often what may be called "liturgical rhymes," i.e., multi-syllabled Latinate words which rhyme only in the repetition of the last syllable. Though the impression is of a learned style, this verse form also has a stately grace, lending itself well to the love speeches of Wisdom and Anima.

1-65. Taken from Heinrich Suso, *Orologium Sapientiae*, translated into English as an anonymous work perhaps as early as 1490 and most commonly titled the "Seven Points of True Wisdom." See Lovatt (47-49) for Suso's availability in England. For sources of *The Play of Wisdom* see Smart. The *Orologium* is probably Suso's Latin translation of his own German dialogue (see Kunzle 28-54). In this work, a fervent disciple engages in a lengthy dialogue with Sapientia, i.e. Wisdom, who speaks alternately as a man and a woman — as the masculine spouse of the Church and the feminine spouse of the human soul. The Corpus Christi College, Cambridge, Ms 268, a parchment book in quarto written in the latter half of the fifteenth century, contains a copy of the *Seven Points of True Wisdom* (the English *Orologium*), which may be slightly closer to the *Wisdom* text than are other extant English mss., though it does not contain the noun *nobley*, found in Ms. Douce 114 and in l. 4 of *Wisdom*; see 4n.

2. imperyall: Not in Suso. The imperial imagery is important to the characterization of Christ enthroned as Wisdom.

4. Euerlastynge Wysdom: Christ, as the second person of the Trinity, was conventionally associated with Wisdom.   Biblical passages justifying this identification include: Isaiah 11.1-2: "Et egredietur virga de radice Jesse, et flos de radice eius ascendet. Et requiescet super eum spiritus Domini: spiritus sapientiae et intellectus, spiritus consilii et fortitudinis, spiritus scientiae et pietatis" ("There shall come forth a shoot from the stump of Jesse, and a branch shall grow out of his roots. And the Spirit of the Lord shall rest upon him, the spirit of wisdom and understanding, the spirit of counsel and might, the spirit of knowledge and the fear of the Lord"; for convenience, translations of Latin Vulgate passages are generally taken from *The New Oxford Bible*. However since this text often takes liberties in its translation, I silently emend the translation when a more literal reading seems preferable. For instance, in the translation above "pietatis" does not literally mean "fear of the Lord," but since it does connote a pious and humble acceptance of authority, I have allowed the translation to stand); in Luke 7.35, Christ appears to personify Wisdom; in Luke 11.31 Christ calls himself "greater" than "the wisdom of Solomon" ("Regina . . . venit a finibus terrae audire sapientiam Salomonis, et ecce plus quam Salomon hic," — "The Queen . . . comes from the ends of the earth to hear the wisdom of Solomon and, behold, something greater than Solomon is here") and Luke 11.49 reports the words of "sapientia Dei" ("Wisdom of God") as part of Christ's teachings. Most signficant, however, was the interpretation of the Prologue to the Gospel according to John which identified Jesus as the *logos* ("word") made flesh. Christ as the *logos* of John 1.1 was associated with certain aspects of Wisdom from the Jewish wisdom literature. See also I Corinthians 1.24, where Paul calls Christ "Dei virtutem et Dei sapientiam" ("the power of God and the wisdom of God").   See Smith (123-65) for literary references to and personifications of Christ as Wisdom. Instances in drama include a reference to Christ as "Patris Sapiencia" in the Chester cycle first pageant of the Fall of Lucifer (1/12; Lumiansky and Mills 1: 2; this form of citation, which will be used for cycle plays throughout these notes, should be read: play 1, line 12 in Lumiansky and Mills, volume 1, page 2). Christ appears as Sapientia in the N-Town Assumption of Mary play, where Mary appeals to his *benygnyté*, and speaks of her allegiance to Christ as a bond of *affye*, terms which correspond to the loving authority and feudal affinities of *Wisdom*:

Maria   O hye Wysdam in youre dygne deyté
        Youre infynyth lovnesse mad oure saluacyon.
        That it lyst you of me, sympilest to take here humanité,
          Wyth dew obeschyauns I make you gratulacyon.
        And, gloryous Lord and sone, yif it like youre benygnyté
                .   .   .   .
        Wyth all myn herte and my sowle, be natures excitacyon,
        To your domynacyon.
          For all creaturis in you don affye. . . .

(41/94 - 98, 101 - 03 Spector 1991 1: 390-91; play ctd. by Smith 147).
See l. 1163n.

Nobley: "Nobility," i.e. "the natural nobility of God." From D; M reads *noble*. The term is taken from the English translation of Suso, which in at least one manuscript confirms the form *nobley*. *The Seven Poynts of Trewe Wisdom* Ms. Douce 114, for instance, reads "þe which name is . . . best accordynge to myne nobleye" (Horstmann 323); see also l. 576.

egalle: Not in Suso. *Egalle* implies "suitable to" or "equal to" the nobility of God.

5. in especyall: Not in Suso.

10-12. Applyede to þe sune by resune . . . . hys hye generacyon: Though quoting the English Suso, the phrasing here alters the syntax of the *Seven Poynts of Trewe Wisdom*, which reads as follows: "Wisdam . . . fallyth to [þe sone] by reson of his generacyon specialy" (Corpus Christi Ms. 268, fol. 56r). *Hye generacyon* implies the high birth of Christ, as the son of God. Cf. Nicholas Heller's translation of Suso's German works, where Christ as Wisdom links his "princely" or "noble" birth to his identification with the *logos* of God: "I am of princely birth, of noble lineage. I am the beloved Word of the Father's heart . . . " (29).

15. & wery patrone: Not in Suso. The patronage metaphor recurs throughout the play. See, for instance, l. 132n, 381-92n, 544-45n, 583-84.

16. Wyffe of eche chose sowle: In Suso Wisdom speaks alternately as a man and a woman: "now as god now as man now as he þat is spowse of hys chyrche and now as sche þat is spowse and wyf of every chosyn soule" (Corpus Christi Ms 268, fol. 56r). As the spouse of the masculine soul, Sapientia is feminine. Though in the play the Soul is feminine, the dramatist keeps the attribution of "wyf" in this reference. It is the one remnant in the play of the alternating masculine and feminine identity of Christ as Wisdom in Suso's dialogue. See ll. 120, 133-34, 289, 1124 for hints of the masculine emanation of the Soul and ll. 17-20n, 79n, and 1103n.

Thus Wysdom begane: This line means either "Thus Wisdom began to speak" or "Thus Wisdom originated." If interpreted in the prior sense, the line indicates that the first 16 lines are a Prologue to the play (as suggested by Chambers 59). If interpreted in the latter sense, the line refers to the genealogy of Wisdom, which the preceding fifteen and one-half lines do trace. See Eccles 203n for a summary of previous interpretations. Both interpretations are plausible. The latter assimilates the line into the dramatic frame of the drama and provides a suitable conclusion to Wisdom's expository tracing of his own lineage. In contrast, the prologue theory may help to account for changes made in adapting the Suso text to the play. The first 16 lines of the play, spoken before Anima enters, constitute Wisdom's prologue to the drama and set the stage for the ensuing dialogue with Anima. Though the Suso work overall is in the form of a dialogue, the 65 lines quoted at the beginning of *Wisdom* are not; in the *Orologium* and in its English translation the *Seven Poynts of Trewe Wisdom* the dialogue exchange of the play forms a lengthy monologue spoken by Sapientia. The dramatist breaks the speech into dialogue after Wisdom's opening soliloquy, which in this reading ends with the actor's indirect allusion to Suso: *Thus Wisdom Begane [to speak]*. This interpretation, of course, effectively reads these lines as a metatheatrical or self-referential stage direction. Such stepping out of the role does occur elsewhere in morality drama, as well as in mystery plays. See, for instance, l. 1163n.

16sd: Anima's costume is intentionally allied with that of Wisdom, since she serves as his Queen. The theological allegory here is particularly rich and multi-valenced, since Anima's role as the Queen of heaven and bride of Christ implies her symbolic association with other female figures.   The play insinuates a link between a conservative theological stance and the established hierarchy of the reigning monarch.   That association is furthered by Anima's costume. Her attire resembles that of the English Queen who on the eve of her coronation is attired in white as a sign of penitence.   According to the document entitled "Little Device for the Coronation of Henry VII," which prescribes a ceremony that seems to have predated Henry's reign [Henry was not married at the time of his coronation], the Queen is to be "arayed in a kirtel of white damaske cloth of gold furred with myniuer pur . . . a Mantell . . . with a greit lase and ii botons and taxselles of white silke and gold." Anima wears a black mantle, for obvious iconographic purposes, as an emblem of her mortal nature tainted by original sin.   Otherwise, her costume exactly parallels that of the Queen.   Both wear a miniver-trimmed white garment and a chaplet or headband, probably a circlet of gold.   Even Anima's two *knottys* (or "bottons") of gold and long *tasselys* find a referent in the Queen's "ii botons and taxselles of white silke and gold." An informed audience could not have missed the association, since the royal marriage of Christ and Anima visually recalls the English King and his Queen in a penitential mode   (See Riggio 1986 9-10). Anima is not only the spouse of Christ; she is also the royal consort of the reigning monarch (of heaven).   Using clothing in this symbolic way is characteristic of the patronage metaphor which will carry throughout the play.

mayde: "virgin." Though Anima represents the spouse of Wisdom, the character also appropriates some of the characteristics of Ecclesia, as the bride of Christ, and the Virgin. (For more information, see Introduction and see Riggio 1989.)

miniver: "little vair," an all-white fur used in ceremonial garments, is a slightly less aristocratic fur than ermine, but is still a restricted fabric, worn on occasion by the English Queen.

cheueler: "wig." Anima wears a wig like Wisdom's.

chappetelot: "chaplet," a rich circlet or coronet for the head (which could be a garland of flowers or a thin band of gold), as a signification of her high office, rather than a crown. (See l. 1064sd when she returns crowned.)

knottys of golde: Either "knots made of cloth of gold" or "gold buttons." The term may signify either. The link between Anima's costume and that of the queen of England favors "buttons." See above.

syde tasselys: "long tassels." The term *syde* consistently refers to long, often floor-length clothing, or as here long tassels hanging from Anima's chaplet. This item, too, connects her costume with that of the Queen of England. For *syde*, see l. 510n.

17. *Hanc amaui et exquisiui*: "This I have loved and have sought. (source: Wisdom of Solomon 8.2 and Suso, *Seven Points of True Wisdom*); see note below.

17-20. Cf. Liber Sapientiae or Wisdom of Solomon 8.2, quoted by Suso: "hanc amaui et exquisiui a iuuentute mea & quisiui eam sponsam mi assumere, & amator factus sum forme illius — þat is to seye: 'sche þis I haue louede & I haue vtturlye sowhte fro myne 3owþe & I haue desyrede for to haue to mye spowse, and I am made a lovere of hir forme and schappe'" (Ms. Douce 114, qtd. by Horstmann 329; in Vulgate "mi assumere" is "mihi eam assumere"). In Suso the feminine Sapientia quotes the biblical passage as referring to the Soul's desire for Wisdom. Here, in contrast, Anima refers to her desire for Christ, her masculine spouse. The love theme is persistent throughout the play. Building on passages from the Wisdom of Solomon and the Song of Songs, as well as the Suso dialogue, Anima is characterized as the *louer* and *spouse* of Christ. The play builds on the tradition in which "contemplative" love poetry echoes and, to some extent, parallels the theologized strain of courtly love poetry initiated by Dante in *La Vita Nuova*. Love poems were written at times in adoration of the Virgin Mary, and mystics often affirmed their "marriage" to Christ. Themes that linked the two traditions include the lover's professed willingness to die for his beloved, modified by the topos in which the woman often does die, thus immortalizing her youthful beauty; the pain and anxiety of a lover's devotion; and the spiritually regenerative power of love. With

Christ as the object of Anima's devotion, the gender lines ordinarily associated with the courtly love tradition are crossed. However, as we have noted, the gender distinctions here are somewhat blurred; Christ as the masculine lover assumes many of the characteristics associated with the feminine Sapientia, and finally it is he who dies for his lover. See ll. 568-73n, 596n, and 1103n.

18. yougthe: "youth." From D; M has *thowte*. This may well be one of the instances in which M's own orthographic practices influences his copying. D distinguishes between þ and y; M does not, and (probably mistaking the "y" for "þ") he transcribes the term *yougthe*, verified by the "iuventute" of the biblical and Suso passages, as the virtually meaningless term *thowte*.

21-24. Cf. Wisdom of Solomon, 7.10-11, quoted by Suso: "Super salutem & omnem pulcritudinem dilexi sapienciam & proposui pro luce habere illam, venerunt mi amnia bona pariter cum illa — 'abouene heele & alle bewte I haue louede wisdam & I haue purposede for to haue hir as for mye lihte, & alle godes haue comene to me with hir" (Ms. Douce 114, Horstmann 329; the Vulgate reads: "Super salutem et speciem dilexi illum et proposui pro luce habere illam quoniam inextinguibile est lumen illius. Venerunt autem mihi omnia bona pariter cum illa . . ."). Note once more that the dramatist has changed the pronouns to accommodate his masculine characterization of Wisdom. The *lyght* of Wisdom and of grace is a persistent theme throughout the play, in which Wisdom is initially identified with light, and, when restored to grace, Anima partakes of that *lyght of grace*. See ll. 917-18n and 1072.

23. he: From D. M reads *ys*. This is one of those instances in which a stray mark from D may have influenced M's reading. A portion of the loop of the *f* in D l. 22 intersects the *h* of *he* in such a way that at a glance the term may appear to be *ye*, which M may have transcribed *ys*. Although this is not the usual D spelling for "is," M does occasionally read his own hand into that of D. He may have done so here.

24. In: From D. In two instances M copies the D *in* as *i*, apparently by choice. In a third instance, after the end of the D text, M once

more transcribes "in" as "i" (l. 1064sd). I have emended the third
occurrence to "in." The consistency of M's use of this convention
suggests that "i" may be an unattested abbreviation for "in," as "a" or
"ad" stand for "and." See ll. 613 and 1064sd.

bewty bryghte: Cf. l. 1092n.

25-26. Not in the Suso dialogue.

27. *Sapiencia specialior est sole.* "Wisdom is more splendid than
the sun" (source: Wisdom of Solomon 7.29 & Suso, *Seven Points of
True Wisdom*); see note below.

27-32. Cf. Wisdom of Solomon 7.29, 26, quoted by Suso: "Sapiencia
speciosior est sole et super omnem disposicionem stellarum luci
comparata inuenitur prior, candor est enim lucis eterne & speculum
sine macula diuine maiestatis & ymago bonitatis illius — þat is to
seye; wisdam is feyrere þanne sonne & in comparisone of hir to liht
she is fowndene passynge aboue alle þe disposicione of sterres, she
is forsoþe þe bryhtnesse of euerlastyne liht and þe mirrour withowt
wemme of goddes maieste & þe ymage of his godenesse'" (Ms Douce
114, Horstmann 329-30. In the Vulgate verse 26 begins "candor est
enim"; Suso does not indicate the break). Once more, the dramatist
reverses the gender of the speaker. Here, too, Sapientia in the
biblical passages and the Suso dialogue is feminine. In the play,
Wisdom is persistently masculine (see "Sources in Context" in
Introduction).

32. image of hys goodnes: The phrase "image of his goodness"
originates in the Wisdom of Solomon 7.26 ("imago bonitatis illius"),
and is quoted by Suso as "ymago bonitatis illius." Christ is cast in the
image of God's "goodness." See ll. 27-32n, 35n, 140n.

33-37. Cf. Proverbs 3.15-16, quoted by Suso: "Melior est sapiencia
euntis opibus preciosissimis & omne desiderabile non potest ei
comparari, longitudo dierum in dextra eius & in sinistra illius diuieie &
gloria — wisdam is bettur þanne manere of moste preciouse godes,
& alle þat may be desyrede may not be in comparisone lyke to hir; þe
lengh of 3eres is in hire right syde and in hir lift seyde richesses &

ioye" (Ms Douce 114, Horstmann 330; the Vulgate Proverbs 3.15 reads: "Pretiosior est cunctis opibus, et omnia quae desiderantur huic non valent comparari"; the term "melior" comes from Proverbs 3.14; allowing for scribal spelling choices [e.g. "u" for "v," etc.] 3.16 reads as Suso quotes it with "divitiae" where Suso has "diuieie"). See also Proverbs 8.11, for a repetition of Proverbs 3.15. Again, in the play a masculine Christ appropriates descriptions attributed biblically and in the Suso dialogue to the feminine Sapientia.

35. in comparyschon to my lyknes: I.e., when compared to the riches inherent in my likeness to God. The noun *lyknes*, added by the dramatist, has its origins in the phrase "lyke to hir [Sapientia]" from the English Suso. For a full list of occurrences and a discussion of "image" and "likeness," see ll. 104n and 140n.

39-40. Not in Suso. Once more, the addition furthers the theme of "sovereignty" and monarchical authority, with its attendant metaphor of patronage, that runs throughout the play.

40. game: "a sport of (divine) love." This term will later be inverted when Understanding (renamed Perjury) plays ironically on this idea of a false game "clepyde wysdom," and Wyll (renamed Lechery) identifies lust as a "game." Of course, the term also implies the dramatic entertainment itself. Cf. Ms. Tanner 407, which contains a small note on an epilogue to a miracle play that ends, "Souereyns alle in same 3e that arn come to sen oure *game* / We pray you all in goddys name to drinke as 3e pas" (fol. 44v). See ll. 603-04n and 612n.

41-46. The English translation of Suso reads: "But nowe, tochinge my loue, beholde wit a ioyefulle mynde howe hable I am to louede, howe louelye to clippede and kyssede of a clene sowle . . . . ffor soþelye I am euer redye to him þat loveþd me for to loue a3enwarde, & wit him I am present in chirche & atte borde, in þe weye & in cloyster & in þe market, so þat þere is no place but þat þere is present charite godde . . . . " (Ms. Douce 114, Horstmann 330).

41. yt ys myrable: "It is a miracle." Not in Suso.

44. of mankynde: Not in Suso.

45. clene sowlys: *Clene* is an adjective which consistently describes the condition of the Soul in the state of grace: as a pure and undefiled lover of Christ, Anima is *clene*. The term will be inverted in the world of sin. See also ll. 54, 176, 284, 289, 954n, 969, 976, and — for the ironic inversion — 494n and 749n.

47-48. Not in Suso.

49-65. Cf. Suso: "for amonge alle oþere spowses þe goddelye wisdam haþ þis sengulere proprete þat sche may be present ouer-alle to þe desyre of hire louere, & alle þe sihynges for hire and desyres & alle-maner dedes & seruyses sche as present knoweþ anone. Also þe sengulere prerogatyfe of mye godenesse and loue is so grete, þat who-so tasteþ þer-of þowh hit be but one lytele drope, after þat he schalle halde alle þe lustes & lykynges of þe worlde but as dritte. Mye love descharges hem þat beþ ouerleyde wit þe heve birþene of sinnes, hit purifyeþ & makeþ clene þe conscience, hit strengþeþ þe mynde & þe sowle, hit 3eviþ fredam to hem þat beþ parfyte & cowpleþ & knitte hem to her euerlastenge beginnynge. And what more: who-so takeþ me into his spowse & loueþ me above alle þinge, he lyveþ wit tranquillyte & reste, he deeþ wit sykernesse, & in a manere he biginneþ here þe blisse & þe ioyes þat schole laste euer worlde wíth-owte ende. We spekene manye þinges & 3ite we faylene in owr wordes: for þe hye worþinesse of mye love þer maye none tunge of menne ne of awngeles pleynlye telle; hit maye be in experience felt, but hit may not be fullye tolde or spokene; & þerefore alle þees wordes of þe makynge of goddelye love beþ but as sodenlye raþere owt caste þan in effecte plenlye fulle spoken" (Ms. Douce 114, Horstmann 330).

50. tastyt: "tastes." D reads *tast*, but D uses the singular form *takith* (M *takyt*) with the pronoun *who* (M. *wo*) at l. 57.

56. yewyt wysdom: "gives wisdom." Cf. Suso's "3eviþ fredam."

63. in experience from: This D reading is closer to Suso's "in experience felt" than the M *from experyens.*

66. wrech: "wretch" or "contemptible person." The D term is difficult to read correctly. It appears to be *wreth*. However, D's "th" and "ch" combinations closely resemble each other; thus, the word bears a strong resemblance to *wreche* (l. 695). It is likely that D himself either intends *wrech* or in his haste has merely mistaken the term for a very similar one. Although *wreth* as a noun related to *wrathe*, meaning "wrath" or anger, is a meaningful term, it does not ordinarily signify a person. *Wrech* is clearly preferable. This entire line is taken from Digby.

69-70. Taken from Suso: "souereynlye fayre and worþi spowse! Why þanne makest þou dissimulacione or feynynge, whye assayest not wheþer þou mayht haue hire in to þi amyke or loue?" (Ms. Douce 114, Horstmann 330). The term *amyke* is ctd. by *MED* as occurring in English only in Suso and *Wisdom* (see Eccles 204n).

69. fayre: "fair." From D; M reads *father*. The rhyme scheme clearly supports *fayre*. However, M tends to give up the rhyme when he feels that grammatical accuracy or sense demand a different term. Here he leaves no doubt that he prefers *father*; M does not distinguish between *þ* and *y*, whereas D does; to clarify his choice in this instance, M transcribes and cancels *faye* (which could read either "faye" or "fathe") before the more explicit *father*. This text returns to the D *fayre*, a choice also made by Furnivall and Eccles, who transcribe *fayer*; see also l. 399n.

71. repeyer: "turn (or resort) to."

77. sanctus sanctorum: "Holy of holies." This term originates in Hebrews 9.3: "Post velamentum autem secundum, tabernaculum, quod dicitur Sancta sanctorum" ("Behind the second curtain stood a tent, called the Holy of Holies"). The reference is to the most holy place of the Temple, the construction of which is described in Exodus 26.31-34. By attributing to Wisdom the status of *sanctus sanctorum*, Anima affirms his identity as the most holy sanctuary for the Soul.

78. to yowr most plesaunce: "for your greatest satisfaction or pleasure."

79. Fili, prebe me cor tuum: "Child, give me your heart" (source Proverbs 23.26 and Suso, *Seven Points of True Wisdom*). Taken from Suso: "And þanne eue*r*lastynge wisdam wit a gladde & graciose chere godelye saluede hym and seyde schortlye in þees wordes: 'Fili, prebe me cor tuum: Sone, 3iffe me þi herte!'" (Ms. Douce 114, Horstmann 331). The term of address hints at the masculine identity of the soul, an echo of Suso's dialogue. Cf. Proverbs 23.26: "Praebe, fili mi, cor tuum mihi, et oculi tui vias meas custodiant" ("My son, give me your heart and let your eyes observe my ways"); see l. 16n and 17-20n.

83. my: D has *myn*, which D consistently prefers before a vowel (or a vocalic *h*). M inconsistently follows this practice, preferring *my* to *myn* in two instances, just as he tends to prefer *a* to *an* before a vowel (see ll. 159 and 786). In the interest of dialectical consistency, this text preserves the M forms. See also l. 385; in ll. 193 and 690 M uses *myn*.

affyance: "betrothed lover." This is one of the terms with which the play inverts the allegory of salvation into the allegory of sin, when Will, whose perversion is lust, turns the concept of betrothal into alliances more suitable to the brothel. See ll. 643n, 657n, 659n, 799n, and (especially) 690n.

84. present: D has *represent*. The M term is more dramatically engaging: Anima "presents" her love to Wisdom as a gift. However, the D term, suggesting that the actor playing Anima "represents" the fervor of the soul's love for God, could make sense as part of a series of metatheatrical references in this section of the play; see l. 101n.

86. Teche me þe scolys of yowr dyvynyte: "Teach me the schools of your divinity." The plural "schools" initially seems an odd choice; the phrase refers to an allegory of learning taken from Suso, where it is made clear that there are various "scoles" of knowledge but that only the "scole" of Christ is worth pursuing: In the English translation of the Suso dialogue between Sapientia and her/his disciple, the disciple visits "diuerse scoles," where he learns the sciences and "alle crafts vndere sonne." In the allegory, these schools occupy one mansion filled with several learned "doctours." But this worldly learning causes the disciple to vomit. He then searches out a second mansion, in which he finds "þe scole [of] soþfaste diuinyte" (Cf. Ms. Douce 114, Horstmann 326-27; also see Smart 12). See ll 99-100n.

87-90. Taken from Suso. After describing three modes of studying and teaching holy doctrine (the "fleshleye," the "bestelye," and the "spirituele and gostlye"), Everlasting Wisdom instructs her disciple as follows: "Mye dere sone, wille þou noht sauere in kunynge to hye, but drede! here me nowe and I schalle teche þe þinges þat beþ profitable to þe: I schalle ȝive þe a chosene ȝifte, for myne doctryne schalle be þi lyfe. Wherefore takynge owr biginnynge of helefulle disciplyne as þe drede of godde, þe wheche is þe beginnynge of wisdam, I schalle teche þe be order VII poyntes of mye loue, wherinne stant souerene wisdam and þe perfeccion of alle gode and rihtwis lyuynge in þis worlde" (Ms. Douce 114, Horstmann 328). The idea that wisdom originates in the fear of God and subsists in the love of God is crucial to the play, which concludes with an appeal to the *doctryne of Wysdom* (l. 1162), a doctrine grounded in love and obedience. Wisdom stresses an epistemological distinction between "sapientia," identified with the intuitive and loving knowledge of God and self, and other more loveless forms of knowledge, called *cunnynge* (l. 87), and associated with "science" (Horstmann 327) which may turn one away from God. Such a concept underlies the characterization of Lucifer in this play. See Ecclesiasticus 19.18-23 for a description of the difference between "sapientia timor Dei" (the "wisdom [which is] the fear of the Lord") and "nequitia et in ipsa execratio . . . Est solertia certa, et ipsa iniqua" ("cleverness which is abominable . . . scrupulous but unjust"). For the idea that wisdom begins in the fear of God, cf. Proverbs 9.10 and 15.33 (where "Timor Domini," or "the fear of the Lord" is called the "disciplina sapientiae," the "instruction of Wisdom") and Ecclesiasticus 1.14 and 19.18-21 (where "timor Dei," the "fear of God," is called "omnis Sapientia," "all wisdom" and contrasted to the "nequitiae disciplina," the "instruction of iniquity," which "non est sapientia," — "is not wisdom.)" The 1947 Roman edition of the Vulgate places these verses beneath a heading entitled "de vera et falsa sapientia," ("concerning true and false wisdom"). The idea that the discipline of studies connected with "scientia" as a form of ungodly or "false learning" is central to the thematic thrust of *Wisdom*, though the link of "nequitia" with "scientia" does not have biblical sanction.

In Isaiah 11.2 "spiritus scientiae et pietatis" ("the spirit of knowledge and piety") connotes goodness; see l. 4n.   See also Eccles 204n. For Mind's later declaration that he will *dysdeyn all oncunnynge*, see 580n; see also ll. 86n, 87-90n, 341-72n, 1154-63, and 1162n.

87. cunnyngys: "logical skills."   The plural is from D; M reads "cunnynge." The OE verb "cunnan" and ME "cunnen" gave rise to the noun "cunnyng" as the equivalent to the L "scientia," or "knowledge," especially that gained through observation or derived from logical skills, as opposed to "sapientia," or wisdom.   Since the fourteenth century the Latin-derived term has been primary. The implication is that having asked Wisdom to teach her the "schools" of his divinity, Anima receives the answer that she should avoid the "schools" or forms of erudite learning in favor of the fear of God and obedience to His will. See ll. 86n, 99-100n, and 156n.

91-92. wedys of synne . . . sowll sprynge: The metaphor of the body as a garden is used also in the Digby *Mary Magdalene*, ll. 1081-83 (Baker et al. 60). *Mary Magdalene* is bound with the partial copy of *Wisdom* in Bodleian Ms. Digby 133. In Shakespeare's *Othello*, Iago — a character who like Lucifer in *Wisdom* exemplifies the demonic wickedness of loveless cunning — plays on this metaphor in his encounter with Roderigo: "Our bodies are our gardens, to the which our wills are gardeners . . . " (I.iii.323-24).

91. flee: The image of weeds *fleeing* initially seems inappropriate to the gardening metaphor. See, for contrast, *Mary Magdalene* in which "þe fowle wedys" are "reynd [plucked] vp be þe rote!" (ll. 1081, 1083 Baker et al 160).   However, by hinting at exorcism, the mixed metaphor in *Wisdom* has a peculiar kind of appropriateness. In both *Wisdom* and *Mary Magdalene*, small devils are actually driven out from under the skirts of a sinning woman.

95-98.   Smart associates these lines with the work which Migne entitles *Meditationes Piissimae de Cognitione Humanae Conditionis* commonly attributed to St. Bernard of Clairvaux, though probably not by him: "Per cognitionem mei valeam pervenire ad cogitationem Dei. Quanto namque in cognitione mei proficio, tanto ad cognitionem Dei accedo" ("Through knowledge of myself, I come to the healthful knowledge of God," Migne 184: 485 [in references to Migne, the numbers, as in 485 here, refer to columns, of which there are two numbered on each page; there are no page numbers]; qtd. by Smart 29; each of these quotations here and subsequently has been verified and in each case capitalization and translation are mine; punctuation is from Migne). Additionally, Smart cites Walter Hilton's *Scala Perfectionis* 1: 40 as a secondary source: "And by the knowyng [of thyn owne soule] to come to the ghostly knowynge of God" (qtd. by Smart 23; in all the Hilton passages, punctuation is mine; for a modern transcription see also Underhill 93). Also see Eccles' citation of Hilton, 1: 40, in which Augustine is quoted as saying "By the knowing of myself, I shall get the knowing of God" (Eccles 204n). These lines continue the theme of intuitive self-knowledge as the key to knowing God.

96. sowle sensyble: "the soul as endowed with the faculty of sensation as well as cognition."

99-100. Anima here maintains the image of herself as a student. See l. 86n.

101. represent here: In a distancing device, Anima acknowledges the theatrical representation of her role. Allegorical drama like *Wisdom* depends in part on the explicit acknowledgment of the dramatic fiction; see ll. 16n, 84n, and 1163n.

102. Wat ys a sowll, will 3e declare?: Of the six major characters in the play, Anima — the only woman — is the one who does not present an expository statement defining her own personality. Instead, in a naive posture, she asks Wisdom to define her identity as a soul. The five masculine characters — Wisdom, Mind, Will, Understanding, and Lucifer — all have self-defining speeches. In *The Castle of Perseverance* and *Mankind*, the other Macro plays, the characters who represent general humanity (Humanum Genus and Mankind) — both masculine — do have self-defining expository monologues. The gender distinction seems clear in this case.

103-70. Smart identifies Hilton's *Scale of Perfection* 2: 1, 2, 6, 13, 12, 31, 9, 26, and 1: 12 as the source of these lines (Smart 18-22; specific passages qtd. in notes below).

104. And not only ymage but hys lyknes ʒe are: Taken from Hilton 2: 1: "For thy soule & my soule and every resonable soule is an ymage, and that a worthy ymage for it is the ymage of God as þe apostle sayth 'Vir est ymago dei'; That is to saye, a man is the ymage of God and made to the ymage and to the lyknes of hym . . . . " (qtd. by Smart 18; also see Underhill 225). See I. Corinthians 11.7 for the reference to the "apostle" Paul ctd. by Hilton: "Man is the image . . . of God." This passage makes specific distinctions between man, who represents the "image and glory" of God, and woman, who "is the glory of man." By representing the feminine Anima as the Soul, cast in the "image of God," the play does *not* confirm this gender distinction.

Cf. Genesis 1.26 for a description of God's creating Adam "in" his "image" "after" his "likeness." In the play there is apparently a distinction between "image" and "likeness," terms which recur throughout. "Image" appears to signify the similarity to God which is permanent and cannot be lost, in contrast to "likeness," which can be effaced through misdeeds. See Hill. Clifford Davidson discusses the importance of "image" and "image theology" in *Wisdom*, noting that St. John of Damascus distinguished between "image" and "likeness" as follows: "Man is created in the image of God. This image is given to him in his spirit and free will. But the image must be revealed in likeness and this is accomplished in freedom and then in the gift of the self in love" (qtd. in Davidson 93). Countering Hill, Bevington argues that in I. 140 the play does pick up from Walter Hilton the idea that the "image" of God may be defaced into an "image of sin"; see Bevington 1986 36-37n; also see I. 140n. See II. 35n, 103, 128, 142, 175, 188n, 214n, 274, 373n, 536, 918n, 1114, and 1131.

105-06. Taken from Hilton: "This ymage made to þe ymage of God in þe fyrst shapyng was wonderly fayre & bryghtful of brennyng love and ghostly lyght, but thorough synne of the fyrst man Adam it was dysfygured and forshapen into another lyknes" (2: 1; quoted by Smart 19; see also Underhill 226). See I. 140n.

108. Wy of þe fyrst man bye we þe vyolence?: "Why do we suffer the consequences of the actions of Adam, the first man?" The term *bye* here is an aphetic variation of *abye*, meaning to suffer the consequences or pay the legal price, a term which still exists in an archaic form in Modern English *abye*.

109-17. Loosely taken from Hilton: "Now it is sooth mankynde, that was hole in Adam the fyrste man, trespassed agaynste God so wonder grevously whan it forfeyted þe specyal byddynge of hym and assented to the false counsayle of the fende that it deserved ryghtfully for to have be departed fro hym and dampned to helle withouten ende . . . . A soule of a chylde that is borne and is uncrystenyd, by cause of orygynal synne hath no lyckenesse of God. He is nought but an ymage of the fende & a brond of helle" (2: 2, 6, qtd. by Smart 19; see also Underhill 223, 243).

110. Was in natur of the fyrst man Adam: "Was present in the essential being of the first man," thus sharing Adam's fallen condition.

111. synne orygynall: That sin which humanity inherited from Adam and Eve, in opposition to *actuall* sin (l. 1112). See ll. 1110-12n.

119-24. Taken from Hilton: "So fer forth that stondynge the ryghtwysnes of god it myght not be foryeven but yf amendes were fyrste made and full satysfaccyon therfore . . . . [No one but Christ could make these amends and he only by taking on man's nature.] Then syth that our lorde Jhesu God & man deyed thus for salvacyon of mannes soule, it is ryghtful that syn sholde be foryeven & mannes soule that was his ymage sholde now be reformed & restored to the fyrst lyknes & to the blysse of heven" (2: 2, qtd. by Smart 19; see also Underhill 228, 231).

119. grace: The favor of a patron — in this case God — which puts one in good standing. This passage suggests that God's *grace*, the gift which makes redemption possible, was forfeited by original sin, to be restored through the God's second gift of *grace*, granted through the Passion of his son. This term recurs throughout the play. Understood theologically, *Grace* is the gift of God making redemption possible; see ll. 119, 172, 203, 223, 317, 524, 893, 946, 1072, 1078,

1138, 1146, 1160; the term also connotes worldly patronage; see ll. 575, 579; for *gracys*, pl., marks of God's favor, see 1028. See ll. 203n, 550n, 723n.

126-30. Taken from Hilton who explains that "Two manner of sins make a soul lose the shape and likeness of God. That one is called original, that is the first sin. That other is called actual, that is wilfully done sin . . . . [T]wo remedies are there against these two sins" (Underhill 243). "One is þe sacramente of baptym ayenste orygynal synne; another is the sacrament of pennaunce ayenst actuel synne . . . . But as soone as [the soule] is crystened it is refourmed to the ymage of God and thorugh the vertue of fayth of holy chyrche sodeynly it is tourned fro the lyckenesse of þe fende & made lyke an angel of heven" (2: 6, qtd. by Smart 19; see also Underhill 243). See ll. llln and 1110-12n.

126. baptem: From D; M reads *bapten*, not a recognized variant of "baptism." The M *n* differs from his *m* by virtue of an upward sweeping loop on *n*; thus, this letter is unlikely to be simply a carelessly incomplete *m*. But the D *m* and *n* differ only in the addition of a final minim to the *m*, and M may have misread in his haste.

132. hys plesant see: That is, the soul is the "seat, throne, or dwelling place" of Christ. The term "see," which implies the dwelling-place of a monarch or of God, continues the metaphor of liveried feudal allegiance carried throughout the play; cf. *The Castle of Perseverance*, where Avarice invited Humanum Genus to "Sit up ryht here in þis se" (l. 834); see also ll. 544-45n.

133. aungell: M reads *a aungell*; D reads *angell*. As in ll. 268 and 328, M adds the indefinite article before a general noun, slightly changing the sense of the phrase. "Angel of light" literally translates Lucifer's name and gives him the singular distinction of his pre-lapsarian attribute of "light," which is the attribute claimed by Wisdom (l. 28).

134. he hathe hys very knowynge: Note that the soul is here referred to as masculine, despite Anima's feminine representation in the play. See also ll. 120, 133-34, 289, 1124 and ll. 17-20n, 79n, and 1103n.

135-40. Taken from Hilton — "For thou shalt understonde that a soule hath two partyes. That one is called sensualyte & that is flesshly felynge by the fyve outwarde wyttes, the which is comon to man & to beest. Of the whiche sensualyte, whan it is unskylfully and unordynatly ruled, is made the ymage of synne . . . whan it is not ruled after reason, for thenne is the sensualyte synne" (2: 13, qtd. by Smart 20; punctuation and indication of omission mine; see also Underhill 272).

135. sensualyte: Eccles defines as "the part of the soul concerned with the senses" and cites Rolle *Psalter* 23, Lydgate, *Reson and Sensuallyte: The assembly of Gods, Mary Magdalene* (where a messenger to Mundus calls himself "Sensuality," l. 394), and Medwall *Nature* (where Sensualyte is a character), along with Hilton (Eccles 205n). See ll. 139, 154, 156n, 295-300n, 478n and 1070.

140. ymage of synne: This phrase, taken from Walter Hilton, challenges Hill's assumption that the "image" of God remains fixed in human reason even when the more vulnerable "likeness" to God is effaced. According to the play, *sensualyte*, or that portion of the soul associated with the senses, may be transformed into an *ymage* of sin, thus effacing the *lyknes* to God by sinful action. Thus, humankind has a choice of *images*. The image of God is implanted in human reason, but through original sin, the human also contains the potential image of foulness. One may actualize the image of God — i.e., approach God through the image implanted in "right reason" — only through faith, love, and obedience, which create a likeness to God. One who does not nourish the image of God must by default develop the *ymage of synne.* See ll. 104n, 142n, 175n.

141-48. Taken from Hilton — "That other partye is called reason & that is departed in two: In the over partye & in þe nether. The over partye is lyckened to a man for it sholde by mayster and sovereyne and that is propyrly the ymage of god. For by that only the soule knowyth god and lovyth hym. And the neyther is lyckened to a woman, for it sholde be buxum to the over partye of reyson, as woman is buxum to man, and that lyeth in knowynge and rulynge of erthly thynges; for to use hem dyscretly after nede, and for to refuse hem whan it is no nede" (2: 13, qtd. by Smart 20).

According to Augustinian doctrine, human reason provides the one direct human link with the divine. Following Hilton, the dramatist identifies reason as *propyrly* the *ymage of God* because it is the vehicle through which one both knows and loves God. However, though the play follows Hilton's further distinction between the *over partye* and the *neyther partye* of reason, the dramatist omits the gender implications of this distinction. To Hilton, the *over partye* is essentially masculine (*lyckened to a man*), and it is precisely the prerogative of masculine authority as *mayster and sovereyne* that *is propyrly the ymage of God*, in contrast to the *neyther parte* of reason, which represents *woman* in her obedience. The dramatist does accept the idea that the higher part of reason leads to knowledge of God, with the *neyther parte* given to knowing *dyscretly / all erthely thyngys* (ll. 145-46). However, with the soul shown as feminine and both Mind (the higher part of reason) and Understanding (the lower part) as masculine, the play omits this gender differentiation between the higher and lower faculties of reason.

141. That: From D; M reads *þe*, but Hilton's "That other partye" supports "that."

147. myghtys bodely: See ll. 1073-77n.

149-50. Thes tweyn do syngyfye / Yowr dysgysynge & yowr aray: Wisdom points to Anima's black mantle and white robe. The distinction between *dysgysynge* and *aray* is central to the play; a *dysgysynge* represents a costume that covers or "disguises" the *aray*, i.e., the livery that defines fealty relationships or social/spiritual allegiances as a relationship of patronage. Anima's *dysgysygne*, her black mantle, hides her *aray*, the white cloth-of-gold robe that allies her symbolically with Christ. As the early name for English masques, *dysgysynge* implies a form of drama as well as modishly new-fangled clothing. (For further discussion of these terms, see Riggio 1989 232-33). CUL Ms. Hh.1.11 contains a sermon that moralizes clothing in a way that recalls the contrast between "disguise" and "array" in the play: "Eueri man & woman temporal & spiritual . . . wil ordeyn for him self clene & honest vesture & clothyng rather þan other ferial dayes of less disguise querfore it semyth us þat be religious persones to be arayed wyth honest clothis pure & semynge wyth all vertuous examplix & quat þei schul be & schal shewe to 3olk" (fols. 130-31). See ll. 324sd, 510n, 551n, 590, 609-11n, 692sdn, and 752sdn.

151-68. Taken from Hilton: "Fayr is mannes soule & fowle is a mannes soule. Fayr in as moche as it is refourmed in fayth toi þe lyckenes of god. But it is foule in as moche as it is medlyd with flesshly felynges & unskylfull styrynges of the [foule] ymage of syn; foule without as it were a beest, fayre within lyke to an angel; foule in felyng of the sensualyte fayre in trouth of the reason; foule for the flesshly appetyte; fayre for the good wyl. Thus fayre & thus foule is a chosen soule, sayenge holy wrytte thus: 'Nigra sum sed formose filie Jerusalem sicut tabernacula cedar et sicut pellis salomonis.' That is, I am blacke but I am fayre & shaply as þe doughter of Jherusalem as þe tabernacles of cedar as the skynne of salomon. That is, þe angels of heven that arne doughters of the hye Jerusalem wonder not on me ne dyspyse me not for my blacke shadowe. For though I be blacke without by cause of my flesshly kynde, as is a tabernacle of cedar, nevertheles I am ful fayre within as the skynne of salomon" (2: 12; qtd. by Smart 20-21; see also Underhill 267-68). See also T. Hoccleve, *Moralization of the Story of Jonathas*: "Right so of the soule, which is in bittirnesse for the wroght offense and synne. wher-of it is seid in the figure and likenesse of the soule: 'Blake y am, but y am fair,' þat is to seyn, blake in body, and fair in soule" (1: 241; qtd. by Smart 21n). See ll. 169-70n.

152. Euery sowll here: Referring to audience. In a manner typical of the morality, the frame of the play opens to include the audience as members of the community of sinning humans represented by Anima. See ll. 488n, 582-89n, 997-1064n, and 1159-63n.

156. infenyt: "infinite," a variation of D *infinite*. Christ once more urges Anima to listen to "true reason," derived from God. The opposition here is not between true and false reason but between the urging of "sensuality," which stirs one to sin, and of "true reason." See also ll. 87n and 135n.

159. a angell: The indefinite article *a*, rather than *an*, is not un-common before a vowel; D prefers *an*; see also l. 333.

162. v prudent vyrgyns: These virgins represent the *v wyttys of my sowll wythinne*, i.e., five inner or spiritual wits. These inwits were thought by some medieval writers to parallel the five outer wits, or physical senses, to create a total of ten wits, which were sometimes identified with the five wise and five foolish virgins in the parable of *Matthew* 25.1-13. In the *Lay Folks' Catechism*, the five inwits were identified as "Wyl. Resoun. Mynd. ymaginacioun. and thogth" (Simmons and Nolloth, qtd. by Smart 42; see Smart for a description of the "ten wits"). These *vyrgyns* wear clothing that identifies them symbolically with Anima: white skirts and mantles, gilded wigs and chaplets. However, as spiritual wits, they do not wear the black mantle of sin, even though they do share the taint of original sin and though she later confesses to sinning in her inner as well as outer faculties; see ll. 1073-77n.

164sd. Nigra sum sed formosa, filia Jerusalem, sicut tabernacula cedar et sicut pelles Salomonis: "I am dark but beautiful, daughters of Jerusalem, like the tents of Kedar and like the skin of Solomon" (*Jerusalem* is *ierusalem* in both M and D; source: Song of Songs, 1.4 and Hilton, *The Scale of Perfection*). From the Song of Songs: "Nigra sum, sed formose, filiae Jerusalem,/sicut tabernacula Cedar, sicut pelles Salomonis" ("I am very dark but comely, O daughters of Jerusalem, like the tents of Kedar, like the curtains of Solomon"). The daughters of Jerusalem are here linked to the five *prudent vyrgyns* of l. 162. By her association with the daughters of Jerusalem, Anima is subtly identified with the figure of Ecclesia, the bride of Christ, often associated with the Woman clothed with the Sun (cf. Apocalypse 12.1-2). Herradis of Landsberg, *Hortus Deliciarum*, Strasbourg: Lib., Bib. de la Villa, fol 225r, contains an illustration of the Song of Songs, 2.15, in which Christ leads a crowned Ecclesia, followed by three daughters of Jerusalem. (See Harrad ed. R. Green pl. 127. This reference was provided by Adelaide Bennet of the Princeton Index of Christian Art.) *Nigra sum . . .* is the first of four chants signifying the state of grace for Anima and her five wits and her Mights. These chants, which involve both processional movement and music, have a stately rhythm that contrasts to the raucous three-part music and the riotous masque dances in the state of sin. For other processions, see ll. 324sd, 996sd, and 1064sd.

169-70. Quod fusca sum, nolite considerare me, / Quia decolarauit me sol Jouis. "Because I am dark, do not look at me, since the sun of Jove has discolored me" (source: Song of Songs 1.5: "Nolite me considerare quod fusca sim, Quia decolarauit me sol" ["Do not gaze at me because I am swarthy, because the sun has scorched me."] *Wisdom* adds *Jouis*). The maiden who speaks in the Song of Songs apologizes for her swarthy color, contrasting her dark exterior to her internal beauty. The dramatist uses the costume of Anima, with its black outer mantle and white inner robe, as an emblem for this contrast between inner beauty and outer blackness. See for comparison Shakespearean sonnets 127, 130 and 131 where Shakespeare plays with the idea of blackness as a term of beauty: "In the old age black was not counted fair, / Or if it were, it bore not beauty's name" (Sonnet 127, ll. 1-2). See also *Titus Andronicus*, IV.ii. *Othello*, a play which in several respects bears comparison with *Wisdom*, affirms the distinction between a black exterior and a fair or virtuous inner self. Referring to Othello's nature, Desdemona says: "I saw Othello's visage in his mind" (I.iii.255); the Duke of Venice says: "If virtue no delighted beauty lack / Your son-in-law is far more fair than black." (I.iii.292-3). In a reference to the scorching sun (one theme of the Song of Songs passage), Desdemona attributes Othello's steadiness of character to his complexion: "I think the sun where he was born / Drew all such humours from him" (III.iv.28-9). See 151-68n, 164sdn.

172. by: An early variant of "be." D reads *be*; see also ll. 287, 304, and 1094.

173. quinque prudentes: "five prudent ones," referring to the five *prudent vyrgyns*. This exhortation to keep their *wyttys five* clean implies a connection between these five feminine inwits and the three masculine "Mights," or faculties of the soul. See ll. 162n, 177n.

175. Ye Godys ymage *n*euer xall ryve: "You shall never rip out the image of God [from your soul]." Both M and D have *euer*. Previous editors, including both Eccles and Baker have assumed this term to be an error for *never*, glossing *ryve* as "tear out [of the soul]." This is the most likely reading, and I have accepted it. However, D's error may have been followed by M partly because of another possible reading for the term *ryve* as an aphetic for the verb *arrive*. The aphetic *ryve* is ordinarily intransitive, signifying *arrive [at]* and used with a preposition, obviously not the meaning implied here. Though otherwise unrecorded, *ryve* could signify the verb *arrive* in its transitive meaning of: "to come to a position or state of mind, to obtain or achieve, as the result of continuous effort" (see *OED* sv. *arrive*, v.^{2}). The sense of this line would then be that the soul that keeps itself clean shall "always achieve the image of God," since the soul is God's *see* or *resting place*. A modernization of l. 175 that preserves the rhyme scheme might be: "God's image in you shall be perpetually alive." Though this reading is an attractive one, the absence of other recorded transitive instances of the aphetic verb *ryve* favors the emendation. See ll. 104n, 140n, 142n, 538n.

177-90. Smart identifies one source for this passage in the pseudo-Bernardian *Meditationes*. These Meditations were published in an English translation by Wynkyn de Worde in 1496 as *The Medytacyens of Saynt Bernarde* (*Minor Poems of the Vernon Ms.*, 2: 511-22; ctd. by Smart 28). Smart cites the Latin original as closer to the play than the translation: "Secundum interiorem hominem tria in mente mea invenio, per quae Deum recolo, conspicio, et concupisco. Sunt autem haec tria, memoria, intelligentia, voluntas sive amor. Per memoriam reminiscor; per intelligentiam intueor; per voluntatem amplector. Cum Dei reminiscor, in memoria mea eum invenio, et in ea, de eo et in eo delector . . . " ("Close to the inner man I find a trinity in my mind through which I recall, know, and desire God. Moreover, these three are memory, intelligence, will or love. Through memory I recall; through intelligence I know; through will I embrace. When I recall God, I find him in my memory, and in that, from him and in him I delight . . . " Migne 184: 485; qtd. by Smart 29; translation mine).

The three *myghtys* or faculties of the soul correspond to Augustine's three-part division into "memoria," "intelligentia," and "voluntas" (cf. *De Trinitate*, 10: 10-12; 15: 21-3; ctd. by Smart 43; see also Eccles 205n). The three "Mights" in the play are Mind, Understanding, and Will. Cf. Hilton: "The soule of a man is a lyf made of thre myghtes, mynde reason & wyl, to the ymage & the lyknes of the blessyd trynyte" (1: 43; qtd. by Smart 24; see also Underhill 100). In the play, Hilton's "reason," corresponding to "ratio" or "intelligentia," becomes Understanding, a translation which echoes writers like Thomas Aquinas and Albertus Magnus, who follow Augustine in naming the second faculty "intelligentia" or its equivalent "intellectus." As in Hilton, the Mights in the play correspond to the Trinity, with Mind allied to God, Understanding with Christ, and Will linked to the holy ghost; see ll. 279-87.

181. 3e thre declare þan thys: Like Wisdom, each of the three "Mights" has a speech in which he defines his own nature. Only Anima does not have an expository, self-defining monologue. Such speeches are characteristic of morality drama; cf. *The Castle of Perseverance*, ll. 157-339, 359-649. In *Castle*, God's monologue is delayed until the end of the play, whereas *Wisdom* begins with Christ describing his own nature. See ll. 1-16.

182. Yowr syngyfycacyon & yowr propyrte: *Syngyfycacyon* implies the full symbolical meaning of the personified character — i.e., what the character *signifies*; *propyrte* refers to the exclusive attribute of each of the Mights. J. J. Molloy explains these terms as follows: "*Signification, property*, and *reason* . . . are technical expressions in the allegorical terminology of Physiologus, the Bestiaries and Lapidaries. The *signification* is the outward sign, arbitrary in use and depending upon the concept allegorized; the *property* or *reason* (*raison d'etre*) is the specific quality emanating from the very nature. *Signification* answers the question: 'What do you represent?' *Property* answers the question: 'What does that do?'" (Molloy 35n).

183-276. In these lines the Mights explicate their *syngnyfycayon* and their *propyrte* (l. 182), i.e., they explain their own significance theologically as attributes of the soul. This section has its counterpart in the world of sin, where each Might agrees to *tell hys condycyons howe*. See ll. 630-52.

183-212. In this passage Mind explicates his own nature. The full passage contains many self-referential comments on the human mind. The import is that although the human mind is created in the image of God, on its own it is a weak and feeble, unstable creation. Contemplating oneself alone, thus, leads to a sense of inadequacy bordering on despair: *Myselff ryght nought than I confes* (l. 201). But using the Mind to contemplate God reminds one of the image of God implanted in the mind and leads, through self-contemplation, to a renewed faith. Thus, the Mind is led to wisdom, defined as humility and obedient devotion to God.

184. The veray fygure of þe deyte: "The truly represented image of God." The term *fygure* derives from the Old French verb, *fingere*, meaning "to mold or form" and it signifies the represented form of God as imprinted in the human. The Mind is the *veray* — or "true" — *fygure* of God, for the human mind bears an imprint of the divine and through the Mind one has access to God. However, the Will — as the faculty of choice which reflects the imprint of the divine will — is also identified as the *fygure* of God, with the exhortation to keep this *fygure* fair in order to retain the likeness to God with which a human is supposed to be born. Of the three Mights, only Understanding, the lower part of reason connected directly with the created world, is not a *fygure* of God. See ll. 211, 214, 241-42, 349 and 359.

188. lyknes: See ll. 35n, 104n, 214n, 274, and 1131. For an inversion of this term, implying a likeness to the devil, see l. 373n; also see ll. 912sd, 1114.

190. Wat grates I ough to God ageyn: "What gratitude I owe to God in return [for the nobility and freedom he has created in me (especially through the power of my mind and its likeness to God) and most of all for the eternal bliss which I will inherit because of God's creation]."

199. vnstabylnesse: From D. M reads *sustabullnes*. A loop from the *y* of *yeers* in the line above (l. 198) has intersected the initial *v* of this word in D, making it appear to a quick reading to look like *s*. Since *u* and *n* are virtually indistinguishable, M has misread the *vn-* as *su-* and mistranscribed the term as a meaningless word *sustabullnes*. Baker and Furnivall read this word correctly in D, whereas Eccles assumed the D term to be *sustabylnesse*. See Introduction: "The Relationship Between the Digby and the Macro Texts" for more information.

193. my: See l. 83n, 385, and 690.

200. fallyngys: "failings." From D. M reads *fallynge*, but the sense of the line "My horrible failings and frailness" supports the plural. In place of *oreble* in this same line, D has the more recognizable *horrible*. For other plural nouns which M transcribes as singular, see ll. 87 and 434.

203. specyall grace: The grace of God necessary for redemption. Such grace is regarded as a gift offered to undeserving humanity, who could never merit redemption. *Grace* is one of the terms in this play which has both a theological and political significance. To be "standing" in *grace* means to be within the favor either of God or of a temporal sovereign. This idea, later Calvinist, is in this context Augustinian. See also ll. 946 and 1138; for references to God's *grace* without the adjective *specyall*, see ll. 119n, 172, 223, 317, 524n, 893, 1072n, 1078, 1146, and 1160; as a term signifying worldly favor, endowed through patronage, see ll. 575n, 579n, and 723n; for *euell grace*, or bad standing which results from choosing an evil patron, see l. 550n.

206. creature: "creator," cited by the *MED* and *OED* as a variant of *creator*. Cf. "Þar-wit com our creature / For to spek wit that traiture" (*Cursor Mundi* 1119; ca. 1300) or "Prayse be to our lorde God my creature" (Berners *The Boke of duke Huon of Burdeux* 436; ca. 1533).

211. fygure: See ll. 184n, 214n, 241-42n, 349-50n, and 359.

212. ow: "ought" or "are bound by duty [to perform]."

213-44. In this passage Will explicates his own nature. Just as Mind attributes his own best qualities to God, Will identifies the source of human will in the divine attribute, i.e., he talks of himself as grounded in God's *wyll*. Here Will appears to speak out of turn, since elsewhere in the play he is the third Might in the speaking order. This speech is unusually difficult to gloss and to translate. Part of the difficulty is the potential confusion of the personified noun *Wyll* as the name of a character, the common noun *wyll* as the human attribute, and the modal verb of the same spelling which recurs throughout. More seriously, the theological argument here leads to convoluted phrases. See ll. 269-74n, 551-716n, 961-68n.

213-18. Smart identifies the source of these lines as the *Tractatus de Interiori Domo, seu de Conscientia Aedificanda*, ascribed at times to St. Bernard and Hugo of St. Victor: "Nam inter omnia Dei dona, quae ad salutem hominis spectare videntur, primum et principale bonum, bona voluntas esse cognosciture, per quam imago similitudinis Dei in nobis reparatur . . . . Quidquid homo facit, bonum esse non potest, nisi ex bona voluntate procedat. Sine bona voluntate omnino salvari quispiam non potest: cum bona voluntate nemo perire potest . . . . Quantum crescit voluntas tua bona, tantum crescit meritum tuum. Fac igiture magnam bonam voluntatem tuam, si vis habere magnum meritum" ("For among all the gifts of God, that which is seen to offer most health and is the principal good, is known as good will, through which the image of the likeness of God is offered to us . . . . Whatever man does, he is not able to be good unless it precedes from good will. Without good will one is not able to be saved; with good will noone is able to perish . . . . By how much your good will grows, by so much your merit increases. Therefore make your good will powerful if you would have great merit" Migne 184: 511; qtd. by Smart 32-33; translation mine).

214. lyknes & fygure: Like Mind, Will identifies the human will as both the *likeness* and the *figure* of God. See ll. 214-220 and ll. 104n, 184n; also see ll. 35n, 103, 128, 142, 175, 188n, 211, 274, 349, 359, and 537-38n. For references of *lyknes* to the devil, see 373n, 912sd, and 1114.

214-20. The idea that sustaining the human likeness to God depends finally on the power of the human will is explained, for example, in a passage in CUL Ms. Dd.14.26, which transcribes a portion of a dialogue once thought to be between Augustine and St. Bernard: "A very clene crysten sowle is full fayre and lyke to ymage of god. Now yf þou couette to know how it standys wythe þi sowle & wheþer it be lyke to þe ymage of god or non þou mayst vausafe þi nowue consciens and loke what þi wylle is for in þat standys alle." See ll. 961-69n.

215. Wyt: "With." Ordinarily, M abbreviates this word as *w*. Three times he expands the abbreviation: twice as *wyt* (here and in l. 975) and once as *wyth* (l. 863). This text follows Eccles and Bevington in expanding the abbreviation as the more familiar *wyth*, though the two to one scribal choice would give slight preference to *wyt*, a choice that would seem to be supported by M's general tendency toward "t" rather than "th" as a verbal ending in words like *fallyt* where D has *fallith* (l. 11), *takyt* for D *takith* (l. 57), *mekyt* for D's *mekith* (l. 85), or *stondyt* for D *standith* (l. 220).

215, 216. goode wyll: Will as the faculty of human choice, fixed on God. See also ll. 231n, 237, and 999. The phrase *goode wyll* is later used ironically; see l. 468n.

spyll: "destroy one's own soul by breaking moral laws."

220-21. For in wyll only stondyt mannys dede / Wyll for dede oft ys take: "For in the will only does human action exist; Will is often taken for the deed," i.e., unwilled human inclination is not sinful. Only in the power of the will lies human accountability; thus, the will to perform an action is often taken for the action itself. The vocabulary has both a legal and a theological ring to it. Cf. "For in the doom of god þe wylle stondeþ for deed and so seyeþ holy wrytte which may not be untrewe þat every good wylle ys accepted as for deede" (*A Sentence to them that be in Temptation*, Ms. Harley 1706, fol. 127; qtd. by Smart 44). Cf. also "Bone voluntas sufficit, si desit operacionis facultas" ("Good will is sufficient if the faculty of charity gives over [to it]"; Augustine, qtd. in *Speculum Christiani* 213); *The Alphabet of Tales*, "Voluntas pro facto reputatur" ("Will for deed is taken" EETS 127: 520); and Margary Kempe, "I receyue euery good wyl as for dede" (212, 339-40; all qtd. by Eccles 206n). See ll. 301-04n.

224. anosyde: "harmed" or "injured." The idea is that the soul can gain grace if it is not harmed by sin. The modern translation "If with sin it is not out-nosed" maintains the rhyme scheme but slightly changes the meaning, to suggest that grace can be pushed out, rather than harmed, by sin.

225. apposyde: "examined" — in the scholastic sense, as derived from Latin *opponere*, "to oppose or argue against." The modern translation "opposed" does not capture the full implication of this term, but deriving from the Latin root *opponere*, the verb "oppose" does mean to "fortify against," hence the implication that Will must be well-fortified against sin before acting on his inclinations. The reference, of course, is once more to Will as the faculty of action, though before acting on its own impulses, the human will must be schooled by reason. A smoother translation, which would vary the meaning even more, might read "Therefore, the Will must be well exposed." See ll. 220-21n and 301-04n.

226. consent: From D; M reads *cosent*. This is the first direct reference in the play to the three-step psychological process of temptation (suggestion, delight, and consent) which underlies the fall from and restoration to grace in the drama. In this process, Will is considered the faculty of *consent* upon whom action for good or ill depends. See ll. 301-04n and 957-76n.

227. lybrary of reson: "the collected learning of reason." Initially, this idea of learning as the key to "good will" seems at odds with Wisdom's earlier advice to Anima to eschew *cunnynge*, or erudite knowledge (l. 87). However, the *lybrary of reson* does not imply erudite knowledge. The phrase instead links the *consent* of Will to the intuitive knowing of God associated with Mind as the higher faculty of reason. Mind's informed judgment leads Will, as the faculty with the power to make choices for the soul, rightly to choose God's law. See also "We xal lerne 3ow þe lyberary of oure Lordys lawe lyght" (N-Town "Presentation of Mary" in Spector 1: 92 — 9/252; qtd. by Eccles 206n at 9/234); see ll. 220-21n, 225n, and 301-04n.

228. take entent: "fix the purpose of the will." The modern translation "And after his judgments to take intent" means literally to fix the purpose of the will to follow the *domys*, or judgments, of reason, represented by Mind, the highest faculty or Might of the Soul.

231. Taken from Hilton's *Scale of Perfection*: "The knyttynge & þe fastynge of Jhesu to a mannes soule is by good wyl" (1: 12; qtd. by Eccles 206n; see Underhill 25).

233. Off hym cummyth all wyll sett perfyghtly: "From God comes all human will that is made firm through spiritual discipline." In this sentence *wyll* is a noun, not a verb. The modern translation "From him comes all power of the will set perfectly" is designed to make clear that the human will is intended by the noun *wyll*.

238-241. "Then this good will, mentioned before, is useful to each creature if he is firmly resolved himself to restore the soul that he has taken spiritual care of." See *cure* in glossary.

241-42. þe fygure: For the second and third time in this speech, Will stresses the idea of the soul as the *fygure* of God, an association also made by Mind; see ll. 184n, 211, 214n, 349-50n, and 359.

245-76. In this passage Understanding explicates his own nature. Like Will before him, he appears to speak out of order, since he is usually the second on the ritual order in which the Mights speak throughout most of the play. Unlike Mind and Will, however, both of whom concentrate on the divine emanations of "mind" and "will," Understanding does not locate his own nature in the divine attribute of "understanding" implied by his name. Instead, in keeping with his identity as the "lower" of the two faculties of reason, Understanding focuses on seeing God through the created world and through knowledge of himself as one of the creatures in that world. See, for instance, *In creaturys hys werkys ben most wonderfully* (l. 257). See 551-716n.

251. How xulde I holly hym: "How should I worship him"; "hallow" (as in "hallowed be thy name") is the modern reflex of the verb *holly*, which means "to hallow, reverence, or worship."

253. I know in angelys he ys desyderable: "I know that to angels he is desirable" *in* has the meaning of "to," but with the implication also of a desire "within" the angels; see also l. 551.

245-64. In this division of the soul, "understanding" is equivalent to "intelligentia," that faculty of the soul through which one is presumed to understand God by understanding his manifestation in angels, saints, and other creatures. The source for these lines is the

Meditationes formerly attributed to Bernard: "Intelligentia intueor quid sit Deus in se ipso; quid in Angelis, quid in sanctis, quid in creaturis, quid in hominibus. In se ipso est incomprehensibilis, quia principium et finis: principium sine principio, finis sine fine. Ex me intelligo quam incomprehensibilis sit Deus; quoniam me ipsum intelligere non possum, quem ipse fecit. In Angelis est desiderabilis, quia in eum desiderant prospicere: in sanctis est delectabilis, quia in eo assidue felices laetantur: in creaturis est admirabilis, quia omnia potenter creat, sapienter gubernat, benigne dispensat; in hominibus est amabilis, quia eorum Deus est, et ipsi sunt populus eius. Ipse in eis habitat tanquam in templo suo, et ipsi sunt templum ejus: non dedignatur singulos, neque universos. Quisquis ejus meminit, eumque intelligit ac diligit, cum illo est. (2) Diligere cum debemus, quoniam ipse prior dilexit nos, et ad imaginem et similitudinem suam nos fecit . . . . Beata anima, apud quam Deus requiem invenit, et in cujus tabernaculo requiescit."

("Intelligence comprehends what God is in himself; what in his angels, what in the saints, what in creatures, what in men. In himself he is not comprehensible, both as beginning and ending: beginning without beginning, ending without ending. Then God is unintelligible to my intellect; since I am not able to comprehend him myself, he himself has created that by which [we can know him]: in angels he is desirable, since they desire to look on him; in saints he is pleasurable, since in him the happy rejoice eagerly; in creatures he is admirable, since he creates all through his power, since God is over them and they are his people. He lives in them as if in his own temple and they are his temple: neither the individual nor the universe is disdained. Whoever remembers him and knows him and loves him, he is with him. We ought to love him, since he first loved us, and he made us in his own image and likeness . . . Blessed soul, with whom God comes to rest, and in whose temple he remains" Migne 184: 485-86; qtd. by Smart 29-30).

The *Wisdom* passage is taken loosely from the *Meditationes*, with some direct translation, as, for instance, *In hymselff begynnyng wythowt begynnyng / Ande ende wythowt ende* (ll. 247-48) from *principium sine principio, finis sine fine*; some additions, as, for instance, *. . . þat xall neuer mys* (l. 248), added for rhyme; or the repeated terms *souerenly* (ll. 254, 259) and *souereyn* (l. 261), which echo the theme of Christ's sovereignty; and some virtually literal transcription, as *in angelys he ys desyderable* (l. 253), from *in Angelis est desiderabilis*; see ll. 177-90n.

247-48. In hymselff begynnyng wythowt begynnyng / Ande ende wythowt ende: Cf. Revelation 1.8 "Ego sum Alpha et Omega, principium et finis."

256. thei: From D; M apparently mistakes D's "i" and transcribes as *per.* See ll. 414n, 584, and 697n.

259-60. By his wysdom gouernyde . . . / And be hys benygnyte inspyryt all soullys: "governed by his wisdom and all souls inspired by his benignity." This construction is from D, from which *his* (l. 259) and *by* (l. 260) are taken. The M lines read "governed by wisdom . . . and his benignity inspires all souls." M has replaced D's *inspired*, clearly a past participle, with the more ambiguous *inspyryt*, which could either be the past participle or the third person present tense of the verb "inspires" with "benignity" as its subject. Either construction is satsifactory, but as the prior text D has more authority in neutral cases such as this.   And there is some consistency in Christ's distancing himself from the "wisdom" of God, which he represents, by clearly attributing wisdom as an attribute to God himself.   Such theatrical distancing is characteristic of the play throughout the theological argument.

265. make reporture: "take note."   The noun *reporture* implies a report or account.   Because *reporture* is obsolete, this phrase is difficult to translate without sacrificing the rhyme scheme.   The modernization avoids this difficulty by altering the term *sure* in l. 264 to *pure*, as follows: "In whom he dwells as in his temple pure. / When this knowledge I comprehend for sure . . . ."

265-74. Not in the *Meditationes*, though Smart connects this passage with the following quotations: "Diligere eum debemus, quoniam ise prior dilexit nos"; and "Quisquis ejus meminit, eumque intelligit ac diligit, cum illo est" (translated ll. 254-64n above; qtd. by Smart 30-31).   See also I John 4.16: "Et nos cognovimus, et credidimus charitati quam habet Deus in nobis. Deus charitas est, et qui manet in charitate, in Deo manet, et Deus in eo" ("And we know and believe the charity which God has in us. God is charity, and he who remains in charity, he remains in God and God in him," also qtd. by Smart 31). Like Will, Understanding speaks out of his normal turn. As the lower faculty of reason, he is subordinate to and linked with Mind, whom he ordinarily follows as the second of the Mights. He is tempted by Lucifer immediately after Mind; in the speeches that define the new personalities of the three Mights in their life of sin, Understanding (renamed Perjury) speaks second (ll. 637-44); his retinue presents the second dance (ll. 717-35); and in the hierarchy within which the Mights are restored to grace, Understanding places second (ll. 933-40). In addition to appearing out of the expected order, Understanding associates himself with charity, thus assuming a connection with a virtue more closely identified with Will, who would normally speak third (see ll. 287, 1133, 1134). The connection between Understanding and charity is probably intended as a foil to Understanding (Perjury)'s association with covetousness as a vice. See ll. 531, 601n, 743-44.

270-72. For Gode ys charyte as awtors tell . . . in hym dwellys: Cf. I John 4.16: "Deus caritas est, et qui manet in caritate, in Deo manet, et Deus in eo" ("God is love, and he who abides in love abides in God, and God abides in him"). See l. 1134n.

270. telles: From D; M reads *tell*. M apparently attempts to "correct" the person of D's verb and in the process loses the rhyme. But using what appears to be a singular verb with a plural subject was not uncommon until the practice became obsolete in the eighteenth century. The use of "es"/"ys" for plural verbs was probably influenced by the fact that the verbal ending "-s" as a plural form spread from Northern English southward in both colloquial and, more occasionally, literary language (see Visser 71-72). The unusual plural *telles* is a "lectio difficilior" ("difficult reading") in comparison to the more common form *tell*, to which M changes this word. The difficult reading weighs as evidence for D's priority as a text (see Maas 13 and Introduction: "Comparison between the Digby and Macro Manuscripts" in this volume); see also l. 722.

**275-76. Blessyde ys þat sowll þat þis speche spellys: / Et qui
creauit me, requiuit in tabernaculo meo**: "Blessed is that soul that
comprehends this saying: And he who created me took rest in me as
a tabernacle" (source: Ecclesiasticus 24.12). Cf. the *Meditationes*:
"Beata quae dicere potest: *Et qui creavit me, requievit in tabernaculo
meo*" ("Blessed is he who is able to say: And he who created me
rests in me as a tabernacle," Migne 184: 486; qtd. by Smart 30, w.
italics from Migne; ctd. by Eccles 206n). *Spellys* in this context means
"comprehends, especially through careful study or observation."

277-82. Taken from the *Meditationes*: "Mens imago Dei est, in qua
sunt haec tria id est memoria, intelligentia, et voluntas . . . . Per
memoriam Patri similes sumus, per intelligentiam Filio, per voluntatem
Spiritui sancto. Nihil in nobis tam simile Spiritui sancto est, quam
voluntas vel amor sive dilectio, quae excellentior voluntas est. Dilectio
namque donum Dei est, ita quod nullum hoc dono Dei est
excellentius. Dilectio namque quae ex Deo est, et Deus est, proprie
Spiritus sanctus dicitur, per quam charitas Dei diffusa est in cordibus
nostris *Rom* v,5, per quam tota Trinitas in nobis habitat" ("The mind
is the image of God, in which there are three parts: that is, memory,
intelligence, and will . . . . Through memory we are like the Father,
through intelligence the son, through will the holy spirit. Nothing in us
is so like the holy spirit as the will or love if not loving delight, which
is the more excellent will. For delight is a gift of God, such that
nothing is more excellent than this gift of God. For delight which is
from God and is God, the holy spirit is said to breath forth, through
whom charity is spread throughout our heart [Romans 5.5] through
whom an entire Trinity lives in us" (Migne 184: 487; qtd. by Smart 30,
with additions from Migne). Note that Mind appears in place of
Memory in the list of faculties in *Wisdom*. And, again, it is worth
noting that in the play this speech, in which charity is identified with
"voluntas" or "will" has been given to Understanding, the allegorical
equivalent of "intelligentiam" rather than "voluntas" in the passage
above. Note, however, that the *Meditationes* connect "dilectio," or
"delight," with the will and in the three-part temptation to sin which the
play dramatizes "dilectio" is the temptation for Understanding, not for
Will (who has the function of "consent"), thus creating another
rationale for the alteration in order of speeches and Understanding's
link to "charity" here in this speech. See ll. 301-04n.

284. symylytude: "likeness." The clean soul's likeness to God lies in its resemblance to the trinity; the three mights in one mind are like the three gods in one god.

285-88. The identities established here carry throughout the play. Mind is identified with *feythe* in the Father; Understanding is identified with *hoppe* in the son Jesus; and Will is linked through *charyte* with the holy ghost. In his just completed monologue, Understanding has linked himself with charity (ll. 269-74; see ll. 265-74n and 277-82n), but from this point on in the play, that virtue is associated primarily with Will (Cf. I Corinthians 13.13; ctd. by Eccles 206n). See also the homily *How Man's Soule is Made to þe Ymage & þe Lyknes of þe Holi Trinite*: "Be ye refourmede wiþ virtewes. þe mynde wiþ belefe. þe reson wiþ hope. and þe wylle wiþ charite. And so ye bene lyche to þe holy trinite" (Ms. Harley 2373, fol. 12b; qtd. by Smart 44). See ll. 1133-34n.

289. Thys: An obsolete variant of *Thus*; see also ll. 812, 817, 839. D has *thus*.

293-94. Traditionally, the three enemies of humankind were identified as the world, the flesh, and the devil. See the pseudo-Bernardian *Meditationes* (Migne 184: 503; ctd. by Eccles 185n).

295-300. Yowr fywe wyttys . . . fre domynacyon: "See that you spare your five wits from [the World, the Flesh, and the Devil], so that they will not let the sensual part of your soul influence your mind. No thing should offend God in any way, and if [the world, the flesh, and the devil] do [tempt you sensually], see that the lower part of reason in no way thereto inclines; then the higher part [of reason] shall have free domination." This passage is difficult. The general sense is that in order to save your five senses from harm, you must protect them against the three temptors (the world, the flesh, and the devil). Otherwise, your sentient self will lead you astray. Nothing you do because of sensuality should offend God, and if your senses should err, make sure that the lower part of your reason (in this scheme, the understanding) does not assent to that error. If you thus protect your understanding from sensual enslavement, you give the higher part of reason free control.

296. brynge to mynde: From D. M reads *brynge not yow byhynde*. This passage is difficult, and it may be that M could not make sense of it. The force of D is to suggest that the five wits (or senses) must be protected against the temptations of the world, the flesh, and the devil. If so tempted, they may try to influence the mind through the senses. This reading is somewhat awkward, but it is preferable to M, which forces one to read *sensualyte* as an indirect object in order to make sense of the line; see note below.

sensualyte: "the sentient part of the soul" (the direct object of the verb *brynge*). For the sake of rhythmic efficiency the modernization has used this term in its more modern sense of "sensuality." A more literal reading of the entire line would be: "so that they [the three temptors] do not bring the sensual portion of the soul to influence the mind." The M *brynge yow not byhynde* requires that one read *sensualyte* as an indirect object of the verb (a reading for which there is no grammatical justification in the line) as follows: "so that they do not mislead you through the sentient part of the soul."

298. þer: an obsolete form of *þey*, meaning "they," which like the earlier *þey* (l. 296) refers to *The Worlde, þe Flesh, & þe Fende* (l. 295). "And if they [the temptors] do, see that the lower part of reason . . . ." The D *ther* could easily be read *thei*. The secretary "r" resembles "i." M persistently has trouble reading the D "i." At line 256 he misread *thei* as *ther*. It was in part the difficulty of distinguishing this letter that led to the addition of the curved tail descending below the line on "i," resulting in the development of the letter "j." See "Editorial Principles." Also see l. 256, 414n, 584, and 697.

þe nether parte of resone: The lower part of reason, here associated with Understanding. See ll. 141-48n and 483-84n.

300. þe ouerparte: The higher part of reason, associated with Mind. Notice that Mind is assumed to have authority over Understanding. See ll. 141-48n, 483-84n, and 1130n.

301-04. The psychology of sin in this play is derived from the medieval tradition which had accreted around the "three temptations" or "three lusts" of I John 2.15-16: "Nolite diligere mundum, neque ea quae in mundo sunt. Si quis diligit mundum, non est charitas Patris in eo, quoniam omne quod est in mundo, concupiscentia carnis est, et concupiscentia oculorum, et superbia vitae; quae non est ex Patre, sed ex mundo est" ("Love not the world, neither the things that are in the world. If any man love the world, the love of the Father is not in him. For all that is in the world, the lust of the flesh, and the lust of the eyes, and the pride of life, is not of the Father but is of the world"). The basic issue in this medieval anatomy of sin is one that persists in modern ethical philosophy: when does one become responsible for one's thoughts and desires? In medieval terms, the question is: when does attraction to the temptations of the world become sin? One of the most typical medieval answers was that found in the Augustinian psychology of sin. Linking the three temptations of I John to the seduction of Adam and Eve in Genesis, Augustine developed a formula for sinning: "suggestion" leads to "delight," which must be confirmed by "consent." Note that the key to this process lies in volitional *consent*. Neither the initial response to suggestions of sin nor unwilled delight in such suggestions is sinful. Sin lies only in consent. For Augustine consenting to sin is a rational act, performed when reason consents to the suggestions put forward by the flesh. (See Augustine, *De sermone Domini in monte secundum Matthaeum*, 1: 12; ctd. by Howard 56). Chaucer follows the Augustinian formula in the *Parson's Tale*: "There may ye seen that deedly synne hath first suggestioun of the feend . . . and afterward the delit of the flesh . . . and after that the concentynge of resoun" (ll. 331 ff; qtd. by Smart 56). Instead of identifying reason as the faculty of consent, St. Bernard identified the *will* as the agent of the soul consenting to sin: "Est Trinitas creatrix, Pater et Filius et Spiritus sanctus, ex qua cecidit creata trinitas, memoria, ratio, et voluntas. Et est trinitas per quam cecidit, videlicet per suggestionem, delectationem, consensum" ("The creating Trinity, the Father and Son and Holy Spirit, from which the created trinity emerges forth, memory, reason, and will. And it is a trinity through whom one falls, that is through suggestion, delectation, and consent" *Sermones de Diversis*, Migne 183: 669; qtd. by Smart 45; translation is as usual mine). The play follows the latter order. The Mind receives the suggestion; Understanding takes delight in the suggestion; but the final affirmation of sin lies in the consent of human will rather than the consent of the rational mind. However, Augustine had at other times identified the human will as the faculty of action or choice. And distinguishing between "the superior reason, the inferior reason, the practical reason, and conscience," Thomas Aquinas created a much more complex formula for consenting to sin, in which finally the will is " 'impregnated' with reason" (qtd. by Howard 64). For allusions to *Will* as the agency of choice see, for instance, ll. 220-21n; also see ll. 226n, 365n, 445n, 497-99n, and 957-76n.

307. Fyght & 3e xall haue þe crown of glory: Cf. *Mankind*, l. 231: "Yf 3e wyll be crownyde, 3e must nedys fyght." See also I Timothy 6.12; I Peter 5.4; and James 1.12, for partial biblical parallels (ctd. by Eccles 206n). See ll. 1115-16n.

309. bound: "bound [by fealty allegiance]." This is the first of several formal statements of allegiance, in which Anima and her Mights are first "bound" to Christ as his vassals with the Mights then pledging their allegiance (and thus, indirectly, Anima's) to Lucifer. See ll. 381-392n, 495n, 497-99n, and 513-15n.

310-23. The topos of God's benefits to man was a popular one. According to Smart, this particular passage has been translated from Bonaventura's *Soliloquium de Quator Mentalibus Exercitiis*: " . . . quantum ego infelix & misera . . . deberem Deum meum, qui me creavit cum non eram, redemit cum perieram, & de multis periculis liberavit me, quando errabam reduxit me, quando ignorabam docuit me, quando peccabam corripuit me, quando constristabar consolatus est me, quando steti tenuit me, quando cecidi erexit me, quando iui duxit me, quando veni suscepit me. Haec & multi alia fecit mihi erit semper loqui, semper cogitare, semper gratias agere, utinam pro omnibus beneficiis suis possem eum laudare & amare" (translated in text; Antwerp 1616 88; qtd. by Smart 33). The Bonaventura passage was taken from Hugh of St. Victor's *De Arrha Animae*: "Et saepe cum mihi consumptus videbar, subito liberasti me; quando peccabam, corripuisti me; quando tristabar, consolatus es me; quando desperabam, confortasti me; quando cedidi, erexisti me; quando steti, tenuisti me; quando ivi duxisti me; quando veni, suscepisti me" ("And often when I saw myself totally destroyed, you suddenly freed me; when I sinned, you took hold of me; when I was sad, you consoled me; when I despaired, you comforted me; when I fell, you raised me; when I stood, you held me; when I was erring, you led me; when I came, you received me" Migne 176: 968; qtd. by Smart 34; translation mine). Lines 310-20 of the play closely follow Bonaventura, with the following additions: *thus gloryus*, l. 310; *Christus*, l. 312; *Jhesus*, l. 313; *by ruthe*, l. 316; *in grace . . . at tyde*, l. 317; *myghtyly*, l. 318; *wyll*, l. 319; *most louyngly*, l. 320. Lines 321-23 do not closely follow Bonaventura, though ll. 322-23 allude to the "beneficiis" and the "laudare" of Bonaventura.

313. reducyde: "led back [to virtue]," a literal translation of the Latin *reduxit* of Bonaventura.

319. wyll: "astray." This adverb, now only Scots dialectal, derives from an ON term meaning "astray" (see glossary). Cf. *Cursor Mundi* "Quen I was wil and out of rest, / Godli ye tok me to rest" (23091) and the Towneley "Judgment" play: "When I was will and weriest, / Ye harberd me full esely" (30/624-25; I wish to thank Martin Stevens for access to this and subsequent Towneley cycle quotations from the forthcoming EETS Towneley text; citations are to play no./line nos.; see Cawley & Stevens and see *Medieval Renaissance Drama Society Newsletter*, ed. Milla C. Riggio, Fall 1994, for a chart comparing line numbers in the Stevens/Cawley edition with the earlier England/Pollard 1897 EETS edition). In the Towneley play this phrase is spoken by Christ as part of his conventional listing of the Corporal Works of Mercy; Christ says that the good souls gave him refuge when he was "astray and most weary." Here, *wyll* (meaning literally rather than spiritually astray) harkens back to Christ's description of himself as a "hospes" ("stranger") in, for instance, Matthew 25.35.

321. oyll of mercy: Not mentioned in Bonaventura, the story of the "oil of mercy" developed apocryphally. In the apocryphal narrative, the oil was associated with baptism and thought to have been brought by Christ. The story is reported as follows in the apocryphal Gospel of Nicodemus: "And when father Adam that was first created heard this, even that Jesus was baptized in Jordan, he cried out to Seth his son saying: declare unto thy sons the patriarchs and the prophets all that thou didst hear from Michael the archangel, when I sent thee unto the gates of paradise that thou mightest entreat God to send thee his angel to give thee the oil of the tree of mercy to anoint my body when

I was sick. Then Seth drew near unto the holy patriarchs and prophets, and said: When I, Seth, was praying at the gates of paradise, behold Michael the angel of the Lord appeared unto me, saying: I am sent unto thee from the Lord; it is I that am set over the body of man. And I say unto thee, Seth, vex not thyself with tears, praying and entreating for the oil of the tree of mercy, that thou mayest anoint thy father Adam for the pain of his body: for thou wilt not be able to receive it save in the last days and times, save when five thousand and five hundred years are accomplished: then shall the most beloved Son of God come upon the earth to raise up the body of Adam and the bodies of the dead, and he shall come and be baptized in Jordan. And when he is come forth of the water of Jordan, then shall he anoint with the oil of mercy all that believe in him, and that oil of mercy shall be unto all generations of them that shall be born of water and of the Holy Ghost, unto life eternal" (James 1955 126-27; see also *Vita Adae et Evae* and *Cursor Mundi*, 1237ff; see Quinn; ctd. by Eccles 207n).

324. thi: From D; M reads *p*ᵘ. Throughout the passage from ll. 310-21, M has transcribed D *thu* (ll. 310, 311, 312, 313, 314, 315, 316, 317, 318, and 319) as *p*ᵘ. At the beginning of l. 321, M copies D *Thu* as *Thu*; in l. 322 he copies D *Thy* as *Thy*. Then in l. 324, with a characteristic carelessness, M transcribes D *thi*, a word which to a quick glance may resemble *thu*, with the familiar abbreviation *p*ᵘ, which he has just used ten times. The preferable reading is D.

324sd. tota pulcra es: Taken from Song of Songs 4.7,11: "Tota pulcra es, amica mea et macula non est in te . . . . Favus distillans labia tua" ("You are all fair, my love; there is no flaw in you . . . Your lips distill nectar"). As quoted by Legg, this antiphon continues with verses taken in an unacknowledged and out of order sequence from the Song of Songs 4.10; 2.11-13; 2.10; 4.8: "odor unguentorum tuorum super omnia aromata iam enim hiems transiit imber abiit et recessit flores apparuerunt vineae florentes odorem dederunt et uox turturis audita est in terra nostra surge propera amica mea veni de libano veni coronaberis" ("And the fragrance of your oils [is better] than any spice. For lo, the winter is past, the rain is over and gone. The flowers appear on the earth; *flowering, they give off fragrance* and the voice of the turtledove is heard in the earth. Arise my love

my fair one and come away from Lebanon, *you will be crowned*"
(italicized phrases additions to translation; see Legg 173; spelling in
Latin passages above normalized to modern Vulgate text, but
punctuation follows Legg; in the Vulgate *odorem dederunt* appears as
dederunt odorem, 2.13; also ctd. by Eccles 207n). These verses are
used as an antiphon for the procession on Trinity Sunday. The music
for this chant may be found in the *Liber Usalis*.

wyght cloth of golde, chevelered & crestyde in sute: The three
Mights are dressed as liveried retainers of Anima. Like Anima, they
wear Wisdom's white cloth of gold and wigs (see 0sd and 16sd).
They are *crestyde in sute*, i.e. wearing crests that identify them with
Anima's "suit" or livery; see ll. 16sdn.

At this point between stage directions, Eccles establishes Scene II.

**Lucyfer in a dewyllys aray wythowt & wythin as a prowde
galonte**: Lucifer appears wearing a devil's costume over the clothing
of a proud gallant. The inner and outer garments parallel the inner
and outer clothing of Anima — the black mantle worn over her white
cloth of gold — with the significant difference that the devil's inner
costume signifies a false rather than a true identity. The primary
reason for wearing the devil's garment over the gallant's costume is
probably to facilitate the costume change in line 380sd. The "gallant"
was typically a pretentious wastrel, whose fine clothing signified his
vanity and pride (see Davenport). For example, Lydgate refers to
"gallantes, dise-pleyers and hasardours" (*Dietary*, qtd. by Davenport
112). The "gallant" particularly symbolizes the decadence of culture
in the fifteenth century, often as associated with the sin of pride and,
thus, with Lucifer. See, for instance, *A Treatise of a Galaunt*: "For in
thys name Galaunt ye may se expresse seuyn lettres for som cause
in especiall, Aftyr the seuyn dedly synnes full of cusydnesse, that
maketh mankynde vnto the deuyll thrall. Was not pryde cause of
Lucyferes fall? Pryde ys now in hell, and Galaunt nygheth nere. All
England shall wayle that eure came he here" (qtd. by Davenport 115).
Davenport points to Barclay's *The Ship of Fools* for a characterization
of the gallant "as symbolic of the world and of man in the world as he
is displayed in the morality plays" (116). Parallels in drama may be
found in characterizations of "New Gyse" and "Nowadays" in *Mankind*;

in the costume of Pride disguised as a gallant named Curiosity in *Mary Magdalene* (496-505); in the Prologue (spoken by Satan) to N-Town play no. 26, often referred to as the opening sequence in N-Town Passion Play I (Spector 1991 I: 248; 26/65-124) and in Medwall's *Fulgens and Lucrece* (Nelson 1/53-56). See Davenport 119, 114, and 118; see also Eccles 207n and Smart 46. The N-Town prologue intriguingly calls to mind *Wisdom*'s renaming of the Mights. The N-Town Satan says that he will give the deadly sins "newe namys, and wyl 3e se why? / For synne is so plesaunt to ech mannys intent. / 3e xal kalle pride 'oneste,' and 'naturall kend' lechory, / And covetyse 'wysdam' there tresure is present" (26/109-12). Stephen Spector has dated Satan's "gallant's" costume between the mid-1460s and about the 1480s, tentatively toward the end of that period. Though the specific clothing styles (e.g., long-spiked shoes and stomachers) Spector uses for dating the N-Town Satan are not specified as part of Lucifer's costume in *Wisdom*, the date Spector has chosen accords well with the probable date of *Wisdom*, which could easily have been written in the 1480s (*Commentary* on N-Town play no. 26, ll. 65-108 in Spector 1991 2: 490-91; I am grateful to Stephen Spector for providing this reference before the publication of his edition). For the ritualized establishment of the new identities of the Mights in *Wisdom*, see ll. 551-760. Note in particular the claim that the *grace* coming from pride gives *curryous eloquens* (l. 579) to Mind (Maintenance), the proclamation of the popularity of *galontys* as *curtely personys* ("courtly persons" ll. 598-99), and the identification of the *ryche couetyse* with *wysdom* (ll. 601-04).

325. At this point the verse pattern changes from Wisdom's eight-line stanza (ababbcbc) to Lucifer's six-line stanza pattern with its shorter lines, more frequent rhymes, and tail-rhyming lines (aaab cccb). These lines, which though they vary in length tend toward eight syllables, contrast with Wisdom's ten to twelve-syllabled lines.

Owt, harow: Thus Lucifer cries in the York cycle 1/97; Satan in York, 30/159; 37/185, 343; devils in the Towneley, Chester, and N-Town cycles, as, for instance, Towneley, 25/98-99: "Sich harow was neuer hard in hell. / Out, Rybald! thou rores"; and "Out, harro, out!". See also N-Town 23/187: "Out! Out! Harrow! Alas! Alas!" (Spector 1991 1: 219). See also the Digby *Mary Magdalen*, l. 722, for the Rex

Deabolus's cry "A! Owt, owt, and harrow" (l. 722) and the devil's cry "Owt, Owt, harrow! I may cry and yelle" (l. 963). (Also see Eccles 207n and Smart 47.)

328. God hath mad man: D has *mad e man*; M copies as *mad a man* (but see l. 268 where M also copies D *made man* as *mad a man*). For a similar reference to the creation of man as an attempt to restore Lucifer's place, see the York cycle 7/23-24 (ctd. by Eccles 207n). For a similar idea, see also the Towneley cycle, 1/261-67, "The ioy that we haue lost for ay, / God has maide man with his hend, / To haue that blis withoutten end, / The ix ordre to fulfill / That after vs left; sich is his will. / And now ar thay in Paradise; / Bot thens thay shall, if we be wise."

332-72. As a parallel to the expository, self-defining monologues of Christ as Wisdom (see ll. 1-16) and of the three Mights (see ll. 183-276), Lucifer defines his own character while outlining his strategy in a declamatory soliloquy.

333. a angell: Cf. l. 159n.

338. whan: M & D — obsolete form of *whom*.

dyspyght: Cf. *Mary Magdalen*, where Satan says: "For at hem [Mannis sowle] I haue dysspyte" (l. 366; also ctd. by Eccles 207n).

341-72. Here Lucifer assumes his character as Anti-Wisdom. That is, just as Christ embodies true Wisdom, Lucifer represents its opposite, worldly knowledge, grounded in loveless *cunnynge*, against which Wisdom warned Anima (see ll. 87-90n). This opposition between true and false knowledge — i.e., between Christ as Wisdom and Lucifer as *wyly . . . knowynge*, is sustained throughout this soliloquy. In his plan to seduce humanity, Lucifer reiterates much of what Wisdom has already said; he describes the Soul in terms which recall those of Wisdom, and he repeats the three-part formula for temptation — suggestion, delectation, and consent — against which Wisdom has already warned the Mights. This parallel emphasizes the focused and specific antithesis which Lucifer presents to Christ in this play. See ll. 349-50n, 357-59n, 363-64n, and 365-67n.

343-45. Smart compares these lines to *The Remedy against the Troubles of Temptations*, attributed to Richard Rolle: "Leo the pope sayth: 'The fende our ghostly enemy aspyeth in euery man what wyse he is dysposed by his compleccyon / and by that disposicyon he tempteth hym'" (Rolle, 2: xliii, qtd. by Smart 49; ctd. by Eccles 207n). A similar idea occurs in William Bond's *Consolatory* printed with Hilton's *Scala Perfectionis*, a source text for *Wisdom*, in Brit. Mus. C.21.b.15: "The enemy when he wold deceyve man / he fyrst consyderyth of what complexion he is.   And so applyeth his ordynaunce & layeth sege to manes soule / where he fyndeth hym most weke. and appte to receyve his suggestions" (n.p.; qtd. by Smart 50).

349-50. fygure . . . symylytude: "figure . . . likeness." By echoing God's description of the three Mights, Lucifer establishes his identity as the antithesis of Wisdom. In these lines, he recalls descriptions of humanity as the *fygure* or *symylytude* of God.   See ll. 184n, 211, 214n, 241-42n, and 284n; see also 341-72n. and 359.

357. In þe soul ben iii partyes, iwys: See ll. 177-78 for Wisdom's introduction of the three Mights: *Thre myghtys euery Cresten sowll has.* Again, Lucifer establishes his credentials by echoing Wisdom; see ll. 341-72n.

359. fygure of þe godhede: Lucifer's remark echoes Wisdom's reference to the three as *applyede to þe Trinyte* (l. 178).

360. þe flesche: By suggesting that he will tempt the flesh, Lucifer follows the Augustinian order of temptation. See ll. 301-04n.

363-64. Again, Lucifer repeats information already provided by Christ. See ll. 226, 290-292, and 341-72n; also see ll. 301-04n.

365-67. suggestyun . . . dylectacyon . . . confyrmacyon: Again, Lucifer echoes Wisdom, who has warned the three Mights against the three-part process of temptation, in which Lucifer makes a suggestion to Mind, offers delectation (or delight) to Understanding, and asks Will for confirmation (or consent). See ll. 301-04n and 341-72n; see ll. 400-99 for the temptation, which follows this formula.

369. That dede xall sew of damnacyon: "That deed shall result in damnation." *Dede* is from D; M reads *dethe*. But Will is persistently associated with "deeds," and Lucifer has just alluded to the "confirmation" of the will as the damning act. *Dede* is superior.

371. this examynacyon: "this interrogation." *This* comes from D; M has *hys*. Either term is defensible. Anima as the soul has elsewhere been identified with a masculine pronoun and her Mights are clearly masculine; see ll. 17-20n, 79n, 120, 133-34, 289, 1103n, and 1124. But within the logic of the play, Lucifer is "examining" or falsely teaching three characters not one. Thus, D's term is perhaps preferable. By identifying himself as the "examiner" of the Mights, Lucifer echoes Wisdom's role of teacher, but more obviously he initiates his plan of putting Humankind on trial. See ll. 86n, 99-100n, 227n, 428n, 445n, 482n, and 539-41n.

373. lyknes: One of the key terms in the play, which functions to identify human "likeness" to good or evil in terms of personal identification with God or the devil. By distinguishing between his own essence as devil and his physical appearance, which may be like or unlike his true self, Lucifer here alters the meaning of this term, which has referred to humanity's *lyknes* to God. For other instances of the term or its variants as referring to the devil, see 538, 912sd, and 1114. For references to the human *lyknes* to God, see ll. 35n, 104n, 128, 188n, 214n, 274, and 536. For a discussion of the term, see l. 104n.

377. Sen I xall schew hym perfyghtnes: "I shall prove to him that perfection is sin." *Sen* is a variant of D *syn*, meaning "sin." Within the contemplative framework of the play, "perfection" derives from the contemplation of God. By using sophistical methods of argument, Lucifer aims to "prove" that perfection itself is sinful. The reference is as deeply ironic as the intention is diabolical. See references to *perfeccyon*, ll. 553n, 1161n.

379. wndyr colors: "under false colors" or "pretenses," with emphasis also on the rhetorical tricks Lucifer will play in applying his sophistry. Using a phrase which implies both "coloring" the truth and taking a false legal plea, Lucifer establishes a link between false logic and corrupt legal maneuvering. Throughout, the play interweaves theology with law, particularly in the interlude of sin where distortions of justice in the courts are prime examples of sinfulness. Such legal misdealing is associated most consistently with Understanding (under his new name of Perjury), though also with Mind (known as Maintenance). Both manipulate the law on behalf of Will (renamed Sensuality, Lechery, or Gentle Fornication), who desires to trick the husband of his lover. See ll. 547n, 717-44, 747, 756, and 785-96.

380sd. galont: See l. 324sdn.

381-92. Mind, Will, and Understanding adopt Lucifer's verse pattern (aaab cccb, with shorter eight-syllabled lines in contrast to their earlier use of Wisdom's verse (ordinarily ababbcbc) with its longer lines and more stately patterns of rhyme). The shift in verse pattern indicates that Lucifer has already exerted influence on the three Mights, though he is as yet unseen by them. In these short, quasi-satirical speeches (apparently affirming piety but ironically linking the Mights with the devil), each of the Mights alludes to his own particular character. Each affirms his allegiance to Wisdom in one of the quasi-legal fealty declarations, but through the parodic form of the verse, each actually defines his vulnerability to the manipulations of Lucifer. See ll. 495n, 497-99n, 513-15n, 527-34n, 551-716n, 551-73n, 574-96n, and 626-52n.

383-84. Mind talks in terms of his *purpos* to pursue Christ's *doctrine*. As the *overparte* of reason, for instance, he is the most theoretical and purely intellectual of the Mights, one who would be concerned with doctrinal questions. See ll. 87-92 and l. 1162n.

385. My: D reads *Myn*; see l. 83n.

386. feyth: "faith." Ordinarily associated with Mind; see ll. 285 and 1118.

387. Hys laws to pursew: As the lower part of reason, identified with the created world, with law and justice, and later with covetousness, or the pursuit of the world, Understanding pledges himself to follow God's "laws."

388. swetter to me: Understanding also emphasizes the sensual nature of his responses, thus foreshadowing his role as the one who delights (or has *delectacyon*) in the temptations of sin.   Such a characterization is also in keeping with his personality as the *nether* part of reason, which is identified with the senses. See ll. 145, 298, 483.

391. Yeldynge vnto hym laude & glory: As the faculty of consent, associated with the Holy Ghost and identified with passion, Will promises to praise God, rather than to engage in any intellectual activity.

392. For hys goodnes: As the third Might of the soul, Will — the faculty of consent — is associated with charity. He here reflects that association in his willingness to praise God for *hys goodnes*. There is nothing specifically satirical about Will's praise in these lines, except the perfunctory nature of his prayer, which results from his adoption of Lucifer's verse form and contrasts greatly to the complicated syntax of his earlier self-expository praise of God (ll. 213 - 44). See ll. 287, 1133-34.

393. fonnyde fathers: "foolish fathers."   By calling the Mights "fathers," Lucifer appears to address them as clerics.   However, Molloy argued that "the apellations of 'father' and 'ser' are . . . titles used for other persons as well [as those in the religious state and the diocesan clergy]; for example there was a custom at Cambridge of addressing the M.A.'s as 'fathers' on certain occasions" (77). Johnston echoed this argument by pointing out that the term "fathers" could be used equally to address "serious secular magnates" (1986 95). Though this is true, the term does not occur in isolation. It is part of a larger argument which Lucifer makes against the contemplative life in his effort to lure the Mights into the world. Whatever the disposition of the entire play toward the value of the contemplative life, in this section there is little doubt that the Mights are treated as cloistered contemplatives.   For an interpretive explanation of this characterization, see l. 431-40n and 553n.

394. Vt quid hic statis tota die ociosi: "And why do you stand here idle all day?" (source: Matthew 20.6) In Matthew Christ asks this question in the parable of the vineyard. By thus associating the life of contemplation with the idleness of those who try but cannot gain work, Lucifer begins his "proof" that virtue is actually wickedness (see ll. 377-78). In the process of making his arguments, Lucifer also subverts the teachings of Walter Hilton. See, for instance, *the Scale of Perfection*, 2: 20, where the refusal to perform acts of penitence is defined as "idleness of fleshlihood" (Watkins 296). See also Wyclif, *On the Council of London*, 1382, in which Benedictine monks are advised not to live lazily, but instead to work with their hands; or, *An Apology for Lollard Doctrines*, attributed to Wyclif (Wyclif ed. Wright 258-59; ed. Todd 106; ctd. by Smart 51).

395. perisshe: "perish." D *pisshe*. D apparently omits the abbreviation for *per*, misled by *pisshe*, an early variant of *piss*, M copies the error and transcribes the word as *pyse*. For another instance of *perish*, see l. 410. A possible but unlikely reading assumes the accuracy of "piss" in both texts, with Lucifer suggesting to the three "fathers" that they will *piss* before they *aspye* ("spy" or understand) the reason for their idleness. Understood figuratively, *piss*, as in "piss away money," could imply that they *will piss [away the day] before they see it*, — before they recognize how they might use it on the devil's business).

or 3e yt asype: "before you know it." The modernization has added the idea of "glory" for the sake of the rhyme, with the implication that the Mights will perish before they attain the end toward which their "idleness" aims.

397. Mynde, Mynde: In keeping with the ritual of seduction, Lucifer begins his temptation by making a suggestion to Mind, who asserts his own position that *He ys not ydyll þat wyth Gode ys*, l. 398.

399. prowe: Lucifer keeps up the fiction of his role as teacher or examiner, an obvious parody of the role of Christ as teacher, with emphasis on the "proof" of Lucifer's premise. For the passage in which Anima asks Christ to *teche me þe scolys of yowr dyvynyte* as her teacher, see ll. 86-178. One major difference in the teaching styles of Christ and Lucifer is Lucifer's emphasis on "proof," a form of logic that belongs to the intellectual world of *cunnynge*, which Christ asks Anima to disdain (l. 87). Christ in contrast puts emphasis on revealed knowledge, gained only from conforming the human will to that of God. For another instance of this same term, see 539-41n; also see ll. 371n, 428n, 445n, and 482n.

yis: "yes." From D; M reads *thys*. Either term would be satisfactory. However, this may be one of the instances in which M reads D in light of his own scribal practices. D distinguishes between "y" and "þ," whereas M does not. But in this instance, M chooses to transcribe the D *yis*, a term which to D can only read "yis" but which in M's text might read either "yis" or "this" with the more explicit *thys*; see l. 69n.

400. suggestyun: See ll. 301-04n.

401-03. Probably taken from Walter Hilton's *Epistle on Vita Mixta*: "And I halde þat hit is good to þe for to vse þis maner in what deuocion þat þou be, þat þou hange not longe þer-vpon, ouþur forto putte from þe þi mete, or þi slepe in tyme, or forto sese any oþur man vnskilfuli, Omnia tempus habent: Al þing haþ tyme" (ch. 27, qtd. by Smart 26). Margaret Beaufort, the mother of Henry VII, had this epistle printed as Book III of Hilton's *Scale of Perfection* by Wynkyn de Worde in 1594 with the following heading: "Here begynneth the table of the thyrde booke of Walter Hylton named Vita Mixta or Scala Perfecciones" (Westminster 1494; *RSTC* 14042). Beaufort, a lay ascetic, appeared to hold the *Vita Mixta* or "mixed life," which allowed for active people to mingle the active and the contemplative life, as a model for lay contemplatives like herself. By arguing for the *vita mixta*, Lucifer undermines its credibility in this section of the play. For l. 401 cf. also Ecclesiastes 3.1; qtd. by Chaucer, "Alle thyng hath tyme," "Friar's Tale," 1475 (ctd. by Eccles 207n). See ll. 405-11n, 413-14n, 417n, 419-27n, 428n, and 431-40n.

404. Be more pleynerly to yowr informacyon: "Be more complete in [— and open to the implications of —] your information." The *MED* glosses the idiom "more plenerli" as "more fully, in greater detail." Trying to seduce Mind with the "suggestion" that religious discipline is a form of sinful idleness, in keeping with his earlier vow to work under "false colors" in order to "prove" perfection to be sin and virtue to be wickedness (see ll. 377-79), Lucifer urges Mind to take more complete account of the "[false] information" he is feeding him. The idea is simple; the clause is difficult largely because *pleynerly to* appears to be unidiomatic; one would expect the pronoun "in" rather than "to." But Lucifer here implies to Mind that he is not completely open "to" the (false) implications of the knowledge he already has.

405-11. Taken from Hilton's *Vita Mixta*, written for men "bounde to þe world be children & seruauns," who do not wish to "give up the contemplative life" and whose "stat askeþ for to do boþe, in diuerse tymes" (Richard Rolle of Hampole 1: 267; qtd. by Smart 26-27; ctd. by Eccles 207n). See 401-03n, 413-14n, 417n, 419-27n, 428n, and 431-40n.

413-14. See Hilton, *Vita Mixta*, "For þou schalt a tyme wiþ Martha be bisy ffor to rule & gouerne þin houshold, þi children, þi seruauns, þi neijebors, and þi tenauntes . . . . A noþur tyme þou schalt wiþ Marie leue þe bisynes of þe world & sitte doun at þe feet of vr lord be mekenes in preyers & holy þou3tes" (Rolle 1: 269; qtd. by Smart 27). For the biblical story of Mary and Martha, see Luke 10.38-42. Lucifer has distorted the biblical parable, in which Christ praises the idle Mary for spending time listening to him when her active sister, Martha, complains. Hilton asserts the need for both the active and the contemplative life. Lucifer overlooks this argument, preferring to denounce all forms of contemplation as empty idleness. See also *Informacio Alredi Abbatis Monasterii de Rieualle ad Sororem Suam*, in which the Abbot uses the story of Mary to persuade "my diere sister, þis is þy party . . . . Maries partye naþeles is y-seyd þe bettere" (*English Studies* 7: 318; qtd. by Smart 53).

414. Maria: From D; M reads *Mara*. This is one of the instances in which M apparently misreads D's handwriting. M sometimes has trouble deciphering D's lower case "i." For instance, in l. 584 he mistakes "i" for "n" and transcribes *streightly* as *strength*; in l. 697 D's "is" appears to M as "y" and he transcribes *discorde* as *dycorde*; again in l. 256 he mistakes *thei* for *ther*. Here the "-ri-" combination looks like "-r-" and M correspondingly transcribes *Maria* as *Mara*.

415. Yet þe lest hade blys for euermore: See *Scale of Perfection*, "For they saye that it is ynough to hem for to be saaf and have the leest degre in heven" (2: 18; qtd. by Eccles 207n; see also Underhill 290; *sauf* has the implication of "saved"). *Blys* refers specifically to the joys of heaven; cf. ll. 192, 216, 244, 358, 877, 1139. The exchange in ll. 413-16 epitomizes the sophistical nature of Lucifer's argumentation. He begins by urging Mind to an active life on the grounds that Martha the active sister pleased Christ. When Mind points out that Mary pleased him much more, Lucifer abruptly ceases to talk of the sisters and turns to the kind of argument put forth by Hilton and others to the effect that the "least" among humanity may inherit the kingdom of God. Lucifer equivocates on the term *lest*, which in Christ's exhoratations refers to the humble, the lowborn, children and others of no recognizable social position. Lucifer implicitly refers to those who are *lest* rigorous in their piety, although *lest* may also imply the conventional medieval conflation of Mary the sister of Lazarus and Martha with Mary Magdalene the repentant prostitute, one of the *lest* whose penitence earned her the kingdom of heaven. The Digby *Mary Magdalene* conflates these two Maries, implying also a link between these two women and the Virgin Mary.

417. Contemplatyff lyff ys sett befor: The contemplative life is valued more highly than the active. Mind's argument in favor of the contemplative life has sparked controversy over the theme of contemplation in this play. Smart assumes that the play was set specifically for "a monastic audience" (Smart 50-54, 80). Agreeing, Gail Gibson argues for a specific monastic location for the play: the Abbey of Bury St. Edmonds (1986 57-58). J. J. Molloy argues against this assumption, in favor of a more popular audience for the play (Molloy xiii.) At the Trinity College *Wisdom Symposium* Alexandra F. Johnston supported Molloy's reading (Johnston 1986 96-101). The Trinity College production of the play was fictionally set in the abbot's palace of the Abbey of Bury St. Edmonds, as one possible location for production. But see Riggio 1986 14-16 for the argument that the ascetic ideals of the play could have been aimed at either a monastic audience or a lay audience. See Introduction. Also see ll. 442 and 452.

418. lore: "religious creed" or "doctrine," — i.e., "My creed does not permit me to believe that the contemplative life is better than the active life."

419-27. For God hymselff wan he was man borre . . . : Cf. Hilton's *Vita Mixta*: "Oure lord for to stere sum men to vse þis medled lyf, tok vpon himself þe persones of such maner of men, boþe of prelates & curates of holy chirche, & of oþur suche as are disposed as I haue seid, and 3af to hem ensaumple be his owne worchyng þat þei schulde vse þis medled lyf as he dude. O tyme he comuned & medled wiþ men, schewyng to hem his dedes [of] merci; ffor he tau3t þe vnkonnyng be his preching, he visyted þe seke & heled hem of heor sores, he fedde þe hungri, & comforted hem þat were sori. Anoþur tyme he lafte þe conuersacion of al worldly men, & of his disciples also, & went alone in to desert vpon þe hulles, & contyned al þe ni3t in preyers as þe gospel seiþ" (Rolle, 1: 269; qtd. by Smart 27). See also Misyn's *The Fire of Love* (1435), a translation of Rolle's *Incendium Amoris*: "[C]ontemplative [Crist] was not in comon maner als sayntis in þis lyf ar contemplatife" (Harvey 49; qtd. by Smart pp. 53-4).

422: relation: "account." *By my relation* means "as far as I know."

428. vita mixta: Cf. Hilton, "þis medled lyf schewed vr lord in himself to ensaumple of hem þat han take þe staat & þe charge of þis medled lyf" (Rolle, 1: 269; qtd. by Smart 27). *Medled lyf* is a translation of the Latin *vita mixta* and refers to a life split between the active and the contemplative modes. Such a split was popular with lay contemplatives during the fifteenth century, particularly among women like Margaret Beaufort, the mother of Henry VII, or Cicely, the Duchess of York, and mother of Edward IV and Richard III. One of the questions which continues to haunt critics of *Wisdom* is why Lucifer champions the *vita mixta*. Assuming that the play was written to counteract apostasy, Smart concludes that the dramatist is attempting to undermine the validity of the *vita mixta*, particularly for the three Mights, whom he assumes to be monks (Smart 55). Bevington argues that the play actually endorses the *vita mixta* through the irony created by Lucifer's distorting Hilton's arguments (1964 51). Both positions are textually defensible. In ll. 393 - 486, when Lucifer is seducing the Mights, the play supports the cloistered contemplative life. By parodying the *Vita Mixta*, Lucifer points toward the idealization of the *contemplatyff lyff* which, as Mind says, *ys sett befor* (l. 417). Later, however, without naming the *vita mixta*, in his nine points of charity, Wisdom — stepping out of his character — adapts a well-known set of religious pointers, formerly attributed to Richard Rolle of Hampole, as precepts for good behavior for the audience (when the Mights are changing costume offstage). The nine points exalt private acts of charity in preference to expensive public endowments or to the rigors of strenuous religious vigil (see ll. 997-1064). Thus, the play presumes that its audience members, at least, are not entirely cloistered. The Mights, as internal faculties, represent the cloistered, devout, and contemplative portion of Anima, the soul who must herself live in the world. In this sense, the play does come close to endorsing a lifestyle similar to that of Hilton's *Vita Mixta*, though such an endorsement is not evident in this section of the play. Here the Mights are being commanded to return to their cloistered lives. Ultimately, the model for contemplation in the play is the kind of internal cloistering recommended, for instance, in documents like *The Abbey of the Holy Ghost*, a lengthy poem written for those who would be contemplatives but by virtue of their public positions must live in the world and who, thus, must build an "abbey" of contemplation inside their own selves. In short, within the allegory of the play the Mights themselves are cloistered contemplatives, but the Soul of which they are the faculties is not. See Introduction: "Sources in Context" in this volume. Also see Riggio 1986 5-6. See ll. 431-40n and 434n.

430. Line taken from D. M reads *I kan not belewe thys ys trew*. This is one of a very few instances in which D and M significantly differ. There is nothing in the D text to account for M's change from an affirmation to a negation, though the cancellation of the partial word *contemp-* (which begins the line below) before line 430 indicates that this alteration occurs at one of the many careless moments in M's transcription. Occasionally, M "corrects" D's text, altering verbal endings, for instance, and thus losing the rhyme scheme. In ll. 431-44, Lucifer does continue to argue insistently and "logically" for his point of view by continuing his attack on the contemplative life. M may have felt it to be too early in Lucifer's "examination" for Mind to affirm Lucifer's position. By almost inadvertently omitting this line, M came close to presenting Lucifer's argument without this one-line break. And he may have felt that the dramatic situation required more conflict at this point; or he may simply have been careless. See ll. 63, 296, and 548.

431-40. When praising the *vita mixta*, Lucifer directly attacks the *contemplatyff lyff*, thus fulfilling his promise earlier to prove *perfyghtnes* (l. 377) to be sin. Discussing this section, Smart points out that "the contemplative life which is described is . . . the life of the cloister, with its rule of silence and its hard discipline; it does not correspond at all with the life of the seculars, and it is much more appropriate to the monks than to the friars, whose business was to go about in the world. We conclude, then, that the Mights are represented as monks" (Smart 51). In a paper delivered at the Trinity *Wisdom Symposium*, Donald Baker counteracts this argument by urging the similarities between the three Macro plays as evidence for similar playing conditions. Baker, for instance, presumes Will to be a student, and thus celibate, rather than a monk (1986 80-81). But the theatrical demands and probable venue of *Wisdom* differ substantially from the other two Macro plays. Overall, the best argument seems to be that the Mights, as internal and thus naturally cloistered faculties, are treated as contemplatives, while Anima the public woman is not. See ll. 428n, 470-78n, 486n, and 553n. Also see Riggio 1985 17-18, 1989 237-41, and Introduction: "Sources in Context" in this volume.

434. Wse harde lywynge & goynge: "Follow a disciplined and difficult life." The adj. *harde* modifies both the verbal substantitves *lywynge* and *goynge*. The term *goynge* has several possibly relevant meanings. It can refer to a departure, specifically to death, a meaning which is hinted at in Shakespeare's "Men must endure / Their going hence, even as their coming hither" (*King Lear*, V.ii.11-12). If understood in that sense, this passage implies that those who follow the contemplative life must lead an austere and difficult life up to and through the passage into death. Or *harde . . . goynge* can refer to the condition of the ground on which one must walk, with metaphorical implications akin to the modern idiom "heavy going." The *MED* also glosses the verb *go* as "live," "conduct oneself," or "follow (a way of life.)" This meaning, glossed as "strict conduct," makes the term *goynge* a virtual synonym for *lywynge* and is perhaps preferable in this instance, though there may be undertones implying "hard living and heavy going right up to the point of death." In terms of *lywynge*, D has the plural *lywyngys*. This term is part of a mini-pattern of plural D nouns that M alters to the singular form. Other plurals seem sensible in the context and have been adopted. In this case only, the M singular seems to correct the D text and has been retained; see also ll. 87 and 200.

dyscyplyne: This term derives from the L. *disciplina*, meaning the instruction of a disciple. Belonging to the disciple, "discipline" is associated with student practice or exercise rather than theory in contrast to the term "doctrine," which is assumed to be the property of the teacher. The emphasis on practice leads to the meaning "chastisement" or, as here, "mortification of the flesh" as well as moral instruction.

437-39. cf. Hilton, *Scale of Perfection* where Hilton points out that "fleshly desires and vain dreads," the contemplative's enemies, will argue that it is perilous to leave the world, "thou shalt falle in to sykenes or in to fantasyes or in to frenesyes as thou seest that som don" (2: 22; qtd. by Eccles 208n; see also Underhill 311-13). This attack on vigils and prayer is answered later by Christ. See ll. 1026-28n.

441. syngler: "solitary" or "lonely"; see ll. 452 and 574n.

442. Be in þe worlde: See l. 417n, 428n, and 470-78n.

vse thyngys nesesse: "make use of the convenient things of the world." The *OED* glosses the term *nesesse* in this line of *Wisdom* as a variant of the archaic word "necesse," meaning "necessary." Though the *OED* does not extend the meaning further, in this context the term implies things "necessary" in the now obsolete sense of "convenient," "commodious," or "useful" (see "necessary," adj., 1c *OED*).

444. Who clymyt hye, hys fall gret ys: A proverbial saying. Cf. "Whoso clyme ouyrhie, he hath a foule fall" (N-Town cycle 41/58;

Spector 1991 1: 389; qtd. by Eccles 208n at 41/32). See also Lydgate, *Minor Poems*, 2: 477, 565, 813; Greene 236; *Religious Lyrics of the Fifteenth Century* 237; *Oxford Proverbs* 282 (ctd. by Eccles 208n).

445. 3e haue reson: As step one in the seduction of the Mights, Lucifer has been making his *suggestyon* to Mind, who represents the higher part of reason. Attributing *reson* to Lucifer suggests that Mind has been seduced by Lucifer, with whom he is to be identified in the hierarchy of the Mights, in which Mind is the "devil's man," with Understanding serving the world, and Will allied with the flesh. Lucifer has won Mind, the most intellectual of the three, through "reasonable" arguments — or what appears to be reasonable logic — but is in truth (from the epistemological perspectives of the play) false reasoning. See ll. 301-04n, 371n, 399n, 428n, 445n, 450n, 482n, and 539-41n.

450. saluacyon: One of Lucifer's tricks in this play is to invert ordinary theological arguments. For instance, in this case, he offers Mind *saluacyon*, rather than attempting to appeal to the pleasure principle as one might expect of a suggestion to sin. Such inversion is characteristic of this Lucifer, who persistently represents a kind of anti-Wisdom, the exact antithesis of Christ as Wisdom. See l. 465; see also ll. 341-72n, 371n, 399n, 428n, 445n, 482n, and 539-41n.

451-61. Here begins the second temptation, that of offering *delectation* or *delight* to Understanding; see ll. 301-04n. In these lines, Lucifer does appeal to the worldly desires of the Soul, offering fine clothing, earthly power, and riches. He also appeals directly to the senses, offering food as an enticement to gluttony and *lust & lykynge* (l. 460) as a fleshly lure. These three enticements — to riches, the pleasures of the flesh, and worldly honors — were conventionally identified with the three temptations of Christ in the wilderness. See, for instance, the *Imitatio Christi*, referred to in manuscripts as *De Contemptu mundi*, or the *De contemptu mundi* written by Erasmus in his youth in which he devotes a chapter each to riches, the pleasures of the flesh, and honors (ctd. by Howard 73).

452. syngler deuocyons: "single-minded devotional exercises," associated with contemplative meditation, with a further implication of singleness or aloneness, in contrast to the vulgarly communal nature of sin. See ll. 417n, 505n.

455. manfull: "stately in appearance"; according to the *OED*, this is an occasional use of this term, which more commonly implies "manliness" in the sense of courage.   In this section on the ostentatious dress of Understanding (Perjury), the implication of costly attire is preferable.   The entire line reads: "What glory it is to be stately in appearance, indeed."

   in dede: "indeed." This term was written as two words until 1600.

462. dylectacyon: See ll. 451-61n.

463. pawsacyon: This term comes directly from late L. *pausationem*, used by Jerome to imply death. Here Lucifer asks Understanding to pause over his delight, but the association with death subtly influences the term; Understanding's "pause" will result in his spiritual death. The idiom "make a pausation" also occurs in the Croxton *Play of the Sacrament*, l. 603.

464. Se & beholde: By impelling Understanding to "see and behold" the world around him, implicitly offering him power and domination over that world, Lucifer reiterates the temptation of Christ from Matthew 4.1-11 and Luke 4.1-13, particularly Luke 4.5. The emphatic formula "see and behold" emphasizes both the act of looking and the implied value of what one is seeing.   See, for comparison, Shakespeare's "Behold and see," *Antony and Cleopatra*, I.i.15.

465. saluacyon: See l. 450n.

466. constryscyon: "contrition" or "sorrow of the heart," but also the hatred of one's sins coupled with the resolve not to sin again.   By arguing that sins destroy contrition, Lucifer frees Understanding to take delight in the suggestion to sin.   Lucifer's argument here is particularly ironic, since "contrition" is the first of the three stages of repentance and will be associated with Understanding later in the play; see. ll. 973, 979.

467. They þat dyspeyer, mercy haue grett compunccyon: Again, Lucifer's inversion of Catholic doctrine is flagrantly ironic, as he pleads that mercy will have pity on one who despairs — the opposite of actual doctrine. Driving the Mights to *despeyer* will be one of Lucifer's primary weapons against them; see l. 542. For the appeal to mercy as part of the process of penitence, see ll. 949-56.

468. Lucifer once more subverts the theological arguments given earlier in the play. See, for instance, ll. 215, 216, 231, and 237.

470-78. In these lines, Lucifer appears to treat Will as a cloistered cleric, arguing that he should give up the contemplative life of the cloisters for an active life in the world. Smart based his argument for the monastic origin of the play partly on this section (Smart 80). For an elaboration of this argument, see Riggio 1985 6-7. For countering arguments, see Molloy who argues that the terms of instruction and of address which Lucifer uses in his seduction of the Mights would be appropriate for lay persons in certain positions as well as for clerics (77); Johnston, who argues that concerns such as "maintenance" in the play imply a secular emphasis (1986 95); and Baker, who argues that the sophistication of the play implies a seasoned group of players, who might well present a play like *Wisdom* before what Baker calls "the groundlings" (1986 80). See ll. 417n, 431-40n, 442, 452n, and 470-78n.

471. of ipocryttys þe syne: See Matthew 6.16, where Christ urges his followers to avoid public shows of piety and in particular not to look "tristes" ("sad") when fasting as the "hypocritae" ("hypocrits") do but instead to fast in private. Arguing that penitence, prayer, and fasting are external rituals, which lead the contemplative to salvation only when coupled with internal commitments, Hilton suggests that such external signs of penitence will fail if they lead to a higher regard for self rather than to true contemplation of God. In this argument, Hilton identifies these virtuous exercises as potentially hypocritical (Hilton, *Scala Perfectionis*, 2: 19-20; also ctd. by Eccles 109n). In his usual style, Lucifer has distorted the theological argument, turning the words of Christ into a mandate against fasting altogether.

472. comun: "common," i.e., that which most people share, ordinary. In its *contemptus mundi* stance, the play (opposing the viewpoint elaborated by Lucifer) equates shared and "common" experiences with sinfulness, limiting virtue for the most part to the isolating individual union with God. See, for instance, ll. 575n, 576n, and 577n. But also see ll. 997-1064 for the play's emphasis on charity as a redeeming virtue.

478. Sensualite: Lucifer has already begun to rename the Mights; "Sensuality" is a fitting name for Will, who is associated with divine love in his state of grace and with lust in the world of sin, especially as *sensualyte* refers to the sentient portion of the human soul; see ll. 135n and 296n. Will later calls himself *Lechery* (l. 747) and *gentyll Fornycacyon* (l. 756). *Lechery* is the name used most consistently.

481. The wyll of þe soule hathe fre dominacyon: For Wisdom's version of this statement, see l. 290.

482. Dyspute not to moche in þis wyth reson: "Don't use logic to argue this case too much." The vocabulary of disputation is essential to Lucifer's purposes, since he styles himself as the "examiner" of the Mights. See l. 371n, 399n, 428n, 431-40n, 445n, 450n, and 539-41n.

483-84. þe nethyr parte . . . ouerparte: Lucifer has already directed his *suggestion* to Mind and offered *delectation* to Understanding. Because he is now attempting to gain *consent* from Will, his appeal to the *ouerparte* of Reason (identified in the play with Mind) seems initially misplaced. However, the consent to sin was regarded by Augustine as a rational act of the higher part of reason. Although in the play Will alone consents to sin, the link with reason as the faculty of consent is subtly insinuated in such references as this. The *nethyr parte* of reason has been associated with Understanding. See ll. 301-04n.

485-92. As Will prepares for the formal ritual in which he will consent to Lucifer's suggestions, the verse form lapses into Wisdom's eight-line stanza (ababbcbc). Throughout this false theological disputation in which he consciously misuses school techniques, Lucifer has inclined to the verse style of Wisdom with its ten to twelve-syllabled lines. But only in this one stanza does he specifically adopt the rhyme scheme associated with Wisdom. See ll. 371n, 399n, 428n, 445n, 450n, 482n, 539-41n.

486. Again, the allusion seems to be to the decision to leave the cloistered life for an active life in the world. See ll. 391n, 401-03n, 417n, and 431-40n.

487. by sent Powle: By using an oath frequently heard in sermons, Lucifer continues to subvert theological discourse (see Molloy 91).

488. þes: The term *þes* implies a theatrical gesture toward some members of the audience. Apparently, the audience must have included clerics who could become the object of Lucifer's satirical scorn; see l. 490n.

490. Ther ys a wolffe in a lombys skyn: The false preacher as a prophet of evil is frequently figured in the image of a wolf in a sheepfold. See, for instance, biblical references in Ezekiel 22.27 and John 10.12. Milton uses this image in his pastoral elegy "Lycidas," ll. 113-31. For the proverbial image of the wolf in a sheep or lambskin, see Matthew 8.15. Also see *Oxford Proverbs* 273 (ctd. by Eccles 208). *Ther*, like *þes* in l. 489, may suggest a theatrical gesture, pointing to someone in the audience. Molloy has proposed the image of the black cloak over the white mantle worn by the Dominicans (Molloy 91; also ctd. by Eccles 208n). If Molloy is right, one could conjecture that at least one Dominican was in the audience, though the symbolism here need not depend on finding such a garment in the audience. Satirizing false clerics was a conventional feature of late medieval literature and sermons. However, putting the satire of *prechors* as false teachers in Lucifer's mouth is a way of undercutting the satire itself, since Lucifer's point of view consistently represents an ironic inversion of that supported in the play. Characteristically, *Wisdom* tends to support the formal, established church somewhat more than the other Macro plays. Although it could be argued that *Mankind* supports the rural clergy, *Wisdom* invests more in the formal sacraments of the Catholic church overall; see ll. 949-56n and 982-91n. The imagery of black-on-white echoes the symbolism of Anima's costume; see ll. 16sd, 149-51n.

491. row ageyn þe floode: A proverbial expression; cf. *Proverbs of King Alfred*, 123-24 (Wright and Halliwell 1: 174; qtd. by Smart 59; ctd. by Eccles 208n); Gower, *Confessio Amantis*, 4: 178a (*Oxford Proverbs* 627; ctd. by Eccles 208n). For a biblical analogue, see Ecclesiasticus 4.26. Will yields to Lucifer's moral seduction by lapsing into a pair of conventional proverbs. By not "rowing against the tide," the Mights prove their willingness to adopt the standards of the common culture, but the staleness of the conventional proverb emphasizes the fatuousness of the Mights' commitment to Lucifer.

492. sett my soule on a mery pynne: "tune my soul for a song of pleasure." This second proverb in as many lines completes the one "Wisdom" stanza in this section of the play. Cf. Medwall's *Nature*, where Pryde boasts that he will "set [man's] hart on a mery pyn" and Worldly Affeccyon says that "thys wyll set [man] on a mery pyn" (Nelson 2-1/864) and Skelton's *The Bowge of Courte*, "Plucke vp thyne herte vpon a mery pyne" (l. 386; qtd. by Smart 59). Also see *Oxford Proverbs* 421 (ctd. by Eccles 208n) and Whiting P215 (ctd. by Nelson 204n). Similarly, in *The Castle of Perseverance*, Humanum Genus vows to "make mery a ful gret throwe" in his new life of sin while he is "but 3onge" (ll. 421, 423). For the term "mery" see note below.

493. than: "that." D reads *that*. *Than* is a ME inflexion of the demonstrative pronoun "that," deriving from the dative singular of OE "þaet."

494. a clene sowll & a mery: Lucifer subverts Wisdom's descriptions of the *clene* soul as *Godys restynge place* and his *symylytude* (see ll. 176, 284). By linking cleanliness of soul to merriment, Lucifer subverts Wisdom's arguments for cleanliness as a product of a contemplative union with God. *Mery* recurs as a term to describe the "active" rather than "contemplative" life which the Mights have now chosen, but which is judged to be thoughtlessly joyful and indulgently sinful, i.e., *mery*. The play's implied attack on the "mery" life is in keeping with the *contemptus mundi* stance throughout. This theme remains throughout sixteenth-century drama, but in the farces it take a different turn. For instance, Mathewe Merygreeke in *Ralph Roister Doister* picks up the Augustinian argument that merriment — or pleasure — leads to long life: "As long lyveth the mery man (they say) / As doth the sory man, and longer by a day" (I.i.29-30). Shakespeare further negates the associations between merriment and sin in *The Merchant of Venice*, where the desire to be "merry" (cf. I.i.48-49) even to the point of unthriftiness — the primary aim of Christian youths like Bassanio, Gratiano, Salano, and Salerio — is echoed ironically in Shylock's "merry sport" and his "merry bond" (I.iii.146,174). For other occurrences of this term in *Wisdom*, see ll. 492, 500, 505, 559, 623, 836, 871; also see 562n and 619-20n.

495. Acorde yow iii togedyr by: Lucifer begins the ceremony which ends this temptation scene by appealing to the virtue of unity, which the discord of the Mights — typical of the world of sin — will later destroy. See ll. 497-99n, 513-15n, 574-96n, 761-80, 805-28n, 1121n, 1130, and 1157n.

497-99. suggestyon . . . Delyght . . . consent: These three lines comprise a formal fealty oath made by each of the three Mights, as each confirms his allegiance to Lucifer. This ceremony completes the transition from the state of grace to the world of sin. The formal nature of the fealty ceremony is typical of morality drama. Cf. *The Castle of Perseverance*, ll. 456-814, esp. 755-63. Also see Riggio 1989 197-200. See ll. 495n, 574-96n, and 761-80n.

497. me: Taken from D. M misreads the D *m* as a *w* and writes *we*. However, each of the Mights takes a formal vow. As the first of the three, Mind agrees to the *suggestyon* with which he has been tempted. Despite the awkwardness of the pronoun *me* in this construction (chosen perhaps for its rhyming value), the D reading emphasizes the symmetry of the vows in which each of the Mights who formally agrees in the first person singular to the pact they have just made. And the use of the oblique case of the pronoun in instances like these where we would expect "I" has historical precedent. *Me* here constitutes a "lectio difficilior" ("difficult reading") which argues for the priority of the Digby text (see Maas 13, Visser 70 and also see Introduction: "The Relationship between the Digby and Macro Texts" in this volume). Such formal ceremonies as this one characterize both *Wisdom* and *The Castle of Perseverance*, in which Humanum Genus must take a formal oath of fealty to King Mundus (see, for instance, ll. 738-50). It could be argued that Mind, as the higher part of reason, speaks for all the Mights. In that case, the more rhetorically attractive term *we* could be acceptable. However, Mind responds specifically to the "suggestion" of Lucifer and in the three-part structure of temptation, it is the higher part of mind alone to which the "suggestion" is made. Furthermore, both Understanding and Will take their own vows immediately afterward, in terms of their own temptations: Understanding agrees to "delectation" and Will "consents" to the seduction; see 497-99n. The formality of the fealty oath here represented argues strongly for the singular pronoun.

500. mery: See l. 494n.

501. Go in þe worlde . . . : See l. 417n.

505. mery: See l. 494n.

let reuell rowte: "Let riotous merry-making reign [throughout a band of merry-makers]." Lucifer consistently praises the communal activities of the world in contrast to the lonely individual acts of penitence which he is attempting to portray as idly sinful. Cf. also "Keepeth revell route as long as it will last," *Ralph Roister Doister*, I.i.48.

506. snowte: Clearly, Mind has already begun to develop animal characteristics as a result of his fealty oath to Lucifer.

508. þe dewyll me spede: A proverbial tag meaning "let the devil assist me." In a way typical of the inversions in the world of sin, Will is playing on the popular expression, "God speed [me, thee, etc.]," which gave rise to the idiomatic "godspeed." See Chaucer's *Knight's Tale,* l. 1700; *Tale of Gamelyn*, 827. In following the lure of Lucifer as a gallant, the Mights clearly do not recognize that they have succumbed to the devil. Persistently throughout this section they allude unconsciously to their actual condition in oaths such as this. See ll. 614n, 619-20n.

509. wysly: Another of the inverted terms; as Anti-Wisdom, Lucifer redefines "wise" action and "wisdom" to suit his purposes. See also ll. 604, 743.

510. syde aray: "long clothes." Throughout the fifteenth century, fashionable short clothing, considered indecent and made the subject of satirical attack, was regulated by legislation. For instance, the sumptuary laws of 1483 repeated provisions of 1463 statutes "that no man shall wear any gown or cloak, which is not long enough when he is standing upright, to reach below his hips" (Baldwin 116). As throughout the play, the moral issue coalesces with conservative aristocratic practice; long clothing was primarily associated with the higher orders of aristocracy and with ecclesiastics; for instance, "social status, rank and age were indicated by the greater length of the garments worn" (Baldwin 75). Cf. *Mankind*, "Master Myscheff, hys syde gown may be tolde," l. 671, and Medwall's *Nature* (Nelson 2-1/755-56 (ctd. by Eccles 208n at ll. 767-68). For *syde*, see l. 16sdn; for *aray* as clothing that identifies fealty allegiance or true character, see 149-50n and 551n.

I yt defye!: The rhyme suggests that this phrase is part of l. 510. In both D and M, it is transcribed on a separate line.

511. happe: This term is taken from D, where it is written as *hap*, with the usual D abbr. for an omitted "m," "n," or doubled "p[e]," superscripted above "-ap." M apparently reads the abbreviation as indicating "m" and transcribes as *hamp*, a meaningless term which has occasioned much commentary. See Eccles 208n.

la plu joly: A French phrase, "la plus joli," i.e., "the most pleasing." The entire clause reads, "We will be fresh and, as it chances, the most pleasing." Using French signifies the decadence of the Mights. See also l. 517.

513-15. In one of several formal fealty rituals, each of the Mights vows allegiance to a new objective: Mind gives his allegiance to *worschyppys*, or honors belonging to a high social position; Understanding to *worschyppys* and *glory*, or worldly honors and position; and Will to the *lusts of lechery*. *Worschyppys* and *glory* are among the terms with both social and theological significance. See also *Contemplations of the Dread and Love of God*, where "rychesse . . . lustes . . . and worshyp" are identified as the "thre thynges" which "men desyre aboue all other worldely thynges" (*Richard Rolle of Hampole*, 2: 81); cf. also *Hymns to the Virgin and Christ* (Furnivall 36-37; qtd. by Smart 57). In Medwall's *Nature*, Pride, called "the swete darlynge of the devyll of hell," is named *Wurshyp* (Nelson 2-1/1208-12; also ctd. by Eccles 209n). See ll. 309n (for Anima's fealty allegiance to Wisdom), 495n, 497-99n, 513-15n, 551-73n, 574-96n, and 626-52n.

516. gyse of Frawnce: "clothes — or guise — worn in France," with a pun on "disguise" as a form of vanity. Like modish new fashions, lechery is associated with France. Cf. the N-Town cycle, "aftyr þe Frensche gyse," (Spector 1991 1: 125, 12/56; also qtd. by Eccles 208n). *Gyse*, which means behavior, manners, or fashion, recalls *dysgysynge*, which masks true identity. See also l. 767n.

517-18. Wyth wy, wyppe, / Farwell, quod I, þe dewyll ys wppe!: "With whee, whip, farewell, say I, the devil is up!" The line break is from D; M transcribes on one line. The lines form a couplet outside the regular meter. The expression is an alliterative interjection, expressing pleasure. *Wy* is an onomatopoeic interjection of no specific meaning; *wyppe* is an adverbial interjection created by using the imperative of the verb *whyppe*, meaning "to leap instantly about." This term is linked to *whip*, n., meaning "a brief span of time"; see l. 552n.

522. wyll: Will remains the faculty of consent throughout the play. Here, the devil urges his own *wyll*.

523-33. Now that the Mights have left the stage, Lucifer shows his true colors. He has made *resone . . . bothe deff & dumme*, i.e., he has rendered true reason impotent, taking away its voice and its power of hearing. But he has done so by cleverly persuading Mind, the most "reasonable" of the Mights, that he has *reson* on his side (see l. 445) and by belittling the argumentative force of reason to Will, the Might who will *take no thought* (see ll. 624 and 660).

524. Grace: One of the terms with both theological and social meanings, which can be inverted in the world of sin.   Lucifer here proclaims that he has put God's *grace* at a distance.   The Mights later look for *grace*, i.e. worldly endowment from a patron; see ll. 575, 579. For Anima's dependence on *grace* from Wisdom, see l. 317.

527-34.   Lucifer now names the three sins which will govern the Mights in his world: Pride, the devil's sin, to be associated with Mind, whose identification in the state of grace is with faith, gained from participating in the power of God the father; Covetousness, the sin of the world, to be identified with Understanding, who is allied with hope, the virtue associated with God the son, in the state of grace; and Lechery, a sin of the flesh, to be identified with Will, who is linked through charity to the love of the holy spirit in the state of grace. Using these sins as umbrellas covering all of the deadly sins was common in medieval literature.   Apparently the three were connected with the three lusts of I John 2.16.   See, for instance, *Myroure of Oure Ladye*:   "Pryde. Couetyse. and flesshely synne. in which ar vnderstonde all synnes, as saynte Iohn sayeth."   A marginal note refers to *Ioan II. Cursor Mundi* also lists "couetise lecchery and pride" as sins that "haþ spred þis world on euery syde"   (*Myrroure of oure Ladye* 99; Morris 103; qtd. by Smart 57).   See ll. 495n, 497-99n, and 551-716n.

529-30. Pryde . . . of all synnys hede: Pride was traditionally the primary sin, associated with Lucifer's fall.   See Morton Bloomfield, *The Seven Deadly Sins*.   During the late middle ages, and especially in the fifteenth century, avarice gained prominence as the primary seducer of humanity, as evidenced in *Wisdom* and *The Castle of Perseverance*.   The sin of pride will link Mind to Lucifer, but in this play pride itself — invested in honor, glory, and material acquisition — has a strong worldly cast to it; see Introduction: "Genre in Context" in this volume.

529. kynde: "the natural character of humanity"; see ll. 575n, 576n, and 927n.

531-32. couetyse . . . enduryth to þe last ende: Covetousness, or avarice (the one sin of the world), was thought to be the sin of old age, though in the fifteenth century it began to take a kind of *de facto* precedence among the sins. In *The Castle of Perseverance* Covetousness, the primary temptor of Humanum Genus, has a separate scaffold of his own. This will be Understanding's sin, linking him to the world. See ll. 562n, 601n and 744n.

533. lechery: This, the sin of the flesh, will be Will's sin.

537-38. lyknes / lyke to a fende of hell: The likeness to God has been effaced, replaced by a likeness to the devil; see ll. 104n, 140n.

539-41. By describing himself as a witness, capable of *prewynge* (l. 541) the soul's guilt, Lucifer continues to identify himself himself with logic (rather than true reason). He has the ability to examine and, finally, assure the condemnation of the soul. Evoking the judgment of God as a court of law in which witnesses appear, he also foreshadows the involvement the renamed Mights are soon to have with the courts. See ll. 371n, 399n, 428n, 431-40n, 445n, 450n, 482n, 485-92n, and 539-41n.

542. dyspeyer: See l. 467n.

543. Wyll clennes ys mankyn: Thus both D and M: "While mankind is undefiled in purity." The clause as it stands seems incomplete, as if a preposition were missing before *clennes*, or as if this n. form should be an adj. The modernization does treat "clean" as an adjective.

544-45. þe soule God ys wythin / þe deuelys place: The feudal metaphor is continued, with the devil represented as taking charge of the *place* or *see* which formerly belonged to God. See l. 132n.

547. colours: The "colors" of rhetoric which disguise the truth. The phrase also implies a legal plea. Lucifer has falsely represented his case. See l. 379n.

   false gynne: False cunning or plotting for evil purposes. The term *gynne* derives from an aphetic for *engin*, and it implies the use of a cunning device. This term is from D. M has misread the first *n*, which resembles the M *a*, and transcribed as *gyane*.

550/550sd. boy . . . shrewed boy: As he departs, Lucifer takes a mischievous boy from the audience with him.   Presumably, he chooses a shrewish or loud and annoying young man of low social rank, probably planted by the actors. Eccles assumes that this is an early instance of the term "boy" in its modern sense of male child (see Eccles 209n). See also l. 913sd, where because of the small size, "boys," i.e. male children, were probably used. Though he may be either young or small or both, the *boy* in this scene may best be linked to the tradition of false or disruptive servants that typically symbolize the discord of the world. Cf. the *garcio*, page to Mundus, in *The Castle of Perseverance*, who inherits the property of Humanum Genus (ll. 2908-68). The most fully developed of the disruptive "boys" in early English drama is Pikeharness, the impudent servant of Cain in the Towneley cycle "Cain and Abel" play. By grabbing the *boy*, Lucifer has given the *Wisdom* audience fair warning of his power. He has also taken with him a disruptive young person who must pay the price for his impudence. E. J. Dobson, who assumes that the term is either used as a direct address to a social inferior or as a term of abuse until the sixteenth century, glosses the word *boy* as "urchin" in this line (141).

euell grace: "Evil grace, " i.e., the bad "grace" or ill-luck that results from choosing a bad patron. The patronage metaphor is continued throughout the play. See l. 723n. On the importance of *grace* as a term that links theology (the "grace of God") to politics (the "grace" of a worldly patron), see ll. 119n, 203n,

551. At this point Eccles establishes Scene III.

551-716. During this interlude of sin, Mind, Understanding, and Will speak in turn in a stylized ritual of hierarchical interaction. Each set of speeches furthers their allegiance to Lucifer. Until l. 716, they do not deviate from the order of speaking: Mind, Understanding, and then Will.   And at l. 716 the order is broken only because Understanding has brought in his dancers; at that point the order of speaking changes, but the ritualized order of the exchange between the characters continues. See ll. 213-44n, 245-76n, and 716n.

551-73. In this first exchange of speeches, each Might celebrates his new fealty, symbolized by a change of clothing and a sudden reliance on pleasure: *new aray* (l. 551); *fresche* (l. 558); and *iolye* (l. 567). Each says *farwell* to a representative attribute of his character in the state of grace: *perfeccyon*, characteristic of Mind as the "higher part" of reason, identified with God the Father and capable of apprehending divinity through his own perceptions of the divine (l. 553); *consyens*, characteristic of Understanding as the "lower part" of reason, identified with Christ as the incarnation of the godhead and with the created world and, thus, linked with human conscience (l. 563); and *chastyte*, characteristic of Will as the faculty of the senses, identified with the Holy Ghost, i.e., with divine love but also with sinful lust (l. 568). See ll. 553n, 563-65n, and 568-73n.

551. new aray: New clothes that signify the change of fealty from Wisdom to Lucifer; see ll. 149-50n, 510n, and 609-11n.

552. Wyppe, wyrre: A second alliterative exclamation; see l. 517n.

care awey: "[drive] care away!" A common expression. Cf. Lydgate, *Minor Poems* (2: 704); *Secular Lyrics* (pp. 4, 34, 39; both ctd. by Eccles 109n).

553. Farwell, perfeccyon: Each of the Mights says farewell to his former life. As the *ouerparte* of Reason, Mind bids farewell to the contemplative life he has left. What constitutes *perfeccyon* in the play is part of the controversy about the possible monastic origins of the drama. For Christians, the ultimate biblical injunction to perfection comes from Matthew 5.48: "Estote ergo vos perfecti, sicut et Pater vester caelestis perfectus est" ("Be you therefore perfect, even as your Father in heaven is perfect"). Within the Christian tradition, "perfection" could be either individual or social. In either case, medieval Christianity defined "perfection" in terms of love, "the most excellent of all virtues" because it leads to God. (St. Thomas 2: q.23, a.6; qtd. by Flew 240). As a play which persistently negates the value of social relationships, *Wisdom* puts forth an ideal of individual perfection. Such an ideal is intrinsically ascetic, "placing immense stress . . . on the worth of the solitary human soul" and closely linked to monasticism (Flew 180). That is the ideal established earlier in the play with its emphasis on the discipline of the cloisters. However, the ideals of individual perfection did in the fifteenth century extend beyond the cloisters to encompass lay contemplatives. Therefore, though the goal of perfection in the play is clearly contemplative, it is not so clear that such a goal was open only to cloistered contemplatives. It appears that the Mights themselves, as internal faculties, are being treated as cloistered contemplatives (on the model of lay contemplation, which allowed for a spiritual or "inner" cloistering of active people) whereas Anima is treated as a person living in the world; see ll. 377n, 393n, 431-40n, 417n, 551-73n, and 1161n.

554. lykly: "having a prosperous appearance, giving promise of success." This entire line means "I seem to myself most promisingly handsome at all times." *Lykly* is from D; M reads *lyghtly*, a term meaning "frivolous, easy to be persuaded" which also implies "contemptible or trifling." If the M term were accepted, this secondary meaning might well constitute an unconscious pun on the part of the speaker with regard to his own new lighthearted personality (see *MED*); "most lyghtly ay" would mean "most frivolous always." However, since Mind is talking about his new clothes, D's term makes perfectly good sense, particularly since it carries an ironic verbal echo of the "likeness" to God which has been lost in this new "likely" appearance. See for comparison the Paston letters where the household retainers of the Duke of York are called "likely men" (1. 265, cited by the *OED* under "likely" 4a). Eccles emends to "lyghly" which he treats as a variant of "lyckely" and glosses as "handsome."

555. It ys but honest, no pryde: Cf. N-Town cycle, 26/111-12: "3e xal kalle pride 'oneste' and 'naterall kend' lechory/ And covetyse 'wysdam'" (Spector 1991 1: 250; also qtd. by Smart 67; ctd. by Eccles 209n). Mind will be associated with pride; see l. 324sdn.

559-62. mery, mery . . . mery: See ll. 492n, 494n.

562. Goode: "goods" or "possessions." The term *goode* is an implied plural.   Understanding, whose sin will be covetousness, here expresses his freedom to sin in terms of acquiring "goods."

563-65. Understanding's retainers wear double-faced masks as a sign of their hypocrisy as jurors. It is fitting that Understanding bid farewell to conscience and talk of letting *truthe . . . slyppe*; see ll. 551-73n.

567. I am so lykynge, me seme I fle: "I am so lustful that I feel like I'm flying through the air." Cf. *The Castle of Perseverance*, where Mundus calls himself a "lykynge lord" who offers "Lust and lykynge" to Humanum Genus for his "ese" (ll. 461, 619). Also see Skelton, *Magnificence*: "Me seme I flye, I am so lyght" (ll. 839-40; qtd. by Eccles 209n). Will, identified with lust, describes himself as "lykynge" or "lustful." See ll. 568-73n.

568-73. Farwell, chastyte: Will bids farewell to chastity. This was one of the lures Lucifer had offered him, though when he was still in a state of grace, he tempted him not with the brothels he will soon visit, but with a wife. See l. 476. Now he is tempted by female *bewte* (l. 571). The inversions of the world of sin are exemplified in his ironic image of *a woman* — considered as an object of lust — as a *heavenly syght*(l. 573). There is a play here on the conventions of courtly and contemplative love, in which female *bewty* is considered *heavenly* in a true sense, i.e., not only because of its physical attractiveness but also because of the virtue of the beautiful woman. Shakespeare plays recurrently on this convention in descriptions of Desdemona in *Othello*, where the idea of woman as a "heavenly sight" has both real and ironic implications. See ll. 17-20n and 1103n. For comments on Will's identification both with true love and false love (i.e., lust), see ll. 551-73n and 609-11n.

574-96. This is the second set of ritual affirmations made by the Mights in their interlude of sin.   Here each defines the worldly pleasures which give him most *solace* (l. 574) or *ioy* (ll. 581, 589). See ll. 495n and 497-99n.

574. syngler: Still focused on one object, Mind has now given up contemplation of God for worldly power and prosperity. The repetition of the term is in keeping with the inversions of the world of sin. See l. 441n.

575. Kynde, fortune, & grace: Soon to be renamed Maintenance, Mind commits sins of pride that lead him to take comfort in *kynde*, i.e., the inherited rights and positions coming from family power — a meaning here and in l. 576 which is at odds to other uses of the term in this play (see glossary); *fortune*, the prosperous condition which attends upon power; and *grace*, the favor of a powerful worldly patron. The attributes here are conventional. Cf. a sermon defining the gifts of *kynde*, *fortune*, and *grace*: "The 3iftis of kynde are theis, noblei of kynrede, gentilnes of blood . . . . The 3iftis of fortune arn . . . lorschipe, worchep and frenschip. 3iftis of grace arn . . . eloquense in speking, coriouste in craft, in reding or such othir" (qtd. in Owst 308). See also Chaucer, *Parson's Tale*, l. 450, which attributes Pride to the "goodes of nature . . . the goodes of furtune, and . . . the goodes of grace" (both qtd. by Eccles 209n). For other uses of *grace*, see 119, 172, 203, 223, 317, 524, 575n, 579n, 893, 946, 1072, 1078, 1138, 1146, and 1160; for similar idioms using *grace*, see ll. 550n, 579n, and 723n; for other meanings of *kynde*, see ll. 529n, 927n.

576. Kynde, nobyll of kynrede: The term *kynde* might imply "natural" as in ll. 529 and 927, but here — as this line makes clear — it refers to noble kindred, i.e., the power of a prestigious family and inherited social position. In this play, family is associated with the accumulation of worldly goods and, thus, with sin. See ll. 575n and 578n.

577. soleyn: "unique," "alone," or "singular." Mind claims to be alone by virtue of his superiority over others. Thus, his noble kindred and prosperous fortune do not bring him community; they isolate him in a different and less healthy way.

578. The prosperity of a good family will *lace* ("entwine") Mind into *worschyppe*, or "worldly renown," owing to his high social position. See ll. 575n and 576n.

579. Grace . . . curryus eloquens: In this usage *grace* primarily means the privilege and personal refinement thought to derive from living under the protection of a worldly lord. But, as the reference to *curryus eloquens* implies, *grace* also connotes charming or pleasing speech. See, for instance, Wyclif, "Who loueth clennesse of herte, for the grace of his lippis shal han the king frend" (*Proverbs*, 1.9). See l. 575n.

580. oncunnynge: When proclaiming a reliance on rhetorical eloquence, Mind disdains *oncynnynge*, i.e., the redeeming innocence of self-knowledge which does not rely on cunning logic. Thus, he rejects the advice given Anima by Wisdom. See ll. 87-90n.

581-88. Understanding casts himself in the posture of a vulgarly rich upstart; his pleasure is in the accumulation of wealth. He portrays himself first as a miser, hoarding up his riches, *To see yt, to handyll yt, to tell yt all* (583). Then he claims social position through his wealth, rather than through his kindred. Whereas Mind claims *grace* and *eloquens* (l. 579), both qualities of social refinement, Understanding claims that he will *bost* (l. 586) of his wealth, again a vulgar display (though Mind himself, who claims "to avaynte" — or boast — of his gallantry in l. 597, is not above shows of vainglory). Finally, Understanding claims that his riches will make him *equall / to hem sumtyme hys souereyngys wer* (l. 587-88). That is, he claims that his money gives him the power to displace those who were his social superiors. This is the typical stance of the social upstart, a problem endemic to capitalism with its potential for accumulating wealth. *Hem* (l. 588) provides actors a chance to engage the audience by pointing to the *soureyngys* (l. 588), either social or ecclesiastical, in the crowd.

584. streightly to spare: "rigidly to save." The idea that Understanding will hoard his wealth, counting it continually and sparing all expense possible, continues the emphasis on miserliness of the preceding lines; *streightly* is from D; because of a persistent tendency to misread D's "i," M reads *strenght*; see l. 414n.

589-96. In keeping with his character, Will assumes the role of the lover; his new *aray* is a *dysgysynge*, or modish new-styled clothing, designed to make him amiable, i.e., loveable. *Dysgysynge* recalls both the mantle of Anima which disguises her true identity and the masque dances which are to come in the play; see ll. 140-50n, 692n.

594. affyable: "agreeable," "compliant," or "of a willing temperament." *MED* glosses this word as "betrothed" in this line, thus erroneously suggesting a link with *affyance* (l. 83). However, *affyable* is linked only through the repeated first syllable to the set of terms, including *affyance*, *affye*, and *affynyte*, which imply alliances in the play. See ll. 643n, 657n, 659n, 690n, and 799n.

596. Be þe smylynge on me wan yt doth remove: "By the smile that remains on me when my lover has gone." This is a difficult phrase. The M *wan* could mean either "when" or "wanness." "Wan" is a term traditionally associated with lovers; cf. the seventeenth century cavalier poet Sir John Suckling's "Why so pale and wan, fond lover / Prithee why so pale?" However, the D *whan* suggests that "when" is the better reading. *Smylynge* is a term associated recurrently with lovers. Cf. Dunbar, "I turne in a tender luke . . . and hym behaldis . . . with hertly smyling" (*Twa Mariit Women* 230). The problem with the meaning as glossed above is that there is no recognizable antecedent for *yt*, and the switch from the third person of *A louer ys son perceyvable* (l. 595) to the first person *me* of l. 596 is unexplained. An alternative, less likely possibility is that the *yt* refers to *smylyng*, and that the passage alludes awkwardly to the courtly love tradition of the pining lover, suggesting "by the smile on [my face] when love does remove it [i.e., the smile]," meaning that love removes the smile from his face, leaving the lover recognizable by his traditional melancholy.

597-608. In this third set of speeches, each of the Mights makes a boast.

598. galontys: "gallants" or "dandies." In boasting of his pride, Mind identifies himself as a dandy, the identity chosen by Lucifer as a disguise when tempting the Mights (l. 380sd). Mind is persistently associated with Lucifer. Mind's aspiration to courtliness is affirmed in this passage in which "gallants," those dandies dressed in the latest

French fashions, are "proclaimed" to be *curtely personys*, "courtly persons."

601. ryche couetyse: Understanding is associated with covetousness as well as with riches. See ll. 527-34n, 531-32n, 562n, and 743-44n.

603. game: One of the inversions in the world of sin. Anima has earlier called Wisdom's speaking of love a *game*. See ll. 40n and 612.

604. wysdom: A typical inversion. Because he is identified with Christ [who is Wisdom] as the second person of the trinity, Understanding defines the false *wisdom*.

"Ware þat," quod Ser Wyly: *Ser* is not in D. Cf. similar names in *Piers Plowman*, C.v.27; also see Sir John Paston, 1473, "Ware that, quod Perse," (qtd. by Davis 136; examples ctd. by Eccles 210n, but note that the N-Town reference ctd. by Eccles at 14/9 is transcribed as "Gyle," not "Wyle" by Spector 1991 1: 139; 14/9. Similarly the Towneley cycle reference cited by Eccles at 13/408 is transcribed by Stevens and Cawley as *Gyle* in Towneley 13/590). *Ser* is not capitalized in M; *Wyly* is not capitalized in M or D.

605. lechory: Typically, Will boasts of and is identified with lechery. See ll. 515, 516, 533, and 747-48n.

609-11. Each Might affirms a commitment to the appropriate vice: Mind to *curyous aray*, or fancy gallant's clothing, such as that worn by Lucifer (Mind [Maintenance] is the devil's man); Understanding to *falsnes*, the sin typical of the deceptions of the world, with whom Understanding (Perjury) is identified; and Will to *lust*, the sin of the flesh with whom Will (Lechery) is closely associated. This pattern continues through l. 676; see ll. 677-84n.

612. game: See ll. 40n and 603n.

614. ewell joy: *Joy* refers to the bliss of heaven and thus by association to the condition of the afterlife; *ewell joy*, "evil joy," hints at the demonic inversion of heavenly bliss. Hence, one reading might at the demonic inversion of heavenly bliss. Hence, one reading might be "let the pains of hell wrack me," the "joy" of hell being in reality pain. The more literal rendering "hellish mirth" captures some of the connotations of this inversion but misses the irony of the term *joy*.

615. sprynge: "jump around," with the implication of dancing. See ll. 747-48n.

617-19. tenowr . . . mene . . . trebull: The Mights sing a three-part song, emblematic of the disunity in the world of sin. Within the play, plainsong symbolizes the unity of God; three-part music, like modish clothing and masque dancing, symbolizes discord. Cf. Towneley cycle play 30 where the devils sing *trebill* and *meyn* (30/715-16). In Towneley, however, three-part music does not carry the same symbolical significance as it does in *Wisdom*. The Towneley shepherds sing *tenory*, *tryble*, and *meyne* in 13/270-72, in a song which, though clearly less exalted than the angels' singing, nevertheless represents their devotion to God (ctd. by Eccles 210n at 13/186-88; qtd. by Smart 69). For an analysis of the function of music in the mystery cycles, see Rastell (1983 and 1989), who argues that music represents divine order in the mystery cycles, in apparent contrast to the dual symbolic function of music in *Wisdom*. For an interesting comparison, see Hildegard von Bingen's *Ordo Virtutem*, where music seems to suggest harmony.

619-20. And but a trebull I owtwrynge / The deuell hym spede þat myrthe exyled: "Unless I ring out a treble, let the devil aid him that exiled mirth." The last clause is ambivalent. It is not clear from the syntax whether *myrthe* is the subject or the object of the verb, i.e., whether "mirth" has been the exiler or the exiled, though probably the latter, particularly in light of a possible pun on the term *exyled*, which may also mean "ravaged," a now obsolete meaning derived from its signification in Old French. Will's point here is that unless he joins in the song by belting out a treble part, he will proverbially ask the devil to assist one of the devil's natural enemies, i.e. one who has "exiled" or "ravaged" mirth. From the perspective of *Wisdom* (and fifteenth century morality drama generally) mirth and merriment naturally serve the devil; thus, an enemy of mirth is an enemy of the devil. In sixteenth century English farces, modelled in part on Latin comedy, the theme of "mirth" continues, but whereas in *Wisdom* mirth or merriment is a clear sign of vice, in later comedy "mirth" can imply "honest" and thus good recreation. See, for instance, *Ralph Roister Doister*, where, echoing Latin comic dramatists Plautus and Terence, the prologue invokes "honest" Mirth: "Than Mirth which is used in an honest fashion; / For Myrth prolongeth lyfe, and causeth health. / Mirth recreates our spirites and voydeth pensivenesse, / Mirth increaseth amities, not hindring our wealth,/ Mirth is to be used both of more and lesse,/ Being mixed with vertue in decent comlynesse / . . . . Which Mirth we intende to use, avoidying all blame" (Prologue 7-11, 13). See l. 494n.

622: to God avow: Not recognizing their true condition as servants of the devil, the Mights continue to make their vows to God. See l. 508n.

623-24. As mery as þe byrde on bow, / I take no thought: Cf. "I am als light as birde on bowe," York cycle, 25/388 (ctd. by Eccles 210n). For *mery*, see ll. 492n, 494n; see also ll. 660-61. By banishing *thought*, Will signals that the Mights have yielded entirely to the *mery* life. It is through *thought*, i.e., through contemplation, that they have formerly known God. As a key to wisdom, thought is the enemy of sin. Will, the faculty associated with feeling rather than with the mind, recurrently evokes this theme of "taking no thought." See ll. 492n, 494n, 660, 890, and 523n.

626-52. The three Mights present a series of self-defining soliloquies in direct contrast to their opening expositions. In those opening statements, they explicated the *syngnyfycacyon* and *propyrte* of their names. In contrast, they now describe their social positions. The order in which the Mights speak reflects the hierarchy of Mind (the higher faculty of reason), Understanding (the *nethyr* part of reason), and Will (the faculty of the senses). Here, as usual, they speak in the order of Mind, Understanding, Will; this is the consistent order in most of the play, although in their opening expository statements the order was changed to Mind, Will, Understanding; see ll. 183-276n, 265-74n.

629-36. Mind is linked with the devil; his sin is pride; his attribute in the world of sin is power, defined in terms of *lordeschyppe*, whom he serves. In his position, he offers *meyntnance* for those who follow him, whom he supports. From his perspective, patronage is the best way to get wealth. In legal terms, *maintenance* signified the wrongful interference in lawsuits, especially by a lord or his liveried followers, basically in an exchange of service for legal protection. Both Richard III and Henry VII passed laws to curb the practice of "livery and maintenance," reducing the number of liveried retainers one could keep. According to David Bevington, "Maintenance . . . was the chief legal abuse of the age. It came into being largely through the breakdown of central authority in England. The medieval peers were trained to violence, and still enjoyed considerable autonomy in their feudal domains. The monarchy had not yet succeeded, as it was to do under the Tudors, in reducing the power of the nobility . . . . Identified by their various liveries, the [all-powerful] factions soon learned to flout common law by interference with courts and juries on their own behalf. In return for service, the chief lords of the realm 'maintained' their liveried retainers against legal action by any power alien to their interests" (1968 30-31; see also Kendall 280-84; Stone 199-203; Elton 19f; ctd. by Bevington 322n). Because of the legislation passed under Richard III (ruled 1483 - 1485) and Henry VII (ruled 1485 - 1509), the emphasis on maintenance as a vice could support the assumption that this play was written in the 1480's, though of course practices of social corruption are well-established by the time they are outlawed by law.

634. schendeschyppe: "shameship," i.e., shameful acts of social life. Notice that in keeping with morality drama conventions, the Mights do at times use terms that imply a moral judgment of their own position.

637-44. Understanding is linked with the world; his sin is covetousness; his attribute in the world of sin is falseness, used in conjunction with the courts to procure wealth. In these lines he defines his own techniques for bribing jurors, practicing simony, taking bribes himself, and swearing falsely to prove a "true" (*try*, l. 641) case false. See ll. 527-34n, 531-32n, 562n, and 743-44n.

638. Enbrace questys of periury: "Bribe jurors to commit perjury." *Enbrace* is a legal term meaning to "incline a jury to be more favourable to one side than the other, by money, promises, letters, threates, or persuasions," i.e., to bribe a jury (Winfield 161). The first legal mention of embracery occurs in 1293 ("De Conspiratoribus Ordinatio," 21 Edward I; ctd. by Winfield 162), at which time it was associated with maintenance. Throughout the fifteenth century, legislation prohibited embracery, including the "Pro Camera Stellata " of 3 Henry VII, c. 1 (1488; ctd. by Winfield 166). Cf. Lydgate, *Dance of Death*, "atte shires questes doste embrace" (481-82); Stow's *Survey of London* says "[in 1468] diuerse persons being common lurors, such as at assises were forsworne for rewards, or fauour of parties, were iudged to ride from Newgate to the pillorie in Cornehill, with Miters of paper on their heads" (Kingsford 1: 191; also see Arnold Williams 45-53, ctd. by Eccles 210n). Both Understanding and Mind are concerned with accumulating wealth through abuses of the legal and judicial systems. Mind works through his power of *lordeschyppe*, whereas Understanding deals more directly with jury-tampering, bribery, etc.; see l. 791n.

643. of myn affye: "loyal to me." The term *affye* is linked to *affyance* and *affynyte*. *Affyance* and *affye* have etymological connections; *affynyte* does not, but is linked to the other two terms both by similarity of sound and parallelism of phrasing. All three suggest alliances based on mutual attraction to or common interest in vulgar activities. See ll. 594n, 657n, 659n, 690n, 799n, and 659n.

653. Mind repeats a claim for the laxity of law in proceeding against *meyntnance*; thus, he affirms his position as one who can grant "livery and maintenance." Cf.°"law goys as lordshipp biddeth hym" (Owst 329; qtd. by Eccles 210n). Note that Mind does presume that there are laws, though unenforced, against maintenance. See ll. 629-36n.

654. Trowthe recurythe not for habundance: "Truth does not collect damages because of wealth," i.e. Truth cannot prevail in suits where it is pitted against wealth. Understanding affirms his commitment to falseness by attacking *trowthe*. *Habundance*, or the accumulation of wealth, is his mode of vice. *Recurythe*, a legal term meaning "to collect damages through judicial action," is one of the terms with both legal and theological implications in the play; for another definition of the verb *recure*, see l. 967n.

655. lust: Following his fellows, Will commits himself once more to the vice of *lust*, noting its prevalence in society; see ll. 567n, 568-73n, 609-11n, 616, and 652.

657. affyance: pledged trust. The term *affyance* is linked etymologically to *affye* and through rhetorical constructions to *affynyte* and *allyance*. See ll. 83n, 643n, and 799n.

659. out of owr allyance: Not allied to us (i.e., not in the circle of supporters created by the bonds that link these sinners together). A similarity of phrasing or rhetorical constructions links this term to *affye*, *affyance*, and *affynyte*; see ll. 690n, 799n, 862n, 643n, and 657n.

660. take we no thought: See l. 623-24n.

664. them: D reads *hem*. This is one of the two instances in which D uses the conservative "h-" in pronouns "their" and "them" where M uses "th-" or "þ-" (see also l. 746). At other times, D appears to have influenced M (who as the scribe of *Mankind* naturally preferred "þ" to "h") to use the conservative "h" form; see ll. 3, 56, 293, 295, 331, 588, 599, 634, 635, 701, 710, 711, 743, 749, and 752sd. Both D and M use *þ-/th-* four times, in ll. 48, 68, 346, and 438. Also see Introduction: "The Relationship Between the Digby and the Macro Texts" for further analysis.

665-68. Reaffirming their previous commitments, the three Mights attribute their success to money. Ultimately in this play as in *The Castle of Perseverance*, the allegiance of sinners to the "world" gives covetousness special emphasis, in keeping with the importance of the sin of avarice in the fifteenth century. Mind (Maintenance) affirms allegiance to *lordschyppe* (l. 665) and Understanding (Perjury) to *law* (l. 666); see 387-88n, 529-30n, 629-36n, 637-44n, and 638n.

669-75. Mind and Understanding claim great popularity for their own vices (maintenance and bribing jurors). Their indication of widespread lawlessness is verified by historians of the fifteenth century. For instance, "It was in vain that statute after statute was passed empowering the justices of the peace to take action against riots, routs, unlawful assemblies, and forcible entries; just as repeated enactments empowered them to proceed against the magnates' giving of liveries of uniform, food, and badges to their retainers. The justices were either too afraid to enforce these statutes or too much in league with the offenders. They can hardly be blamed for lack of zeal when even royal judges were sometimes to blame" (Myers 142). To take an example from early in the fifteenth century: in 1411 Robert Tirwhit, a justice of the King's Bench, invaded a property to settle a dispute and, when charged by Parliament to explain his crime, pleaded ignorance of the law (ctd. by Riggio 1974 201; see E. Williams xvi-xvii and Myers 200). R. W. Owst points out that medieval sermons fiercely denounce "officers of gret men that wareth lyverethes," whose liveries "may be safely trusted to shield them from any just penalty in the courts for their misdeeds." (Ms. Roy. 18, B. xxiii, fol. 142; qtd. by Owst 325; ctd. by Molloy 115). See ll. 629-36n, 637-44n, 745n, and 761-62n.

672, 78. Mayntnance: See ll. 630-36n.

676. ys take nought a hede: "is paid no attention at all." Instead of *nought a*, D has *non*. In this M construction, *a* is an indefinite article with the noun *hede*. *Nought* is an adverb.

677-84. In these lines the three Mights join together in a general celebration of their sinful lives. In contrast to the clarity of their expository self-definitions, here they do not speak only for their own vices. Now they praise each other under their newly personified names. For instance, in ll. 677-80, Will speaks for the prominence of *Mayntnance* and *Periury*, now personified by Mind and Understanding, whereas in ll. 681-82 Mind praises the reign of *Lechery*, personified by Will.

679. reynande: "arraigning," i.e. bringing indictments in court. The implication is that because of the power of Maintenance and Perjury, there are more false legal cases brought now than ever before. Glossing *reynande* as *flourishing*, Eccles and Baker assume that *Ther* is an error for *Thei* in both D and M, with the implication that "They [the vices] have never reigned so powerfully before." However, since *reynande* is an aphetic for *arreyning*, or *arraigning*, the Ms. line makes sense as it stands.

680. Seth Gode was bore: Cf. *Minor Poems of the Vernon MS*, "Seþþe þe tyme þaet god was boren, þis world was neuer so vntrewe" (2: 685); *Peter Idley's Instructions to His Son*, "I reporte me yf now vsed be pride inordinate; Neuer more I trowe sith God was born" (2: B, 22-23; both ctd. by Eccles 210n).

685. There is a marginal notation in both D and M, reading *va*, apparently an abbreviation for *vacat*, indicating that the dances were at some point cut, perhaps for purposes of production; see l. 784n.

686. retenance: "retinue." Cf. "Alle þis Riche Retenaunce þat Regneden with Fals Weoren bede to þe Bruyt-ale," (Langeland, *Piers the Plowman*, A.11,35); "And so he assembled eal his retynance and went & spake vnto ham of þe Kyngus honour" (*The Brut, or the Chronicles of England* 218: 258).

687. by contenance: Probably "masked, as in a mime," suggesting that the dancers enter in a dumb show, deriving from *contenance* meaning "expressive movement, sign, gesture." Cf. Towneley cycle, "Thay knew by contenaunce that thare kyng / Was done to dede" (26/116-17; N-Town 27/348sd and 28/80sd, "be contenawns," Spector 1991 1: 276, 289; glossed as "appearance, countenance" by Spector, 2: 572; in play 28, the reference to "contenawns" occurs in a passage in which actors are described as "dysgysed in odyr garments," but there is no specific reference to masking); see also, "The pageantes wear so obscure . . . because all was cuntenaunce, and no wordes" (*Archaeologia*, 31: 328 [document dated 1468]; ctd. by Eccles 210n. Note that Eccles cites the Towneley occurrence at 26/114 and the N-Town stage directions at 27/669*a* and 28/972*a*). However, *contenance* also means "patronage," and it is possible this expression *Cummynge in by contenance* means "coming in by patronage," i.e. as a patronized group. It is clear that each of the sets of dancers belongs to one of the three Mights.

690. of myn affyance: "of those pledged to me," i.e., that group belonging to me by fealty bond. This is the term by which Anima identifies Wisdom as her betrothed (*my hertys affyance*, l. 83). In this instance, M has followed D in using *myn*, rather than *my*, as the possessive pronoun. See ll. 83n, 193, 385, 643n, 657n, 659n, and 690.

691. Meyntnance: Mind has now been renamed; in keeping with his affinity with lordship and his sin of pride, identified with worldly power, he is named *Maintenance*. Cf. *Jacob's Well*, for "meyntenauns of pletynges & of strives" as a branch of Pride (qtd. by Eccles 211n). See 629-36n, 634, 653n, 671, 678, 693-96n, 700-06n, 714n, 724sdn, 745n, and 761-62n.

692sd. dysgysyde: "masked," as if for a formal masque dance. This term also implies clothing in a new-fangled mode. The *sute of Mynde* is a livery, apparently with a crest, belonging to Mind in his newfound role as a maintaining lord. The *lyouns rampaunt* echo and parody the theme of royalty associated with Wisdom. The Trinity College production used a Throne of Solomon as the staging area for Christ as Wisdom. The twelve gilded lions on that throne were then parodied by the rampaunt red lions worn as part of the livery of these dancers. Smart conjectured that the lions were intended to symbolize the livery of the Duke of Suffolk and the Duke of Norfolk, who both had lions as their badges (89). The lion was, however, prominent in the English royal crest and was such a commonplace symbol of pride that this particular attribution is not fully convincing. See, for instance, Hilton's *The Scale of Perfection* "The proud man is turned into a lion for pride, for he would be dreaded and worshipped of all men" (2: 14, tr. in Underhill 276; ctd. by Eccles 211n). Similarly, the *rede berdys* parody the gilded beard of Wisdom. Red, particularly in association with black, was widely regarded as the devil's color. Red beards often appeared on Judas in portraits and were worn by Judas in the cycle plays (Mellinhoff 31-46 and Molloy 115). In the Coventry *Destruction of Jerusalem*, soldiers apparently wore "red cotes" (Ingram 304). Cf. *Handlyng Synne*, where men of wrath are "rede as blode" (10229-30; qtd. by Eccles 211n). See ll. 589-96n.

warders: heavy club-like symbols of authority which parodically recall the more elegant sceptre of Christ in the opening stage directions; see 0sdn.

vi: see ll. 696-77n.

her mynstrall, trumpes: The symbolical instrument for these dancers is the trumpet, which is both the instrument of *jugemente* (l. 703) — with ironic implications of the last judgment — and battle. Thus, it is appropriate for maintaining false pleas in court and for the dancers who symbolize the sins of wrath, envy, and pride.   The musicians (*mynstrall*, with an implied plural), are virtually identified with the instrument, *trumpes*, in this designation;   see also ll. 702-04.

693-96. Mind (Maintenance) has six retainers whose names recall the three deadly sins associated with the devil: wrath, envy, and pride. Each dancer answers to his name.   According to Eccles, treatises on sin codify "Disdain and Stubbornness (*Indignacyon* and *Sturdynes*) under Pride; Malice and Discord under Envy; and Hastiness and Vengeance (*Wreche*) under Wrath" (211n).   For *hastiness* meaning *sudden rage*, cf. "He waxed ny3e wood by hedy hastynesse" (*The Life and Martyrdom of St. Katherine of Alexandra* 77).   *Wreche*, meaning "vengeance," was in common usage through the mid-fifteenth century; cf. Belial, "Wyth werkys of wreche I werke hem mykyl wrake" (*The Castle of Perseverance*, l. 203).   See ll. 716 and 630-36n.

696-97. Each renamed Might includes himself with his retinue, for a total of seven (six dancers plus the patron — in this instance, *Mayntennance*).   The number seven recalls the seven deadly sins, which are represented by the three troups of dancers.   Moreover, by identifying *seven* as a number of *discorde* and *inperfyghtness*, the dramatist plays on and inverts the traditional Catholic identification of *seven* with completion or perfection, an association having its origins in the story of creation.   See ll. 692sdn, 724sdn, 752sdn, 912sdn, 725-33n, 753-56n.

697. discorde: From D; M reads *dycorde*, apparently misreading D's "-is-" as "y," which it resembles; a similar error may account for *dyvygurde* (l. 901), although this latter term is a recognized variant of *dysfygure* and so has been retained in this text. See l.414n. It is, of course, possible that *dycorde* is an unattested variant of *dyscorde*, but without other authority for the term, this edition uses the D form.

698. yomandrye: "a company of young vassals." The metaphor of feudal patronage carries throughout the play, with the dancers seen as retainers of their patrons; see l. 692.

loweday, to dres: *loweday*, a translation of ML *dies amoris*, designates a day appointed to settle disputes, and by extension the agreements signed on such a day. Cf. Lydgate, "Fyghters, brawlers, brekers of lofedayes" (*Assembly of Gods* 692). However, the term also implies a *day of lovemaking*, and in this devil's dance the two terms are intermixed, with a further play on the term *dres*, which means both *to redress* a wrong and *dres* for the game. The implication is that this group of "dressed" or costumed dancers, serving as the retinue of the dandy Mind (Maintenance), will give false testimony even on a *loweday*. Since they use the law falsely and they represent wrath, envy, and pride, their antics ironically invert the intentions of harmony implied by the term. This is one of the typical inversions of the world of sin. Because *loweday* as a day for redressing legal wrongs is not well known, the modernization links the legal disputes and the idea of lovemaking in a way that slightly alters and simplifies the complex meaning of the line. (See also Bennett; ctd. by Eccles 211n.)

699. Ande þe deule hade swore yt: "If the devil had sworn to it." As the devil's men, this troupe will testify falsely and "maintain" any suit to which the devil has sworn himself. Cf. Caesar in the Towneley cycle 9/94-96 (ctd. by Eccles 211n at 9/83-84). See ll. 629-36n and 700-06n.

700-07. These lines explicate the meaning of trumpets as emblems of perverted power and war. The allusion to judgment calls to mind the paintings of the Last Judgment, with trumpets blowing at the corners of the earth. That allusion is parodied in the reference to *jugement*, which is assumed here to be connected with the court system and, specifically, with judgments rendered because of Maintenance (*Mayntement* from D, l. 706; M reads *meyntnance*), or false support of court cases. The allusions to battle also suit the role of Mind (Maintenance) as a powerful secular lord who wages battle; they are likewise appropriate to the sin of wrath, which leads to fighting. Linking *menstrellys* with *trumpys* (ll. 701-02) once more identifies the instrument with the musician. See ll. 630-36n, 692n, and 698n.

700. þe deullys dance: This is the devil's dance, because Mind (Maintenance) is the devil's man. Cf. also Dunbar, *Dance of the Seven Deadly Sins* (referring to Stubbes, *Anatomy of Abuses*, ed. Furnivall 147; ctd. by Eccles 211n).

705. expedyent: fitting, as a symbol for Pride or Maintenance, whose dancers they are.

706. þes meny of Mayntement: troupe serving Mind renamed as "Maintenance." The term *Mayntenment*, a personification for Mind (Maintenance), is taken from D, who obviously uses it for the value of the rhyme with *expedyente* (l. 705) and *Madam Regent* (l. 707); recurrently less mindful of the rhyme scheme, M changes to the more familiar *meyntnance*.

707. Madame Regent: Eccles may be right in assuming this is the name of a dance. However, no such dance has as yet been identified, and reading the entire line, one may conclude that the directive to *blow* should be given to the minstrel, who may be comically called *Madame Regent*, perhaps parodically disguised as a woman. Or a term like *Madam Regent* might refer ironically to some particular woman of power, such as Margaret Beaufort whose influence as the Queen mother of Henry VII was considerable or Margaret of Anjou (the mad Margaret of Shakespeare's *Richard III*) who attempted to hold the power of her imbecile husband Henry VI for their son Edward by claiming full honors for herself and her son when on progress throughout the countryside. See, for example, the *Coventry Leet Book*, where the Queen demanded to "be met yn like forme as the king" (14 March, 1457). Whether a specific historical reference is intended or not, the term parodies the idea of a ruling woman as a perversion of power and lordship, one of the many satirical inversions of power and sovereignty associated with mind in the world of sin. Cf. Prudentius, *Psychomachia*, where Pride is represented as a woman warrior, identified as *regina* (l. 199). Also see Jonson, *Bartholomew Fair*, I.v. 18-19, "You think you are Madam Regent still, Mistress Overdo, when I am in place?" (ctd. by Eccles

211n). For more information on the ironies implied by "women on top," see N. Davis, *passim*.

714. Mayntnance: Both the character of Mind (Maintenance) and the legal practice. See ll. 629-36n.

716. When introducing his dancers, Understanding speaks out of turn for the first time since he gave his expository self-defining monologue in ll. 245-76; see ll. 551-716n.

718. Jorowr in on hoode berith to facys: Each of these dancers wear a double-faced mask as an emblem of hypocrisy. (Cf. Lydgate, *Minor Poems*, 1: 69; 2: 450, 758, 775; *Peter Idley's Instructions to His Son* 85, 215; *Oxford Proverbs* 679; ctd. by Eccles 211n); Cf. also Skelton's *Magnyfycence*, "Two faces in a hode couertly I bere" (qtd. by Smart 69). See l. 724sd.

719. Fayer speeche & falsehede in on space ys: "Flattering speech and deceit are together in one space," i.e., in one dancer wearing two masks. See ll. 725-33n.

721. Quest of Holborn: Furnivall identifies the quest of Holborn as a "wardmote quest," but according to Eccles that "was a jury of inquiry which . . . did not try [offenders]." The Holborn quest was probably a jury presided over by the sheriff and justices of Middlesex, who met in High Holborn, where a new Quest House was built about 1590 . . . opposite Grays Inn Lane" (Furnivall 168; also see Riley 36-39, 257-60; E. Williams 1232; Jeaffreson 70, 77-78; ctd. by Eccles 211-12n). Milton McC. Gatch suggests that the emphasis on Holborn, born out further by the reference to *Sent Audre of Ely* (l. 832), suggests that the play may have been performed in the bishop of Ely's palace in Holborn (358-59). The *Quest of Holborn* is the choice location for both the dancers of Mind (Maintenance) and Understanding (Perjury). The repeated reference does suggest some local satire. See 731 and 832.

722. rechases: From D; M reads *rechase*. The D form, which insures the rhyme, is an implied 3rd person plural of the verb meaning to "chase, as in a hunt," with the implication that the full line means

"This jury always takes to the hunt against justice." This is one of the instances in which M foregoes rhyme for the sake of what appears to be grammatical specificity, replacing D's "singular" form. But, though a "lectio difficilior" ("difficult reading"), the implied plural was not uncommon in the late fifteenth century (see Visser 70-72 and Introduction: "Comparison between the Digby and Macro Manuscripts" in this volume); see also l. 270n.

This line has occasioned various readings. Baker suggests that D *thei rechases* is an error for *ther rechase*: "the final *r* of *ther* was easily confused with *i*, for almost invariably both scribes . . . used the secretary *r* as a final letter" (Baker et al. 222n). The *OED* suggests *theire chases is* as a possible reading, noting also that the meaning here may be a transferred meaning of the verb *rechase*, taken from hunting (suggested by the hunting implications of the term *quest*): "to chase (a deer) back into the forest." Eccles associates the term with the verb *recheat*, citing Chaucer, *Book of the Duchess*, 379 and *The Master of Game* where *rechase* means "recheat, blow the horn to call together the hounds" (212n). However, D's form is satisfactory as is. Also see l. 908n.

723. harde hys grace ys: According to the *OED*, *hard grace* is a term meaning either "ill-will" or "a stroke of ill-luck." In either case, the phrase connotes the loss of favor from a patron; the idea is that those against whom the false jurors marshall their forces will suffer ill-luck, i.e. they will receive bad judgments at court. See l. 550/550sdn, 575n, and 669-75n.

724sd. Again, there are six dancers, with Understanding (Perjury) making up the contingent of seven. This troup wears jurors' hoods. See ll. 696-97n, 718n, and 752n.

vyseryde dyuersly: literally "wearing different visors," but as explicated in the text at l. 718, here it appears to mean "wearing masks with two faces turned in different directions." See ll. 692sdn, 718n, 733n, 717n.

hattys of meyntnance: The dancers wear liveried hats, as a reflection of the patronage of Understanding (Perjury). Identifying *meyntnance* with the followers of Understanding (Perjury) suggests how closely the sins of the first two Mights accord with each other. Mind is renamed Maintenance, as the vice of lordship. However, because of its association with the courts, this particular crime is also identified with Understanding (Perjury). According to Eccles, the Commons petitioned in 1377 against the giving of hats by way of livery for maintenance (Rotuli Parl. 3: 23; Eccles 212n). Legislation against the abuses of Maintenance was passed throughout the latter part of the fifteenth century. See ll. 629-36n.

her mynstrell a bagpyp: Partly because of its swelling shape, the bagpipe was often associated with the sin of lust. But it was also regarded as an instrument of vanity, a symbol for "an inflated and senseless talker; a windbag" or "a long-winded monotonous speaker" (*OED*). Cf. Henry Crosse, *Virtues Commonwealth*: "the bagpipy of vanitie, like a windie instrument, soundeth nothing but prophaneness" (c. 1603, pub. Grossart 1878 103). Once more, the instrument and the musician are assimilated to each other in the emblem. See ll. 692sd, 752sd.

725-33. These six dancers are followers of Understanding (Perjury). They follow Avarice (or Covetousness), the sin of the world, with each representing an offense which will gain an advantage at law. *Raveyn*, taken from L. *rapina*, "seize," implies robbery or greed. Cf. Prudentius, *Psychomachia*, where *Periuria (Perjuries)* and *Commenta (Falsehood)* are among the ten followers of *Avaritia*; *Fraus*, or deceit, also plays a role in the attack of the vices (ll. 258, 464-65). D has *falsehed* where M has *falsnes*; see also *falsehede*, l. 719. Molloy compares St. Gregory, *Moralia,* whose seven daughters of Covetousness include *perjurium, fraus, proditio, fallacia,* and *violentia* (31: 45; ctd. by Eccles 212n). See ll. 693-96n, 718n, 719n, 744n, and 753-56n.

731. Quest of Holborn: See l. 721n.

an euyll endyrecte: "an indirect [or] twisted evil." Associating the term *endyrecte* with *Entret* in 796, Eccles emends it to *entyrecte* and glosses it as "salve, plaster" from OF *entrait, entret*: "A jury should remedy wrongs, but this jury is an evil plaster or ointment which takes bribes to plaster wrongs and oil its own palms. Cf. *Hick Scorner* 267, 'And with an oyntment the iuges hande I can grece'" (Eccles 212n). Baker accepts Eccles' emendation and his association of the term with *Entret*: "the word in this context would then mean an evil of bribery (i.e., salving or greasing the palm)" (Baker et al. 222n). This emendation is unnecessary; *endyrecte* is an adjective, deriving from OFr *indirect*, meaning "crooked" or "dishonest," modifying *euell*, a noun.

734. Now dance on, ws! All the worlde doth on ws wondyr: The first clause of this line, the same in D and M, does not make good sense. The first *ws* is probably an error resulting from D anticipating the prepositional phrase *on ws*; M copied the error. The line should probably read *Now dance on! All the worlde doth on ws wondyr*. As it stands now, the first *ws* makes sense only as a term of direct address, meaning "Now dance on, us [i.e., those of our company]," but the pronoun is awkward in this usage. I have maintained the reading in the line but emended the modernization.

739. swere & starre: "swear and stare," an alliterative phrase denoting intense rage. Cf. *Minor Poems of the Vernon Ms*: "þe leuh bigon to stare and swere / And seide þer com none such child þere" (75).

740. Though: From D; M *thouht*. D transcribes as *though*, but with a crossstroke through the second *h*, which to a quick look suggests *t*. Apparently misreading, M transcribes the term *thouht*. This would be the only instance of M transcribing the word *thought* as *thouht* (an obsolete form of ME *thought*). If the M reading were correct, the line could be read "[All] thoughts [of those who swear and stare] are false, both to a greater and lesser degree." This reading is not as satisfactory as the D reading ("Although everyone is false, both the richer and the poorer"), nor is it clear that M intends this word. He may simply have misread D in his haste.

741-42. Wyche wey to þe woode wyll þe hare / They knowe & þey at rest sett als tyghte: "Which way will the hare go to the woods? [These covetous tricksters] know and they sit tight, waiting for their victim as securely as in a dense woods." The term *tyghte* means "firmly," "closely," "securely," or as "densely as a woods." The idiom *at rest sett als tyghte* thus means "remain comfortably fixed, as securely as in a dense woods." The expression *wyche wey to þe woode wyll þe hare* has a proverbial ring to it.

743-44. Some seme hem wyse / For the fadyr of vs, Covetyse: "Some think them wise because of Covetousness, the father of us." This troupe of dancers is liveried to Understanding (Covetousness; sometimes called Perjury). The image of the patron as *fadyr* ironically recalls recurrent references to God the father, although it is Mind who is most often associated with God the father, rather than Understanding. Identifying Covetousness as the "father" of sinners does, however, reinforce the primacy given to this sin of the world throughout the Macro plays. In *The Castle of Perseverance*, for instance, Covetousness has his own scaffold, along with the World, the Flesh, the Devil, and God. For references to God as father, see ll. 122, 279, 285, 989, 1096. For comments on avarice as the primary sin, see ll. 531-32 amd 637-44n.

745. Mayntnance and Periury: the renamed Mind and Understanding. See l. 630-6n, 637-44n, 653n, 669-75n, 671, 677-84n, 678, 691n, 693-96n, 700-6n, 714n, 724sdn, and 725-33n.

746. þer: D reads *here*. This is one of two instances in which D uses the conservative "h" form in pronouns where M has "þ." More often, M follows the conservative D practice. See l. 664n.

747-48. sprynge of Lechery / Þat to me attende: "The troupe of dancers that attend on me, Lechery." A *sprynge* is a dance. Here, the dance and the troupe are conflated. Will, renamed Lechery, now introduces his dancers. See ll. 561, 615n.

749. stewys clene rebaldry: "the clean ribaldry of the brothels." The ironic reference to *clene*, meaning "pure," echoes the similar ironic inversion in *a clene sowll & a mery* (l. 494). The irony is particularly sharp since Anima as a pure and undefiled lover of Christ is persistently called *clene*. The ironic implication of calling bawdy love play of the brothels *clene rebaldry* is obvious. For references to *clene* as a term denoting genuine moral purity, see ll. 45, 54, 81, 174, 176, 284, 289, 954, 969, and 976.

752. They may sey wyth tenker, I trow, lat amende: "They may say with the tinker, I believe, let it mend itself." As itinerant craftsmen repairing small household objects, tinkers developed a reputation as bunglers, which led to a number of derisive proverbial expressions, as, for instance, "to swear like a tinker," "a tinker's curse," or as here "let it mend [itself]." The term "tinker" became a virtual synonym for "vagrant."

752sd. Will (Lechery)'s dancers are apparently women. Female dancers were not uncommon, particularly in the kinds of masked dances which are being parodied at this point in the play. At Cambridge University, for instance, women dancers were recorded as coming from St. Mary's Parish at least from 1429-30 on (see Nelson 1989 2: 735), and women regularly danced in later masques. The number of dancers is slightly ambiguous; D and M indicate *vi women in sut dydgysyde as galontys*, and *iii as matrones*. This could mean that there are nine dancers, six disguised as gallants and three as matrons. However, the formula for the previous two sets of dancers, which have included six dancers each, suggests that there are six dancers, with the number *iii* probably omitted before *dysgysyde as galontys*; this would mean that half the dancers are disguised as gallants and half as women. When the dancers are introduced below, the names are ambiguous enough to confuse the numbers a little, but there are at the most seven possible dancers, not nine.

dysgysyde: "disguised" — refers to the costuming and implies a dramatic genre, the *dysgysygne*, as the early masque was called, as well as costumes. See ll. 692sdn and 753-56n.

wondyrfull vysurs conregent: "very fine visors of a livery that suggests the regent." The *OED* lists this passage as the only instance of *conregent*, meaning "ruling together." The definition does not make particularly good sense in this line. Eccles emends the term to *congruent*, an emendation which Baker notes as possible but does not adopt. The phrase *wondyrfull vysurs* indicates "very fine masks"; thus the meaning I have suggested. The term *Madame Regent* has already insinuated that the power of a regent may be parodied by associating it with a woman. Here, once more, the women dancers may be wearing masks that associate them parodically with royalty. Or *wondyrfull vysurs conregent* may simply mean "beautiful masks of one livery." For *Madame Regent*, see l. 707n.

here mynstrell a hornpype: The musical symbol of the dancers of Will (Lechery) is a hornpipe. This term may refer to any one of several instruments in the fifteenth century. See ll. 757-78n.

753-56. Like Mind (Maintenance) and Understanding (Perjury) before him, Will (Lechery) introduces his dancers and explicates their names. This process is not as precise as it was for the two earlier Mights. Though the stage directions specify *vi* dancers (l. 752sd), Will does not enumerate his retinue or count himself specifically among them as Mind (Maintenance) and Understanding (Perjury) do (ll. 696, 733) but using the formulas developed in the earlier dances, it follows that six dancers symbolize the three sins of the flesh: sloth, gluttony, and lechery. They are introduced as couples, probably with a *gallant* and a *matron* in each couple, as follows; the *slepers*, *Rekleshede* and *Idyllness* (sin of sloth) are couple one; *Surfet* and *Gredynes* (sin of gluttony) are couple two, and *Spousebreche* and *Mastres* (i.e. "Adulterer" and "Mistress," sin of lust) are couple three; Will apparently calls himself *jentyll Fornycacyon*. *Mastres*, a variant of *mistress*, most commonly meant a ruling woman, and the term may hint at the perversion of gender felt to adhere in a ruling woman (See N. Davis) and previously alluded to in *Madam Regent* (l. 707). However, here the term appears primarily to have the modern meaning of "mistress" as a "lover who illicitly replaces a wife." Cf. "Called in my countre a traitouresse . . . . Of newe defamed and namyd a maistresse" (Lydgate *Bochas* 1924-27). All of these sins represent their master, Will, who — probably making up the seventh member of the company — is apparently called *jentyll Fornycacyon*. This latter attribution is ambiguous; this term could refer to one of the dancers, but the division into couples makes that unlikely; see l. 752sd and 759n.

757-78. hornpype: a term referring to several instruments, sometimes so-called because the mouthpiece was made of horn. Eccles assumes that this piece of horn made the instrument a fit emblem for cuckoldry (see Eccles 212n). As with previous minstrals in the play, the term here actually designates the musician who played the hornpipe. The meaning is slightly confused here, however, by the fact that *OED* glosses this term as "a raucous dance, associated with merriment," for this line of *Wisdom*. However, the next instance of this meaning recorded in the *OED* does not occur until the late sixteenth century. And the *MED* does not give the meaning of *dance* for the term *hornpype*. There is in a capital at Vezelay a sculpture showing profane music, with a devil playing a wind instrument (possibly a hornpipe), to a woman whose hair stands high on end, with another woman hiding her naked genitals. (See Salet plate 29; I am grateful to Michael Davis for this reference).

759. Thre fortherers of loue . . . quod Bete: Will (Lechery)'s dancers are recurrently divided into groups of three. They are disguised, [three] as gallants, three as women. They are named in three sets of two (*Rekleshede & Idyllnes*, *Surfet & Gredynes*, and *Spousebreche & Mastres*, ll. 753-55). And now they are called *thre fortherers of loue*; apparently, each couple is regarded as a unit. Cf. Skelton, "Furders of loue, with baudry aqueinted" (1: 386; ctd. by Eccles 212n, who also identifies various possibilities for the nickname *Bete*, which is most likely a casual nickname for a woman, colloquially associated with shrewish speech). See ll. 753-56n.

760. dance of þis damsellys: Apparently, an obscene dance, performed by the six women *dysgysyde* as gallants and matrons in the suit of Will (Lechery). The constellation *caprae saltantes*, or dancing goats, was associated with lecherous dances. *Dancing damsel* was also a phrase meaning "dancing girl" (cf. *OED* under *dancing*).

761-62. *Meyntnance* is consistently associated with Mind; here Understanding (Perjury) allies himself with the first Might. He provides the bribes for jurors which makes *meyntnance* possible. See ll. 629-36n, 672-78, 630-66n, 637-44n, 653n, 654n, 669-75n, 691n, 693-97n, 696-97n, 700-06n, 714n, 724sdn, and 745n.

763-78. In these lines, Will (Lechery) — as the spendthrift who represents mindless pleasure — battles with Mind (Maintenance) and

Understanding (Perjury) as the faculties associated with making and keeping money and power. The dissension is reflective of the disharmony which in the allegory of the play inevitably accompanies godlessness. It pits the higher and lower parts of reason against sensory experience (represented by Will, the character who will *take no thought*). Thus, for this portion of the play, there is a break between "reason" (Mind and Understanding, the two faculties that represent the higher and lower portions of reason) and "passion" (Will). See ll. 624, 660.

765. Whom breydest þu vs of þin aqueyntance?: "To whom do you reproach us among your acquaintance?" Since it is very likely that the verb *breydest*, a shortened form of the now obsolete verb "abraid," would have carried a pun on the colloquial meaning of "abraid" to "ejaculate," this question may informally be rendered: "For whom do you jerk us off among your friends?" The "acquaintance" to whom Will is referring are of course those allied to Mind and Understanding. The *vs* of this passage refers to Will and his dancers.

767. here gyse ys of France: "This costume is from France." Called *harlottys*, Will (Lechery)'s female dancers are associated with the fashions of France, persistently a metaphor for vulgarity, extravagance, and sinfulness in dress as well as for sexual laxity. Cf. the N-Town Cycle "Joseph's Doubt": "Olde cokwold, þi bowe is bent / Newly now aftyr þe Frensche gyse" (Spector 1991 1: 125; 12/55-6; also see Smart 65). See l. 517n.

775. Dompe deuys, can ye not dare?: "Mute disguised dancing device, can't you get up the courage to fight?" *Deuys*, or "device," refers either to a heraldic device or a dramatic device; it can also signify a "disguise"; in this context, it probably refers to the troupe of dancers as a disguised dramatic device, with "device," the commonplace term designating the machinery of later masques, here used to indicate the costumed dancers themselves. *Dare* has its obvious meaning of showing courage. Will (Lechery), who has just been attacked by his fellow Mights, pleads for help from his *menye* of dancers. They clearly do not help him, since in the next line he banishes them from the room; see 776n. This line has occasioned various readings. The *MED* erroneously glosses it as "dompe Denys," presuming *deuys*, spelled *denys*, to be the personified name of one of the dancers. Similarly, Furnivall glosses *dompe* as "Master"; Eccles glosses this term as "dumb," or mute, while glossing *dare* as "remain quiet." *Dompe* may mean "mute," but as a sb., it may also refer to a dance, a subtextual inference relevant in this context. The M *u* and *n* are difficult to distinguish from each other. Thus, the word could be *denys*. However, the personification is not necessary, as the more obvious reference to the dramatic device of the masked dancers fits the context perfectly.

776. owtwarde, on & tweyn!: With ellipsis of the verb go, this phrase means "Go out, move on and get out!" *Tweyn* in this instance is a verb meaning "separate." Will (Lechery) dismisses his useless dancers. An alternative possibility is to gloss *on* as "one" and *tweyn* as "two" and to suppose that Will is sending his dancers out of the room in pairs.

780. all at on: As the Mights patch up their differences, they parody the process of atonement, or at-one-ment (the regaining of godlike unity), which is required for redemption.

783-84. He þat ys yll wywande, / Wo hys hym, by þe bon!: Cf. the Towneley cycle, referring to wives, "wo is hym that is bun," (13/116; ctd. by Eccles 213n at 13/64). The proverb "by þe bon" is of obscure origin; it may have to do with dicing, or it may be a corruption of the Old Testament prophesy upon the dry bones into which God breathed life for the prophet Exekiel. Cf. Ezekiel 37.1-5, esp. 4: "Et dixit ad me: Vaticinare de ossibus istis, et dices eis: Ossa arida, audite verbum Domini" ("Again he said to me, 'Prophesy to these bones, and say to them, O dry bones, hear the word of the Lord'").

787. chevesaunce: From OFr *chevance*, acquired wealth, this term means "a stratagem to make a profit."

789. Westmyster: "Westminister Hall," where the courts of King's Bench, Common Pleas, and Chancery were all held. The courts of Westminster were typically objects of satire for their corruption. Cf. *Mundus et Infans*, ll. 575-82 (ctd. by Smart 63). See also Stow 2: 118 (ctd. by Eccles 213n).

790. Þe nex terme: "the next legal term," of which there were four — Hilary, Easter, Trinity, and Michelmas (see Eccles 213n).

791. retornys . . . enbraces . . . recordaunce: All associated with devices to extract illegal profit in court. *Retornys* are "writ returns," reporting the extent to which a writ has been carried out; *enbraces*, derived from the verb *enbrace*, to bribe a jury, means "jury briberies"; *recordaunces* are the "acts of giving false testimony." See ll. 638n and 795-96n.

793-94. parvyse . . . A Powlys: "the enclosure or court in front of a church, especially of St. Paul's Cathedral [where lawyers met]." Eccles glosses *A* as *of* and cites *Mankind* (ll. 127, 272), *Minor Poems of the Vernon MS.* (i.407), and *Cursor Mundi* (1367) as other early instances of this meaning (Eccles 213n).

795-96. Mind (Maintenance) identifies three personifications of legal malpractice as a retinue of his liveried retainers (*menye*). The term *meny(e)* has been used previously to identify the troupes of dancers of each of the Mights. *Entret* means "supplication," "negotiation" — here with the implication of being falsely suborned; *Jugepartynge* is "sharing wealth with judges," i.e., bribing judges; *To-Supporte* means "to give financial support," obviously to legal officials. Eccles associates *endyrecyte* (l. 713), which he emends to *entyrecte*, with *entret*, but this emendation is unnecessary, as the two terms are different; see ll. 706, 709, 715, 735, 781, and 731n.

797. Ande euer þe latter, þe leuer me: "The later I come, the happier I am." Will (Lechery) persistently identifies himself with pleasure rather than acquisition. While Mind (Maintenance) and Understanding (Perjury) are meeting clients and making illegal profits in the law courts, Will (Lechery) comes to the city only at night, in search of pleasure.

799. to my affynyte: "to meet companions allied to me," or alternatively "with the companions allied to me." The term *affynyte* recalls terms *affyance* and *affye*. See ll. 643n, 690n.

800. stews: Brothels. Eccles notes that the most common stews were on the Bankside. In Medwall's *Nature*, Bodyly Lust goes to "tother syde" of the water to "þe stews" (Nelson 2/179, 183). Cf. also *Mundus et Infans* (592-93) and *Cock Lorel's Boat* (ctd. by Eccles 213n).

801-04. Mind (Maintenance) chides Will (Lechery) for his spendthrifty ways. This exchange does not, as previously, lead to a fight. Will (Lechery) defends himself, saying that he does at times *take amendys*, i.e., "exact a fine," from those who have offended no one.

804. engrose: M *engose*. E amends to *engrose*. *Engrose vpe* means to "collect for oneself from all quarters."

805-28: In two sets of ritual speeches, the three Mights once more define their specific functions in their new identities, with Mind (Maintenance) arresting and exacting forfeit where he does not get a profit; Understanding (Perjury) indicts and acquits for his own advantage; Will (Lechery) has *lest care* (l. 814), since he only requires *met & drynke & ease* (l. 814), rather than work. In the second set of speeches (ll. 817-29), each Might brags of the money he will spend on a feast to celebrate. See ll. 381-92n, 383-84n, 387-88n, 391-92n, 495n, 497-99n, 513-15n, 527-34n, 551-716n, 551-73n, 574-96n, and 626-52n.

809. Thow þey curs, nether þe wers I fare: "Although they curse, I neither fare the worse," i.e., "I do not fare the worse for their cursing." This is perhaps the best reading for a difficult line. If transcribed as *nther*, this term is obviously an error, but for what? The best solution may be to presume a missing "e" before the "-th," at which there appears to be a slight scribal overstroke, as if to correct some unspecified error. The term *nether*, "neither," may be used as a conjunctive adverb without a second negative particle (though the recorded occurrences of this usage postdate *Wisdom* and despite the fact that the M scribe does not use the term *nether* in this sense elsewhere in the play). Other possibilites are twofold: 1) Because of the similarity between *u* and *n*, the term could be transcribed as *uther*, which may be either singular ("other") or plural ("others"). Thus transcribed and repunctuated, the line might well read: *Thow þey curse uther þe wers, I fare*, meaning "Though they curse others worse, I carry on well," implying that "though those who lose in court curse others even worse, their curses do not affect me; I carry on well." This transcription provides an awkward but possible meaning for the ms. as it stands. However, this would be the only instance in which M begins a word with *u*, his preference being *v* or *w*. 2) Eccles transcribes as *uther* but emends to *neuer*, "never," with the implied reading: "Though they curse, never the worse I fare," essentially the same as the reading proposed above with the more familiar negative particle "never." Though this may be an acceptable emendation, M is clearly not trying to write *neuer*, he consistently abbreviates *euer* and in the one instance in which he writes *neuer* (*neuerþeles*, l. 9), he similarly abbreviates the word. Moreover, D's "th" combination, which can resemble "ch," could not be mistaken for "eu"; see l. 66n.

811. yff nede were: "if necessary." That is, I will acquit those wealth will help to advance me, not because of justice.

812, 817. Thys: Variant of *thus*; see ll. 289n and 839.

819. Set a noble: Lay out a noble [for the meal]. A *noble* is an English coin first minted by Edward III, usually worth 6s.

824. For euer I trost Gode wyll send: Cf. the proverb "Spend and God will send" (Whiting 76; ctd. by Eccles 213n).

826. cosyn: The term, which implies any kind of kinship, may imply an incestuous lusting after a kinswoman as well as lechery on the part of Will or it may simply and ironically suggest a "friend" or sexual partner; see l. 834.

828-31. In this exchange, Will (Lechery) again identifies himself as the spendthrift; the Mights once more threaten to fight, in a minor display of the discord that characterizes their worldly state.

832. Sent Audre of Ely: Saint Audrey of Ely, a saint I have been unable to identify outside the play. The reference to Ely in East Anglia helps to locate this play in that region. See l. 721n.

834. cosyn Jenet N.: "kinswoman Jenny N." The *N.* in this formula stands for *nomen* and is an invitation to fill in the blank with a name. Cf. the Banns of the N-Town cycle plays: "A Sunday next yf þat we may,/At vj of þe belle we gynne oure play / In N-town . . . " (Spector 1991 Proclamation/525-27, 1: 21). As before, *Cosyn* may imply a kinswoman or a "friend" or sexual partner. See l. 826n.

836. mery: This term has consistently identified the life of sin. See ll. 492, 494n, 500, 505, 559, 562n, 623, and 871.

838. dysprawe: "libel" or "slanderously declaim." A rare variant of ME *dysprayse* meaning "to address someone with great contempt," "to declame" or "speak scandously" against someone. This verb can also be transitive; cf. "and all þi comaundementys he depravyd" (*The Castle of Perseverance*, l. 3265).

839-40. How myght make hym thys to lawe. / I wolde onys haue hym in þe wyrry: This is a difficult passage. Eccles emends *how* to *who*, with the implication that "whoever might make him [go] to law" would put the *chorle* (l. 835) into Will (Lechery)'s grasp. But if one reads l. 839 as a continuation of the sentence begun in 838 *Than þe chorle wyll here dysprawe*, the entire passage may mean "Then the churl will here scandalously declare how he might go to court with this. I would like to have him once by the throat." In this reading Wyll (Lechery) is asking his friends to help him avenge himself against the threats of the churlish husband.

839. thys: an obsolete variant of *thus*; see also ll. 289, 812, and 817.

840. wyrry: "stranglehold," apparently a noun derived from the verb meaning "to kill by strangling." Thus, *in þe wyrry* means to hold "in a killing grasp."

841-48. Mind (Maintenance) offers to redress the injury done to Will (Lechery) by the threats of the jealous husband; using his power, he will rebuke the churl so that he fears for his life; and if that fails, he offers physical punishment *on hys bodye* (l. 846).

843. wery: Bevington and Eccles read *very*, with Eccles emending to *wery*. However, the ms. reads *wery*, though because the second loop of the *w* is difficult to see, it is easy to mistake the initial letter for *v*.

846. abye: "suffer a penalty for." The legal term "aby" (or "abye"), though archaic, is still in use. The modernization — "On his body the price he'll pay" — does not quite capture the full legal significance of "aby," but it does avoid the archaic term; also see l. 768.

849-56. Understanding (Perjury) offers a better remedy, which is to use the courts to gain revenge. The plan of each Might furthers the parodic trinitarian allegory of: a) abused power (embodied in Mind [Maintenance], who initially represented God the Father, now the devil's man), b) greedy misuse of the courts (epitomized by Understanding [Perjury], who initially was linked with Christ, now the vassal of the world), and c) uncontrolled lechery (reflected in Will [Lechery], initially identified with the Holy Ghost, now in the power of the flesh).   The strategy that Understanding/Lechery proposes is basically to have the husband in question indicted in more than one jurisdiction at the same time so that he cannot be present to answer the trumped-up charges. Thus, he will lose the case by default. Each of the strategies is designed to achieve this end; see l. 851n.

850. to pes for fyght: "to keep the peace because of a trumped-up charge of fighting." This is the legal pretense for arrest in the first jurisdiction.

851. in another schere hym endyght: "After arresting him, indict him in another shire." To have someone indicted simultaneously in two courts was a common legal ploy guaranteed to be successful; since one had to be physically present to answer the charges, the second indictment necessarily brought conviction. Sir John Paston faced a similar form of double jeopardy; after inheriting the property of Sir John Fastolf, he was jailed twice by coexecutors who forced him to defend his claims to the property in court in London at the same time that he defended the property itself in the East Midlands. (See Bennet 1-26; see also Riggio 1974 204-05n.)

853. þe Marschalsi: According to Eccles, "the court held before the steward and the knight-marshal of the king's household" (Eccles 214n). Cf. *The Complaynt of Roderyck Mors*, "The court of the Marshyalsee I can neyther thynck, speake, nor write, the slendernesse and vnreasonable chargys of that court" (qtd. by Smart 63).

854. þe Amralte: The court of the Lord Admiral (identified by Eccles 214n; see *Select Pleas in the Court of Admiralty*, ctd. by Eccles).

byght: "sharply accuse."

855. A preuenire facias: *Preuenire facias* is apparently an error for *praemunire facias*, originally a writ by which the sheriff was summoned to charge a person who attempted to prosecute in a foreign court a suit belonging to the courts of England; later, the offense was asserting papal jurisdiction in England, thus denying the ecclesiastical supremacy of the English crown. This writ was based on a statute of 16 Richard II (see *OED*, under *praemunire*; also see Eccles 214n). The legal ploy is to create a trap by establishing multiple jurisdictions. The writ of *praemunire*, which affirms monarchical authority in opposition to papal jurisdiction, implicitly reinforces a central theme in the play — the authority of the crown, whether divine or secular.

858. þe crose & þe pyll: "the head and tail of a coin," so called because a cross was stamped on one side of some coins; the under side of the minting apparatus was called a *pyll* or *pile*; hence, the reverse side of the coin, opposite to the *crose*, was called a *pyll*. The term originated as a French phrase *croix et pile*. The entire phrase means "I will distort the meaning of it with the head and tail of a coin," i.e., the legal wrongs can be hidden under the cover of money.

862. allyede: "firmly allied, well-connected." Money — as bribery — triumphs over social connections so that no matter how well-positioned or firmly allied one's adversaries may be, bribery will win the case. This term recalls *affyance, affye, affynyte* as terms which suggest the alliances of kinship and maintenance that characterize the world of sin in this play. See also ll. 643n, 657n, 659n, 799n.

864. seyer: Eccles is right in glossing this term as "speaker," i.e., spokesman, rather than *assayer* or "one who tries," despite the *OED* citation of the term as meaning "one who tests." The key term is *replyde* (l. 863), which introduces the idea of "speaking [legally] on one's behalf."

866. the: "thrive" or "prosper," from OE *þion*.

868. Now go we to the wyne: "Now let's go to the wine." This line provides an opportunity to engage the audience in the drama; assuming that the play is being staged as a banquet masque, the tables provide a ready source of wine. See ll. 949-56n.

871. Mery, mery, all mery . . . : Cf. ll. 492, 494n,

873. At this point Eccles establishes Scene IV.

O thu, Mynde: Whereas at the beginning of the play, Christ spoke directly to all three Mights, from this point on, during the call to repentance, Christ as Wisdom communicates directly only with Mind, the "higher" part of reason and the Soul herself. Understanding (the *nethyr* part of reason) and Will do not directly see or hear God. Mind communicates the suggestion to Understanding, who in his turn speaks with Will, in a descending order of the Mights — from the higher part of reason to the lower part of reason to the will, which is the faculty of consent but must act on information provided by the other Mights. As the higher part of reason, Mind is more easily persuaded to see the fault in their lifestyle, while the other two are still looking for thrills.

889-92. Will uses a conventional argument, putting off consideration of death until a later age. Cf. the persuasion of Malus Angelus in *The Castle of Perseverance*, "þou art forty wyntyr olde, as I gesse. / Goo ageyn . . . / And pleye þe a whyle wyth Sare and Sysse . . . . " (ll. 1571-84). See l. 897n.

897. pyttys brynke: "on the edge of the grave, facing death." *Pyt* means "grave"; it may also refer to hell, and here the implications are that death will bring damnation. Cf. *The Castle of Perseverance*,

"Late men þat arn on þe pyttys brynke . . . do penaunce . . . " (ll. 1581-33).

901. dyvyguryde: A rare variant of *dysvyguryde* (*OED*); according to the *MED*, the verb *dysvygure* specifically means "to blemish (the soul)." This is its use here. See also l. 117. It is possible, however, that M has once more misread D's "-is-" as "y" and so transcribed the term "disfygure" as *dyvygure*, an error more likely to occur because it is a variant of the term. Without this portion of the D text, it is impossible to know for certain what the D term was. See ll. 414n and 697n.

902sd. Furnivall refers to the Soul as masculine from this point on. Because of this, Theodore Spencer assumes that Anima has changed gender since the play began (56; ctd. by Eccles 214n). Such an assumption is unfounded; Anima clearly remains a feminine character. For instance, Wisdom later calls her his *syster, spowse dere* (l. 1085). However, she has from the beginning represented the masculine as well as the feminine soul. And in the Suso dialogue, from which the opening section of the play is quoted, the Soul is masculine. In addition to the implication here, remnants of the Soul's masculine identity appear elsewhere in the play, as in the masculine pronoun: *to hys fyrste lyghte*, l. 120; see also ll. 79n 133, 289, and 1124. Her costume at her entrance here should suggest her deformity — resembling but more horrible than the natural guise of Lucifer.

906. Godys own place: The feudal metaphor continues throughout the play. The soul, which has earlier been called *His [i.e., Chrystys] restynge place, his plesant see* (l. 130), is once more identified as *Godys own place*.

908. rechace: "call to the hunt." This term is synonomous with *recheat*, sb., "the act of calling together the hounds for a hunt," or "notes sounded in order to call the hounds together." Though the metaphor is mixed, the line suggests that by defoulling "God's own place" (l. 906) the Mights have given the hunt over to the devil, making his *rechace* possible. In the image, humanity as a secure possession of God's has become the prey of the devil's hunt. The link to the hunting horns implies the trumpet blasts which signify judgment, alluded to in the emblematic use of the trumpet as the *mynstrall* (l. 692sd) for the devil's dance. See ll. 701-06n, 722n.

909-10: See 912sdn below.

912sd. vi: The number six in this stage direction was emended by Eccles to vii, following the suggestion of Molloy 136 (see Eccles 214n). However, although it is clear that seven deadly sins are implied, the formula established during the formal masques applies here as well. In that formula, *vi* dancers represent sins in three different dances; in each instance, the seventh sin is represented by the Might who controls the dancers. See, for instance, *Her entur vi dysgysyde in þe sute of Mynde; . . . And þe viite am I Mayntennance. / VII ys a numbyr of discorde & inperfyghtnes* (ll. 692sd, 696-97). Similarly, here *vi small boys in þe lyknes of dewyllys*, added to the defiled character of Anima herself, represent the seven deadly sins which fill her soul. It is interesting that Wisdom has for the first time addressed *man*, urging him to take pity on his *Soule*, rather than speaking to Anima herself. Anima is apparently identified with the deadly sins which *in yowr soule be* (l. 910). By linking each of the Mights with their dancers and Anima with the sins in her soul, the play carries on the metaphor of feudal lordship and vassalage, though Christ's reference to *As many dedly synnys as ye haue vsyde, / So many deullys in yowr soule be* (ll. 909-10) complicates the formula of 6, rather than 7, devils in this case.

913-24. Eccles cites parallels to the appeal of Christ based on the Good Friday service, as, for instance, in "Goddis Owne Complaynt" in Furnivall 17, 86-93; 151-75 (see Eccles 214n).

917-18. bronde of hell . . . ymage of lyght: "firebrand of hell . . . image of light." The *ymage of lyght* is the characteristic feature of the goddess Sapientia; Humanity has been cast in this *ymage*, but has converted the *ymage of lyght* into a firebrand of hell. For Wisdom and the imagery of light, see ll. 27-32n and l. 1072n.

927. noble kynde: "the nature of humanity, ennobled by its likeness to God"; see l. 529n; for an inversion of this term in the world of sin, designating the inherited rights and positions coming from family power, see ll. 575n and 576n. See also l. 4 where Christ describes his own *nobley*, i.e., "nobility."

935. dysyrynge: "desiring." Eccles emends to *dysyrvynge* ("deserving"), on the assumption of a scribal error. It is possible that M has omitted a D "-v-" or misread a D "-rvi-" as "-ry-." M does have trouble reading the D "-i-" correctly; see ll. 256n, 414n, 584n, and 697n. Though the emendation makes sense, the term as transcribed here suggests that a penitent sinner *desires* punishment as a way of atoning for sin.

940. He ys resurreccyon & lywe: "He is resurrection and life." Cf. John 11.25: *Ego sum resurrectio et vita* ("I am the resurrection and the life").

946. þe yiffte of hys specyall grace: "the grace of God as the gift which makes salvation possible for humanity." See 1l. 119n, 203n.

947. recurable: "recoverable" or "redeemable." As a legal term, the verb *recure* means "to obtain possession of" or "to collect damages through judicial action." Here while it implies the "curing" of illness in the *seke soule* (l. 947), it also continues the metaphor of feudal possession, of the soul as God's *see*, lost and now to be recovered. This is one of the legal terms with theological implications that characterize this play, which persistently reflects the points of interchange between legal and theological terminology; see l. 654.

949-56. These lines imply theatrical action. Together with her three Mights, Anima calls for "Mercy." Then she wonders why she has not been transformed into her original self. In this exchange the play deftly modifies the appeal to mercy which in *The Castle of Perseverance* constitutes the only act of penitence on the part of the character representing humanity. In that play, Humanum Genus's last words are: "A word may I speke no more. / I putte me in Goddys mercy" (ll. 3006-07). The soul which emerges after death ("Anima") affirms the importance of this call: "'Mercy,' þis was my last tale / þat euere my body was abowth. / But Mercy helpe me in þis vale, / Of dampnynge drynke sore I me doute" (ll. 3009-11). This deathbed plea for mercy is sufficient justification for Mercy and Peace to plead for and ultimately save his soul in the debate of the four daughters of God: "A mone I herd of mercy meve / And to me, Mercy, gan crye and call" (ll. 3129-30). Similarly, in *Mankind*, the agent of redemption is named Mercy. Relying upon the unmediated appeal to mercy emphasizes the role of the individual in the process of redemption and is, thus, characteristic of fifteenth century theology. The importance of the private appeal to mercy in the later Middle Ages is reflected in songs such as *Mercy Passes All Things* and *Ay Mercy, Gode* (Brown 125 ff., 149-50; ctd. by Bloomfield 168, 265n). In contrast, *Wisdom* relies more on ecclesiastical authority as the key to redemption. For a discussion of the importance of the individual as his own mediator with divinity in the late Middle Ages, see Ullman 143-45. See also Riggio 1974 206. See 868n and 982-89n.

954. clene: *Clene* is one of the terms which consistently applies to the Soul in the state of grace and is inverted ironically in the world of sin. See also ll. 45n, 54, 176, 284, 289, 969, 976 and, for ironic contrast, 494n and 749n.

957-76. Wisdom provides the formula for Anima's restoration to grace. Continuing the metaphor of the *seke soul* (l. 947), he offers *þis medsyne* (l. 970). He makes it clear that forsaking sin alone is not sufficient to salvation (see ll. 957-59); nor do prayers and acts of penitence alone merit salvation (see ll. 965-66). Wisdom's formula emphasizes *contricyon* (ll. 961, 973), *confessyon* (l. 974), and *satysfaccyon* (l. 976) — a symmetrical three-part answer to the three stages of seduction to sin (suggestion, delectation, confirmation) which Wisdom warns against earlier in the play and which Lucifer employs. Each of the three Mights has a particular responsibility in this process of penitence: *By Wndyrstondynge haue very contrycyon, / Wyth Mynde of yowr synne confessyon make / Wyt Wyll yeldynge du satsyfaccyon* (ll. 973-75). The division of penance into contrition, confession, and satisfaction was a common convention, perhaps attributable to Peter of Lombardy, "In perfectione autem poenitentiae, tria obseruanda sunt, scilicet, compunction cordis, confessio . . . satisfactio operis" ("In completing penitence, therefore, three things are to be observed, namely, sorrow of heart, confession, [and] . . . satisfaction through deeds" *Quatuor libri sententiarum*, Libre IV, Dist. 16; qtd. by Smart 73). CUL Ms. Hh.I.11 contains a sermon which moralizes on articles of clothing, with particular emphasis on *contricion* and *confession*: "3e haue a smok & be þat is understonden contricion & confession is þe first & principal wei of contriccion to god," (fols. 130-32). See ll. 226n, 301-04n, 365n, 445n, 497-99n, and 1011-12n.

This process of penance was forecast at the beginning of the play. CUL Ms. Dd.14.26, which transcribes a portion of a dialogue once thought to be between Augustine and St. Bernard, reports that a Soul grounded in faith and having turned away from deadly sin, which has been shriven and taken penance "wyt contricion & sorowe of herte" is "reformed to þe lykenes of þe ymage of god." See ll. 214-20n.

959, 965-67. Cf. Hilton's *Scale of Perfection*, 2: 7: God "abydeth not grete penaunce doynge ne paynful flesshly sufferyng or he foryeve it. But he askyth a lothynge of synne & a ful forsakynge in wyl" (qtd. by Eccles 215n; see also Underhill 245-46).

961-62: The syntax in these lines is difficult, since the clause *who þat haue may* (l.961) appears to be incomplete, as if a verbal phrase like "put sins away" (see l. 960) is to be understood, with l. 962 explaining that contrition will purge sins because "it is the purger and cleanser of sin." To preserve the rhyme and rhythm in a meaningful English sentence, the modernization ("But true contrition — whoever has that may / Know that is the purger and cleanser of sin") adds the verb "know," for which there is no justification in the original text.

980sd. Hic recedunt demonos: "Here the demons leave." This Latin stage direction is partially bracketed in the right margin beside ll. 979-80, the first two lines of Wisdom's speech. The placement may imply that the six small devils are driven out by Wisdom's spoken command.

982-91. modyr Holy Chyrche . . . Holy Chyrch . . . modyr chyrche . . . modyr Holy Chyrche: *Wisdom* gives more emphasis to the institutional structures of the established church than other English morality plays, despite *Mankind*'s reliance on the power of the rural clergy. In *Wisdom*, the individual plea to mercy must be followed by a more formal reconciliation to the Church itself, through the process of *confessyon*. The conventional designation of the church as "mother" plays a thematic role in this play, as in *The Castle of Perseverance*. In these plays the "worldly" claims of family and kinship are negated in favor of the individual's association with the church itself as a surrogate family: Anima is the "spouse" of Christ; the only "mother" in the play is the church, and — in contrast — *kynrede* (l. 756) is one of the attributes of vice, associated with sin. See Milla Riggio 1974 203-06. See l. 576n, 949-56n, and 1078.

986. charter of pardon: The charter of pardon, gained through confession to Holy Church and directly associated with the passion of Christ, is associated with the medieval *Charter of Christ*. Dating from the fifteenth century are at least a dozen representations of the *Charter of Christ*. These take the form of legal documents, particularly of a last testament in which Christ bequeathes the gift of redemption to the penitent. These charters simulate legal instruments in their formal apparatus; they frequently have seals pendant on them, and they are "witnessed" in a quasi-legal fashion. Brit. Mus. Addit. Ms. 37049, fol. 23r, for instance, contains a *charter of Christ* "witnessed" by the earthquake that occurred at Christ's crucifixion, the broken stones, the rent veil of the temple, and the dead raised from their tombs. (See Wormald 280-81 fig. 1; see also Spalding.) In addition to the pictorial *charters of Christ*, there were also various other *charters* which took the same form. For instance, CUL Ms. Ff.5.45 contains a *charter of heaven* offered as "þe chartre of this herytage & þe bulle of this euerlastyng pardon"; this charter "is oure lord Jhesu Crist, wreten wyth al þe myhte & vertu of god." The charter characteristically presents the metaphor of God's skin as the "parchment" on which the pardon of humanity was written; this "parchment" was "streyned & drawen" more on the gibbet than any parchment prepared for writing. Pierced by five thousand wounds, made by "nailes & sharp spears" instead of "pennes," the body of Christ becomes the formal instrument by which pardon is granted to humanity (fol. 64a). Brit. Mus. Ms. Addit. 24343 contains a similar charter entitled *Carta Redempcionis humanae*, framed in imitation of a land grant and offering redemption as a heritage of Christ's passion (fol. 6B). Both the charters in Mss. 37049 and 24343 are identified as "gyfen at calvery þe fyrst day of þe gret mercy." Similarly, though more formally, the Brit. Mus. Ms. Addit. 5960 contains a *Carta [Jesu Christi] de liberatibus mundi*, also written in imitation of a land grant, sealed in the presence of the three Marys and *John the prophet*, notarized by Matthew, Mark, Luke, and John. In a passage that probably served as the model for this image in *Wisdom*, Walter Hilton further associated the *charter of pardon* with "contrycyon betwene god and [man]," saying that redemption cannot be gained "but yf he have a charter made by holy chyrche yf he may come therto. And that is the sacrament of penaunce the whiche is his charter & his token of foryevenes" (*The Scale of Perfection*, 2: 7; qtd. by Eccles 215n; also see Underhill 247). See ll. 982-91n, 1077-78, and 1101-04n.

989. O, fadyr of mercy ande of *comfort*. M *mercy*. The rhyme scheme calls for a term rhyming with *resort* in place of the second *mercy* in this line. Furnivall and Eccles emend to *comfort*. This emendation is supported by the association of this line with 2 Corinthians 1.3-4: "Pater misericordiarum et Deus totius consolationis, qui consolatur nos in omni tribulatione nostra." ("Father of mercy and God of all consolation, who comforts us in all our troubles.") This Latin line is quoted by Mercy in *The Castle of Perseverance*, l. 3313. Cf. also "O Fadyr of Mercy and God of Comforte," (N-Town cycle 11/73 in Spector 1991 1: 114; also qtd. by Eccles 201n).

996. contricyon: For the importance of *contrition* in the process of penance, see ll. 957-76n.

996sd. Magna velud mare contricio, contricio tua, contricio tua: quis consoletur tui? Plorans plorauit in nocte, et lacrime ejus in maxillis ejus.: "As great as the sea is contricion, your contricion, your contricion: Who will console you? Crying he cried in the night and his tears were great in him" (source: Lamentations 2.13 & Holy Thursday service). As the stage directions indicate, this mournful chant — the third and penultimate chant in the play — comes from the liturgy of Maundy Thursday. The text is taken from Lamentations, a small psalter of laments over the fall of Jerusalem, attributed (probably incorrectly) to Jeremiah 2.13 ("Magna est enim velut mare contritio tua") and 1.2 ("plorans ploravit in nocte, et lacrymae eius in maxillis eius"; "For even as vast as the sea is your contrition; weeping she cries in the night, with tears covering her cheeks.") According to Molloy, these verses are sung during the first nocturn of Matins for Holy Thursday and may be meant to indicate a procession "similar to that for the reconciliation of penitents on Holy Thursday in at least some of the cathedral churches" (Molloy 150).

997-1064. These lines are taken from translations of the *Novem Virtutes*, formerly ascribed to Richard Rolle. Of the extant manuscripts of the *Nine Virtues*, none is identifiably the source of the play, though each of the nine points is consistent in most versions. As introduced in CUL Ms. Ff.vi.33, these virtues are spoken by Christ: "Thes be the ix virtues that our lord Jhesu cryst answeryd a sely creature þaet was lyvyng in flessch & blode in the yer of our lord miiixlv" (fol. 33v). In general, *Wisdom* adds lines to each point, particularly 1003-04, 1011-12, 1018-20, 1026-28, 1035-36, 1049-52, and 1062-64 (ctd. by Eccles 215n and verified by manuscript readings). The thematic import of the nine points — that God prefers real sorrow of heart, reflected in human charity and private penance, to self-lacerating forms of penitence — is consistent with Wisdom's stance throughout the play. And with one exception (l. 1018), each of the added lines supports themes of the play. Except for point eight where there is no addition, the added lines also complete poetic stanzas. See ll. 1003-04n, 1005n, 1011-12n, 1013 . . . 1057n, 1018n, 1019-20n, 1026-28n, 1035-36n, 1049-52n, and 1062-64n.

As identified in subsequent notes, the scribe himself indicates the paragraph breaks in this passage. Throughout this section, the actor playing Wisdom distances himself from the role by continually quoting God; see ll. 997, 1005, 1013, 1021, 1029, 1037, 1045, 1053, 1057. In punctuating the sermon, I have enclosed the nine points attributed to God in quotation marks. In those cases where the additions to the nine points seem to constitute a commentary on a given point, using the forumla "*Lo, . . . ,*" I have closed the quotations before this phrase, treating the addition as a gloss on the point itself; see ll. 1011-12n. Though in l. 1007, Wisdom talks of *þe passyon of me Ihesus*, he later quotes *Cryst* as his source without identifying himself with Christ (l. 1045).

Though the actor distances himself from the role of God, he need not distance himself from the audience in delivering this sermon. In fact, the acknowledgement of his role as actor [or, for the moment, preacher] may give him an opportunity to close the gap between the audience and "God." By playing these lines directly to the audience, one can overcome the remoteness of their didactic tone and signal the difference between this sermon and the rest of the play. Such interaction with the audience also complements the direct audience interaction in the world of sin. The primary theatrical justification of the lines, of course, is to allow Anima time for her confession (and, not incidentally, for her costume change).

1003-04. These added lines reinforce the theme of sinful acquisition in the play. Since they seem integral to point one, they have been included in the direct quotation.

1005. Though the added lines in 1003-04 complete a poetic stanza, the ms. does not indicate a paragraph break here. It has been added in this text for consistency, since paragraph breaks are indicated between each of the subsequent points. See l. 1013 . . . 1057n.

1011-12. Lo, contrycyon ys a soueren remedy . . . : These lines introduce a formula by which moral tags beginning with *Lo* are added to several points. These tags complete the poetic stanza and reinforce themes of each point; here the lines harken back to the theme of *contrycyon*, *confessyon*, and *satysfaccyon*. See ll. 957-76n, 1019-20n, 1026-28n, 1035-36n, 1062-44n.

1013, 1021, 1029, 1037, 1045, 1053, 1057: A paragraph sign appears in the lefthand margin before each of these lines, indicating a break between each point. With the exception of point three, each of the nine points is precisely one poetic stanza long.

1017. þrywe: M. *prywe*, probably an error for *þrywe*, "thrive."

1018. In þe space of days jornye: This added line does not appear to have thematic significance. It may have come from a version of the *Nine Virtues* no longer extant. Extant mss. give other measurements, and they often differ from each other, as, for instance "as many roddys as myght growe on an acre of lond," (Trinity College Library Ms. O.2.53 [Cambridge University] fol. 24) or "wyth as many yerdys as my3te grewe in all þe woodys of the worlde" (CUL ms. Ff.vi.33). The reference to a measurement of time, rather than space — "a day's journey" rather than "an acre of land" or "all the woods of the world" — is in itself odd and unexplained by any of the *Nine Virtues* manuscripts I have been able to examine.

1019-20. Lo, who suffyryth most for Gode ys most lewe: / Slandyr, repreve, only aduersyte: "Lo, one who suffers most for God is most dear: Slander, reproof, and also adversity." Line 1020 identifies the kinds of sufferings — withstanding slander and public reproof and any kind of adversity because of one's faith — which make a Christian dear to God. *Only* means either "and also" or "any." These added lines once more complete the verse stanza by returning to and rephrasing the theme iterated in ll. 1013-14.

1023. kyngys: Probably an error for *knyghtys*. Manuscripts of the *Nine Virtues* generally identify *knyghyts* or, in one instance, *armyd men* (CUL Ms. Dd.11.89), or in another simply *men* (CUL Ms Ii.iv.9, fol. 64) instead of kings in this point, though like the apparent addition in l. 1018, the reference to "kings" may point to an unexamined or now lost manuscript as the source for this portion of the play. It is possible that the dramatist made the alteration for thematic reasons, since the role of kings is relevant to *Wisdom*, a play in which no references to knights occur.

1026-28. Again, the added lines complete the poetic stanza; they also reinforce the theme of this point — the virtue of waking. This echoes and corrects the inversion of a theme ironically introduced by Lucifer in ll. 433-44, in which the fasting, waking, and praying of the contemplative life is equated with idleness or, worse, madness. See ll. 431-40n.

1035-36. Again, this added moral tag completes the poetic stanza and reinforces the theme of pity and compassion as a virtue — one of the deeds of mercy identified here as necessary for redemption.

1049-52. These lines are not found in the extant mss. of the *Nine Virtues* examined for this edition. Their addition again completes the poetic stanza, but they do not echo a theme of the play. It may well be that these lines, like ll. 1019-20, are taken from a different, possibly lost, version of the *Nine Virtues*. Existing mss. stress the creation of a "new chyrtye" (CUL Ff.vi.33), rather than the laceration of the naked body. The *Lo* formula is not used for this point.

1053-56. This point comprises only half of the usual eight-line stanza. It does not have a moral tag or added lines of any kind.

1059. pyler of tre: A post or pillar made of wood, perhaps suggesting a cross in imitation of Christ. Mss. of the *Nine Virtues* ordinarily indicate either a *pilar* or a *tre* for this point rather than a *pyler of tre*, as, for instance, "make a piler rechyng up to the heven stykyng full of rasors" (CUL Ff.vi.33) or "lever than yowe yode vpon a tre that tyl heue stode that were dreuyn ful of scharpe resorys" (CUL II.iv.9, fol. 65b).

1062-64. This added moral tag again completes the stanza, but it concludes the entire nine points rather than reinforcing the last point specifically. The direct address of l. 1064 — *Remembyr thes poyntys, man . . .* — reinforces the idea of playing these virtues directly to the audience.

1064sd. The *v wyttys* are the five *prudent vyrgyns* (l. 162) who formed part of Anima's retinue in the original state of grace. Here they return with her and the three Mights, all of whom are now crowned as a sign of their full restoration to grace. They sing the fourth and last chant of the play, taken from the Vulgate Psalm 115.12-13 (Protestant Psalm 116). According to Molloy, the replacement of the Lamentation of Jeremias, sung in departure (l. 996sd), by this chant from Psalms may indicate that Anima has received the Holy Eucharist as well as the sacrament of penance because "this psalm has been associated with the Communion of the Mass from the ninth century" and "the two verses from this psalm are still said by the celebrant of the Mass after he has received the Body of Christ and just before he drinks the precious blood" (Molloy 157).

commynge in: The Ms reads *commynge I* with a line separating these directions from the Latin lines of the chant. Eccles emends to *i[n]*. Throughout the play, M recurrently abbreviates D *in* as *i*; this was likely another of those instances. See ll. 24, 63, 133, 164sd, 264, 338, and 613.

all hauyng on crownys: Anima and her Mights are now all crowned, as a sign of their restoration to grace and their likeness to Christ. At the beginning of the play, Anima merely wore a coronet, rather than a crown. See also ll. 0sdn, 16sdn, and 1115-16n.

Quid retribuam Domino pro omnibus que retribuit mihi? Calicem salutaris accipiam et nomen Domini inuocabo.: What shall I give to God for all he has given me? I will accept the cup of health [i.e., salvation] and I will call on the name of God (source: Vulgate Psalm 115.12-13, sung by mass celebrant since the 9th century C.E.; Protestant Psalm 116); see headnote to this line.

1065-82. In these lines, Anima summarizes the process of penance ordered for her by Wisdom earlier in the play. Cf. *Than wyth yow iii þe Soule dothe crye / 'Mercy, Gode!' — Why change I nowte?* (ll. 949-50). The cry of mercy was supplemented by a more formal confession and plea for penitence from *modyr Holy Chyrche* (ll. 982, 1078). In summarizing this process, Anima reiterates the importance of the institutional Church in the process of penitence — an important theme in this play, somewhat in contrast to other morality plays. Once more *Holy Chyrche* is identified as a *modyr*; the only kinship of importance in the play is that of the individual with God (as spouse, father, brother) and with the established Roman Catholic church (as mother). Once that idea has been made clear, the final plea is conventionally to mercy, taken from Psalm 107.5: "magna est super caelos misericordia tua" ("For thy compassion is great above the heavens"; Protestant Psalm 108.4, where "misericordia" is translated as "steadfast love")). See ll. 949-56n and 982-91n.

1072. lyght of grace: "light that emanates from divine grace." Anima shares the *lyght* that characterizes Wisdom. See ll. 21-24n, 917-18n.

1073-77. As used here specifically, the term *tweyn myghtys* is slightly confusing. *Myghtys* have previously signified the three *faculties of the soul* — Mind, Understanding, and Will (see ll. 177, 277) — or the physical senses, as *bodylye myghts*, l. 147. Apart from the terminological distinction, however, the description of the soul here follows that in ll. 135-48 where Wisdom divides the human *sowll* into *tweyn partyes*: *sensualyte* and *resone*. Sensuality rules the *owtwarde* *wyttys*, or five senses, which must be controlled if the soul is to remain in a state of grace. *Resone* (l. 141) is regarded as the other one of the two *partyes* of the soul (l. 141). Now in 1073-77 one *myght* is identified with the *inwarde wyttys*, which earlier in the play have been represented by the five *prudent vyrgyns* in *kertyllys & mantelys* (ll. 161-64sd), and one with the *outwarde wyttys*, i.e. the *v wyttys bodyly*, ₊which do not appear as characters in the play. The phrase here harkens back to the *tweyn partyes* of l. 135 rather than to the characters of Mind, Understanding, and Will, typically regarded as *myghtys*. See ll. 162n, 164n, and 177-90n.

1077-78. See ll. 949-56n and 982-91n.

1081-84. These four lines form an abbreviated stanza, with the abab rhyme scheme characteristic of the first four lines of a normal stanza.

1081. Magna est misericordia tua: "Great is your pity."

1083-91. Taken from the Song of Songs 4.9: "Vulnerasti cor meum soror mea, sponsa; vulnerasti cor meum in uno oculorum tuorum . . . " ("You have wounded my heart, sister, bride; you have wounded my heart in one of your eyes"). The *Wisdom* text quotes these lines with an uncommon addition of the noun "ictu," "blow, stroke, or thrust," in the last phrase which should literally be translated "in one stroke of your eyes" where the text translates *in þe tweyn syghtys of yowr ey*. The two "eyes" of the soul were often identified with reason and love. Cf. "*Vulnerasti cor meum in uno oculorum tuorum (Cantic. iv.9)*. Duos nempe oculos habet anima . . . . dexter oculus est amor . . . intellectus, quem sinistrum diximus" ("*You have wounded me in one of two eyes [Song of Songs 4.9]*. To be sure, the soul has two eyes . . . the right eye is love . . . [and] reason which we call the left," from the anonymous *Tractatus de Charitate*, Migne, 184: 592; qtd. by Smart 75, w. italics and citation from Migne). Cf. also the first draft of a speech prepared by John Russell, Bishop of Lincoln and Lord Chancellor, who speaks of a twin eye — "oculus . . . geminus" — "quorem dexter est intellectus, sinister affectus" ("in which the right is intellect, the left affection" Nichols 55; qtd. by Smart 76). Smart has trouble explaining the *Wisdom* translation of *ictu oculorum tuorum* as the *tweyn syghtys of yowr ey* (l. 1086). Molloy also recognizes this problem, explaining the interpolation of the term *ictu* by reference to love's wounds which enter through the eye (Molloy 162). Though he does not develop the argument, Molloy's suggestion makes sense if one understands that the play is dealing with "inner" as well as "outer" sight. At this point of reconciliation, it is appropriate for Wisdom, as the divine lover, to allude to the wounds of love, implied by the verb *vulnerasti* and the noun *ictu* as wounds inflicted by the inner as well as the outer sight of Anima, i.e. as a blow struck by the *tweyn myghtys* of the Soul, cited by Anima several lines earlier, with the implication that "reason" is identified with the "inner eye" while "sensuality" is linked with outer sight. The allusion to the notion of an inner vision, corresponding to the outer vision of the eyes, was a commonplace of medieval theology, dating back at least to Augustine, who placed primary emphasis on the inner vision. Wisdom here tells Anima that she offended him not only by sins of the flesh but also through the perversion of her mind and understanding. Now that she has repented, she is dearer to him than ever before. See ll. 17-20n and 1103n.

1092. bewtys bryght: The restoration of Anima to her original condition recalls Anima's description of herself as *made all bewty bryghte*, l. 24.

1093-1106. Wisdom appeals to his own passion as redemptive, his guiltless *wyttys* (l. 1095) — or five senses — making restitution for the impotent senses of Anima, the ordinary human soul; to verify this claim, he iterates the pains each of his senses has undergone in the crucifixion. Juxtaposing the moment of Anima's redemption with that of Christ's Passion serves both theological and dramatic purposes. It is imperative that the staging of the play contain a visual referent to the Passion at this point — if only in the momentary assumption of the position by Wisdom. For an illustration of the crucified Christ with a punctured body and for commentary on the theological implications and the dramatic opportunities in this passage, see Riggio 1989 234-46 and fig. 1.

1099. *sm*elte: M *felte*. Wisdom repeats the term *felte*, which occurs in ll. 1099 and again in 1101. This term has been questioned. The down stroke of M *f* is indistinguishable from *s*, and the cross-stroke of *f* in *fe* combinations appears as an extension of the *e* rather than a separate stroke. Thus, Bevington transcribes the term in 1099 as *selte*; assuming a scribal error for *smelte*, Eccles emends to *smelte*. However, the *felte* of 1099 is identical to *felte* in 1101 — and very different from other M *se* combinations. M does not connect his *s* to *e* at the beginning of words. See, for instance, the words *second* (l. 1005) and *see* (ll. 185, 298, 501, 503, 650, 725, etc.). Obviously the term in the text is *felte*, though *smelte* would clearly be preferable: One smells, rather than feels, a stench, and the sense of smell has otherwise been omitted from the list. The resemblance between M's *s* and his *f* may have contributed to this error, in which M incorrectly anticipates the *felte* of 1101. In any case, the emendation is surely justified by the sense of the line.

1101-04. A *Charter of Heaven* in CUL Ms. Ff.5.45 describes the Passion of Christ in terms that are intriguingly similar to the description Christ gives of himself in this passage. Since Christ himself invokes the *charter of pardon* (986) as the key to penance and since the various *charters of pardon* or *charters of Christ* portray his body, punctured by its 500 wounds, as the parchment on which the charter is written, this charter or one very similar to it may well be the source for this description of Christ's Passion: "The prente of this seal is þe shap of oure lord Jhesu hangyng for oure synne upon the cros as we may se by *the ymage of þe crucifyxe*. He hath *his hede bowed don redy to kyse* all them þ^t verrily turnen to hym. *He hath his armes spred a brood redy to clype hem. He is nayled foot & honde to þe cros*, for he wil dwelle wyth hem euer & neuer wende away fro man but yf man forsake hym first thorough synne. *He hath al his body spred a brood* to gyf hymself holy to us clewyng to hym. And vtterly he hath his syde opened & *his hert cloven for oure sake*" (fol. 65b; punctuation, capitalization, and italics to emphasize passages that directly resemble the text of *Wisdom* are mine). *Carta Redempcionis Humane* or *Charters of Human Redemption* — also called *charta [Jesu Christi] de libertatibus mundi* — which portray Christ's body as the punctured parchment are found in Brit.Mus.Ms.Addit. 37049 fol. 23; Addit. 24343 fol. 6; Addit. Ch. 5960; and Ms. Harley 6840 fol 239b. See ll. 986n and 1106n.

1103. swet herte: The metaphor of divine lovers is continued throughout the play — and should be attended to in the staging of *Wisdom*. The idea of contemplative *love* as a spiritual parallel to certain courtly love conventions is actualized in a powerfully affectionate and physical way. Christ embraces Anima; he offers his life for her; her love is the motive for his *clowyn* heart. The linkage of love and death further echoes the major themes of the contemplative and courtly love traditions. See ll. 17-20n.

1106. full of holys as a dovehows: Introducing the Passion at this point recalls the *Charter of Pardon* (or *Charter of Christ*), in which Christ's punctured body becomes the parchment on which the pardon for humanity is written. Christ's wounds, which were thought to have numbered 500, were often depicted as a rash-like perforation of his body. The Charter in Brit. Mus. Ms. Addit. 37049, fol. 23r, provides a particularly graphic representation of the body of Christ as *full of holys as a dovehows* (l. 1106). Eccles cites the *Ayenbite of Inwyt*, Rolle's *Meditations on the Passion, Orologium*, and Margery Kempe as providing analogues to the *dovehous* image (Eccles 216n). See 986n and 1101 - 04n.

1107. plesynge: Eccles emends to *plesere* for the sake of the rhyme.

1110-12. synnys orygynall . . . synnys actuall: The contrast between *orygynall* and *actuall* sins is between the single sin of Adam and Eve which corrupted all human nature, and those sins actually committed by individual persons. The term "actuel . . . senne" was used in English as early as 1315 by William of Shoreham to describe "senne nau3t of thy ken" (107; qtd. by *OED* "actual," 1). The term "original sin" derives from the French "peche originel," and is ordinarily a singular term, deriving its meaning from the one great sin of Adam and Eve. Cf. "The grete Senne original, Which every man in general Upon his berthe hath envenymed" (Gower, *Confessions*, 3: l). Earlier in the play, Wisdom has described *synne orygynall* (l. 111) to Anima. The plural here is difficult to account for. The probable explanation is that when both original and actual sins are considered together, the plural noun can be used, as, for instance, in a sixteenth century treatise: "the lambe that taketh away our sinnes, original and actual" (Northbrooke). In *Wisdom*, "sins original and actual" has been divided into two separate phrases, *synnes orygynall* and *synnys actuall*, though there remains only one original sin. It is, of course, true that the concept of "original sin" does encompass the seven deadly sins, which are represented in this play. It is possible that the plural here reflects that assimilation of various sins into the one great sin of Adam and Eve. See ll. 111n, 125-30n.

1111. sakyrment of penance: The "sacrament" of penance, assumed by Robert Potter to be central to the morality drama tradition, has been the focus of attention in the play since Anima's cry for mercy in l. 950. (See Potter 30-57.)

1113:   Crystys own specyall: "Christ's own special [place; possession; or beloved]" Cf. *Crystys own specyall, / Hys restynge place, hys plesant see* (ll. 131-32).

1114. lyknes of þe fende: See ll. 373 and 912sd; for the term *lyknes* referring to the "likeness" of God see ll. 35, 104n, 128, 188. 274, 536.

1115-16. crownnys victoryall, / To regne in blys: The *crownnys* are a sign of restoration to grace. Having fallen in sin, Anima and her retinue are now elevated to a position even higher than that in which they began. They now share the throne with Wisdom, reigning *in blys*, i.e., in paradise. The metaphor of sovereignty obviously furthers both the theological and the social allegory of the play, in which established sovereignty has full authority. See 0sdn, 16sdn, 415-16n, and 1064sdn.

1119-20. Nolite conformari huic seculo / Sed reformamini in nouitate spiritus sensus vestri: "Do not be conformed to this world but be reformed in the newness of your spiritual feeling" (source: Romans 12.2 + Hilton's *Scale of Perfection* 2: 31). Romans 12.2 reads: "Et nolite conformari haec seculo, sed reformamini in novitate sensus vestri . . . . " *Wisdom* adds the term *spiritus* and changes *conformari* to *confirmare*, a probable scribal error for *conformare*. This verse and the two in subsequent stanzas are quoted in the same order in the *Scale of Perfection*, without the alterations made in *Wisdom* (ctd. by Eccles 216n; see also Underhill 367). Each of the three Mights now affirms his reformation in terms of the virtue with which he has primarily been associated; Mind here affirms his restoration through *feyth*. See ll. 285-28n, 1125-26n, 1133-34n. But also see l. 1121n.

1122. reforme in gostly felynge: "be restored in spiritual affection." One might have expected this reference from Will, associated with love and charity and identified with the Holy Ghost, rather than from Mind, who has been ordinarily associated with the *ouerparte* of reason. This is but one of several such intermingling of the expected qualities of each Might which in this concluding scene may represent a final unity or coming together of the faculties in one integrated and harmonious soul. But the specific justification for associating "ghostly feeling" with Mind comes from Hilton who in *The Scale of Perfection* compares the reformation of faith (see l. 1118) with "the higher reforming that is in feeling" and links that to "two manner of feelings: one without . . . another within of the ghostly wits, the which are properly the mights of the soul, mind, reason and will" and concludes that "Your reason, that is properly the image of God through grace of the Holy Ghost . . . then is . . . reformed in feeling" (modernized by Underhill 366-68). Thus, as the master Might (and the only one to whom Christ communicates directly in the last portion of the play), Mind speaks for all three when he talks of "reforming" in "ghostly feeling," i.e., of approaching God through love, which from the perspective of the play is the highest form of Wisdom and thus the final reformation of reason. This idea is furthered in l. 1130. See ll. 300n, 483-84n, and (especially) 1130n.

1124. Mercy: Now that the penitential process has taken place, with emphasis on confession and the absolution of the *modyr holy chyrche* (l. 982), Mercy is given pride of place as the prime mover in the redemption of the Soul. See ll. 949-56n, 982-91n, 1065-82n.

1125-26. Understanding is restored through *hope*, the second of the cardinal virtues associated with the Mights. See ll. 285-88n, 1117-18n, 1133-34n.

1127-28. Renouamini spiritu mentis vestre / Et induite nouum hominem, qui secundum Deus creatus est.: "Be renewed in the spirit of your mind and put on a new man who is created in the likeness of God" (source: Ephesians 4.23-24 and Hilton's *Scale of Perfection*). Ephesians 4.23-24 reads: "Renovamini autem spiritu mentis vestrae, et induite novum hominem, qui secundum Deum creatus est . . . . " Cf. "ye shall be refourmed not in bodily felynge ne in ymaginacion but in the over partye of your reason" (Hilton, *Scale of Perfection*; ctd. by Eccles 216n).

1129-30. Ye be reformyde in felynge, not only as a best / But also in þe ouerparte of yowr reasun: Understanding extends the idea begun by Mind in 1122, once more affirming that the "higher" feeling is that associated with reason rather than with sensuality. It is peculiar to have Understanding invoke the *ouerparte* of reason, since he has been associated with the *nethyr parte* of reason. The medieval divisions of the mind or soul into three parts or faculties did, however, take several forms, in some of which *intelligentia* (here associated with Mind) is the second faculty. This may also be one of those moments in which the intermingling of the Mights signals the final unity of the soul; see l. 1122n; also see ll. 300n and 483-84n.

1133-34. Will is restored through *charity*, the third of the virtues associated with the Mights. See ll. 285-88n, 1117-18n, 1125-26n.

1134. Wyth charyte ys Gode verely: "God truly is with charity." From John 4.16. This same passage is quoted earlier in the play by Understanding, who in the opening expository declamations of the Mights associates himself with charity, probably as a counterforce to his later identification with covetousness. See l. 270n. Also see ll. 1121n and 1130n. Eccles emends *Wyth* to "Whyche."

1135-36. Exspoliantem veterem hominem cum actibus suis / Et induite nouum, qui renouatur in agnitionem Dei: "Put off the old man with his practices, and you have put on the new man, who is renewed in the knowledge of God" (source: Colossians 3.9-10). Colossians 3.9 reads: "exspoliantes vos veterem hominem cum actibus suis . . . . " The seven-line stanza pattern and abbreviated rhyme scheme of ll. 1132-39 in M suggest that a line has been omitted from this stanza at this point. Furnivall inserts "et induentes novem, eum qui renovatur in agnitionem" ("and you have put on the new nature, which is being renewed in knowledge," from Colossians

3.10). As Eccles points out, the line does not fit the rhyme scheme. However, the corresponding line from the *Scale of Perfection* (2: 31, ctd. by Eccles 216n; see also Underhill 368), which adds "Dei" ("of God") after "agnitionem" ("knowledge"), not only fits, but is apparently translated in the text (l. 1138). The reliance of *Wisdom* on Hilton at this point of the play is so close that it is almost certain this line belongs in the text as l. 1136. Furthermore, the added line follows a pattern of two-line Latin quotations, primarily taken from Walter Hilton, in the four speeches of Mind, Understanding, Will, and Anima in ll. 1117-48. The quotations not only occur in the same place in each stanza (as ll. 3-4 of the stanza), but they echo each other so strongly that it is possible to conjecture the M spellings of the missing line from terms in previous lines (e.g., *nouitate* in l. 1120 and *Et induite nouum* in l. 1128, the latter phrase repeated precisely in the conjectural l. 1136).

1138. renuyde in Gode knowynge ageyn: "renewed through your restored knowledge of God." Within the marriage metaphor of the play, the "knowing" of God has a dimension of intimacy, at once marital and spiritual, that is akin to the intimate knowledge of the self as well as the "knowing" of one's beloved. This line translates the Latin text of Hilton interpolated as l. 1136 in this text. Cf. "ye shal be renewed in þe knowynge of god" (Hilton, *Scale of Perfection* 2: 31; ctd. by Eccles 216n; see also Underhill 368); see ll. 95-98n and 1136n.

1143-44. Suavis est Dominus uniuerses, / Et miseraciones ejus super omnia opera ejus.: "God is sweet to all and his pity is above all his works" (source: Psalm 144.9; Protestant Psalm 145.9). "Suavis Dominus universis; et miserationes eius super omnia opera eius" ("God is good to all the world, and his pity is above all others").

1152. Justificati ex fide pacem habemus ad Deum.: "Justified by faith, we have peace in God" (source: Romans 5.l + *Scale of Perfection*). Romans 5.1 reads: "Justificati ergo ex fide, pacem habeamus ad Deum . . ." ("Justified by faith, we have peace from God"). As Eccles points out, *Wisdom* follows the *Scale of Perfection*, "As saynt poul sayth: 'Justificati ex fide pacem habemus ad deum' /

That is: we that arn ryghted & refourmed thorugh faythe in cryst hathe pees & accorde made betwyx god & us" (216n).

1154. Timor Domini inicium sapiencie.: "The fear of God [is] the beginning of Wisdom" (source: Proverbs 1.7; cf. Psalm 110.10 (New Oxford 111.10); Ecclesisticus 1.16, and Job 28.28). Proverbs 1.7 reads: "Timor Domini principium sapientiae."

1155. speaker's name — [Wysdom]: At this point in the manuscript, between ll. 1153 and 1154, M has drawn a line, appearing to signal a change of speaker, but has neglected to add a name. When such a line occurs without a speaker's name, it is only used to separate spoken lines from stage directions. Even in those instances, the line marks the end of a character's speech. The only exception occurs after l. 396 where M has copied a line inadvertently drawn in by D one line before the end of a speech by Lucifer. D has lightly cancelled the line. M does not cancel the line, which occurs at the end of a page, but he does write in Lucifer's name again at the top of the succeeding page, to indicate that Lucifer continues to speak. No such indication of speaker is provided at l. 1154. It would be strange for Anima, as the representative of humanity, to offer the benediction that concludes the play. In both *The Castle of Perseverance* and *Mankind*, the closing benediction is spoken by the figure representing divine authority: God the Father in *Perseverance* and Mercy in *Mankind*. The same convention should apply in *Wisdom*.

The strongest argument against the change of speaker initially appears to be the third person references to the *lorde Jhesu* in the benediction — particularly in l. 1163: *grawnt þat for hys passyon* (underlining mine). However, Wisdom refers to himself in the third person during his prologue (ll. 9-16). He has spoken in the third person both of God and of Christ in the sermon on the nine virtues (ll. 997-1064). These closing lines, which constitute a benediction for the audience, may be regarded as an epilogue that parallels the prologue. Moreover, the pronoun *hys* is problematic even if one assumes that Anima is speaking, for she would have no reason to talk of *hys passyon* if she were addressing Christ directly.

Not only would it be unconventional for Anima rather than Wisdom to provide the benediction in this play, but as a feminine manifestation of the Soul Anima has not even been given an expository self-defining monologue in the play. Thus, it would be astonishing should she now have the authority to conclude the drama. Wisdom would have spoken last in l. 1115, some 48 lines before the ending of the play — not a likely conclusion. Moreover, the interplay between Anima and Wisdom is theatrically effective when these final lines are assigned to Wisdom. Anima ends by drawing a conclusion taken from Proverbs (l. 1152), and Wisdom picks up this thematic thread in the opening lines of the benediction (ll. 1153-54), exhorting the audience, whom he alone has the authority to command, to learn the lesson of the play.

1155-56. Vobis qui timetis Deum / Orietur sol justicie: "For you who fear God, the Son brings forth Justice" (source: Malachi 4.2 and Hilton's *Scale of Perfection*). Malachi 4.2 reads: "Et orietur vobis timentibus nomen meum Sol justitiae" ("And for you, fearing my name, the sun of Justice shall come forth" — partially translated in text). Eccles points out that *Wisdom* follows the version in the *Scale of Perfection* (*"Vobis qui timetio Domini orietur sol justitiae"* 2: 26, Underhill 332), together with Hilton's explanation: "ye true sonne of rightwysnes that is our lorde Jhesu shal sprynge to you that dreden hym; that is to meke soules . . . " (qtd. by Eccles 216n; also see Underhill 332).

1158. on: "one." The *Scale of Perfection* has *our* at this point (Underhill 334). Eccles emends to *owr*. It is possible that M may have misread his source at this point. But *on lorde Ihesu* does reiterate the emphasis on the oneness and unity of the soul (and of God) which characterizes the condition of salvation established at the end of the play. That is, in his opening monologue Christ emphasized his role as a member of the Trinity (ll. 1-16) just as the Mights emphasized their distinctive functions in their opening expositions (ll. 183-276). Toward the end of the play, the Mights begin subtly to intermingle their identities, just as Christ here claims a "oneness" of his role as God. see ll. 1121n, 1130n, and 1134n.

1160-64. These closing lines are spoken directly to the audience, echoing earlier direct audience addresses. Cf. *Euery sowll here þis ys no nay* (l. 152); see also 16n, 152n, 488n, and 997-1064n. The authority of the benedicton once more confirms the likelihood that these lines are spoken by Wisdom.

1162. perfeccyon: In the framework of the contemplative tradition, from which the source documents of *Wisdom* are taken, *perfeccyon* ordinarily signifies contemplative union with God. See ll. 377n and 553n.

1163. doctryne of Wysdom we may sew: The final statement harkens back to Mind's affirmation in ll. 381-44: *My mynde is euer on Ihesu / . . . Hys doctrine to sue . . . .* The *doctryne of Wysdom* itself recalls Sapientia's introduction in Suso's *Orologium Sapientiae*: "myne doctryne schalle be þi lyfe. Wherefore takynge owr biginnynge of helefulle disciplyne at þe drede of godde, þe wheche is þe beginnynge of wisdam." Thus, the play ends where it begans, with Wisdom affirming the *doctryne* taken from Suso, the teaching of *Jhesu* as articulated throughout the play. It is a doctrine that begins with the fear of God (*Timor domini inicium sapiencie*, l. 1153) and centers on the love of the worshipper for God (*above all thynge 3e loue me specyally*, l. 58) and the love of God for humanity (*The hye worthynes of my loue / Angell nor man can tell playnly*, ll. 62-63). Ultimately, it is grounded in obedience — in the conformity of the will to God — which constitutes true "wisdom" in this play. See ll. 87-90n.

1164. Sapiencia patris: "The wisdom of the Father," i.e. Christ. Cf. Luke 12.50: "et sapientia Dei dixit" ("And [Christ] the wisdom of God said.")

grawnt þat for hys passyon: It is partly through his Passion that Christ manifests the wisdom of God the Father. In his Epistle to the Corinthians, Paul identifies the crucified Christ as the *sapientia a Deo*, i.e. the *wisdom from God*: "nos autem praedicamus Christum crucifixum" ("however, we preach Christ crucified," Corinthians 1.30, 23). This last line constitutes a prayer to Christ, probably spoken by the actor who has been impersonating Christ as Wisdom throughout the play. Thus, in a manner typical of allegorical Christian drama the epilogue breaks the fictional frame of the play, separating the actor from his role as he invokes the blessing of Christ, the *Sapiencia patris*, for the assembled audience. Both *Mankind* and *The Castle of Perseverance*, the other two Macro plays, end with a prayer spoken respectively by Mercy and by God the Father. Neither of those concluding speeches breaks the dramatic frame, as happens here. But other Digby plays do end with epilogues which explicitly break the frame to invoke blessings for the audience; see, for instance, *The Conversion of Saint Paul*, *Mary Magdalene*, and *The Killing of the Children* (Baker et al. 23, 95, 115); see also l. 16n.

GLOSSARY

Compiled with the help of
Editorial Associate Melanie Kulig

Except for proper names, which are glossed in endnotes, all terms in *Wisdom* appear in the glossary. When a proper name is included in an idiomatic expression, it appears in the glossary as well as being identified in the notes. Etymologies of all terms are given in brackets [ ]. All instances of terms that occur fewer than 50 times in the text are cited by line number. When a term occurs more than 50 times in the text, the first five occurrences and the last occurrence are cited by line, with . . . indicating omitted instances of that word. All variants of such terms are listed. All terms taken from the Digby text (D) are cited (even for words with more than 50 occurrences); these are indicated by an * and followed in parentheses by the M reading, thus: "(M = _____)." When no such parenthetical notation occurs, the reader may assume that there was no M equivalent for the D term; all such instances are glossed in textual footnotes. An * in the etymology, however, conventionally signifies a conjectured, rather than a recorded, early form of the word. Because the language of this play reinforces the interactive link between religious allegory and social history, definitions which have specific theological and/or legal significance are emphasized. The primary sources for both etymologies and meanings are the *Oxford English Dictionary* and the *Middle English Dictionary*. A specific meaning quoted directly from the *Oxford English Dictionary* is indicated by *OED*, with specific quotations taken from the *Middle English Dictionary* indicated by *MED* in the etymologies or definitions. In the course of preparing this glossary some incorrect definitions were discovered in both the *OED* and the *MED*. These are not systematically indicated, but this glossary may be presumed to take precedence over other dictionaries as the primary source of meanings for terms in this play. Idiomatic phrases are cited when appropriate, with the headword in an idiom indicated by " ~ ." Idiomatic expressions are cross-referenced to every word in the idiom. Verb forms — person, tense and number — are specified only when they are in some sense distinctive. When a variant of a word has the same meaning as the definition which immediately precedes it, the definition is not repeated, though specific line references are cited. As in the text all yoghs are transcribed as *3*.

In terms of alphabetization, vocalic *y-* words are listed interchangeably with *i-* words in the I/Y section; consonantal *y-* words are in the Y section following X at the end of the alphabet. *Th-* and *þ-* words are listed sequentially as "th-" in the T section. Medial *-y-* is listed as if *-i-*. *Ȝe-*, with the yogh transcribed as *ȝ*, is listed with *ye* under Y.

Abbreviations for the glossary:

```
*    = in etymologies, conjectured early form of word
       in body of glossary, term taken from Digby text
a.   = adjective
adv. = adverb
AFr  = Anglo-French
assoc. = associated
aux. = auxiliary
c    = century
C. de Rol. = Chanson de Roland
comp. = comparative
Com  = Common to (Rom=Romance; Teut=Teutonic;
             WG=West Germanic) languages
conj. = conjunction
D    = the Digby text
De Civ. Dei = Augustine's De Civitate Dei
dem. = demonstrative
E    = English
e    = early (eME=early Middle English, etc.)
ellip. = elliptical
esp. = especially
ety. = etymology
f.   = from
fig. = figuratively
Fr   = French
Fris = Frisian
imp. = imperative
IndoEur = Indo-European
indef. art. = indefinite article
inf. = infinitive
infl. = influenced
int. = interjection
intens. part. = intensifying particle
intr. = intransitive
G    = German
Goth = Gothic
l    = late (lL=late Latin, etc.)
L    = Latin
lit. = literature
```

LG = Low German
M = (in definitions) the Macro text
M = (in etymologies) Modern (L=Latin; LG=Low German;
      Swed=Swedish)
ME = Middle English
MED = *Middle English Dictionary*
medL = Medieval Latin
ModE = Modern English
n. = noun
neg. part. = negative particle
nom. = nominative
O = Old (E=English; Fr=French; Fris=Frisian; HG=High German;
      N=Norse; NFr=Northern French; Nor=Northumbrian;
      Teut = Teutonic)
obs. = obsolete
OED = *Oxford English Dictionary*
orig. = originally
pa. = past tense
pl. = plural
popL = popular Latin
poss. = possibly — or — (as part of speech) possessive
pp. = past participle
pr. = present tense
pred. a. = predicate adjective
prep. = preposition
prob. = probably
pron. = pronoun
prp. = present participle
quasi-sb. = quasi-substantive, word used as if a noun
refl. = reflexive
rel. = relative
sb. = substantive (designates an a. or v. used as a noun)
Scand = Scandinavian
sg. = singular
subj. = subjunctive
superl. = superlative
Teut = Teutonic
theo. = theological (meaning)
tr. = transitive
ult. f. = ultimately, i.e. originally, from
v. = verb
var. = variant
vbl. = verbal
w. = with

A

a, indef. art. [*OE an, one*] a, an, used frequently in the modern sense, always before consonants in all instances; 3 before vowels, ("a angell", 159; "a ordenance", 786), Osd(*), 16 sd, 20, 40, 102 . . . 462* (M = **in**) . . . 1129; see **best**, n.; **clene**; **fowll(e)**; **hede**; **maner(e)**; **pynne**; **tak(e)**; **tyme**.

a, int. [*Obs. dialectical form of o! or ah! for which a!/eh! is still a common expression of surprise, admiration or invocation*] ah!, oh!, 39, 77, 83, 173, 463.

a, conj. Obs. form occasionally occurring before a consonant, meaning **and**, 825, 1071.

abey, **abye**, v. [*a- away, out + OE bycgan, buy; cognate with G usbujan, redeem*] abye, suffer a penalty for, 768, 846.

abhomynable, a. [*OFr abhominable f. L abominari, deprecate as an ill omen; E = abhominable (15-17c) f. L ab homine, inhuman, bestial; permanently affected meaning of the word*] offensive, beastly, 540, 942.

abyde, v. [*OE abidan*] remain, stand fast, continue, particularly to remain in the service of; metaphor linking the body, cross, and temple, 1103.

abye; see **abey**.

able, v. [*OFr (h)able*] enable, 945.

aboue, **abowe**, adv./prep. [*a + OE bufan, above, atop*] adv., from heaven, 63, in heaven, 284; prep., "~ all," more than, 21, 29, 58; "~ all þis," first of all, chiefly, 290; see **dysposicyon**; **experience**.

abowt(e), adv. [*OE on-butan, on or by the outside; replaced OE ymb-utan (13c)*] around, 0sd, 724sd; "þe worlde (. . .) ~," all the world, everywhere in the world, 464, 501.

abrode, adv. [*OE on, a + brad, broad*] widely, 453, 1102. see **sprede**.

acorde, v./n. [*OFr acorder f. IL accordare; in lit. bnng heart to heart, reconcile*] **acorde**, v., agree, (to a false covenant), 829; "~ togedyr by," imp., be in agreement (implying false unity), 495; **acordyt**, 3 sg. pr., well-suited to, 557; "~ best in especyall," is particularly appropriate, 5; **acorde**, n., harmony, suggesting a formal religious covenant, 1151; **acordance**, n., compliance (especially with the will of God, here ironically with reference to the devil), 689.

actual, a. [*OFr actuel f. IL actualis, of or pertaining to action*] existing in fact, real; "þe synnys ~," (theol.) sins committed by one's own act (opposed to original sin), 1112.

acumberyde, v. pp. [*OFr encombrer*] burdened, harassed by the devil, 396.

aduersyte, n. [*OFr aversité f. L adversitatem, opposition*] adversity, misfortune, 1020.

affyable, a. as n. [*OFr affable (lit 14c) ult. f. L affari, speak to; MED glosses this word in Wisdom as "betrothed," thus erroneously suggesting a link with affyance*] agreeable, compliant, of a willing temperament, 594.

affyance, n. [*OFr afiance ult. f. afier, trust*] betrothed lover, 83; pledged trust, 657; "of myn ~," pledged to me, 690; see **affynyte**.

affye, n. [*OFr afye f. IL affidare*] trust, loyalty; "of myn ~," followers, those bound to me, 643; see **affynyte**.

affynyte, n. [*OFr affinité; not related to afier, though similarity of phrase suggests parallels between the terms affyance, affye, and affynyte*] natural liking or attractiveness; "to my ~," to (meet) companions allied to me by temperament, 799.

aftyr, prep./adv. [*OE æfter*] prep., in compliance with, 228; after, 1002, 1044; adv., following, 324sd.

age, n. [*OFr aäge/eäge f. L ævum, an age*] age, 890; see **tender**.

ageyn, adv./prep. [*OE onðe(a)n, opposite, facing; extended to suggest opposition, reversal, or repetition; the contrastive meaning "against" derived from the genitive ending -es of OE a3en*] adv., once more, as before, 119, 380sd, 772, 1138; back [under], 912sd; in return, 73, 190; prep., against, 491, 529, 661, 722; see **kynde**.

agre, v. [*OFr agreer f. L adgratare, make agreeable*] assent, 497.

ay, adv. [*eME aðð/ai/ei*] at all times, on all occasions, 554, 677; "~ whan," every time, always (referring to a series of separate incidents), 345; see **lykly**.

ayer, **hayer**, n. [*OFr (h)eir*] heir, 159, 244.

alas, int. [*OFr (h)a las, wretched, weary*] alas, 912.

all, a./n./pron. [*ComTeut all(e); not found outside Teut*] all, used frequently in the modern sense, 8, 21, 23, 24, 29 . . . 530* . . . 1064sd; in compounds:

"~ day," all the time, continuously, 153; "~ cum þey not," if they do not come, 329; "~ in ~," all together, 754; "~ wey," in every way, 958; see **aboue**; **dyspyght**; **dysposicyon**; **on(e)**; **thynge**; **thys**; **werkyst**; **worlde**.

allyance, n. [*OFr al(l)iance (14c), ally*] alliance, bonds created by shared worldliness, 659; **allyede**, v. pp., firmly allied, well-connected, 862.

allthow, conj. [*ComTeut OE all + þe(a)h; circa 1400 one word*] even though, 7.

als, adv. [*Intermediate form between OE al-swa and ModE as*] as, 742; see **tyght(e)**.

also, adv. [*OE al (all) + swa (so), wholly so*] also, likewise, 11, 426, 694, 703, 1130.

am, v. 1 sg. pres. of verb **be** [*Origin obscure*] in active and passive uses, 3, 43, 45, 82, 183, 213, 309, 332, 336, 341, 368, 534, 564, 567, 570, 628, 631, 648, 696, 879; modal verb in 1 sg. pr. perf., have been, 20, 28; see **bownd(e)**; **fownder**.

amende, v. [*OFr amende f. emendare, free from faults*] correct, reform, 713, 892; refl., mend (itself) 752; **amendyde**, pp., reformed, atoned for, 936; **amendys**, n. pl., reparation, fine, (theol.) penance, atonement; "take ~," exact a fine, 802; see **let(t)**.

amyable, a. [*OFr amiable*] worthy of love, 43, 536, 590; see **dysgysynge**.

amyke, n. [*L amicus, friend*] beloved (a title for Wisdom), 70.

amys(e), adv./pred. a. [*a, prep. of manner + miss, failure*] adv., "do ~," act sinfully, 75; led astray, (implying sin), 874; pred. a., sinful, wrong (used ironically), 403.

an, indef. art. [*OE an*] an, 731; see **euell**.

and(e)/&, conj. [*OE and/ond*] and, used frequently in the modern sense, 0sd(*), 2, 6, 8, 11 . . . 496* . . . 511* . . . 547* . . . 645* (M = a) . . . 733* (M = a) . . . 1162; if, 451, 699, 769, 800, 856; then, 330; **ande**, spelling not used in D; used in M only at beginning of lines except for 627, 769, 1124; see **by(e)**; **choppe**; **clene**; **cros(e)**; **day**; **fayer(e)**; **fende**; **go**; **hedyr**; **lere**; **lyff**; **lyknes**; **mercy**; **mynde**; **resurreccyon**; **so**; **starre**; **tassyelys**; **tweyn**; **vyolence**; **w(h)at**.

angell, n. [*eTeut adoption f. L angelus infl. by OE engel; 14-15c forms in au-, which show Fr influence, appear in D but not in M*] angel, 62, 159; "~ of lyghte," Lucyfer, 333; **angelys**, pl., 253.

anoyntyde, v. pp. [*OFr enoinf*] annointed, 321.

anosyde, v. pp. [*ME anoisen OFr nuisir ult. f. L nocere, injured*] harmed, 225.

another, a. [*OE an other; originally two words meaning a different or a remaining*] another, 851.

anow; see **inow(e)**.

answer, v. [*OE andswaru, a reply or rebuttal to a sworn oath*] answer, 420; **answerys**, 3 sg. pr., 692sd.

apere, v. [*OFr apareir f. L apparere, come forth into view*] become evident, 301; appear, seem, 539; **apperythe**, 3 sg. pr., appears, 902sd.

aplye, v.[*OFr aplier f. L applicare, fold*] submit, devote, 513; **imp.**, 446; **applyede**, pp., "~ to," referred to, connected with, 10, 178.

appeyere, v. [*OFr ampayre, worsen; spelled im- after L impeiorare late 15c*] injure, 860.

apperythe; see **apere**.

apposyde, v. pp. [*OFr oposer used in common scholastic sense of L opponere, argue againsf*] examined, 225.

aqueyntance, aqweynttance n. [*OFr acointance*] acquaintance, 763; familiarity, 658.

aqwyt, v. [*OFr aquiter f. IL acquitare, settle*] discharge, acquit, 811.

aray, n.[*OFr arai f. arayer arrange, prepare, order*] clothing which signifies fealty relationships or social/spiritual allegiances, 150, 324sd; "new ~," a new suit of clothes designating a change of allegiance f. Wysdom to Lucyfer, 551; "syde ~," long clothing associated with piety, 510; "curyous ~," costly vulgar clothing associated with worldly sin, 609.

are, v. 2 sg. of verb **be** [*Origin obscure*] are, 104; **art**, 2 sg. pr., 319, 905.

are, adv.[*OE ær/ME ar(e); partly represesents ON ´r or OE ' r without umlaut; ´r results from loss of stress*] before, 810.

arest, v. [*OFr arester f. IL adrestare, detain*] intr., seize, 805; tr., arrest; "~ . . . to pes for fight," arrest for fighting (as a pretense of keeping the peace), 850; see **fyght**.

aryght, adv. [*OE a- + rihf*] immediately, straight away, 853.

arome, adv. [*OE on rum(e)*] at a distance, 524; see **put**.

art; see **are**, v.

as, conj./prep./adv. [*OE all-swa, wholly as; see als; also*] conj., as, 64, 100, 167, 168, 270, 361, 479* (M = **at**), 485, 489, 516, 730, 1034, 1036; as if, 130; "~ . . . ~," as . . . as, 9, 129, 242, 341, 558, 566, 623, (elliptical) 652, 909, 969, 1010, 1017; prep., 16sd, 158, 159, 289, 1106, 1124, 1129.; adv. phrase; "~ for," for, 22; "~ in hys tempull sure," in his secure temple, a metaphor linking the body with God's temple, 264; "~ streytly," as strictly, 1033; see **best**, n.; **in**; **longe**; **many**; **tyght(e)**.

aschamyde, pp. as pred. a. [*OE asceamod; ME form probably combines OE 3esceamod + ME yschamed*] ashamed, 628.

asythe, n. [*Northen variation of assethe f. OFr a(s)set f. a(s)sez enough; see* **sethe**] reparation, satisfaction; "mak/made ~," make/made atonement for sinfulness, 1094, 1096; see **suffycyent**.

aske, v. [*ComTeut OE ascian*] ask (of), 80, 1054; ask for, 814; pray for, 983.

aspye, v. [*OFr espier*] know by looking, perceive, 395; **espyede** pp., perceived, discovered, 857.

assende, v. [*L ascendere, climb*] ascend, (with spiritual implications), 252.

assyduly, adv. [*OFr assiduel f. L assiduus*] constantly, 256.

at, prep. [*ComTeut OE æf*] at, 526, 539, 564* (M = **a**), 742. 764, 780, 789, 793, 822, 948; "haue ~," go at (it), 615, 627, 869; "~ þe best," at its best, 622, 700; see **eas(e)**; **jug(e)ment(e)**; **last**; **nought(e)**; **on(e)**; **rest**; **tyght(e)**.

atastyde, v. pp. [*OFr ataster*] tasted, experienced, 568.

atawnt, adv. [*OFr autant, as much as possible*] excessively, 606.

attende, v. [*OFr atendre f. L adtendere, stretch*] tr., pay attention to, 100; intr., "to me ~," attend upon or serve me, 748.

auctoure, n. [*OFr autor, later auteur; auct- became the ordinary spelling (15-16c); further corrupted to act- from medL confusion of auctor and actor; auth-, at first a scribal variant of aut-, appeared in E circa 1550*] creator, with the implication of teacher, 99; **awtors**, pl., writers, authorities, 270; see **souere(y)n**.

avawnt(e), **avaynte**, v. [*OFr* *ava(u)nter* f. *IL* *vanitare*, boast (cf. Augustine), ult. f. *vanare*, lie] vainly display, 586, 597; as a n. (of lechery) 605; Mynde, Wyll, and Wndyrstondynge each make a boast as one indication of their worldliness.

avawnce, v. [*OFr* *avancer* f. *popL* *abanteare* f. *IL* *abante*, away; form *advance* derived from mistaking *a-* for a form of *ad-*] advance, improve (term also used to describe service under a king or in support of war; here it refers to advancement through manipulation of law, rents, etc.), 790.

avaynte; see **avawnt(e)**.

avoydyth, v. tr. 3 sg. pr. [*OFr* *e(s)vuidier*, empty ouf] purges, 979.

avowe, v. [*OFr* *avouer* ult. f. *L* *advocare*, call upon; in feudal times to call upon as a patron, defender, or clienf] an oath, 625* (M = **ma vowe**); "to God(e) ~," I swear, 562, 622, 889.

awake, v. [*OE* *awæcnan*, wake up; confused in form with *lOE* *awacian*, watch, keep awake] be alert, become vigilant, bestir, 977.

awey, v. [*OE* *a-we3an*, *MED*] imp., brush, get away, remove, 500, 552; wash, take away, 960; see **care**.

awey, adv. [*OE* *a-we3*] away, 125; see **wasche**.

awtors; see **auctoure**.

ay-; listed as if **ai-**.

B

bagpyp, n. [*eME* *bagge* poss. f. *ON* *baggi*, bag, bundle + *OE* *pipe*, musical tube, related in verb form to *L* *pipare*, chirp] bagpipe. 724sd.

balle, n. [*ME* *bal(le)* f. *ON* *böllr*; no OE form known; *ME* *balle* coincides in form with *OFr* *balle*, often erroneously thought to be its source; may be related to *L* *follis*, a thing blown up or inflated] ball, orb, symbol of royal power; only instance cited by MED of "ball" meaning "orb", 0sd.

baptem, **baptyme**, n. [*OFr* *baptême/baptesme*] baptism. 126* (M = **bapten**), 1109.

bare, a. [*ComTeut/OE* *bær*] bare, naked, 770, 815, 1042, 1052.

batell, n. [*OFr* *bataille* f. *IL* *battuere*, beaf] battle, 703.

be, **by**, v. most common form of irreg. v. **be** [*OE* <u>*beon*</u>, <u>*wesan*</u> f. *3 surviving OTeut inflexions:* <u>*beo;*</u> <u>*es;*</u> <u>*wes;*</u> *forms* <u>*am*</u>, <u>*is*</u>, <u>*are*</u>, <u>*was*</u>, <u>*were*</u>, *derive from these verbs*] used frequently in the modern sense, most commonly where we would use **are** in 3 <u>pl</u>. <u>pr</u>. 3, 133, 137, 263, 277, 304 . . . 448* . . . 600* . . . 1076; <u>inf</u>., to be, 455, 603; <u>inf</u>. <u>w</u>. <u>pp</u>., 222, 225, 227, 229; <u>inf</u>. <u>w</u>. <u>fut</u>. <u>aux</u>., 511, 556, 793; 1 <u>pl</u>. <u>pr</u>., 892, 600*, 1149; 2 <u>formal pl</u>. <u>pr</u>., 114, 117, 1090, 1092, 1107, 1108, 1113, 1129; 3 <u>sg</u>. <u>pr</u>., 7, 36, 224; 3 <u>pl</u>. <u>pr</u>., 163, 171; <u>subj</u>., 46, 668, 816, 862; <u>imp</u>., 442, 506, 782, 971, 1138; <u>pass</u>., 115, 138 . . . 1150; **ben**, 3 <u>sg</u>. <u>pr</u>., 257, 357, 690, 708; 3 <u>pl</u>.<u>pr</u>., 3, 364, 470, 574, 708, 1074; <u>pp</u>. <u>w</u>. <u>aux</u>. in <u>perfect tense</u>, has existed, 109; **by**, are, 172, 304; **by**, inf. w. imp., 495; **by**, <u>cond</u>., be, 641; **bene**, 3 pl. pr., 56; **bethe**, 3 pl. pr., 178; **beynge**, <u>prp</u>., being, 959; <u>vbl</u>. <u>sb</u>., existence, 283; see **acorde**; **ber(e)**; **fame**; **hert(e)**; **holde**; **how(e)**; **lyke**; **must**; **neuer**; **reconsylyde**; **reforme**; **rewlyde**; **ryche**; **serue**; **worlde**.

be, prep.; see **by(e)**.

beer; see **ber(e)**.

befor(e), prep./adv. [*OE* <u>*beforan*</u>, *from the front; originally an adv. which gained the force of a prep. over time*] <u>prep</u>., above, more than, 291, 998; before, in front of, 895, 948; <u>adv</u>., above, 417; previously, 237; in front of, 324sd, 1064 sd; **byfor**, prep., 179; see **set(t)**.

begyle, v. [*OE* <u>*be*</u> + *OFr* <u>*guile*</u> *related to ME* <u>*wile*</u>, *a cunning or deceitful trick*] trick, beguile, 376.

begyn(ne), v. [*OE* <u>*beginnan*</u> *rare; more common OE form was* <u>*on-ginnan*</u>] begin, originate, start (over);. <u>tr</u>., 306, 717; <u>intr</u>., 119, 161, 627, 943, 977; **begynnyt**, 3 sg. pr., 223; **began(e)**, 2/3 sg. pa., 16, 103, 332, 347, 428, 969; **begynner**, n., founder, originator, 236; **begynnyng(e)**, <u>vbl</u>. <u>sb</u>., beginning, entering into or bringing into existence, 90, 247.

behynde, **byhynde**, adv. [*OE* <u>*behindan*</u>] behind, 16sd; see **lace**.

behest, n. [*OE* <u>*behæs*</u>] promise, 1126.

beholde, v. [*OE* <u>*bihaldan*</u>; *in other Teut langs.* = *"hold"; implication of "watching" restricted to E*] look (around), fix eyes on, see, 1 <u>sg</u>. <u>pr</u>., 246; <u>inf</u>., 254; <u>imp</u>., (Wysdom urges inner seeing, first of his own beauty, then of the disfigurement of the soul), 42, 902, 911; (Lucyfer urges looking around at the world), 458, 464.

behoueable, a. [*OE* <u>*behoflan*</u> + *-<u>able</u>, be of use*] useful, 238.

beyght, n. [*OE* <u>*bat*</u> *influenced by ON* <u>*beit*</u>, *pasture* + <u>*beita*</u> *food, especially used to entice prey*] bait, 730.

belewe, v. [*eME bileven* f. *be* + *OE 3elefan; be-* compound appeared in 12c as *beleeve; believe (17c) is an erroneous spelling probably modelled after Fr relieve*] believe, 418; **beleve**, 430* (M = **belewe**).

belowyde, pp. a. [*ME biloven, love*] beloved, 13.

ben(e); see **be**.

benefyttys, n. pl. [*AFr benfet* f. *L benefactum, good deed; in lit. (a thing) well done well* f. *bene facere, to do well; 1st syllable assimilated to L (15-16c)*] benefits, 186, 322.

benygnyte, n. [*OFr benignité ult.* f. *L bene, well* + *genus, born of a kind*] kindness of disposition (especially in superiors), 260; as a term of address, "yowr ~," your graciousness, 39.

berde, n. [*ComTeut OE beard*] beard, 0sd; **berdys**, pl., 692sd; see **sypres**.

ber(e), v. [*ComTeut OE beran*] display, wear, carry, 166, 602; "~ wp," uphold, 699; **bor(r)e**, pp., "be ~," are born, 115; "was (man) ~," when Christ was born as a mortal child, 419, 680; **born** pp., "~ wpe," upheld, 669; **beer**, implied 3 sg. pr., wears, 718.

beschrew, v. [*be* + *OE scræwa, malignant being (Teut); modelled on the mammal shrew*] invoke evil upon, curse, 506.

beseke, v. [*ComTeut be* + *OE secan*] seek after, 970.

besy, a. [*OE bisi3*] industrious, 406.

besynes, n. [*OE bisi3nis*] effort, activity, (indicates contemplation), 441.

best, adv./superl. a. [*ComTeut OE betst, reduced to best by assimilation of -t- to following -s-*] adv., most appropriately, 5; best, 468; superl. a., 443, 622, 700; 825; see **acorde**; **at**.

best, n. [*OFr beste* f. *L bestia; replaced OE deór; in early usage, included men; later indicated animals excluding humans*] beast; "as a ~," as an animal without reason, 158, 1129.

bethynke, v. refl. [*ComTeut OE bibencan*] bethink, think about; "yow ~," consider, 899.

bett, v. inf. [*ComTeut OE beatan*] beat, 771.

better, comp. a./adv. [*ComTeut OE betera*] comp. a., better, 33, 477, 787; comp. adv., 849.

betwyn, prep. [*OE betweon(um)* f. *bi sǽm tweònum; in lit = by the seas tweyn*] between, 794.

betwyx, prep. [*ME betwixe(n) (12c)* f. *OE betweoxan, final syllable lost 15c*] between, 1151.

beware, v. imp. [*be v. + ware, compound f. OE warian + OE wær, cautious*]; as early as 1300, beware written as one word] be aware of, careful of, 291, 293.

bewty, n. [*OFr beuté*] beauty of spirit, moral purity, 21, 24, 168; **bewte**, physical attractiveness, 571; **bewtys**, pl., aspects of spiritual beauty (plural has the force of a collective noun implying total beauty), 1092;   see **bryght(e)**.

by, **be**, prep., adv. [*OE bi, bi3, be; originally an adverbial particle of place*] used frequently in the modern sense; through, by means of (which), from, because of, 10, 75, 95, 117, 123 . . . 260* . . . 600* . . . 1131; w. prp., 95, 153, 155, 160, 252; by (as first term in an oath), 422, 487, 493, 556, 784, 832, 903, 923; adv. "~ & ~," on and on, continuously, 751, 1032; see **bon**; **contenance**; **relacyon**; **reson(e)**; **set(t)**; **towchynge**; **tru**.

bycause, adv. [*OE bi + OFr cause (13c)*] because, 12.

bye, v. tr. [*Aphetic variation of abye f. OE byc3(e)an origin unknown; not found outside Teuf*] suffer the consequences of, 108; buy, obtain for money (but with the unconsciously ironic implication of ultimately paying the price for the sinfulness of worldly lordship), 665; **bought**, pp., "ys ~," has been bought, 762.

byfor; see **befor(e)**.

byght, v. [*ComTeut OE bitan*] bite, find fault, sharply accuse. 854.

byhynde; see **behynde**.

byrde, n. [*OE brid ONorth bird, fledgling; not found elsewhere in Teuf*] bird, 623.

bytyme, adv. [*ME by(-)time; properly a phrase*] in good time. 691.

bytterly, adv. [*OE biterlice*] bitterly, 768.

blake, a./sb. [*OE blæc/blac; in OE confused with blac, shining, white*] black, 16sd, 151, 153, 167; ellip. as sb., "þe deullys ~." spiritual blackness caused by sin, 979.

blame, n./v. [*OFr blame/blamer f. lL blasphemare, revile, reproach*] n., blame, culpability, 113; v. inf., blame, accuse, 601.

blyne, v. [*OE blinnan, cease, leave off*] tarry, 549.

blys, n. [*OE bliðs; the meanings of bliss and bless mutually infl. each other, so that ME blys refers more to heavenly joy than to blitheness*] supreme delight (as a title for Wisdom), 70; the perfect joy of heaven, 192, 216, 244, 358, 415, 877, 1116, 1140; see **regne**.

blyssyde, pp. a. [*OE bl(o)edsian; not found elsewhere in Teuf*] hallowed, consecrated, blessed, 156, 275.

blode, n. [*OE blod*] blood, 1043.

blow, v. [*OE blawan*] blow, 702; imp., sound the horn, 707.

body, n. [*OE bodi3*] body, the corporeal part of a human, 411, 485, 504, 770, 1004, 1016, 1051, 1106; **bodye**, 846; **bodyly**, a., bodily, 1076; **bodely**, a., of the body, 147; see **myght**.

boy, n. [*ME boi, boy origin obscure; originally this term = a male servant and then evolved in meaning to = a young male, especially a child*] boy, person of low rank) 550, 550sd; **boys**, pl., male children, 913sd.

boldly, adv. [*OE bald + -ly; not found outside Teuf*] boldly, 669.

bon, n. [*ComTeut OE ban*] bone; "by þe ~," idiomatic expression of unknown origin, perhaps having to do with dicing, or possibly a corruption of a prophesy on the *bones* of God, 784; **bonys**, pl., bones, 1052.

bore; **born**; **borre**; see **ber(e)**.

bost, v. [*ME bosten, not found before 1300; prob. of Germanic origin (MED)*] make a show, vainly display, boast, 586.

bothe, adv./a. [*eME baðe*] both, adv., 157, 523; a., 617.

bought; see **bye**.

bow, n. [*ComTeut OE boh; akin to OHG buog, shoulder, foreleg; meaning "bough of a tree" restricted to E*] bough, 623.

bowhede, v. pp. [*OE bu3an; originally a strong verb: by 13c began to develop weak pa. and pp. through confusion w. OE be3an, bend, cause to bow*] bowed, 1105.

bownde, pp. a. [*ComTeut OE bundan; replaced by pp. bound (15c)*] bound; "am ~," bounded by, particularly with respect to Christian doctrine or monastic rules; also implies a bond of marriage, 309.

brede, n. [*OE bread, rare; in 12c replaced OE hlaf, Mod E loaf*] bread, 1034.

breydest, v. 2 sg. pr. [*ComTeut OE* _bre3dan_, *move quickly; "to reproach" may be a special sense of this v.; akin to ON* _bregða_ *or a shortened form of v.* _abraid_ *(15c) f. OE* _upbredan_] reproach, upbraid (probably infl. by the colloquial meaning "to ejaculate," which was current for the verb **abraid** until the 16th century), 763.

bren, n. pl. [*OE* _bræw_] eyebrows, 196.

brennynge, prp. a. [*OE* _brinnan/bærnan;_ *developed into 4 verb stems:* _bern-_, _brin(n)-_, _barn-_, _bren(n)-;_ *the fourth variant akin to ON* _brenna; esp. in IME_] burning, 281.

brybe, n. [*ME* _bribe_ *(lit 14c esp. Chaucer); ety. obscure, poss. f. OFr* _bribe_, *bread given to a beggar or f. OFr* _briber_, *agent-noun meaning vagabond or thief*] bribe, 737, 762; **brybys**, pl. (fig.), those willing to be bribed, 675.

bryght(e), a. [*ComTeut OE* _beorht;_ *lost in all langs but E*] bright; "bewty(s) ~," beauty gleaming with moral purity, 24, 1092; **bryghtnes**, n., brilliance, radiance, 30; gaudy splendor, 375.

brynge, v. [*ComTeut OE* _bringan_] bring, 197, 356, 366, 374, 617, 916, 925; "~ . . . byhynde," mislead, 296; **bryngyt**, 3 sg. pr., brings, 189; **bryngyth**, 3 sg. pr., brings, 267; **bryngeth**, 456* (M = **bryght**); **brought(e)**, pp., brought, 23, 520, 952; see **mynde**.

brynke, n. [*ME* _brink_ *not found in OE; akin to MLG* _brink_, *edge of a field, side of a hill*] edge, brink, 897; see **pyttys**.

bronde, n. [*ComTeut OE* _brande_, _brond_] brand; "~ of hell," firebrands or torches of hell, 917; **brondys**, pl., 114.

brought(e); see **brynge**.

browys, n. pl. [*OE* _bræw_, _bru_] eyebrows, suggesting artificial eyebrows or possibly bangs, Osd; see **bren**.

burthen, n. [*OE* _byrðen;_ *-d- circa 1100*] burden, 53.

busche, n. [*ME* _busk_ *akin to OHG* _bush_] bush, 1050.

but, conj./prep./adv. [*OE adv./prep.* _be-utan_, _buta(n)_, *on the outside, without; ME* _boute(n)_, *weakened to* _bute(n)_, *then* _but;_ *usage as conj. closely linked to prep.*] conj., however, 414, 488, 916; although, 758; unless, 484, 619; but (used in a contrastive sense), "~ not," but not, 64; not/nouhte . . . ~," not . . . but, 87-88, 801, 1046-7, 1121-2; "~ yff," only if, 363; "~ only," except, 206; "~ for . . . yt" but, 373-4; "~ þat," unless, 920; prep., but, 283, 813; "not only, ~ also," 104, (implied) 961, 1130;

except, 235, 572; adv., merely. only, 305, 555, 612. 650, 651, 816, 890; anything but, 831; see **lytyll**; **only**.

by-; listed as if **bi-**.

C

cache, v. [*ONFr cachier* f. *L captare*, seek, catch; *replaced OE læcc(e)an*] subj., 1 sg. pr., catch (the gout), 507.

call, v. tr. [*ComTeut ON kalla, cry, shouf*] call out for, 1098.

cam, see **com(e)**.

can, kan, v. [*OE cunnan; OTeut sense = to know, be mentally able*] aux. w. inf., am/is able to, can, 62, 65, 68, 210, 250, 430*, 447, 449, 775, 836, 966; 1/3 sg. pr., know 841; know how to, 792, 848, 849; "yet ~," still know, have not forgotten, 342; **cowdys**, pa. subj. 2 sg., are able to, 1034.

care, n./v. [*ComTeut OE: c(e)aru/carian*] n., concern over, 737; worry, responsibility, 813; w. elliptical imp., "awey ~," banish care, (used by Lucyfer), 500; "~ awey," (echoed by Mynde), 552; v., worry, have a regard for, 664; "yff (þat) I ~," for all (that) I care, 507, 663.

caren, n. [*ONFr caronie poss.* f. *L caro, flesh*] dead flesh, carrion, 1099.

cast, v. refl. [*ON kasta, cast, throw; replaced OE weorþan*] firmly resolve, 239; "~ no dowte," have no fear, 502; **castynge**, prp.. resolving; "euer ~ me," always maintaining a firm resolution, 339.

cause, n. [*OFr cause (13c)* f. *L causa, reason, motive, lawsuit*] reason, ground for action, motive, 432, 629; legal case, 641; see **w(h)y**.

cedar, reference to Kedar; see **tabernacull**.

celestyall, a. [*OFr celestial ult.* f. *L cælum, sky, heaven*] celestial, divinely beautiful, 129.

certen, a. [*OFr certain ult.* f. *L cernere, decide, determine*] certain, 876.

change, v. [*OFr changer* f. *IL cambire, exchange*] change clothes, (esp. in refl. use) 375, 510; be transformed, 950; since clothing identifies character, these two meanings work together in the play; **chonge**, exchange, trade, bargain, 639; see **choppe**.

changeable, a. [*OFr changeable*] variable, 360.

chappetelot, n. [*Probable error in D & M for OFr chappelet (MED)*] headress worn as a sign of office, 16sd; **chapp(e)lettys**, pl., 164sd, 1064sd.

chargys, n. pl. [*OFr charge f. lL carrica*] dependents, 407; responsibilities, 410.

charyte, n. [*OFr charité ult. f. L caritatem*] charity, virtue; first associated with Wndyrstondynge as a foil to covetousness; 269, 270, 271, 272, 274; linked to Wyll as a manifestation of divine love, 287, 1134; used by Wysdom, 1062; divine grace; "in ~," in charity, i.e., in or through God's grace, 1133; see **loue**.

charter, n. [*OFr chartre, map, card*] a written document granting ownership (here used fig. for granting pardon), 986; see **pardon**.

chastyte, n. [*OFr chastété (13c) f. L castitatem*] chastity, 476, 568.

chere, a. [*OFr chier f. L carum, dear*] precious, 1047.

chere, n. [*OFr ch(i)er f. lL cara, face*] mood, 819.

cherysyste, v. 2 sg. pr. [*OFr cherir, value highly*] cherish, 914.

cheueler, **cheweler**, n. [*OFr cheveleure*] wig, 0sd, 16sd; **cheuelers**, pl., 164sd; **chevelered**, pp. a., wigged, 324sd* (M = **theveleryde**).

chevesaunce, n. [*OFr chevance, acquired wealth*] device, stratagem to gain a profit, 787.

chylderne, n. pl. [*OE cild*] children, 406.

cheweler; see **cheueler**.

chyrch(e), n. [*OE cir(i)ce*] church, 15, 982, 984, 988, 991, 995, 1078; word appears more frequently in Wisdom than in any other morality play; see **holy**; **modyr**.

chonge; see **change**.

choppe, v. [*Probable variant of ME chapien f. ceapian*] barter; "~ & chonge," buy and sell (perhaps the earliest recorded use of this idiom), 639.

chorle, n. [*OE ceorl, a man without rank, (not a nobleman)*] base, low-bred fellow, 835, 838; **chorlys**, pl., 848.

chose, pp. a. [*OE ceosan; OE coren; pp. assimilated in ME (12c) to chosen*] chosen, 16.

cyte, n. [*OFr cité*] city, 798.

clene, a./adv. [*ComTeut/OE clæne*] a., pure, undefiled, unmixed, 81, 954, 969, -976; "~ sowlys/sowll/soule," undefiled soul(s), 45, 176, 284, 289; Lucyfer mocks the association of purity with the soul: "a ~ sowll & a mery," a clean and merry soul, 494; a similar ironic echo is heard in "stewys ~ rebaldry," the pure ribaldry of the brothel, 749; adv., "purfyethe ~," cleanses completely, 54, 174; see **kepe**.

clennes, pp. a. [*OE clænnes*] made clean, undefiled in purity, 543.

clense, v. [*OE clænsian*] cleanse, 932; **clensythe**, 3 sg. pr., 126; **clensyde**, pp., 1110, 1112; **clenser**, vbl. sb., purgative, cleanser, 962.

clepe, v. [*OE clipian*] call, summon, 692; **clepyde**, pp., called, named, 3, 136, 141, 269, 282, (ironic) 604; see **loue**.

clere, adv. [*OFr cler f. L clarum, bright; sense of moral purity peculiar to E; through association with OE clean*] distinctly, entirely, with clear vision, 1087.

clerkys, n. pl. [*OE cler(i)c*] learned men, 1036.

clymyt, v. 3 sg. pr. [*OE climban*] climbs, 444.

closyde, pp. a. [*OFr clos- (stem of clore) f. L claudere, shut; associated with ME clusen f. lL cl(a)usa, enclosed place*] entombed, 1004.

cloth(e), n. [*OE clað*] cloth; "~ of golde," cloth of gold, fabric (usually silk or wool) woven with gold thread, wires, or strips, 0sd. 16sd. 324sd; **clothynge**, n., clothing, 474, 1064sd.

clowyn, pp. a. [*ComTeut/OE clif(i)an, cleofian*] cloven, split into pieces, 1104.

clumme, a. [*Origin uncertain; poss. related to OE clumian, murmur*] silent, 521.

cognycyon, n. [*L cognitionem f. cognoscere, know*] knowledge. perception gained from higher intuition, 143; **congnycyon**, cognition. 1132.

colo(u)rs, n. pl. [*eMe colur f. OFr color f. L colorare, imbue with color or hue*] implying both rhetorical colors which cloak the truth and a false legal plea, 379, 547; **coloryde**, pp. a., colored, misrepresented, 673.

com(e), **cum**, v. [*ComTeut OE* <u>*cuman*</u>] come, arrive at, approach, 274, 320, 329, 525, 693, 721, 753, 798, 1153; humbly submit (myself), 1082; **cam**, 3 sg. pa., were descendants of, 112; **commyth**, **cummyth(e)**, 3 sg. pr., comes, 153, 380sd, 881; derives or arises from, 154, 233, 460; **commynge**, prp., entering, 1064sd; **cummynge**, prp., deriving from, 687, 1070; see **all**.

comfort(e), n. [*OFr* <u>*confort*</u> *(lit 11c);* replaced *OE* <u>*frofor*</u>, *particularly in enumerating the "comforts" against temptation*] encouragement, solace, succour, 205, 704, 989** (Ms = **mercy**); **comfortede**, v. 2 sg. pa., strengthened, 316.

comyn, **comun**, n./a. [*OFr* <u>*comun*</u> *poss. f. L* <u>*communis*</u>] <u>n</u>., shared experience, 443, 751; <u>a</u>., ordinary, prevalent, that which many people share, 472, 652; see **lyff**; **wey**.

comly, a. [*OE* <u>*cymlic*</u> *f.* <u>*cyme*</u>, *exquisite, fine*] becoming, 454* (M = **comunly**).

comparys(ch)on, n. [*OFr* <u>*comparaison*</u> *ult. f. L* <u>*comparare*</u>] comparison, 28, 35.

compassyon, n. [*OFr* <u>*compassion*</u> *(lit 14c) ult. f. L* <u>*compati*</u>, *feel pity*] compassion, solicitude, 1029, 1068.

compellys, v. 3 sg. pr. [*OFr* <u>*compeller*</u> *f. L* <u>*compellere*</u>, *drive*] compels (one), urges irresistably, 273.

compleccyons, **complexccyon**, n. [*OFr* <u>*complexion*</u> *(lit 13c) f. L* <u>*complexionem*</u>, *twined together*] nature resulting from blending of humors, temperament, 343, 557.

co[m]pleynnyng, prp. a. [*OFr* <u>*complaign*</u>- *stem of* <u>*complaindre*</u> + -<u>*yng*</u> *f. L* <u>*complangere*</u>, *lament, bewail; orig. to beat the head or breast as a sign of grief*] lamenting, 996.

comprehende, v. [*L* <u>*comprehendere*</u>, *seize*] conceive fully or adequately, 250; include, comprise, 715; **comprehendyde**, 3 sg. pa. (theo.), w. reference to God's omniscience: encompassed, 937; that which is perceived by the senses (as opposed to the spirit), 1075.

compunccyon, n. [*OFr* <u>*compunction*</u> *(lit 12c) f. L* <u>*compungere*</u>, *prick; in Christian writing = sting of conscience*] contrition, 467.

comun; see **comyn**.

comunycacyon, n. [*OFr* <u>*com(m)unicacion*</u> *f. L* <u>*communicare*</u>, *make common, share, impart*] communication, 426.

conclusyon, **conclusyun**, n. [*OFr conclusion ult. f. L concludere end, close*] judgment, conclusion, 1153; proposition derived from logical reasoning, 446, 478.

condescende, v. [*OFr condescendre f. L condescendere, stoop; in medL = to be complaisant or compliant*] accede, yield, 711.

condycyons, n. pl. [*OFr condicion f. L condicere, declare*] the whole affecting circumstances of a character's (new) life, 626; see **howe**, a..

confes, v. [*OFr confesser (lit 12c) f. lL confessare, acknowledge, disclose*] admit, confess, 201; **confessyon**, n., formal confession of sins, (2nd step toward penance) 974, 986; for other steps to penance see **contricyon**; **satisfye**.

confyrmacyon, n. [*OFr confirmacion ult. f. L confirmare, strenghthen, establish*] consent, 367; see **consent**.

conforme, v. [*OFr conformer (lit 13c) f. L conformare, shape*] submit, fashion, 88, 1121.

congnycyon; see **cognycyon**.

coniecture, n. [*OFr conjecture ult. f. L conicere, throw together*] scheming, plotting, 354.

conregent, a. [*L con + regent f. pp. of L regere, rule*] of one livery; "wonderfull vysurs ~," very fine masks of one livery (perhaps masks suggesting regency), 752sd.

consell, n. [*OFr conseil ult. f. lL consulere, deliberate*] instruction, 923.

consent, n./v. [*OFr consente/consentir f. L consentire, agree*] consent, third term in the three-part process of sin (suggestion, delectation, consent); n., 226* (M = **cosent**); v., most directly associated with the Wyll, 303, 363; 1 sg. pr., give a formal consent, thus completing the process of sin (implies a formal covenant), 499; **confyrmacyon** has similar implications.

conseruynge, v. prp. [*OFr conserver f. L conservare, keep*] preserving; "~ in peyn," preserving through justified suffering, 1140

consyens, n. [*OFr conscience f. L conscientia knowledge within oneself; in ME conscience replaced earlier ME inwit, inward sense of right and wrong; not related to OE inwit meaning deceit*] conscience, 219, 521, 563; col. pl., conscience, 729.

conteynys, v. [*OFr* *contenir* f. *L* *continere*, *hold together*] contains, 1010.

contemplacyon, n. [*OFr* *contemplacion* *(lit 12c)* f. *L* *contemplare*, *observe*, *behold*] contemplation; "in ~," living a contemplative life, 421.

contemplatyff, a. [*OFr* *contemplatif* f. *L* *contemplare*, *observe*, *behold*] contemplative (life, as contrasted to the active or the mixed life), 417, 431; see **lyff**.

contenance, n. [*OFr* *contenance*, *(Ch de Rol)*, *manner of holding oneself*] expressive movement, sign, gesture, facial expression; "by ~," masked, as in a mime, 687.

contente, a. [*OFr* *content* ult. f. *L* *continere*, *hold together*] satisfied, compensated, content, 82.

contynuall, a. [*OFr* *continuel* f. *L* *continuus*] continual, 1126.

contrauersye, n. [*OFr* *controversie* *(14-16c)* f. *L* *controversia*, *dispute*] debate, contending of opponents, 305.

contricyon, **contry(s)cyon**, n. [*OFr* *contriciun* f. *L* *conterere*, *rub*, *grind*] contrition, sorrow of the heart, hatred of one's sins coupled with the resolve not to sin again, 466, 961, 996, 1011; first of three steps to penitence, (others being **confessyon** and **satysfaccyon**) associated with Wndyrstondynge, 973, 979; **contryte**, a., crushed by sin and so brought to complete penitence, contrite, 990, 1090; see **confess**; **satysfye**.

convenyent, a. [*OFr* *convenient* *(15-16c)* ult. f. *L* *convenire*, *unite*, *meet*] suitable, appropriate, 6, 701.

conversacyon, n. [*OFr* *conversacion* *(lit 12c)* ult. f. *L* *conversari*, *keep company with*] frequent exchange, conversation, 425; **conversant**, a., common, familiar, 607.

corecte, v. 3 sg. pa. [*L* *correct-* pp. stem of *corregere*, *set right*] corrected (a fault in conduct), disciplined, 315.

cosyn, n. [*OFr* *co(u)sin*] kinswoman; "~ of myn"/"my ~." kinswoman or kindred spirit, potential lover (used in a bawdy sense), 826, 834.

couetyse, n./a. [*OFr* *coveitise*] n., avarice; the sin of the World associated with Wndyrstondynge, 531; a., avaricous, greedy, 601; **covetyse**, n., avarice (personified), 744.

cowdys, see **can**.

craft, n. [*ComTeut/OE cræft; ety. uncertain, original meaning in other Teut langs = power, strength, virtue; meaning a skilled occupation restricted to E*] artifice, 861.

creator, n. [*OFr creato(u)r; replaced OE scieppend, the being who created all things*] God as creator, 74; see **creature**.

creature, n. [*OFr creature (11c) f. L creatura, thing created*] created being, human person 26, 65, 72, 74, 109, 195, 238, 262, 351, 876, 905, 1146; a rare spelling of God as creator, 206; **creaturys**, pl., created beings, human creatures, 105, 112, 257, 261, 390; see **euery**.

credyble, a. [*Fr credible (15c) f. L credere, believe*] reliable, credible, 99.

cresten, a. [*OE cristen f. L christianus; in ME infl. by OFr crestien & AFr cristien, (12c); replaced by christian (16c)*] Christian, 177; **crysten**, n.(imp. pl.), Christians, 212.

crestys, n. pl. [*OFr cr(i)este (lit 13c) f. L crista, plume, tuft*] heraldic insignias worn as identification livery, 692sd, 1064sd; **crestyde**, pp. a., wearing crests as badges of fealty, 324sd.

Cryst, Crystus, n. [*OE crist; rarely if ever, spelled with -h- before 1500 in E*] Christ, 312, 1045, 1145; **Crystys**, poss., "~ own specyall," Christ's own special (possession or abode), 131, 1113.

crye, v. [*OFr crier f. L quiritare, cry aloud*] shout, sing, 323; lament, entreat, pray, 949, 1065, 1077, 1089; **cryenge**, prp., shouting, 550sd.

crysten; see **cresten**.

cros(e), n. [*OE cros f. L crucem; replaced OE rod, rood; infl. by OFr crois (11-15c)*] Christian cross, 0sd; head of a coin, (term resulted from stamping across the surface of a coin); "~ & pyll," the head and tail of a coin, 858.

crown, n. [*AFr coroune f. L corona, wreath, chaplet*] crown, 0sd, 307; **crown(n)ys**, pl., 1064sd, 1115; **crownyde**, v. pp., crowned, 1124; see **imperyall**.

cum; **cummynge**; **cummyth(e)**; see **com**.

cumpeny, n. [*OFr cumpagnie*] a band of retainers, 746.

cunnyngys, n. [*Not recorded in OE; vbl. sb. of* canne,*(OE* cunnan*/ME* cunnen*)* = L scientia, *have knowledge of; common since 14c; see* **oncunnynge**] erudite knowledge, clever skill (as opposed to intuitive self-knowledge); "to sauour in ~ to excellent," take pleasure in too much learning or cleverness, i.e., take pride in skills or acquired forms of knowledge as opposed to intuition, 87*.

cure, n. [*OFr* cure *f. L* cura] care, spiritual charge, anxiety, 53; "hath take of ~," has taken custody of, has spiritual care of (possibly implying that the curative process has already begun), 240.

curlyde, pp. a. [*ME* crulled *(14c) f.* croll *a. (1300), curly*] curled, 0sd; see **sypres**.

curyous, **curryus**, a. [*OFr* curius *(Ch de Rol) f. L* curiosus, *studious, attentive*] subtle, sophisticated, 579; costly, 609; see **aray**; **eloquens**.

curs, n./v. [*IOE* curs, *origin unknown/*cursian] n., curse, 872; v. intr., utter a curse, 808; curse, 809 (poss. tr., see **fare**).

curtely, a. [*OFr* cort, c(o)urt, *court, enclosure + -ly; associated with L* curia, *an assembly held by a sovereign*] courtly, refined, 599.

custume, n. [*OFr* custume *(11-12c) f. L* consuetudinem] habitual use, 520; **custummaly**, adv., customarily, 14.

cut, v. 2 sg. pr. [*Origin uncertain; first recorded in 13c replacing OE* ceorfan] cut, 1061.

cy-; listed as if **ci-**.

D

day, n. [*ComTeut/OE* dæȝ] day, 153, 810; **day(e)s**, pl., 1033; "yerys & ~," years and days, i.e. the period of time, 198; poss., day's. 1018; see **all**.

dalyance, n. [*OFr* dalier, *casually pass time + -*ance] sport, play, 785.

dame, n. [*OFr* dame *(lit 11c) f. L* domina, *lady, mistress*] mother, 115.

damesellys, n. pl. [*OFr* dameisele] young, unmarried women (used slightingly); "dance of þis ~," obscene dance, 760.

dammyde, v. pp. [*OFr damner (legal and theo.) + -yde f. L damnare, pronounce adverse judgment on*] condemned to hell, 118, 1123; rendered a judgment against, 724; **dampnabyll, damnable**, a., subject to damnation, punishable, 364, 541; **damnacyon**, n., damnation, 369.

dance, daunce, n./v. [*OFr dance/dancer*] n., dance, 685, 700, 760; v., 708, 732, 734; **dansaunde**, prp. a., dancing, 777; see **damesellys**.

dare, v. [*OE durran*] dare, 601, 714; have courage in battle, 775.

dasche, v. [*ME daschen, (13c); poss. f. ON daske, beat*] strike violently, 774.

daunce; see **dance**.

daunte, v. tr. [*OFr danter (lit 12-14c) f. L domitare, tame*] subdue, control, 611.

declare, v. [*OFr desclairer infl. by L declarare, formally state*] declare, explain, 102, 181.

dede, n. [*OE dæd, ded*] deed, act (opposite to idea or intention), 369* (M = **dethe**), 403; associated with Wyll, the faculty of consent, 218, 220, 221, 232; **dedys**, pl., deeds, actions, 364, 1062; see **in dede**.

dede, pp. a.; **dedly**; see **dey**.

deface, v. [*OFr desfacier f. des- + face, face (n.)*] disfigure (yourself), 174.

deff, a. [*ComTeut OE deaf*] deaf, 523* (M = **dethe**).

defyle, defoule, v. [*OFr defouler f. lL fullare, stamp with one's feet; by 14c associated with E foul a., soiled, rotten*] corrupt, morally pollute, 380, 906; **defowlyde, dyffowlyde**, pp., 130, 927.

dey, v. [*eME deðen akin to ON dayja; not found in OE lit*] die, 60, 882; **dede**, pp. a., dead, 534; **dedly**, a., deadly, "~ synne(s)," sg. or pl., deadly sin(s), 545, 909, 980.

deyte, n. [*OFr deite f. L deus, god (term formed by Augustine. De Civ. Dei VII., i., after divinitas)*] deity, 156, 184.

delectacyon, dylectacyon, n. [*OFr delectation ult. f. delectare, please, entice*] delight, 1066; as the second of three stages of temptation (**suggestyon, delyght, consent**) is associated with Wndyrstondynge, 366, 451, 462; "ys more ~," gives greater pleasure, 1031; **delyght** has the same connotations; **dylectable, delectable**, a., 255, 591; see **ples**.

delyght, n./v. [OFr *delit/delitier* f. L *delectare*, please, entice; erroneously spelled after *light* (16c)] n., delight, pleasure, 498, 571; v., delight, linked with Wndyrstondynge, 302; see **delectacyon**.

dere, a. [ComTeut/OE *deore*] precious, beloved, 1085, 1104.

derknes, n. [OE *deorcnes*] spiritual darkness, oblivion, darkness of hell, 118.

descendyde, v. pp. [OFr *descendre* (lit 11c) + -*yde* f. L *descendere*, descend] fallen down (from the guilt of sin), descended from heaven to hell, 939.

desyderable, a. [OFr *desirable* ult. f. L *desiderare*, long for] precious, object of desire, 253.

deth(e), n. [ComTeut OE *deab*] death, 123, 124, 539, 876, 1002, 1025; see **dede**.

dett, n. [OFr *det(t)e*] (theo.), a debt incurred through sinfulness, 194.

deuell, deule, deull, dew(y)ll, n. [OE *deofol*] devil, 370, 396, 508, 518, 620, 699, 782, 919; **deuelys, deullys, dewyllys, poss.**, 324sd, 546, 700, 908, 979; **deullys, dew(y)llys, pl.**, 372, 910, 912sd; see **blake**; **place**; **rechace**; **spede**.

deuys, n. [OFr *devis*, division + OFr *devise*, heraldic device, conceit] heraldic design or emblem, mechanical device; disguise or fashion in dress; "dompe ~," mute dramatic device, referring to "disguised," i.e. masked dancers (as a kind of miming device), 775.

deuocyons, n. pl. [OFr *devocion* (lit 12c) ult. f. L *devovere*, devote] acts of worship, 452.

dew, a. [OFr *d(e)u*, orig. pp. of *devoir*, owe] proper, suitable. 401, 434; **du**, that which is owed, 975; **duly**, adv., properly, rightly, 144, 410; see **dyscyplyne**; **satysfye**; **tyme**.

dewoydyth, v. 3 sg. pr. [OFr *devoyder* akin to medL *disvacuare*, empty] leaves, goes away, 380sd.

dyd(e); see **do**.

dyffolwyde; see **defyle**.

dyfye, v. tr. [OFr *defier* f. medL *diffidare*, distrust] renounce, reject, 510.

dyght, v. pp. [OE *dihtan* f. L *dictare*, dictate] prepared (Wysdom referring to his own death) 123; pass., created (Lucyfer referring to the creation of man), 337; refl., direct (ourselves), 995.

dylectable; **dylectacyon**; see **delectacyon**.

dylygens, n. [*OFr* diligence *ult. f. L* diligere, highly value or esteem] persistent effort, 1041; "do yowr ~," perform necessary penance diligently, 931.

dyne, v. inf. [*OFr* dis(g)ner *f. IL* disjejunare, break a fast] eat, dine, 827; **dyner**, n., dinner, 822.

dynge, v. [*Not recorded in OE; prob. f. ON; akin to Icelandic* dengja, hammer] strike a blow, 774.

dyrke, a. [*OE* deorc; no corresponding adj. in Teut] black from sin, 166; see **schadow**.

dyschargethe, v. [*OFr* descharger] releases, frees from liability, 54.

dyscheyit, n. [*OFr* deceyte *ult. f. L* decipere, trap, ensnare; -sch difficult to account for, though dischayte is listed by the MED as one variant] deceit (personified), 727.

dyscyplyne, n. [*OFr* discipline *f. L* disciplina, instruction of disciples] moral and mental training, 89; "~ dew," appropriate mortification of the flesh, 434; **dyscyplynyde**, v., 2 sg. pa. refl., mortified (your own flesh), 1016.

dyscorde n. [*OFr* descord (12c), discord (14-15c)] discord, strife, (personified), 695; **discorde**, 697* (M = **dycorde**).

dyscrey, v. [*OFr* descrier *f. L* discrier, cry] denounce, challenge, 859.

dyscretly, adv. [*OFr* discret(e) + -ly (12c lit) *f. L* discretus, separate, distinct] discretely, i.e., as separate parts of a whole through the processes of observation or experience, rather than as one indivisible body of revealed knowledge, 145; see **know(e)**.

dysdeyn, v. [*OFr* desdeigner *f. L* dedignare, reject as unworthy] despise, 580.

dysfygure, **dysvygure**, v. [*OFr* desfigurer *f. L* disfigurare, mar] deform, blemish (the soul), 353; refl., transform (your own) appearance, 1114; **dysvyguryde**, pp. a., deformed, tarnished. 117. **dyvyguryde**, pp., a recognized variant of **dysfygure**, (OED), defiled. 901.

dysgysynge, n. [*OFr* de(s)guise, disguise; (lit 11c)] clothes which conceal true identity, opposite to **aray**, 150; newfangled clothing of elaborate fashion; "fresche ~ to seme amyable," a new gallant's costume used to create the appearance of a lover, 590; **dysgysyde**, v. pp., dressed for a mimed public performance (masque or disguising). 692sd, 752 sd.

dysyer(e), n./v. [*OFr desir/desirer* f. L *desiderare, long for*] n., desire, longing, 254, 519; v., desire, 87; **dysyryde**, pp., desired, 34; **dysyrynge**, prp., longing (for a means of penance), 935.

dyspeyer, n. [*OFr despoir*] despair, the condition of hopelessness that prevents one from receiving redemptive grace, 439, 542; used ironically by Lucyfer as a precondition for receiving God's grace, 467.

dyspyght, n. [*OFr despit* f. L *despicere, look down upon*] contempt, disdain; "haue in most ~," hold in contempt, 338; "doyst . . . me all ~," treat me with complete contempt, 921.

dyspyse, **dyspyes**, v. [*OFr despicer* f. OFr *despire* + L *despicere, look down upon*] scorn, 612, 1039; treat as unworthy, 204.

dyspytuusly, adv. [*OFr despiteus* + *-ly*; *after 1400 associated with piteous and spelled -uous*] mercilessly, 842.

dysporte, n. [*OFr desport ult. f. L desportare, divert, amuse*] sport, game, 688.

dysposicyon, n. [*OFr disposcion (lit 12c) ult. f. L disponere, arrange; associated with dispose in meaning though not etymologically related*] arrangement; "off sterrys aboue all þe ~," above all the ordering influence of the stars, 29; **dysposyde**, pp. a., regulated, controlled, 222; inclined, 344; "for the ~," made provisions for thee, 1002.

dysprawe, v. [*Rare ME variant of disprayse f. OFr de(s)preiser slander, disparage, MED*] slanderously declaim, 838.

dyspute, v. [*OFr desputer (lit 12c) f. L disputare, dispute, discuss*] "~ . . . in þis," formally argue about this, 482.

dystroyt, v. 3 sg. pr. [*OFr destruire f. L destruere, demolish*] diminish, destroy, impair spiritually, 458, 466; **dystroythe**, destroys (sins), 1012.

dysvygure; **dysvyguryde**; see **dysfygure**.

dyuersly, adv. [*OFr divers* + *-ly (lit 11c) f. L diversus, turned different ways*] variously; "vyseryde ~," wearing different masks or (more likely) masks with two faces turned in different directions, 724sd.

dyvyguryde; see **dysfygure**.

dyvyne, **dywyn**, a. [*OFr devin f. L divinus, pertaining to a deity*] godlike, 31; devoted to theology, 470; see **merowre**.

dyvynyte, n. [*OFr devinité*] theology, 86.

dywyn; see **dyvyne**.

do, v. [*OE don*] do, act, perform, 75, 412, 493, 509, 931; as aux., 149, 207, 305, 685, 884; inf., 230; w. implied v., 298, 960; **doyst**, 2 sg. pr., does, 880, 921; **doth(e)**, 3 sg. pr., 71, 119, 292, 301, 578, 596, 734, 949, 1015, 1028; **dyd(e)**, 3 pa., 386, 1095; **do(n)**, pp., 913, 915, 1117; see **amyse**; **dylygens**; **dyspyght**; **only**; **trespas**.

dobullnes, n. [*OFr do(u)ble + -nes f. L duplus, twice as much*] duplicity (personified), 726.

doctryne, n. [*OFr doctrine (12c) f. L doctrina, teaching, learning*] doctrine, system of dogmas, instruction, 383, 1163.

doyst; see **do**.

domynacyon, n. [*OFr domination (12c) ult. f. L dominari, rule over*] lordship, sway, 31, 300, 370, 456, 481; see **fre(e)**; **merowre**.

domys, n. pl. [*ComTeut/OE dom*] judgments, statutes (both legal and moral) 228, 995.

dompe, a. [*OED: first found in early 16c; origin obscure; MED links form to OE domb, cf. dumme*] a. (rare) derived from the sb., which may mean dazed, struck dumb, but also a mournful or plaintive melody or song, a dance; hence, a., struck dumb, possibly = silent dancing (troupe), 775; see **deuys**.

doth(e); see **do**.

doughters, n. pl. [*ComTeut OE dohter*] daughters; "~ of Ierusalem," women of Jerusalem associated with the five "prudent virgins" as inner senses, 165; see **vyrgyne**.

dovehows, n. [*ON dufa + OE hus*] dovecote, 1106.

down, adv. [*OE dun(e); aphetic form of adune f. OE of dune, off the hill or height*] down, 16sd, 1105.

dowte, n. [*OFr doute*] fear or doubt, 502; adv. phrase, "no ~," no doubt, 468; **dowtles**, adv., without doubt, 882. see **cast**.

drawte, pp. a. [*eMe draht poss. f. OE dreaht, though not recorded(MED); in lME spelling drawt appeared*] drawn out, "~ notys," notes slowly sung or drawn out, 996sd.

drede, v./n. [*eME* *dreden;* *probable aphetic variation of OE* *andreden*] v., fear, standing in awe of, 88, 1159; n., something to be dreaded, drudgery, 432; fear of danger, risk, 805; awe-inspiring fear (of God), 90; fear of the consequences of sin, 895, 898, 903, 916; **dredys**, v. 3 sg. pl. pr., dread, 632; **dredfull**, a., fearful, 123; see **tak(e)**.

dres, v. [*OFr* *dresser* f. L *derigere*, direct, straighten] inf., arrange, redress an injustice, aray in suitable clothing, 698; see **loweday**.

drynke, v./n. [*ComTeut OE* *drincan/drinc*] drink, v., 606; n., 814, 1100; see **menglyde**.

drywande, v. prp. [*OE* *drifan* + *-ande;* *not found outside Teut*] rushing, 782.

droppe, n. [*OE* *dropa*] drop, 50.

du, duly; see **dew**.

dumme, a. [*ComTeut OE* *dumb*, speechless; *this meaning restricted to OE, ON, & Goth; in other Teut langs it also = stupid, deaf*] mute, silent, 523.

durable, a. [*OFr* *durable* f. L *durabilis* (rare) f. *durare*, endure] lasting, 324.

dwell, v. [*OE* *dwellan*] dwell, remain, 116, 340; **dwellys**, 3 sg. pr., 272; **dwellyt**, 3 sg. pr., 264, 271; see **indwell**.

dy-; listed as if **di-**.

E

eas(e), **es**, n. [*OFr* *eise/aise* f. IL *!asia*, origin uncertain] ease, gratification, 411, 814; "at ~," comfortable, well-to-do, 564.

eche, **yche** a./pron. [*3 OE roots:* *ælc*, *3ehwilc*, *æ3hwilc*] a., each, 7, 16, 238, 262, 284, 626, 751, 1044, 1146; pron., each (actor), 692sd.

egalle, a. [*OFr* *egal* f. L *æqualem;* *in E (14-16c)*] suitable to, 4.

ey, n. [*OE* *eage*] eye, 963, 990; "tweyn syghtys of yowr ~," the twin sights i.e., inner and outer vision of your eye, 1086.

ellys, adv. [*OE* *elles*] otherwise, 506; "not ~," nothing more, 80.

eloquens, n. [*OFr* *eloquence* *ult. f. L eloqui, speak fluently*] graceful style; "curryus ~," sophisticated, learned style (as an affectation associated with worldliness), 579.

enbrace, v. tr. [*OFr embracer, instigator f. OFr embrasser, set on fire*] legal term meaning to bribe or otherwise influence a jury; "~ questys of periury," bribe jurors to commit perjury, 638; **enbraces**, n. pl., briberies, 791.

ende, n./v. [*ComTeut OE ende*] n., death, final judgment, 532, 875; "wythowt(yn) ~," (theo.) without end, enduring perpetually out of the range of time, 47, 191, 907, 1116; "~ wythowt ~," he who creates the final end, but is himself without end, 248; v., end, 1162; **end(e)les**, a., eternal, 93, 324, 935; adv., continuously, without stopping, 323; **endelesly**, adv., eternally, 1123; **endyn**, v. 3 pl. pr., "~ yll," come to a bad end, die in sin, 878; see **last**.

endyght, v. [*OFr enditer f. lL indictare, declare against*] indict, 810, 851.

endyrecte, a. [*OFr indirect f. L inirectus, (Quintilian)*] indirect, crooked, dishonest, 731; see **euell**.

enduyde, pp. a. [*en + OFr douer; (AFr legal term (15c) f. L dotare, to endow*] endowed (by God), with virtue, 382, with grace, 1139.

endure, v. [*OFr endurer f. L indurare, harden*] indure, continue in a particular state, 243, 761; **induyr**, 1148; **enduryth**, 3 sg. pr., 532.

eng[r]ose, v. [*M engose Probable Ms. error for engrose f. AFr engrosser, f. ML ingrossare, to thicken*] gather; "~ vpe," collect for oneself from all quarters, 804.

enmy(e), n. [*OFr enemi f. L inimicus, unfriendly*] enemy, the devil as an adversary of God, 914, 922; **enemyes**, pl., adversaries, foes, 293* (M = **enmyes**).

entent, n. [*OFr entent f. L intentus, a stretching out; in lL of attention or will*] intent; "take ~," fix the purpose of the will, 228.

enteryd(e); **entre**; **entreth(e)**; see **entur**.

entret, n. [*OFr entrait(i)er*] negotiation, intervention, supplication (personified), 796.

entur, v. [*OFr entrer f. L intrare*] enter, 692sd; **entreth(e)**, 3 pr., 16sd, 324 sd, 724sd, 1064sd; **entre**, v., 752sd* (M = **entreth**); **entreth**, 3 sg./pl. pa., enter, 0sd* (M = **enteryde**), 164sd* (M = **enteryd**).

envy, n. [*OFr envie ult. f. L invidere, look contemptibly upon*] envy, 326.

equall, a. [*L æqualis* ult f. *equus, level, even*] socially equal to, 587.

erys, n. pl. [*ComTeut OE eare*] ears, 758.

ermyn, n. [*OFr (h)ermine*] black-flecked white fur; in 15c restricted to use by the royal family, 0sd; **ermynnyde**, v. pp., lined with ermine, 0sd.

erre, v. [*OFr errer* f. *L errare*883; **erryde**, 1 sg. pa., 313.

erthe, n. [*ComTeut OE eorþe*] earth, 1146; "in ~," on earth, 3; **erthely**, a., earthly, not divine, 146.

es; see **eas(e)**.

eschew(e), v. [*OFr eschever* akin to *OHG sciuhen, shun/OE sceoh, shy*] eschew, avoid, 435, 1161.

especyall, adv. [*OFr especial*] in particular, 5, 581; "in ~," above all else, 968; see **acorde**.

espyede; see **aspye**.

eternall, a. [*OFr eternal* f. *lL æternus*] eternal, without beginning or end, 7, 128.

euell, euyll, ewell, ewyll, n./a. [*OE yfel; ME uvel; related to root of OE up(p) & ofer, hence meaning "overstepping proper limits", "exceeding due measure"*] n., evil, ill deeds, 778, 1046; "an ~ endyrecte," an indirect evil, 731; a., ill, bad, hellish, (associated with the devil), 550, 614; see **grace**; **joy**.

euer, adv. [*OE æfre; not found in other Teut langs*] ever, at any time, 21, 352; always, 46, 67, 76, 192, 243, 263, 339, 381, 384, 421, 433, 505, 609, 648, 722, 766, 824, 1140, 1148; in each instance, increasingly, 797; **euermore**, adv., always, from this time onward, 415; even more, 569; see **cast**; **lewe**; **new**; **neuer**; **ryve**.

euerlastynge, a. [*OE æfre + OE læstan*] everlasting, 4, 8, 308.

euery, a. [*OE æfre/ælc*] every; "~ creature," all God's creatures, 109, 876; "~ (. . .) sowll/soule," all Christian souls, 152, 1160; **euerywere**, adv., everywhere, 684.

euyll; see **euell**.

evyn, ewyn, adv. [*OE efne; by assimilation of emne + efen*] exactly, 538; fully, 1052.

evyncresten, n. [*OE efne-* + *OE cristen;* akin to *OFris ivinkerstena*] fellow christian, 1039.

ewell, ewyll; see **euell**.

examynacyon, n. [*OFr examination* ult. *f. L examinare, weigh accurately*] trial, interrogation, 371.

example, n. [*OFr example* ult. *f. L eximere, take out*] example, 424.

excellens, n. [*OFr excellence* ult. *f. L excellere, rise above others*] dignity, eminence, 1040; **excellent**, a., haughty, sophisticated, 87; see **cunnynge**.

exyled, v. 3 sg. pa. [*OFr exilier (12c) f. lL exiliare*] exiled, cast out, expelled, — or — (possibly) ravaged, brought to ruin, 620.

expedyente, a. [*OFr expedient* ult. *f. L expedire, forward matters*] fitting, proper, 705.

expellyt, v. tr. 3 sg. pr. [*OFr expeller (15c) f. L expellere*] drives out, 920.

experyens, n. [*OFr experience* ult. *f. L experiri, put to the test*] experience, direct communication; "felt in ~ from aboue," learned from direct spiritual contact with God, 63.

exposycyon, n. [*OFr exposition* ult. *f. L exponere, put forth, display*] meaning, explanation, 26.

expres, a./adv. [*OFr expres(se)* ult. *f. L exprimere, form, press out*] a., truly depicted, 695; adv., clearly, unmistakably, 396, 443.

ey-; listed as if **ei-**.

F

face, n. [*OFr face f. popL facia, form, figure*] face, 179, 948; imp. pl., 895; **facys**, pl., 718.

fadyr, father, n. [*ComTeut OE fæder*] God, as father in heaven, 122, 1096; Christ as God, 989; first person of the Trinity, 279, 285; progenitor (ironic contrast to God the Father), 744; **fathers**, pl., revered men, 393; see **suffycyent**.

fay, n. [*lOFr fei ult. f. L fidere, trust; var. of feith; see feythe*] faith, "by my ~," assuredly, by my faith, 556.

fayer(e), a./adv. [*ComTeut OE fæ3er*] a., beautiful, splendid, free from blemish, 129, 159, 187; handsome or attractive by virtue of possessing a liberal fortune, 459; "fowll(e) & ~, " foul and fair, evil and good, 151, 157; "~ frut," fair fruit, legitimate offspring (the products of morally sanctioned mating, in contrast to the **fowll pollucyon** of fornication), 477; with reference to argumentation -- legitimate, equitable; "~ speche," legitimate legal argumentation (in opposition to **falsehede**), 719; adv., 242; **fayre**, n., "soueren ~," fair or splendid sovereign (reference to Christ as king), 69* (M = **father**); **fayrest**, superl. a., 105, 1113; see **fowll(e)**.

fayre; see **fayer**.

fall, n./v. [*ComTeut OE feallan*] n., fall from grace, 444; v., suffer a reversal in fortune, 318, 582; **fallyn**, var. of **fall**, 3 pl. pr., fall, drop through suffering or sin, 438; **fallyngys**, vbl. sb., failings, human errors, 200* (M = **fallynge**); **fallyt**, 3 sg. pr., "~ to," is appropriate to, 11.

fayll, v. [*OFr faillir, be wanting*] fail, 436.

fals(e), a. [*lOE fals ult. f. L fallere, deceive*] false, deceitful, 354, 547*, 550, 603, 642, 740; **falsnes**, n., that which is false, 610, 699; **falsehed(e)**, n., falsehood, 726 (personified) 719; **falsly**, adv., falsely 673; see **gynne**.

fame, n. [*OFr fame f. L fama, report*] fame; "be in most ~," be highest in reputation, 598.

fare, v. [*ComTeut OE faran*] The context suggests either of two possible meanings: a) tr., tread under foot, or intr., get along (well), prosper, 809.

farwell, v. [*OE faran + wel(l); phrase treated as one word*] farewell, say goodbye, tr., 521; intr., 518; inter., 512, 553, 568; **farewell**, inter., 563.

farre, adv. [*OE feor(r) akin to ON fiarre; -e spelling related to OE feorran (13-14c), from a distance*] afar, 881.

fast, v. [*ComTeut/OE fæstan*] fast, abstain from food 433. **fastyde**, 2 pr. pa. subj., fasted, 1032; **fastynge**, prp. as sb., fasting as a religious observance, 402.

father(s); see **fadyr**.

fawowre, n. [*OFr favo(u)r ult. f. L favere, regard with good will*] grace, benevolence, 209; see **mynde**.

febyll, v. [*OFr feble f. L flere, weep over*] grow weak, 438.

fede, v. refl. [*OE fedan*] inf., feed, 459.

feer, n. [*Aphetic variation of 3efer*] party, group of companions; "be thys ~," by this company of fellows (an oath sworn upon the friendship of the three Mights), 821.

feet, **fete**, n. pl. [*ComTeut OE fet*] feet, 1042, 1103.

feyntnes, n. [*OFr feint, feigned, sluggish*] fraility, weakness, 437.

feyth(e), n. [*OFr feit f. L fidem, trust (early use restricted to religious faith)*] belief grounded in the affirmation of the will; opposed to intellectual assent to religious truths; often viewed as the exercise of a special faculty of the soul, 285, 1082; or as the key to redemption; associated with renewal and reform, 386, 1118, 1150; "~ verray"/"veray ~," true faith, redeeming faith, 127, 971.

fele, v. [*OE (3e)felan akin to OHG foulen, handle, grope*] feel (pleasure), 462; (theo.) to have spiritual communion with God, 1072; **felt(e)**, pp., felt and therefore known (only), 63; 1 sg pa., felt (physical pain), 1101; **felynge**, n., perception based on spiritual experience, 95, 1129; "flechly ~," fleshly feeling, carnal desire, 136; "wyche ~," the desire which, 154; "~ of synne," sinful desire, 158; "gostly ~," spiritual desire, 1122; see **experience**.

felycyte, **felycite**, n. [*OFr felicité ult. f. L felicitare, make happy*] felicity, the joys of heaven, 25, 72; happiness in worldly pleasure, 570; in a spiritual state of bliss, 1064.

felynge; **felt(e)**; see **fele**.

fende, n. [*ComTeut OE feond*] a fiend, demon, 528, 538, 902sd, 904; "þe ~," the devil, 1114; "the worlde, þe flesche, & þe ~," the world, the flesh, and the devil -- in Christian doctrine, the three traditional enemies of humankind, 294; see **fowll(e)**.

fer(e), n. [*OE fær*] n., fear, 844; "for ~," in fear of, 582; **feerfullnes**, n., state of being fearful, 374.

fervowre, n. [*OFr fervour f. L fevere, heated*] ardor, 84; **ferwent**, a., passionate, ardent, 85.

fete; see **feet**.

few, a. [*ComTeut OE feawe*] few, 649, 659.

fyght, v./n. [*OE feohtan/feoht(e)*] v., fight, 307; inf., 339; n., (those that engage in a) fight, 704; "for ~," as a result of fighting, 850; see **arest**.

fygure, n. [*OFr figure ult. f. fingere, form, mold*] represented form of God, 349, 359; (an attribute of Mynde), 184, 211; (of Wyll), 214, 241, 242; see **lyknes**.

fylyde, v. pp. [*OE !fylan f. OTeut !fuljan, foul*] defiled, 987.

fylthe, n. [*OE fylð*] uncleanness, that which corrupts morally, particularly with reference to: sexual desire, 52/original sin, 111; related to **fowll(e)**.

fynde, v. [*ComTeut OE findan*] receive, experience, discover, 205.

fyne, a./adv. [*OFr fin ComRom fino ult. f. L finire, finish; ComRom word passed into all Teut langs*] a., highly ornate, expertly fashioned, 474; adv., fully, 829.

fyrst(e), a./adv. [*ComTeut OE fyrst*] a., first, 108, 110; previous, former, original, 120, 1064sd; adv., first, at first, 0sd, 115, 126, 692, 725, 850, 1079, 1109; see **arest**; **lyght(e)**; **natur**.

fyue, **fyve**, **fywe**, **v**, a. [*ComTeut OE fif*] five; most frequently written as **v**, 137, 162, 163, 164sd, 324sd, 453, 1064sd, 1076, 1093, 1095; **fyue**, 479; **fyve**, 173; **fywe**, 295; see **vyrgyne**; **wyttys**.

flatter, v. [*Origin uncertain; poss. f. OFr flatere, flatter or f. OE flatter, an onomatopoeic expression indicating light, repeated movement*] flatter, win favor through obsequious speech or conduct, 489.

flechly; see **flesche**.

fle(e), v. [*ComTeut OE fleon, associated with !fleugan, fly*] flee, run away from, escape, 91, 870, 875; fly through the air, 567.

flesche, n. [*OE flæsc*] flesh, body, (opposite to spirit), 360, 611, (personified), 755, 1061; associated with the **worlde** and the **fende**, (devil) as one of the temptations of humankind, 294; **flechly**, adv., of the flesh, 136; see **fele**; **fende**.

floode, n. [*ComTeut OE flod*] tide, current, 491.

foly, n. [*OFr folie f. fol, foolish*] foolish lack of wisdom, sinfulness, 140, 235, 393, 1137.

folke, coll. n. [*OE folc*] people, (implying inferiors), social followers, 632.

folowyng(e), prp. adv./prp. a. [*OE fol3ian, fyl3an*] prp. adv., following in (entrance), 324sd; prp. a., 1064sd; attending upon, 795.

folwude, v. 3 sg. pa. [*OE flowan*] gushed forth, 1043.

fondnes, n. [*ME fonned + -nes*] foolishness, 438; **fonnyde**, a., foolish, 393.

for, prep./conj. [*OE for; not used as a conj. before 12c*] used frequently in the modern sense, 9, 22, 23, 73, 89 . . . 1147; to be, 20; because of, for the sake of, 166, 654, 744, 1043, 1164; "~ to," in order to, 192, 431, 664, 1140; see **arest**; **as**; **but**; **dysposicyon**; **fer(e)**; **fyght**; **reuerens**; **sew(e)**; **vyolence**.

forfett, a. [*OFr forfet f. medL fors factum, fine ult. f. lL forisfacere, transgress*] crime or transgression wilfully committed for which one may be held legally responsible, 806; see **preue**.

forgett, v. [*OE for3ietan*] overlook, 449.

foryeffnes, **foryewenes**, n. [*OE for3ifennys f. for3ifan + -nes*] forgiveness, remission, pardon, 987, 1082.

forme, n. [*OFr forme f. L forma, shape*] form, semblance, the shape of dramatic representation in the play, 749.

fornycacyon, n. [*OFr fornication ult. f. L fornicari*] fornication (personified), 756; see **jentyll**.

fors, v. [*OFr forcer*] attach importance to, pay attention to, 606, 656; hesitate, 739; all occurrences with negative particle - **no/nought/not**.

forsake, v. [*OE forsacan, contend, dispute*] 3 sg. cond. pr., renunciate (sin), 959; pp., repudiated, 1090.

forsothe, adv. [*OE forsoð, truth*] truly, 30.

forthe, adv. [*OE forð*] forth; "holde ~ ði wey," keep to your present course, continue on the same path, 885.

fortherers, n. pl. [*OE fyrðr(i)an + -ers*] promoters, 759.

fortune, n. [*OFr fortune*] prosperous worldly condition, success, inherited wealth, 575, 578.

fowll(e), a. [*OE ful; see fylthe; defoule*] harshly polluted sound, 758; unclean, rotten, impure, 932; foul, used in opposition to **fayer(e)**, 151, 157, 158-9;" ~ **pollucyon**," the moral pollution of fornication (in contrast to the legitimate offspring, or **fayer frut**, of marriage), 477; **fowler(e)**, comp., fouler; "~ þan a/ony fende," fouler than a fiend, 902sd, 904; see **fayer(e)**.

foundon; see **fownder**.

[**fourth**], appears as **iiii^te**, ellip. a. as sb. [*ComTeut OE feorða*] fourth, 1021.

fownder, n. [*OFr fonder f. L fundare, lay the foundation or framework*] creator, 733; **founders**, pl., 393; **foundon**, v. pp. pass., "am ~." was created, 28.

fre(e), a. [*ComTeut OE freo; linked to OE freon, to love; see frende*] independently guided by one's cognitive faculties, not subject to the devil, 187; free, 290; noble, 1023; "~ domynacyon," unconstrained control, (used by Wysdom with reference to reason), 300; (used by Lucyfer cunningly with reference to Wyll), 481; **frely(e)**, adv., freely, openhandedly, without constraint, 499, 502, 828; see **wyll**, n.

freellness, n. [*OFr freele* + *-ness*] moral weakness, 200; **freelte**, n., fraility, 75.

frely(e); see **fre(e)**.

frende, n. [*ComTeut OE freond*] comrade, 888; loving patron, 914; **frendys**, pl. companions, 1009; **frendeschyppe**, n., patronage, 633.

fresche, a. [*OE fersc (obs. by 14c) replaced by fre- prefix as of 13c; poss. infl. by OFr fresche*] lively, lustily dressed in the latest fashion, 511, 558, 590, 648; **freshest**, superl., 556; see **dysgysynge**.

fro(m), prep. [*OE from*] since, 18; from, 63, 68, 295, 881, 912 sd, 1070; out of, 118, of 1110, 1112; see **experience**.

frut, n. [*OFr fruit ult. f. L frui, enjoy*] "fruit," i.e., offspring, 477; see **fayer(e)**.

full, a./adv. [*ComTeut OE full*] a., complete, 26, 122, 1082; "~ of," filled with, 168, 570, 1060, 1068, 1106; adv., very, fully, 45, 941, 972; see **set(t)**.

furred, pp. a. [*OFr fuerre*] lined or trimmed with fur. 0sd*.

fy-; listed as if **fi-**.

G

gaff; see **yeue**.

gay, a. [*OFr gai*] gay, lascivious, decked out in finery, 648.

gall, n. [*OE 3ealla*] bitter substance, the drink given Christ on the cross, the bitter drink of death, 1100; see **mengylde**.

galont(e), n. [*lOFr galant (14c) f. galer, make a merry show; in E the n. preceded the a.*] dandy, fop, 324sd, 380sd; **galontys**, pl., 598, 752sd.

game, n. [*ComTeut OE gamen*] pleasure, amorous play as a source of mirth (referring to God's love), love relationship, 40; referring to amusement or sport as a worldly pleasure, 603, 612.

3e; see **ye**.

gederyde, v. pp. [*OE gæd(e)rian influenced by OE (to)gædere, together*] gathered, 766.

gees, v. [*ME gessen*] intend, 361.

geet; see **get**.

generacyon, n. [*L generationem f. generare, generate*] origin, ancestral line, 12; procreation, 460; "hye ~," royal or noble birth (as the son of God), 12.

get, v. [*ON geta; in OE compound formations -3ietan*] imp. pp., get, 560; inf., 636, 792; **gett**, procure (in order to), 867; subj. pr., gain, 677; **geet**, imp., attain, 502; **gettys**, 2 sg. pr., profits, 801; see **goode**.

geue; **gyff**; see **yeue**.

gyde, n. [*lOFr guide (14c) f. OFr guie*] guide, spiritual benefactor, 319.

gynne, n. [*Aphetic variation of OFr engin*] cunning; "false ~," plotting for evil purpose, 547* (M = **gyane**).

gyse, n. [*OFr guise*] fashion, behavior, manners; "~ (. . .) of Fra(w)nce," newfangled clothing, as symbol of sin imported from France, associated with high fashion, 516, 767.

gytely, adv. [*Poss. variation of gyte, gyde, n., kind of dress, (fig.) splendour f. OFr guite, some article of clothing*] splendidly, 16sd.

glade, a. [*OE gl*æ*d infl. by OHG glat, smooth*] joyous, 559.

glory, n. [*OFr glorie f. L gloria, glory*] honor of God, bliss of heaven, 307; honor owed to God, 391; worldly honor, 514, 1121; **gloryus**, a., divinely splendid, 128, 188, 310, 907; **gloryosest**, superl., 351.

go, v. [*ComTeut OE gan (defective verb)*] continue, proceed (in life), 319, 883; go, 371, 773, 996sd; imp., 501, 509, 868, 970, 988; "~ ther," take that, 774; **go(o)**, travel, 549, 878; **gost**, 2 sg. pr., 874; **goth**, 3 sg. pr., 550sd; **goyng(e)**, vb. sb., exiting; "harde lywynge & ~," strict life and difficult vigils, 434; a., proceeding, passing, departing, 324sd, 1064sd; gerund phr.,"þe ~ (owt)," 324sd, 996sd, when exiting; see **wey**; **well**, adv.; **worlde**.

God(e), n. [*ComTeut OE god*] God, used frequently in the modern sense, 14, 90, 96, 98, 103, 190* . . . 1151; second instance of **gode**, 231; see **goode**; **godys**, pl., 283; sg. poss., 118, 175, 176, 203, 335, 906, 1126; **godhede**, n., divinity, 94; deity, 214; all 3 persons of the Trinity considered as one God, 359; **godly**, a., divine, 65; adv., coming from God, 1088; see **avowe**; **hye**; **know(e)**; **offende**; **place**; **ryve**; **save**; **syght(e)**; **wet(e)**.

gode, a.; see **goode**.

goyng(e); see **go**.

golde, n. [*ComTeut OE gold*] gold, 0sd, 16sd, 324sd, 1001; see **cloth(e)**; **sypres**; **tasselys**.

goode, a./n. [*ComTeut OE god*] a., good, pious, 211, 215, 216, 237, 468, 480, 486, 488, 819, 822, 823, 999, 1027; **gode**, 231; n., imp. pl., goods, wealth (possibly also implying the abstract "good," i.e. the pleasure that comes from obtaining wealth), 562; "ge(e)t ~," obtain wealth, 502, 560, 636, 792; **goodys**, pl., 1003, 1009; "grett ~," great wealth, 867; **goodnes**, n., divine purity, 23, 32, 203, 392; **goodly**, a., well decked out, 380sd; see **mynde**; **vse**; **wyll**, (n.).

gost, n. [*ComWG OE gast*] spirit; "holy ~," holy ghost (3rd person of the Trinity), 282, 287; **gostly**, a., spiritual, 1122, referring to the "inwarde wyttys" or spiritual senses, 1074; see **fele**.

goth; see **go**.

gouernyde, v. pp. [*OFr governer f. L gubernare, steer (a vessel), hence, rule*] ruled; "~ most souerenly," governed by sovereign authority, 259.

govell, n. [*OE gafol MED*] usury, 602.

gownyde, pp. a. [*OFr goune* f. *L gunna*, *skin or fur*; *a garment of fur permitted for elderly or infirm monks. (Boniface 8c)*] dressed in a gown, 724sd.

gowte, n. [*OFr gout(t)e* f. *L gutta*, *drop*] gout, 507.

grace, n. [*OFr grace* f. *L gratia*, *good will*] grace; the gift of God making redemption possible, 119, 172, 203, 223, 317, 524, 893, 946, 1072, 1078, 1139, 1147, 1161; worldly favor, the good will endowed through worldly patronage, 575, 579; "euell ~," ill-luck, as the result of choosing a bad patron, 550; "harde hys ~ ys," bad is his luck, adverse are the judgments rendered against him in court; ("harde ~" is defined by the OED as meaning "ill will" or "a stroke of ill luck"), 723; **gracys**, pl., marks of God's favor, 1028; see **specyall**.

grante, **grawnt**, v. [*OFr graänter* ult. f. *credere*, *entrust*] 1 sg. pr., agree, 869; 3 sg. pr. (invocation), grant, bestow on humanity, 1164.

grates, sb. pl. [*L grates*] thanks, 190.

grawnt; see **grante**.

gredy, a. [*OE grædi3*] greedy, 675; **gredynes**, n., greediness (personified), 754.

gret(t), a./adv. [*ComWG OE greaf*] a., great, big, adundant, 49, 76, 217, 218, 312, 374, 432, 444, 467, 631, 636, 655, 658, 867, 1024, 1041; **grete**, 448*; **grettly**, adv., greatly, 413, 934, 1035; see **goode**; **tender**; **vse**.

grewe, a. [*OFr grief*, *MED*] grevious, 1016.

gronde, n./v. [*ComTeut OE grund*] n., ground, foundation, 236; v., ground, establish, 944.

grow, v. [*OE growan*] grow, 1017.

gy-; listed as if **gi-**.

gret(t), a./adv. [*ComWG OE greaf*] a., great, big, adundant, 49, 76, 217, 218, 312, 374, 432, 444, 467, 631, 636, 655, 658, 867, 1024, 1041; **grete**, 448*; **grettly**, adv., greatly, 413, 934, 1035; see **goode**; **tender**; **vse**.

grewe, a. [*OFr grief*, *MED*] grevious, 1016.

gronde, n./v. [*ComTeut OE grund*] n., ground, foundation, 236; v., ground, establish, 944.

grow, v. [*OE growan*] grow, 1017.

gy-; listed as if **gi-**.

grow, v. [*OE growan*] grow, 1017.

gy-; listed as if **gi-**.

H

ha, inter. [*Exclamation common to Gr, L, Mod Rom, & Mod Teut; not recorded in E until circa 1300*] ha, 463, 500*.

habundance, n. [*OFr (h)abundance ult. f. L abundare, flow away from in waves; h-spelling appeared in E & Fr (14c) due to confusing the root with L habere, have*] prosperity, wealth, 654.

had; see **haue**.

hayer; see **ayer**.

hale, n. [*OE alu*] ale, 473.

halse, v. inf. [*Ety. uncertain; variant of OE heals, neck; or OE halsian,invoke the divine*] embrace, in the sense of sexual fondling, 594; spiritual embracing, 1102; **halsyde**, pp., embraced, 44.

hap[pe], v. [*ME happe(n) f. ON hap, chance*] hap, 511** (D **hap**, w. abbr. for "-pe" omitted; M = **hamp**).

hande, honde, n. [*ComTeut OE hand, hond*] hand, 0sd. 692sd; "in ~," present before all men (in the guise of Maintenance, Perjury. and Lechery), 683; **handys**, pl., 1102.

handyll, v. inf. [*OE handlian*] touch, handle, 583.

hangynge, prp. [[*OE hangian*] infl. by OE hon & ON hengian] hanging, 16sd.

hante, v. [*OFr hanter (lit 12c); origin uncertain*] use, wear, 609.

harde, a. [*ComTeut OE heard*] harsh, 434; unlucky, punitively harsh, 723; see **go**; **grace**.

hare, n. [*ComTeut OE hara*] hare (used proverbially to suggest
setting a trap, in which this term figuratively represents a person), 741.

harlottys, n. pl. [*OFr harlot, herlot; 13c masculine; 15c feminine*] idle players,
scoundrels, beggars, evil women, 767.

harow, inter. [*OFr haro(u), origin obscure*] indignant or angry cry,
325.

has(e), **hast**,; see **haue**.

hastynes, n. [*OFr hasti* f. *OFr hastif, impetuous, hurried*] sudden rage, rash anger
(personified), 694.

hath(e), **hat**, see **haue**.

hatyst, v. 2 sg. pr. [*OE hatian*] hate, 914, 924.

hattys, n. pl. [*OE hæt*] hats; "~ of meyntenance," headgear that identifies
relationship, designed in the livery of one's patron, 724sd.

haue, v. [*ComTeut OE habban, hæfde, hæfed*] have, possess; used frequently in
the modern sense, 18, 22, 48, 93, 95 . . . 1151; "~ to my spowse," to
receive and retain as my spouse, indicating continued possession, 19;
"~ in . . . dyspyght," hold in contempt, 338; w. gerund, "knowyng ~,"
279/"~ knowynge," have knowledge, gain understanding, 93, 280;
had(e), had, 130, 415, 425; previously possessed, 342; subj., 564, 699;
pp., 1027; **has(e)**, has, 177, 576; **hast**, has, 321, 908, 917, 1003;
hath(e), has, have, 13, 53, 109, 134, 143, 191, 240, 266, 328, 370, 396,
406, 481, 657, 664, 738, 746, 864, 978, 1078, 1096, 1117, 1124; **hat**,
401; **hauyng**, prp., having; "~ on," wearing, 1064sd; **hawynge**, prp.,
wearing, 0sd; see **at**; **cure**; **dyspyght**; **mynde**; **reson(e)**; **resurreccyon**;
sew(e); **stedfast**; **spowse**; **wondyr**.

he, pron., 3 sg. nom. masc. [*OE he, hi*] used frequently in the modern sense, 23*
(M = **ys**), 59, 134, 145, 218, 232 . . . 969; **hem**, obj., 331, 339, 588, 940;
hym, obj., 11, 23, 52, 111, 112 . . . 345* . . . 998; **hymm**, 256, 414, 533;
hys, poss., 1 sd, 12, 32, 67, 68 . . . 1164; **his**, 0sd*; **hymselff**, 247, 249,
419, 758; see **as**; **grace**; **hestys**; **howe**, a.; **lyght(e)**; **lyff**; **lyknes**;
passyon; **pe(o)ple**; **reson(e)**; **schew**; **spede**; **wey**; **w(h)o**.

hede, n. [*OE hedan, v., guard, care for; no OE n.*] heed, notice, 457, 676, 900;
"take ~," pay attention, 457; "take ryght nought a ~," paid no attention
to at all, 676.

hede, n. [*ComTeut OE heafod*] head, 0sd, 1105; chief, principle, 530.

hedyr, hydyr adv. [*OE hider*] "~ & theyder," hither and thither, this way and that, 199, 732.

hele, n. [*OE hælu*] health, spiritual well-being, 21; **heelfull**, a., wholesome, 89.

hell(e), n. [*OE hel(l), ON hel; in Scandanavian mythology, the proper name for the goddess of the infernal region*] hell, 114, 336, 372, 538, 548, 878, 917; see **bronde**.

hem, pron., 3 pl. obj. [*OE hi(o)m, heom; dative pl. in all genders of **he**; after 1500 **them** became the standard form*] 3, 56, 293, 295, 599, 635, 710, 711, 743, 759, 803, 1098, 1159.

hende, a. [*Aphetic variation of OE 3ehende, at hand*] gracious, offering the grace of God, 45.

hens, adv. [*ME hennes f. OE hionan*] hence, away from here, 767.

herbys, n. pl. [*OFr erbe (lit 11c) f. L herba, herbage; circa 1475 h- spelling in common use*] herbs, nourishing plants, 92.

her(e), adv. [*ComTeut OE her; origin uncertain*] here on earth, 428, 429, 1099; here in this place, (direct reference to playing space, to actors, or to members of the audience) 101, 152, 179, 405, 551, 558, 566, 698, 728, 731, 735, 781, 838, 1105; at this point (in the play) 16sd, 164sd, 324sd, 380sd, 550sd, 692sd, 724sd, 752sd, 902sd, 912sd, 996sd, 1064sd.

her(e), pron., 3 sg. nom. fem. [*OE hire*] her, referring to a pretty woman as a possible lover, 815; referring to the holy mother church, 988, 992.

her(e), pron., 3 pl. poss. [*OE hiera, heora; genetive pl. in all genders of **he**; **their** prevalent after 1500*] 634, 692sd, 701, 724sd, 749, 752sd, 767, 804, 1064sd.

here, v. [*ComTeut OE hieran*] hear, 1089; **herde**, 1 sg. pa., heard, 810, 1098.

hert(e), n. [*ComTeut OE heort*] heart, 81, 85, 569, 967, 990, 1085, 1089, 1103, 1104; **hertys, poss.**, 83; **pl.**, 708; **hertyly**, adv., devoutly, 1006; see **swet(e)**.

hestys, n. pl. [*OE hæs f. OTeut haitan, call upon by name*] command; "in hys ~," under his orders, 716; rhyme scheme suggests possible mistake for hettys, heats, rages.

hewy, a. [*OE hefi3 f. hafian, heave*] heavy, 53; weary, 316.

hewyn, n. [*OE he(o)fon*] heaven, 116, 122, 159, 1146; **hewynly**, a., heavenly, 340, (used ironically to describe sinful pleasure), 573.

hydyr; see **hedyr**.

hye, a./adv. [*ComTeut OE heah; reduced to hi3, high, hy (14c)*] a., exalted, divine, 12, 25, 61, 1088, 1145; adv., high, 444; **hyghly**, adv., greatly 436; **hyg[h]ly**, (ms. hyghly), greatly, 981; see **offende**; **worthy**.

hyghly; see **hye**.

hyght, v. intr. pa. [*ComTeut OE haten*] am called, 334.

hym(m); **hymselff**; **hys**; **his**; see **he**.

holde, v. [*OE holden*] support, defend, 723; imp., assemble, hold [forth in your dance] together, 728; hold, grasp, restrain, 773; continue on, 885; pp., "be/ys ~," to be considered, 585, 651; **holdyn**, pp., held; "be ~," be considered, 832; **holdyste**, 2 sg. pr., sustains, 317; see **forthe**.

holy, a., [*OE hali3*] holy, 282, 287, 348, 1026; "~ chyrch(e)," Holy Church, 982, 984, 991, 1078; sb., (implied pl.) holy men and women, 426; see **gost**; **modyr**.

holys, n. pl. [*OE hol(h)*] holes, 1106.

holl, a. [*OE (3e)hal*; spelling with h- appears 15c] whole, healthy, restored to spiritual well-being, 187.

holly, v. [*OE hal3ian*] hallow, worship, treat with reverence and awe (OED), 251.

honde; see **hande**.

honest, a. [*OFr honeste (lit 12c) ult. f. L honestare, honor*] worthy of respect, fitting, 555.

hood(e), n. [*OE hod*] hood, head covering distinguishing vocation (often worn around the neck), 718; "ryall ~," royal hood. Osd": **hodys**, pl., 724sd.

hop(p)e, n. [*lOE hopa f. tohopa*] trust, 286, 1126; **hoope**, "~ of." hope for, 823.

hornepype, n. [*ComTeut OE horn + pipe*] an obs. wind instrument partly made of horn; term may also refer to the musician who plays the instrument or the music of the instrument (MED), 752sd, 757.

horryble, horrybyll, horrybull, a./adv. [*OFr (h)orrible* f. *L horrere, abhor*] **a.**, horrible, hideous, 902sd, 912sd, 926; adv., horribly, 896, 951; **oreble**, a., horrible, 200.

how(e), adv. [*OE hwo, hu*] how much, to what extent, 43, 187, 188, 454, 896, 901, 979; in what way, 93, 119, 146, 251, 458, 560, 615* (M = **haue**), 788, 839, 852, 927, 947; "~ be þis," how can this be, 621; "~ seyst thowe," what do you say, 888.

howe, a. [*OE hoða* f. *huðu, a parallel formation of OHG hugu*] prudent, politic; "tell hys condycyons ~," describe his politic, worldly circumstances (achieved through self-protective prudence), 626.

humanyte, n. [*OFr humanité (lit 12c) ult.* f. *L humanus*] humanity, 166; see **schadow**.

hurde, v. [*OE hordian*] hoard, 582; see **wp(pe)**.

hurle, v. [*Origin uncertain; akin to IG hurreln*] hurl, drive out, 767; harass, 856.

hy-; listed as if **hi-**.

I/Y

(Vocalic *y*- words only; consonantal *y*- after X)

I, pron. 1 sg. [*OE ic*] used frequently in the modern sense, 3, 18, 20, 22, 24 . . . 1153; see **care**; **lytyll**; **mynde**; **n[e]ther**; **schew**; **schrew**; **trow**; **tweyn**.

i; see **in**.

yche; see **eche**.

ydyll, a. [*OE idel*] idle, lazily unoccupied, 398; **idyllnes**, n., idleness (personified), 753.

yf(f), prep. [*OE ʒif*] if, 1, 39, 58, 224, 292, 298, 355, 363, 436, 507, 508, 614, 663, 811, 845, 919, 986, 1009, 1023, 1041, 1049, 1056, 1059; **iff**, 239; see **but**; **care**; **were**; **wrynge**.

ygnorans, n. [*OFr ignorance (lit 12c) ult.* f. *L ignorare, not to know*] ignorance, inherited sin (cleansed by infant baptism), 1109; **ignorant**, a., sinful state characterized by a lack of wisdom, 314.

yll, ill a./adv./n. [*eME* *ill* f. *ON* *illr*] **a.**, evil, 303; poorly, 783; adv., badly, 769, 878; n., evil; "~ wrought," brought evil about through their behavior, i.e., behaved badly, in a sinful way, 953; see **ende**; **spede**; **wyff(e)**.

ymage, n. [*OFr* *image* (lit 13c) f. *L* *imago*, *imitation*, *statue*; f. *the same root as imitari*, *copy*] image, particularly the image of God, 103, 104, 140, 142, 175, 918; **image**, 32; for similar terms see **fygure**; **lyknes**; **ryve**.

imperyall, a. [*OFr* *imperial* ult. f. *L* *imperium*, *command*, *absolute power*] imperial, worthy of an emperor, 2; "~ crown," 0sd.

impotent, a. [*OFr* *impotent* f. *L* *impotens*, *without power*] ineffectual attempt to make amends or do penance for an offense (MED), 1094.

in, prep. [*ComTeut OE* *in*] used frequently in the modern sense in, 1 sd, 3, 5, 16sd, 35 . . . 1161; D 24* (M = i), 63*, 133* (M = i) . . . 164sd* . . . 338* . . . 613* (M = i) . . . 1159; on, 3; among, 253, 255; within, 185; to, 253, 515; through, 1086, 1140; "as ~ ," as if in, 264*; "~ þe," while, 324sd, 996sd; "~ thys," through, because of this (sacrifice), 1107; adv., in 380sd, 456; i[n], adv., contracted as i (same construction at 24, 613, w. **in** taken from D), 1064sd; **yn**, prep., 72; see **acorde**; **as**; **charyte**; **contemplacyon**; **conseruynge**; **cunnynge**; **dyspyght**; **dyspute**; **erthe**; **especyall**; **experience**; **fame**; **hande**; **hestys**; **kynde**; **lyff**; **maner(e)**; **know(e)**; **mynde**; **natur**; **reforme**; **regne**; **reioys**; **seker**; **store**; **sut(e)**; **tender**; **tru**; **wyrry**; **wysdom(e)**; **wys(e)**; **worlde**.

inclyne, v. inf. [*OFr* *encliner* f. *L* *inclinare*, *bend inward or towards*; *ME* *encline* *was replaced by* *incline* *circa 1500*] change your course, 469; favor, 475.

incomparable, a. [*OFr* *incomparable* f. *L* *incomparabilis*] incomparable, infinite, 535.

incomprehensyble, a. [*OFr* *incomprehensible* (lit 13-14c)] beyond the bounds of reason or intellect, unfathomable, incomprehensible, 94, 249.

in dede, adv. phrase [*in + dede; see dede*] indeed (until 1600 written as two words), 455.

indignacyon, n. [*OFr* *indignation* ult. f. *L* *indignari*, *regard as unworthy*] scorn (personified), 693.

induyr; see **endure**.

indwell, v. [*in- + OE* *dwellan; in Wyclif rendering L* *inhabitare*] exist in, remain in, 880.

inestymable, a. [*OFr inestimable* f. *L inæstimabilis*] immeasurable, 593.

infenyt, a. [*OFr infinit(e)* f. *L infinitus, unbounded*] infinite, 156.

informable, adv. [*OFr enformer or L informare, give form to*] as an informant, 539.

informacyon, n. [*OFr informacion* f. *L informationem*] instruction, (a key to Lucyfer's false teaching); information based on cunning persuasion and sensory perception rather than love and intuition, 404, 449, 461, 479; communication of instructive knowledge, 423.

innumerable, a. [*L innumerabilis*] innumerable, 322.

inow(e), n./adv. [*OE ӡenoh*] n., enough, 564*(M = **now**), 856; adv. 368; **anow**, adv., 416; **ynowe**, adv., 886.

inperfyghtnes, n. [*OFr imparfait*] imperfection, sinfulnes, 697.

insyght, n. [*[OE in- + OE (ӡe)sihð; originally meant internal sight, synonymous with "inwit", internal vision*] perception based on internal sight, 189.

inspyryt, v. 3 sg. pr. [*OFr inspirer (lit 12c)* f. *L inspirare, breathe into*] fills, imbues, 260.

instruccyon, n. [*OFr instruction* ult. f. *L instruere, furnish with information*] instruction, 483.

instrumente, n. [*OFr instrument (14c)* ult. f. *L instruere, outfit, equip*] musical instrument, 703.

insuffycyens, n. [*OFr insufficience* f. *IL insufficientia*] inadequacy, 193.

intellygens, n. [*OFr intelligence* f. *L intelligentia, understanding*] the highest faculty of mind, 928.

into, prep. [*in (adv.) + to (prep.); written as one word when in and to refer to the same place*] into, 281* (M = **in**), 375, 439, 520, 721, 955, 1001, 1047, 1061; until, 106.

invy, n. [*OFr envie* ult. f. *L invidere, look maliciously upon*] envy (personified), 716.

inwarde, a. [*OE inweard*] internal, inner, 1074; see **wyttys**.

ioy; see **joy**.

ioly; see **joly**.

ipocryttys, n. pl. [OFr *ipocrite* f. eccIL *hypocrita*, *dramatic actor, pretender*] hypocrites, 471.

ys, v. 3 sg. pr. [see *be* v.] used frequently in the modern sense, 6, 9, 33, 35, 38 . . . 1158; **is** (all f. D), 66*, 176*, 430* (M = **ys**), 473*. 546*, 672*, 720*; see **bye**; **delectacyon**; **euer**; **grace**; **holde**; **nede**; **w(h)o**.

yt, pron. [OE *hif*] used frequently in the modern sense, 11, 41, 63, 64, 89 . . . 1036; **it**, 55, 459, 511*, 555, 651, 720*, 1089; see **but**.

iwys, adv. [OE *3ewis*; *often written as two words with capital I*] certainly, as I well know, 357, 1063.

J

(In manuscripts, transcribed as I, extending below line; see Editorial Principles)

jelousy, n. [OFr *gelosie, jalousie*] sexual jealousy, 847.

jentyll, a. [OFr *gentil, jentil, high-born, noble*] having chivalric or aristocratic character, as prescribed by Christian ideals, 188; well-born, of high social position, 832; "~ Fornycacyon," noble fornication (ironic), 756.

jerowry; see **jorowr**.

joy, ioy n./v. [OFr *joie/joir* f. *gaudere, rejoice*] n., happiness. esp. gained from the joy of loving God, 37, 60, 308, 1145; as a title for Wysdom, 70, 83; prideful, lustful, or avaricious pleasure, 561, 572, 581, 589, 593; "euell ~," hellish or illicit mirth, 614 [note: **joy** could in the fifteenth century mean a comic drama, a meaning which could be relevant to this difficult phrase]; v., take pleasure, 256; **joys**, n. pl., joys of the flesh; "joy of ~," highest of all fleshly pleasures, 593; **joyfull**, a., joyful, 42; see **souere(y)n**; **wrynge**.

joly, a. [OFr *joli(f)*] "la plu ~," French phrase = the most pleasant experience, 511; **iolye**, jolly, merry, 566.

jornye, n. [OFr *jomeé, day's travel, work*] journey 1018.

jorowr, n. [AFr *jurour* f. OFr *jureor*] professinal juryman, 718; **jorours**, pl., 724sd; **jerowry**, n., false testimony, 637.

jugepartynge, n., [OFr *juge* ult. f. L *jus* right, law + OFr *parte* f. L *partire, share, divide*] sharing wealth with judges, i.e., judge-bribing (personified), 796.

jugemente, n., [*OFr jugement*] judgment; "to þe ~," to announce legal judgment, 702; **jugment**, "at þe ~," at the day of final judgment, 948.

K

kan; see **can**.

kepe, v. [*Ety. obscure; poss. f. lOE cepan; no related words in cognate langs.*] tr., keep, preserve, 435; refl., "~ yow clene," remain, keep yourself pure, 174; **kept**, 2/3 sg. pa., maintained, 242; guarded, watched, 312; pp., observed, kept to, 403; see **sylence**.

kertyllys, n. pl. [*OE cyrtel f. L curtus, short coat (as opposed to a long gown)*] women's skirts, 164sd.

kynde, n. [*OE 3ecynde*] n., nature, natural character of humanity 927; inherited right, 575, 576; "in no ~," in no way, 297; nature; "ageyn ~," contrary to, or in violation of, nature (OED), 529; see **noble**.

kynge, n. [*ComTeut OE cyning*] term = king (also designates reigning queen, though gender implication here not clear); (theo.), one of the elect, 289, 1124; secular king, 618; **kyngys**, pl., 1023.

kynrede, n. [*lOE cynrede (MED)*] of family or race, 576; see **noble**.

kys, v. [*OE cyssan*] kiss, as a token of lust, 594; as a token of reconciliation with God, 1105; **kyssyde**, pp., "~ of," kissed by (referring to humanity's contemplative or mystical relationship with God), 44.

knaue, n. [*OE cnafa; originally a male child employed as a servant, hence, one of low condition*] vulgar rogue, 835.

knelynge, prp. [*OE cneowlian*] kneeling, 16sd.

knett, v. [*OE cnyttan*] 1 sg. pr., knit (brows), 196; pp., interwoven, 231.

knottys, n. pl. [*OE cnotta*] knots, 16sd; see **tasselys**.

know(e), v. [*ComTeut OE (3e)cnawan*] know by experience; "God(e) (. . .) ~," know God from personal experience, 98, 210; know, understand, 253, 343, 359, 670, 742; imp., "~ not yow," know you not, renounce you, 563; **knowyt**, 3 sg. pr., comprehends, 26; "~ dyscretly," understand (the created world) as separate parts of a whole, through the circumspect knowledge of his own experience, 145; **knowyng(e)**, **knowenge**, prp. as sb., comprehension, understanding, 93, 265, 279, 280, 342, 953; "very ~," 134, 933; "~ of," (gerund phrase), clear understanding of: yourself, 95, 97, 252; God, 160, 252; reason, 155; "in Gode ~," knowledge of God, 1138; see **haue**.

ky-; listed as if **ki-**.

L

la; see **joly**.

labour, n. [*OFr labo(u)r*] toil, work, as contrasted to meditation, 402, 409; **laberyde**, **laboryde**, v. 2/3 sg. pa., worked, 427; suffered pain, 1041.

lace, v. [*OFr lacier* f. popL *!laciare, ensnare*] entwine, (myself), 578; **lasyde**, pp. a., "~ behynde," laced at the back, 16sd.

laddys, n. pl. [*ME ladde, origin obscure*] servants; "ye ~," members of a retinue, 708.

lake, v. [*ME lac* akin to MIG *lak*] disparage, find fault with, 165.

lame[n]tabull, a. [*OFr lamentable* f. L *lamentari, passionately grieve*] mournful, 996sd.

lande, **londe**, n. [*ComTeut OE land, lond*] kingdom, country; "þis ~," this land, England, 682, 732.

lanys, n. pl. [*OE lane*] narrow streets, walkways between walls or houses, 799.

large, a. [*OFr large* f. L *larga, bountiful*] ample, lavish, 640.

lasyde; see **lace**.

last, sb./superl. a. [*OE latost, syncopated in ME; latest is a new formulation*] sb., last; "at þe ~," at the end of life, 526; a., "to þe ~ ende," at the point of death, 532.

lat, adv. [*ComTeut OE læf*] late in the day, 798; **latter**, comp., later, 797; see **lewe**.

lat, v.; see **let(t)**.

laude, n. [*OFr laude f. L laudem, laus*] praise, 391; **laudable**, a., worthy of praise, 589* (M = **delectable**).

law, n. [*IOE lager f. prehistoric ON !lagu, something laid or fixed*] law, legal system, 653, 673, 713; favorable legal decision, 666; **lawe**, "to ~," involve in a legal proceeding or court of law, 839: **laws**, pl., laws of God, 387; **leefull**, a., legitimate, morally correct, 408.

lawde; see **lorde**.

lechery, n. [*OFr lecherie*] lechery, 516, 533; 681, 747 (personified); **lechory**, 605; see **sprynge**.

lede, v. [*ComTeut OE læden; related to OE liðan, go, travel*] lead, "~ . . . lyff,"/"lyff . . . ~," lead, continue in a particular kind of life, 472, 812, 886; 3 sg. pa., led, 420.

leeffull; see **law**.

left(e), v. 3 sg. pr. [*ON lypta*] raise, lift, 939; see **wp(pe)**.

le(y)fte, a. [*OE left, lyff*] left (hand), 0sd; left (side), 37.

lende, v. [*OE lendan*] assent to, continue in a particular course; "þerto ~," persevere (in an activity), MED, 299.

lengthe, n. [*OE leng(u)*] length of time; "the ~ of þe yerys." long life, full duration of time, (cf. Proverbs VII, 16) 36.

lere, v. [*OE læran*] learn, 303; teach (a lesson), 848: **lernyde**, a. as sb., learned; "~ & lewyde," the educated and the ignorant. implying everyone, 682.

les, comp. a. as sb. [*OE læs, adv.*] those of a lower station: "~ & mare." less and more, persons of all ranks, the lower and higher. i e. everyone, 740; **lest**, **superl**. **a.**, smallest, 50, 813; **sb.**, lowest in rank. 415.

lesynge, vbl. sb. [*OE læs*] "wythowte ~," without doubt. (MED). 139.

lessun, n. [*OFr lecon ult. f. L legere, read*] lesson, 100: **lessons**, pl., 303.

lest; see **les**.

let(t), v. [*ComTeut OE lætan*] tr., hinder, 887; intr., leave off, give up, 51, 452; w. inf. phrase, let, allow, 453, 565; imp., 505, 613, 626, 664, 773, 779, 938, 956, 1039; "~ se," let us see, come forth, 691, 693, 707, 725; **lat**, refl., "~ amende," let it mend (itself), 752.

leue, leve, lewe, v. [*ComTeut OE lætan*] leave, give, 409, 785, 891; leave off, cease, 845, 847; imp., 441, 470, 476.

leuer; see **leve**.

leve, lewe, a. [*OE leof f. Aryan root meaning both "believe" & "love"*] dear, 1019, 1091; **leuer**, adv., beloved; "þe ~ me," = "lief I ware," glad would I be: "euer þe latter, þe ~ me," the later I arrive, the happier I am, 797.

leve, v.; **lewe**, v.; see **leue**.

lewyde, a. as sb. [*OE læwede; ety. obscure; originally a lay person, but remotely linked to "lewd" and "lay"*] unlearned, 682; see **lere**.

lybrary, n. [*OFr librarie ult. f. L liber, bark; original substance upon which Romans wrote*] collected learning, 227.

lye, v. [*ComTeut OE licgan*] lie in misery, 951.

lye, v. [*ComTeut OE leoȝan*] lie, utter falsehood, 489, 642, 750.

lyff, lyue, lyve, lywe, n./v. [*ComTeut OE lif f. Aryan root lo(i)þ, last, endure*] n., life; sinful life, 886, 891; "hys/my ~," one's personal life as a good or bad exemplum, 423, 812, 843, 992; "owr ~," i.e., the lives of the myghts treated collectively, 930; "in . . . ~," while alive 171, 999; the contemplative life (as opposed to the mixed or active life), 417, 420, 431; "þat ~," the mixed life, 429; "comun ~," an ordinary secular life, 472; "on ~," alive, 792; "resurreccyon & ~," resurrection and eternal life, 940; **lyue**, v., live, 877; **lywyt**, 3 sg. pr., lives. 405. **lywynge**, prp. as sb., living, manner of life, 434; see **go**; **lede**; **on**. (adv.).

lyght(e), n./a./adv. [*OE leohf*] n., light, the brightness of God. 22, 28, 30, 260, 918, 1072; "hys fyrste ~," original brightness, punty. 120; "a angell of ~," an angel of light (Lucyfer), 333; a., "hert ys/hertys ben (. . .) ~," lighthearted, with heart(s) free from sorrow or care. but also with the implication of being morally light, i.e., taking pleasure from sin, 569, 708; adv., of little value, 923; **lyghtlyer**, comp. adv. more easily, 792; see **angell**; **set(t)**.

lyke, a. [*OE ȝelic*] like; "~ to," similar to, having the same qualities as. 16sd, 538, 928; "by ~ to," resemble, 172.

lykly, a. [*on the model of ON liklig-r*] prosperously handsome in appearance, giving the promise of success, "most ~ ay," most handsome on all occasions, 554* (M = **lyghtly**).

lykynge, prp. a./vbl. sb. [*OE licung*] prp. a., amorously disposed, 567; vbl. sb., object of desire; **lykynge / lykyngys**, "lust/ys and ~," lust(s) and sensual pleasure(s), 51; pl., 460.

lyknes, n. [*OE licness*] actual semblance of God, 35, 104, 128, 1131; "to (. . .) hys ~," in God's own image, 188, support 274, 536; likeness of the devil, 373, 912sd, 1114; "~ & fygure," both the actual semblance and the represented form, 214; for similar terms see **fygure**; **ymage**.

lyouns, n. pl. [*L leo(nem); adopted in all Teut langs*] lions, 692sd.

lyst, v. [*OE lystan*] please to, wish to (w. inf.), 837.

lytyll, a./adv. [*OE lytel*] a., little, small, 465; adv., "I reke but ~," I care little if, 816.

lyue; see **lyff**.

lo, inter. [*OE la*] lo, behold, 38, 179, 274, 277, 288, 400*, 551, 566, 615, 698, 709, 735, 979, 1011, 1019, 1026, 1035, 1062.

loke, v. [*OE locian*] look, see clearly, examine closely, 894, 902.

lombys, n. poss. [*ComTeut OE lamb, lomb*] lamb's, 490.

londe; see **lande**.

longe, a./adv. [*ComTeut OE long*] a., long, tall, 770; adv., long period of time, 978; "as ~ as," as long as, within a conditional period of time, 242.

longe, v. [*Aphetic variation of OE 3elang, at hand, dependent on*] belong, 686.

loose, v. [*OE losian f. los*] subj., lose, 677.

lorde, n. [*OE hlaford f. hlafweard, bread-guardian*] Lord God, 107, 268, 286, 309, 322, 925, 955, 977, 1082, 1142, 1158; **lawde**, used to denote an exclamation or plea directed to God, (MED), 323; see **souere(y)n**.

lord(e)schyppe, n. [*OE hlaford + -scype*] the patronage of a lord; associated with Mynde, 630, 635, 665.

lore, n. [*OE lar*] doctrine, religious creed, acquired learning, 418.

lore, v. [*ME louren poss. f. OE !lurian*] scowl (at), 326.

lought, v. 3 pl. pa. [*ME la3henn f. lah*] abase (themselves), bow down, 503.

loue, **love**, **lowe**, n./v. [*OE lufu*] n., love, esp. contemplative love of God, 40, 41, 48, 49, 54, 61, 65, 66*, 71, 84, 85, 266, 268, 282, 916, 1006, 1013, 1021, 1088, 1104; "~ clepyde charyte," love of God, called charity, 269; sexual desire, 592; love of pleasure, comfort, 759; v., 47, 58, 267, 735, 1057; **louer**, n., lover, 20, 595; God as lover and paternal guardian, 74; **louers**, **lovers**, pl., 47, 67; **lou(ev)yt**, **lowyt**, 67, 144, 494; **louyth**, 66*; **louyde**, 22; 2 sg. pr., **lowyste**, **louyst**, 913, 924; **lowyde**, a., beloved-- as a designation prefixed to a personal name or designations, equivalent to the "trusty and well-beloved" of English charters, particularly characteristic of royal and feudal documents (OED), 261; **louely**, a., lovely, gracious, 43; **louyngly**, adv., lovingly, 320* (M = **louynly**); see **souere(y)n**.

loweday, n. [*OE lufu* + *OE dæs; in ML dies amoris (Du Cange)*] a day set aside for aimably settling disputes; a day of truce; "wyth ~ to dres," implies both a loveday to arrange or dress up for and the chance to redress an injury through false legal moves (with perhaps a pun on the idea of *love* as a debased commodity in this world of sin), 698.

lowly, adv. [*OE lah* + *-ly; see lought*] meanly, in a lowly manner, 503; **lowest**, superl. a., the lowest, 336.

lust, n. [*ComTeut OE lusf*] lechery, lust, the sin associated with Wyll, 460, 568, 611, 616, 652, 655; **lustys**, pl., 51, 516; see **lykynge**.

ly-; listed as if **li-**.

M

ma; see **may**.

madam, a. [*OFr ma dame; ety. related to Italian madonna; ML mea domina*, my *lady*] madam; " ~ Regent," Madame Regent, possibly the name of a dance (MED) but more likely a parody of women in power, probably referring to the mynstrall, 707.

mad(e); see **mak(e)**.

madnes, n. [*Aphetic variation of OE 3emæd(e)d*] madness, insanity, 439.

may, v. [*ComTeut OE m__æg*] can, may, be able; aux. w. inf. or pp., 34, 57, 63, 73, 78, 89, 93, 95, 116, 161, 202, 215, 418, 486, 496*, 533, 549, 752, 761, 788, 860, 861, 864, 892, 916, 936, 947, 961, 965, 1063, 1080, 1141, 1149, 1163; **myght**, 1/3 sg. pa. subj., might, 839, 875, 915, 919, 1017.

mayde, n. [*Shortened form of OE m__æ3den, maiden*] virgin, 16sd, unmarried girl, 816.

mayde, v.; see **mak(e)**.

maynten, v. [*OFr maintenir f. L phrase manu tenere, hold in one's hand*] su; ort a legal accusation, 700; **mayntnance**, **meyntnance**, n., in legal terminology = wrongful interference in lawsuits, especially by a lord or his followers as a result of trading (political) influence, 634, 653, (personified) 671, (personified) 678, 691, 714, 745; **meyntenance**, 724sd, 761; **mayntennance**, (personified) 696; **mayntement**, n., maintenance; "meny of ~," retainers kept by Mayntenance, 706* (M = meyntnance); see **hattys**.

mak(e), v. [*ComWG OE macian*] make, 265, 372, 866; cond., 367 inf., 365, 371, 447, 537, 605, 685, 954, 974, 1094; imp., 463; **makyt(h)**, 55, 91, 129, 204, 459, 562, 577, 587, 616, 969; **mase**, makes, 579; **mad(e)**, made, 122, 268, 310, 390, 523, 528, 535, 918; pp., made, designed, 24, 114, 140, 258, 328, 907, 908, 917, 972, 1096; **mayde**, pp., 187; see **asythe**; **pawsacyon**; **report**; **suffycyent**.

males, n. [*OFr malice ult. f. L malus*] malice (personified), 694.

malewrye, n. [*OFr mal, a./adv. f. L male, ill, bad (used as a prefix in E more commonly after 16c) + wyre, rare sb., bad twist f. OE wri3oam, turn, twist out of shape*] bad twist, unlucky chance, misfortune, 667.

man, n. [*ComTeut OE man(n)*] a human being, man as a generic term for humanity, 14, 62, 101, 108, 110, 121, 215, 268, 328, 338, 343, 348, 349, 360, 373, 419, 424, 454, 459, 475, 486, 587, 612, 626, 714, 792, 859, 882, 885, 912, 968, 1053, 1063, 1064, 1147; adult male, 405, 408; **men**, pl., people, 503, 599, 603, 606, 633, 736; **mannys**, poss., 220; **mankyn(de)**, n., humankind, 44, 543, 997; **manfull**, a., stately in appearance, 455; see **ber(e)**; **natur**.

maner(e), n./a. [*OFr maniere f. L manus, hand*] n., "a ~ of," a degree (of), 462; "in þis ~," thus, in this way, 1045; a., kinds of, 466.

manfull; see **man**.

mankyn(de); **mannys**; see **man**.

mantyll, n. [OE _mentel_ infl. by OFr _mantel_ (12c)] mantle, long gown or cloak, 0sd*, 16sd, 912sd; **mantelys**, pl., 164sd.

many, a. [ComTeut OE _mani3_] many, 348, 548, 724, 910, 1017, 1028; "~ on," (in ME often written as one word = mani3on, OED) many a one, 893; "as ~," so many, 909; see **tyme**.

mare; see **mor(e)**.

marre, v. [ComTeut OE _merran_] perplex, 346.

mase; see **mak(e)**.

mastres, n. [OFr _maistresse_] mistress] (personified derogative term) probably implying an illicit lover, 755.

matrones, n. pl. [OFr _matrone_ ult. f. L _mater_, mother] matrons, married women (as opposed to virgins), 752sd.

me, pron., 1 sg., obj. [OE _me(c)_] used frequently in the modern sense, 6, 48, 54, 61, 83 . . . 311* . . . 316* . . . 321* . . . 1098; **me**, used as subject of verb, 497* (M = we); **w. imp.**, 507* (M = I); **my(n)**, poss. pron. as a., used frequently in the modern sense, 2, 4, 18, 19, 22 . . . 1145; **myself(f)**, pron., 185, 195, 201, 202, 204*, 554, 1080; see **affyance**; **affye**; **affynyte**; **attende**; **cast**; **cosyn**; **dysgysynge**; **dyspyght**; **fay**; **haue**; **lewe**; **lyff**; **mynde**; **pynne**; **pley**; **ples**; **relacyon**; **reuerens**; **save**; **seme**; **spede**; **spowse**; **tak(e)**; **trespas**; **tru**; **wrynge**.

mede, n. [OE _med_] reward, bribe, recompense for services rendered to the Lord God, (religious), 217; to a human lord, (secular), 672, 730, 806, 862.

medsyne, n. [OFr _medecine_] medicinal remedy (used fig. to suggest spiritual remedy), 970.

meyntenance; see **maynten**.

meke, a. [eME _meoc_/ON _miuk-r_, soft, pliant, gentle] courteous, gentle, merciful, 81, 972, 1065; **meknes**, n., gentleness of spirit, humility, 1159; **mekyt**, v. 3 sg. pr., calms, humbles, makes meek, (poss. infl. by **make**), 85.

men; see **man**.

mene, n. [OFr _me(e)n_ ult. f. L _medius_, middle] middle voice in song, 618.

mengylde, pp. a. [*IME* _mengel_ f. _meng_ f. Du _mengelen_] mixed; "drynke ~ wyth gall," Biblical reference to the drink mingled with gall, Christ's bitter drink, (cf. Matthew 27:34), 1100.

meny(e), n. [*OFr* _meyne_] body of retainers, retinue of (liveried) dancers, 706, 709, 715, 735, 781, 795; **menys**, poss., 729; see **mayten**.

menstrall; **menstrellys**; see **mynstrell**.

menyver, n. [*OFr* _menu vair, little vair_] white fur, used in ceremonial garments, 16sd.

mercy, n. [*OFr* _merci_ f. *L* _mercedem, reward; in Christian L often =_ _misericordia_] mercy, pardon, the forgiveness of God offered in response to penitence, often contrasted to justice, 76, 321, 920, 945, 956, 983, 1015, 1068, 1079, 1124; falsely offered by Lucyfer as a reward for despair, 467; as a penitent cry, 950, 1077; "of ~ ande of [comfort — Ms. mercy]," second instance of **mercy** in this line a probable scribal error for **comfort**, 989; **mercyfull**, a., merciful, 1132; see **comfort**; **oyll**; **tak(e)**.

mery, a. [*OE* _myr(i)3e_] thoughtlessly joyful, indulging in a life of sin, 492, 494, 500, 505, 559, 562, 623, 836, 871; see **clene**; **pynne**.

merowre, n. [*OFr* _mirour_ ult. f. *L* _mirare, look at_] model, reflection; "~ of þe dyvyne domynacyon," reflection of God's majesty, 31.

mest; see **most**.

met, n. [*OE* _mete_] meat, food, 473, 814.

mete, a. [*ME* _mete_ prob. f. OE _3emæte, commensurate_] fitting, suitable, 757.

mevyngys; see **move**.

my(n); see **me**.

myght, v.; see **may**.

myght, n. [*OE* _miht_] power, 258, 920; strength, 726; **myghtys**, pl., "thre/iii ~," faculties of Mynde, Wyll, and Wndyrstondynge (personified), 177, 277; "tweyn ~," inner (i.e. spiritual) and outer (i.e. physical) "wits" or senses, 1073, 1077;
"~ bodely," bodily mights: Mynde, Wyll, & Wndyrstondynge (personified), 147; **myghty**, a., powerful, 630, 671; **myghtyly**, adv., so as to make strong, 318.

mylde, a. [*ComTeut OE* _milde_] merciful, 982.

mynde, n. [*OE 3emynd, memory, intellecf*] frequently personified as a faculty of the soul; mind, thought, 42; cognitive aspect of the soul, often as a reflection of God, 55, 197, 199, 204, 209, 210, 212, 381, 513, 881; the higher part of reason, one of the three faculties of the soul, 180, 183, 278, 279, 285, 301, 324sd, 358, 365, 527, 692sd, 873, 899, 902, 933, 952, 957, 974, 993, 1064sd; "Wen in myselff I haue ~ & se," When I look inward and take note of my own mind, 185; "haue (. . .) ~,"/ "in ~ . . . haue," have in mind, remember, 208, 833, 1117; "bryngt/brynge to (. . .) ~," bring to mind, recall, remember, 189, 916, 925; "haue ~ of," take note of, be aware of, recall to your mind, 397* (M = "haue ~ of"); "~ to ~ bryngth þat fawowre," mind as a reflection of God brings that grace to the unstable human mind, 209; "goode ~," uncorrupted mind, 211; **myndys**, coll. pl., minds, 346; see **tak(e)**.

mynstrell, n. [*OFr menestral, attendanf*] musician (playing symbolical instruments), 724sd, 752sd, 757; **mynstrall**, 692sd; **menstrellys**, pl., 701.

myrable, a. [*L mirabilis* f. *mirare, wonder*] marvellous, 41.

myrthe, n. [*OE myr(i)3þ*] joy, 620.

mys, v. [*OE missan*] cease to be, 248.

myschance, n. [*OFr meschance*] disaster, 766.

myselff; see **me**.

mysfare, v. 2 pl. pr. [*OE misfaren*] go wrong, 496*.

moche, a./adv./sb. [*Shortened form of muchel* f. *OE micel, greaf*] a., many, 1010; (used with coll. n.), 632; **adv**., greatly, a lot, 9, 414, 600*, 1004; "to ~," too much, 482; **quasi-sb.**, many; "so ~ reynande," so many formally accusing (others) of crime, 679; see **set(t)**.

modyr, n./a. [*ComTeut OE modor*] n., mother, 1056; a., "~ (holy) chyrch(e)," mother (holy) church, 982, 988, 991, 1078; typical of morality plays, the nurturing family is connected with the Church rather than with kindred.

monye, n. [*OFr moneie* f. *L moneta, Roman goddess of the minf*] money, 666.

moque, v. [*OFr mocquer, mock*] to make sport, 822.

mor(e), **mare**, comp. a./adv./sb. [*ComTeut OE mara*] a., more, greater, 97, 1022, 1031; adv., more, a greater degree, 98, 404, 414, 646, 681, 915, 1000, 1008, 1015, 1040, 1048, 1055, 1058, 1062; "no ~," no longer, 491, 779; not more than this, 606, 814; **mare**, sb., those of high social rank, 740; see **delectacyon**; **les**; **pleynerly**.

mornyth, v. 3 sg. pr. [*ComTeut OE murnan*] frets, pines, 835.

mosyde, v. pp. [*ME masen* f. *amased (MED)*] deceived, confounded, 348.

most, superl. a./adv. [*ComTeut OE mæsf*] superl. a., most, the greatest amount or degree, 78, 338, 598, 657; adv., 6, 19, 99, 195, 255, 257, 259, 267, 320, 344, 536, 537, 554, 589, 684, 902sd, 930, 996sd, 1019, 1104; **mest**, 1131; see **dyspyght**; **fame**; **gouernyde**; **lykly**; **ples**; **wys(e)**.

move, v. [*AFr mover* ult. f. *L movere*] impress, 1015; **mevyngys**, prp. as sb., promptings, 226* (M = **mevyngye**).

mowyntenys, n. pl. [*OFr montaigne*] mountains, 1001.

must, v. [*OE moste*] must, be compelled to; aux. w. inf., 218, 433, 665, 666, 867, 983; "~ (. . .) be," w. pp., 222, 225, 227, 229; **mut**, 2 pl., 1160; see **nede**.

my-; listed as if **mi-**.

mor(e), **mare**, comp. a./adv./sb. [*ComTeut OE mara*] a., more, greater, 97, 1022, 1031; adv., more, a greater degree, 98, 404, 414, 646, 681, 915, 1000, 1008, 1015, 1040, 1048, 1055, 1058, 1062; "no ~," no longer, 491, 779; not more than this, 606, 814; **mare**, sb., those of high social rank, 740; see **delectacyon**; **les**; **pleynerly**.

mornyth, v. 3 sg. pr. [*ComTeut OE murnan*] frets, pines, 835.

mosyde, v. pp. [*ME masen* f. *amased (MED)*] deceived, confounded, 348.

most, superl. a./adv. [*ComTeut OE mæsf*] superl. a., most, the greatest amount or degree, 78, 338, 598, 657; adv., 6, 19, 99, 195, 255, 257, 259, 267, 320, 344, 536, 537, 554, 589, 684, 902sd, 930, 996sd, 1019, 1104; **mest**, 1131; see **dyspyght**; **fame**; **gouernyde**; **lykly**; **ples**; **wys(e)**.

move, v. [*AFr mover* ult. f. *L movere*] impress, 1015; **mevyngys**, prp. as sb., promptings, 226* (M = **mevyngye**).

mowyntenys, n. pl. [*OFr montaigne*] mountains, 1001.

natur, n. [*OFr nature* f. *L natura; replaces native E kind*] nature, the essential qualities and properties of a person or thing (*OED*); "in ~ of þe fyrst man," in the essential being of the first man (thus sharing Adam's fallen condition), 110.

ne, neg. part./intens. part. [*OE ne*] neg. part., nor, 966; correlative, "not . . . ~," neither . . . nor, 64; "~ . . . ~," not . . . nor, 852; intens. part., "~ not," not at all, 1046.

nede, n. [*ComTeut nied*] need, necessity, 458, 811; "þat ys ~,"/"þat ~ ys," what is necessary, needful, 504, 807; **nedy**, a., needy, 1030; **nedys**, adv., "must ~," of necessity, 867; **nedyt**, v. intr. 3 sg. pr., is necessary, 148, 662; see **were**.

neybur(e), n. [*OE neah3ebur*] fellow human, especially a fellow Christian, 1014, 1030, 1046.

ne(y)ther, **nethyr**, comp. a. [*ComTeut OE neoþera*] lower; "~ parte," lower part (of reason), represented by Wndyrstondynge, 145, 298, 483.

neke, n. [*OE hnecca limited to Teut langs; rare in OE; more common was OE hals*] neck, 0sd; **nekys**, pl., 724sd.

nesesse, a. [*ad.* f. *L necesse*] commodious, convenient 442.

n[e]ther, conjunctive adv. [*obs. var. of neither, ME adaptation of OE nawðer, nauðer, prob. inf. by either; ordinarily a neg. part. in a list requiring at least one alternative, neither may be used as a conj. adv. without a second negative particle; the earliest such usage cited in the OED occurs in Shakespeare; it is not a precise parallel; though otherwise unattested this early, this seems to be the usage here*], neither, "~ þe wers I fare," neither [for that] do I fare the worse, i.e., I do not fare worse [though they curse], 809.

neuer, adv. [*OE næfre* f. *ne* + *æfre, ever*] never, at no time, 68, 130, 174, 248, 380, 663, 668, 681, 810, 831, 836, 859, 866, 936, 985, 1095, 1114; **[n]euer**, (both M & D = **euer**), never; "be . . . ~ so," no matter how (it) may be, 641, 862; "~ so," never before so, 679, 1091; **neuerþeles**, adv., nevertheless, 9.

new, a./adv. [*ComTeut OE niwe*] a., new, different, fresh, 551, restoration to a former state, recovery from decay or disease, 1071, adv., anew, fresh, 943; "euer ~," continually, 433; see **aray**; **resurreccyon**.

nex(t), adv./a. [*OE neahsf*] adv., proceeding thereafter, 324sd; a., next, 790.

nyne, **(ix)**, a. [*OE ni3on*] nine, 830, 998.

nyse, a. [*OFr nice f. L nescius, ignorant*] foolish, 476; **nysyte**, n., trifling folly, 651.

no, a./adv./inter. neg. particle [*Reduced form of OE nam, non*] a., no, 26, 65, 116, 152, 215, 297, 299, 304, 447, 468, 502, 555, 572, 597, 606, 608, 612, 624, 660, 714, 737, 792, 805, 806, 861, 887; adv., 491, 779, 814; inter., 399, 831; **non**, a., no, 362, 658; adv., not, 980; **nought**, adv., nought, 676; **cast**; **dowte**; **kynde**; **mor(e)**; **nay**; **thynge**; **thought**; **wys(e)**.

nobley; see **noble**.

noble, n. [*OFr noble*] an English coin first minted by Edward III, worth 6s 8d, 819; **nobles**, pl., 828

nobley, n./a. [*OFr noble f. L nobilis; OFr form the direct result of combining L root (g)no, know + OFr suffix -ble f. L -bilis, given to, able to*] n., natural nobility of God, 4* (M = **noble**); a., high ranking, admirable; **noble**, a. "~ kynde," human nature ennobled by likeness to God, 927; n., high social rank; "~ of kynrede," a high ranking family, 576* (M = **nobyll**).

non; see **no**.

nor, neg.conj. [*Probable contraction of nother*] nor, 62, 216.

not, adv./sb. [*Contraction of noughf*] adv., used frequently in the modern sense, 64, 66*, 87, 104, 138 . . . 496* . . . 1121; sb., nothing, 35, 80, 194; **nowt(e)**, adv., 107, 950; see **all**; **but**; **ellys**; **know(e)**; **ne**; **only**; **rewlyde**; **tak(e)**.

notys, n. pl. [*OFr note f. L nota, mark*] musical notes, 996sd; see **drawte**.

nought(e), a./n./adv. [*OE nowihf*] a., immoral, evil, 201, 310, 924; n., nothing, 234, 268, 628, 967; immoral or vicious end, 356; "to/at ~," to/at nothing, having no value, 764; adv., not at all, 656, 676, 803; **nouhte**, n., 801; see **nought**; **ryght**; **set(t)**; **tak(e)**.

now(e), adv. [*OE nu*] now (at this time or in this place), 14, 43, 341, 420, 451, 519, 527, 559, 598, 607, 613, 621, 644, 649, 651, 671, 678, 683, 685, 717, 727, 728, 734, 745, 777, 780, 833, 868, 900, 925, 987, 1088, 1090, 1092, 1109, 1111, 1113, 1125, 1133, 1149, 1153, 1160.

nowt(e); see **not**.

numbyr, n. [*OFr nombre*] number, 697.

ny-; listed as if **ni-**.

O

Q, inter. [*Not found in OE; variation of a!; see a*] oh!; used in direct address to Christ 69, 70, 74, 93, 99, 989, 1065, 1066, 1067, 1145; direct address to Mynde, 873.

obeysance, n. [*OFr obeissance (lit 13c) ult. f. L obedire, obey*] worshipful obedience, 81.

of(f), prep. [*OE of*] used frequently in the modern sense, 0sd(*), 2, 7, 12, 15 . . . 265* . . . 1157; by, 3, 44, 261, 1080; (born) from, out of, 110, 115; from, 111, 112, 124, 233, 268, 288, 538; at, 865; for, 823, 988, 1030; about, 1142; "~ owrselff," by/in ourselves, 234; "~ thys," in this, 436; spelling **off** is used at the beginning of lines only in M, not in D); see **affyance**; **affye**; **angell**; **bronde**; **cloth(e)**; **cosyn**; **cure**; **damesellys**; **dysposicyon**; **doughters**; **ey**; **enbrace**; **fele**; **full**; **gyse**; **gold(e)**; **hattys**; **hop(p)e**; **ioy**; **kys**; **know(e)**; **lengthe**; **maynteyn**; **maner(e)**; **mercy**; **merowre**; **natur**; **ne(y)ther**; **noble**; **oyll**; **pardon**; **penance**; **pyler**; **quest**; **reforme**; **reioys**; **reson(e)**; **schadow**; **set(t)**; **sew(e)**; **sypres**; **sprynge**; **tabernacull**; **tasselys**; **tender**; **vsande**; **wondyr**.

offence, **offens**, n. [*ME offence ult. f. L offensa, hurt, a striking against; ME offens f. OFr offens, injury, wrong*] offense, transgression, sin, 926; "Adamys ~," Adam's original sin in eating the apple, 106.

offende, v. [*OFr offendre, strike against*] sin against God, 297; "~ gode hyghly," greviously offend God, 436; strike against, offend, 710; **offendys**, 3. sg. pr. intr., 803; **offendyde**, 1/3 sg. pl. pa. tr., offended (God), 934, 981, 1073; pp. intr., sinned, 1093.

oft(yn), adv. [*ComTeut OE oft*] often, 221, 1054.

oyll, n. [*OFr oyle (15c); replaced OE ele*] oil; "~ of mercy," healing oil promised to Adam, thus, salvation through Christ (MED), 321.

olde, a. [*ComTeut OE ald*] former, existing from long ago -- or great, abundant (colloq., see OED), 956; "~ synnys," past sins, 1137

on, prep./adv. [*OE an, on*] prep., on, in, at, 381, 492*, 565. 596. 623, 692sd, 765, 817, 846, 897, 1037, 1064sd; adv., 533, 734, 776, 1064sd; "~ lyue," alive, 792; see **lyff**; **pynne**; **pyttys**; **tweyn**; **syde**; **wys(e)**; **worde**.

on(e), a./pron. [*ComTeut OE* _an_] a̠., one, 135, 277, 283, 324sd*, 703, 718, 719, 1006, 1021, 1064sd. 1158; orie everlasting wysdom (personified), 8; pron., 558*, 562, 566, 893, 1074; "all at ~," be at one, united in harmony, (a demonic parody of atonement), 780; see **many**; **worde**.

onclennes, n. [*OE* _onciænnes_] moral impurity, 650.

oncunnynge, n. [_on_ + *prp. of OE* _cunnan, know_] redeeming ignorance, ability to believe without cunning or without the kind of scholastic logic or courtly elegance which Lucyfer affects (here identified by Mynde as a fault), 580.

ony, a./adv. [*OE* _æniȝ_] a̠., any, 351, 618, 904; adv̠., any, 915; see **fowll(e)**.

onys, adv. [*Genetive form of* a̠n, _on_] once, 520; once and for all, 840.

onkynde, a. [*OE* _uncynde_] unnatural, 905.

only, adv./a. [*OE* _ænlice, similar, unique, or excellent_] adv̠., only, solely, 206, 220, 229; "do not ~ ," alone do not, 960; "not ~ . . . but," not only, but also, 104, 1129-30; a̠., and also (or possibly any) 1020; see **but**.

onthryvande, prp. a. [*OE* _on_ + *ON* _þrifask, thrive_] unworthy, unprosperous, 781.

onto, prep. [*ME variation of* _until_ *f. ON* _und, up to, as far_] unto, 207, 1098; to, 592; within, 1055; **vnto**, unto, 391*.

opynly, adv. [*ComTeut OE* _open_ + -_ly_] openly, 670.

or[1], conj. [*OE* a̠r] before, 226, 395; see **þa(e)t**.

or[2], conj. [*Phonetically reduced form of* _other, conj. (obs.)_] or, 109, 218, 677, 738, 816, 1007, 1009, 1017.

ordenance, n. [*OFr* _ordenance_ ult. f. L _ordinare, ordain_] plan, established method (of a court), 786; **ordenyde**, 3 sg. pa., established, destined, 191, 475; pp̠., 243; **ordynatly**, adv., duly, properly, systematically or in due order, 138; see **rewlyde**.

ordure, n. [*OFr* _ordure_ f. _ord_, filthy, foul; cf. L _horridus_] dung, 52.

oreble; see **horrybyll**

orygynall, a. [*OFr* _original_ ult. f. L _oriri, arise from_] original; "synne ~," original sin, 111, 126; "synnes ~," possibly with reference to actual and original sins, 1110.

other, a./pron. [*ComTeut ober*] a., other, 141, 407, 1064sd; pron., other (one), 1075; (implied) pl., others, 709, 998; **uther**, pron. as pl., other persons, 809.

ouerparte, n. [*OE ufer(r)a + OFr part; properly 2 words*] the higher faculty (of reason), 300, 484, 1130; see **ne(y)ther**.

ough; see **owe**.

out, owt, adv./inter. [*ComTeut OE uf*] adv., displaced, out (of), 524; out (direction), 324sd, 912sd, 996sd; inter., alas!, 325, 903; **owtewarde**, a., outward, having to do with the body rather than the spirit, 137; **owtwarde**, a., outward, 1075; adv. w. ellipsis of v., (go) outside, 776; see **go**; **wyttys**.

outhe, adv. [*origin obscure; according to OED, poss. f. OE uf + with; term recorded by the OED only as meaning "above" or "over"; in this instance obviously a variant of D. out*] outside, 659.

ow(e), v. [*ComTeut OE a3an,pay homage to*] 1 sg. pr./3 sg. pl., ought, am/are bound by duty (to do), 100, 212; **ough**, 1 sg. pr., 190*.

own, a. [*OE æ3en; originally pp. of a3an; see ow(e)*] own, 131, 906, 1113; see **Cryst**.

owyr, n. [*OFr ure, ore f. L hora*] hour, 1021.

owr, pron. 1 pl. poss. [*ComTeut OE ure*] our, 70, 75, 229, 286, 659, 686, 762, 930, 935, 991, 1142; **owrselff**, imp. pl., ourselves, 234, 936; see **lyff; of(f)**.

owt; see **out**.

owtwrynge, v. [*Variation of OE outringen (MED)*] ring out, sing out loudly, 619.

oy-; listed as if **oi-**.

P

pacyenly, adv. [*OFr pacient ult. f. L pati, suffer*] patiently, humbly, 1013.

pardon, n. [*OFr pardon ult. f. IL perdonare, grant, concede*] granting of mercy, forgiveness of sins; "charter of ~," a document granting pardon, equivalent to a "bulle of pardon," 986.

parte, n. [*OFr part* f. *L partire, share, divide*] part, portion of the whole (used particularly in reference to the faculties of the soul) 141, 145, 245, 298, 483; **party(e)s**, pl., 135, 357, 994, 1061; see **ne(y)ther**.

parteners, n. pl. [*Variation of AFr parcener* f. *OFr parçon, partition; infl. by* **parte**, *n.*] parteners, (referring to the Soul and her faculties), 308.

parvyse, n. [*OFr parevis*] enclosure or court in front of a church, in this instance, St. Paul's Cathedral, where lawyers met, 793.

passante, prp. a. [*OFr passant*] excelling, surpassing (others), 610.

passe, v. [*OFr passer (lit 11c), go, proceed*] exceed, 830.

passyble, a. [*OFr passible*] capable of feeling emotion; "yowrselff ~," your sentient self, 97.

passyon, n. [*OFr passion ult.* f. *L pati; in L primarily a Christian term (possibly introduced by Tertullian)*] passion: "þe/thy/hys ~," the crucifixion of Christ, 1007, 1069, 1163; "~ wyke," Easter week, 996sd.

patrone, n. [*OFr patron (13c) ult.* f. *L pater, father*] lord, superior, protector, 15.

pawsacyon, n. [*lL pausationem* f. *pausare, pause; St. Jerome uses in the sense of death (OED)*] pause; "make a ~," (at this point) take a rest, with the ironic implication of leading oneself toward death, 463.

pe(a)s, n./v. [*OFr pais (lit 11c)* f. *L pax, peace*] n., peace, amity, 1151; v. inf., to make satisfaction or amends for, 850; see **arest**.

peyn, n. [*OFr peine (lit 11c)* f. *L poena, punishment, penalty*] justified grief, 193; suffering inflicted for a crime or offense, 935, 1043; justified suffering, 1140; **peyn(y)s**, pl., pains, 1012, 1016, 1063, 1101; see **conseruynge**; **vyolence**.

penance, n. [*OFr pen(e)ance* f. *L pænitentem*] penance, penitence, a ritual atonement central to the action of morality drama, 471, 512, 965; "sakyrment of ~," sacrament of penance (one of the seven Roman Catholic sacraments), 1111.

peny, n. [*OE pening, peni3 (lit 15c); penny emerged 15c*] penny, (1/12 of a shilling), 870; a small coin of unspecified amount, 999.

pe(o)ple, n. [*AFr poeple ult.* f. *L populus*] people, 1097; "hys ~," the people of God, 263.

perceyvable, a. [*OFr percevable ult. f. L percipere, take possession of, seize*] perceptible (by the senses), recognizable, 595.

perell, n. [*OFr peril (lit 10c) ult. f. L experiri, trial*], peril, jeopardy, 312, 900.

perfyghte, a. [*OFr parfit(e) (lit 11c) ult f. L perfectus*] spiritually perfect, 56; **perfyghtly**, adv., "sett ~," fixed through spiritual discipline, 233; **perfyghtnes**, n., perfectness, the practice of contemplative life (used ironically with malicious overtones), 377; **perfeccyon**, n., spiritual perfection, the goal of the Christian life, achieved primarily through contemplation, 553, 1162; see **schew**.

performyt, v. tr. 3 sg. pr. [*AFr perfourmer prob. f. OFr parfournir*] carries through, perfects, 232.

perysche, v. [*OFr periss- f. perir f. L perire*] intr. 3 pl. pr., are forgotten, 410; **perysschede**, 1 sg. pa., languished, 311; **perrysschyt**, tr. 3 sg. pr., withers up, 1089; **p[er]isshe**, 395* (D = **pisshe**; M = **pyse**); see **pyse**.

periury, n. [*AFr perjurie (11c) ult. f. L perjurare, swear*] perjury, 638, 674; (personified), 678, 733, 745; see **enbrace**.

perlys, n. pl. [*OFr perle f. medL perla*] pearls, 0sd.

perpetuall, a. [*OFr perpetuel ult.f. L perpetere, aim, seek*] perpetual, eternal, 60.

perrysschyt, see **perysche**.

person(e), n. [*OFr persone f. L persona, personage, person*] person of the Trinity, 7, 1142; **personys**, pl., persons of social distinction, 599; see **souere(y)n**.

perteynynge, prp. [*OFr partenir f. L pertinere, extend*] pertaining, 592.

perverte, **perwert**, v. [*OFr pervertir f. L pervertere, distort, corrupt*] turn aside from correct religious beliefs (MED), 292; misdirect, 362: **perverse**, 3 sg. pr., pervert, turn aside from true meaning, 379.

pes; see **peas**.

pyctowre, n. [*L pictura, painting*] representation, likeness. 350.

pyler, n. [*OFr piler f. L pila*] pillar; "~ of tre," wooden pillar or post, with poss. implications of a cross (in imitation of Christ's passion), 1059.

pyll, n. [*OFr pile (lit 12c)*] tail of a coin, 859; see **crose**.

pynne, n. [*IOE pinn*] a peg used as a fastener, as on a musical instrument or a drinking cup; "sett my soule on a mery ~," fix my attention on pleasure with the implication of re-directing the soul into sinful merriment, 492.

pyse, v. [*OFr pissier, origin uncertain, poss. onomatopoeic*] piss or waste (away): M transcription of D **pisshe**, a probable error for **perisshe** (emendation of D accepted in this text); see **perysche**.

pyte, n. [*OFr pitet (11c); clerical adaptation f. L pietas, piety; in IL "pity" and "compassion" directly linked to piety*] pity, the disposition of mercy or compassion, 912, 1029, 1035.

pyttys, n. poss. [*OE pytt*] pit; "on þe ~ brynke," on the verge of death, 897.

place, n. [*OFr place ult. f. L platea, broad way, open space*] place, allotted space, 327, 337, 340; "þe deuelys ~," Satan's abode, 546; "hys/Godys . . . ~," the soul as God's natural dwelling place, 132, 176, 906; **placys**, pl., places, locations, 649; "þis ~," acting area, 721; see **reforme**; **rest**.

playnly; see **pleyn**.

pley, v./n. [*OE ple3ean/ple3a*] v. 1 sg. pr. refl., play; "~ me," amuse myself, 837; n., amusement, 887.

pleyn, adv. [*OFr plain f. L planus, flat*] simply, purely, unconditionally, 992; **playnly**, adv., clearly, fully, 62.

pleynerly, adv. [*f. plener(e), adj; f. OFr plener f. L plenus, full*] fully, completely, "more ~ to," more fully accurate (or complete) in, 404.

pleyntuus, a. [*OFr plentivous*] bountiful, 1146.

ples, v. [*OFr plaisir f. L placere, agreeable*] please, satisfy (God), 998; **plesyst**, 1040, 1048; **plesyt(h)/(e)**, 1000, 1008, 1035, 1055, **plesyde**, 413, 414,; pass., 440, 468, 1062; **plesant**, a., pleasant, 132, 1058; **plesaunce**, n., satisfaction (of God), 1022; "to yowr most ~," for your greatest satisfaction or pleasure, 78; **plesynge**, vbl sb., source of pleasure; "my ~," to my satisfaction, 1107; see **delectacyon**, **delyght**.

plu; see **joly**.

poynt, n. [*OFr point f. L punctum, a specific place in time or writing; ComRom/OFr pointe f. medL puncta, to pierce. in ME two senses combined; evolution of meaning restricted to E*] point, rule, provision, 1005; **poyntys**, pl., 998, 1064.

pollucyon, n. [*OFr* *pollution* ult. f. *L* *polluere*, soil, defile] desecration, especially through fornication, 477.

pompyus, a. [*OFr* *pompeux* f. *L* *pompa*] processional ostentatious, 1121.

pore, a./n. [*OFr* *poure* f. *L* *pauper*] a., poor, lacking in wealth, plain, 676; sb., the poor, 1000.

pouert, n. [*OFr* *poureté* ult. f. *L* *pauper*] poverty, 667.

powre, n. [*OFr* *poeir* f. popL *potere*, be able; modern spelling f. 14c] power, 324.

pray, prayer(s); see **prey**.

praty, a. [*OE* *prætti3* f. *prætt*, n., trick, wile] pretty, 815.

prechors, n. pl. [*OFr* *prech(e)or* ult. f. *L* *predicare*, proclaim] preachers, 488.

precyus, a. [*OFr* *precios* f. *L* *pretiosus*] costly, valuable, 0sd, 454; **precyosnes**, richness, 33.

prey, pray v. [*OFr* *prier* f. clL *prerare*, entreat] tr., pray to, 988; intr., pray, 433, 1054; **preyde**, 427; subj., 1056; **prayer, preyer**, n. formal prayer, part of monastic discipline, 402, 411, 966; **prayers**, pl., 471.

prerogatyff, n. [*OFr* *prerogative* (lit 14c) f. *L* *prærgotiva*, previous choice of election] sovereign right, 49.

presens, n. [*OFr* *presence* (lit 12c) f. *L* *præsentia*, presence] inner being, inner sight, 929.

present, v. [*OFr* *presenter* (lit 11c) f. *L* *præsentare*, place before] present, give, 84.

present, adv. [*OFr* *present* (lit 11c) f. *L* *præsens*, prp. of *præesse*, be at hand or before] present, 8, 46, 1099.

presumynge, prp. [*OFr* *presumer* f. *L* *præsumere*, take] usurping, taking possession without right, showing arrogance, 335.

preue, preve, prowe, v. [[*OFr* *prover* f. *L* *probare*, test] tr prove by argument, 399, 642; **prove**, 378* (M = **provyt**); intr., "~ forfett." prove (the goods) forfeited (to me), i.e. win the legal case, 806; **prewynge**, prp., proving logically, 541.

pryde, n. [lOE *pryto* adopted f. OFr *prud* circa 1000] pride as deadly sin, 529, (personified) 716; ostentation, 555; **prowde**, a., proud, vain, 324sd.

prykkys, n. pl. [*OE pric(c)a*] thorns, 1060.

prynce, n. [*OFr prince (lit 12c)* f. *L princeps*, a., first; as sb. = leader, sovereign ruler] prince, 267.

pryncypall, a. [*OFr principe* f. *L principium*, origin] primary, foremost, 288.

prywe, v. [*Probable error for brywe* f. *ON brifask*] thrive, flourish, 1017.

procedyth, v. 3 sg. pr. intr. [*OFr proceder* f. *L procedere*, advance] proceeds, takes loyal action, 653.

proclame, v. [*L proclamare*, cry out, especially in defense before a judge] proclaim (them to be), praise (them as being), 599.

profyght, v. intr. [*OFr profiter*] profit, benefit, 457, 1004.

propyrly, adv. [*OFr propre* ult. f. *L propriare*, make one's way] suitably, specifically, 9; intrinsically, as a reflection of his (God's) own being, 142.

propyrte, n. [*OFr propriété* f. *L proprius*, own, proper] exclusive attribute, charaterizing feature, 1, 182.

prosperyte, n. [*OFr prosperité* ult. f. *L prosperare*, succeed] prosperity, 37.

proteccyon, n. [*OFr protection* ult. f. *L protegere*, protect] protection, 988.

prowde; see **pryde**.

prove; **prowe**; see **preue**.

prudent, a. [*OFr prudent* f. *L prudens*, skilled] wise, discerning; "~ vyrgyns," prudent virgins, identified with the five wits, (associated with the daughters of Jerusalem), 162; **prudentes**, n. pl., "quinque ~," five wits, 173, identified with the prudent virgins of l. 162.

pure, a. [*OFr pur(e)* ult f. *L purare*, cleanse] pure, uncorrupted, clean, 55, 219, 267; **puryfyethe**, v. 3 sg. pr., purifies, 54; see **clene**.

purfyled, pp. a. [*OFr porfiler* ult. f. *L pro/per* + *filum*, thread] trimmed, bordered, 16sd.

purge, v. [*OFr purgier (lit 12c)* f. *L purgare*, cleanse] expurgate, purify, 305; **purger**, vbl. sb., purifier, that which removes the stain of sin, 962.

puryfyethe; see **pure**.

purpull, a. [*ONor purple ult. f. L purpura, early name of the shellfish yielding Tyrian purple; modern spelling replaced OE purpur(e) 15c*] royal purple, 0sd.

purpos, v. [*OFr purposer*] resolve, 384.

purs, n. pl. [*OE purs*] purse, moneybag, 804.

pursew v. tr. [*AFr pursiwer ult. f. L prosequere, follow*] comply with, 387.

pussychaunce, n. [*OFr puissance (lit 12c)*] an armed force, 1024.

put, v. [*IOE putian*] tr., put, cause to be, 955; intr. pp. pass., "~ arome," sent away, put at a distance, 524.

py-; listed as if **pi-**.

Q

qwytte, v. [*OFr quiter f. medL quitare, absolve*] repay (for injury done), 849.

R

rampaunt, a. [*OFr rampant f. ramper (12c) crawl, climb, origin uncertain*] standing on the hind legs, 692sd.

raveyn, n. [*OFr ravine f. L rapina f. rapere, seize*] robbery, rape, **greed** (personified), 727.

rawe, v. intr. [*OFr raver, rare variant of rêver, dream*] declaim in a poetic rapture, 837.

reasun; see **reson(e)**.

rebaldry, n. [*OFr rebau(l)derie*] debauchery, 749; see **clene**.

rebuk, v. [*ONFr rebuker, beat*] reprove, 842.

receyuyde, v. pp., trans. [*OFr recoivre f. L recipere*] received. 1115.

rechace, n. [*Poss. f. OFr !rachas f. !rachat, recheaf*] call to summon hounds; "made þe deullys ~," turned into a hunting ground for the devil, 908.

rechases, v. [*OFr rechasser (13c)*] drive out, chase back; possibly meaning to call the hounds together (in which case, see **rechace**), implied pl., 722* (M = **rechase**).

reclusyde, v. pp. [*OFr reclurer f. L recludere, seclude*] enclosed, cloistered, 911.

recognycyon, n. [*L recognoscere, identify, recognize*] knowledge, acknowledgment of obligation, 1087.

recomendynge, v. prp. [*OFr recommender, rare variant of recommander*] refl., entrusting (myself), 324.

reconsylyde, v. pp. [*OFr reconciler (12c) f. L reconciliare, reunite physically or in thought of feeling*] reconcile; "be ~," be restored to harmony, 984.

recordaunce, n. [*OFr recordance (MED)*] giving (false) testimony, 791.

recure, v. [*L recurare, recover*] (law), obtain possession of, 217; **recurythe**, 3 sg. pr., collect damages through legal action, 654; **recurable**, recoverable, redeemable, 947.

reddure, n. [*ONFr reddure ult. f. L rigida, unyielding*] harsh treatment, 76.

rede, a. [*ComTeut OE read*] red, 692sd.

rede, v. [*ComTeut OE rædan; same word as ModE v. read*] intr., counsel, advise, 469, 1036.

redy, a. [*eME rædi3 prob. f. OE (3)ræde put in order, prepare*] already prepared, easy, 644; **redyly**, adv., easily, willingly, 820.

reducyde, v. 2 sg. pa. [*L reducere, restore*] led back to virtue, restored to God, 313.

reforme, v. [*OFr reformer f. L reformare*] intr., be restored, 1122; **reformynge**, prp., "in ~ of my place," to restore my place, as a replacement for me, 337; **reformyt(h)(e)**, 3 sg. pr. tr., restore, reform. 120, 127, 968; **reformyde**, pp., 1109, 1118, 1124, 1133; "be ~." (you) are reformed 1092, 1107, 1111, 1129, 1150.

refreyn, v. [*OFr refrener (12c) f. L refrenare, bridle*] restrain, 1038.

refusyde, pp. a. [*OFr refuser f. L refusum, pp. of refundere, pour*] rejected, 148.

regall, a. [*OFr regal(e)* or *L regalis* f. *rex, king*] regal, royal, 0sd.

regent, n. [*OFr regent* f. *L regare, govern, rule*] regent, 707; see **madam**.

regne, reyn(ge), v. [*OFr regner* ult. f. *L regnum*] live in glory (in heaven), 263; "in blys (. . .) ~," live in the perfect joy of heaven, 192, 1116, 1140; **regyn**, n., reign, 760; see **moche**.

reynande, prp. [*OFr aresnier* f. *L adrationare: ad,* to + *rationare, reason, talk; reyne* is an aphetic variation of English verb *arreyne*] arraigning, formally accusing of crimes, 679.

reysyst, v. 3 sg. pr. [*ON reisa*] tr., raises, lifts up, 318;

resythe, intr., rise up, is elevated, 231.

reioys, sb. [*OFr rejoiss-* f. *rejoir*] rejoice; "in ~ of," in celebration of, 613.

reke, v. intr. [*ComTeut OE reccan*] care, 808, 816; see **lytyll**.

rekleshede, n. [*OE recceleas + hede*] recklessness, carelessness, appears to be identified with sloth (personified), 753.

relacyon, n. [*OFr relation (14c)* or *L relationem*] account; "by my ~," as far as I know, 422.

reles(s)yt, v. 3 sg. pr. [*OFr relesser* f. *L relaxare, relax*] remits, alleviates, 967, 1012.

reme, n. [*OFr reaume, realme* ult. f. *L regalis*] realm, 162.

remedy(e), n. [*AFr remedie, remedy* f. *L remedium, make well. heal*] deliverance from sin, remedy, 841, 931, 1011; see **souere(y)n**.

remembyr, v., imp. [*OFr remembrer* f. *lL rememorari, mindful*] remember, 1064; refl., "~ the," take heed, bethink yourself, 873.

remene, v. [*Poss. f. OFr remener, bring back* or f. *re-* + *OE mænan, have in mind, remember*] recall, bring back, 956.

remove, remowe, v. [*OFr remouvoir* ult. f. *L removere*] remove, take away, disappear, 68, 596.

rende, v. [*OE rendan*] rend, tear (to pieces), 533; **rent**, pp., flayed, 1052.

renew(e), v. tr./intr. [*ME re-* + *neuen* f. L *renovare*] tr., renew, restore, 386; intr., be restored, 668, 1160; **renuyde**, pp., 1138.

renne, v. [*OE rinnan*, rare variant; or *irnan* + *OE æman; ME form infl. by ON renna*] run, 1049; **rennyt**, 3 pl. pr., 912sd.

rent; see **rende**.

repeyer, v. [*OFr repeirer* f. IL *repatriare*] return, resort, 71.

replicacyon, n. [*OFr replication* ult. f. L *replicare*, *unfold*] reply, rejoinder, 447.

replyede, v. pp., [*OFr replier (law)*] answer a charge or complaint; pass., is answered, responded to in court, 863.

report, v. [*OFr reporter* f. L *reportare*, *carry back*] describe (as), name, 603, 730; **reporture**, n., report, account, 355; "make ~," take note, 265.

reprehende, v. [*L reprehendere*, *rebuke*, *seize*] condemn, 714.

represent, v. [*OFr representer (12c)* f. L *repræsentare*, *place before*, *exhibit*] symbolize, represent dramatically, 101.

repreve, n./v. [*AFr repris* f. *reprendre*, take back, resume; *insertion of v and change of vowel difficult to account for, (OED)*] n., clemency, forgiveness, 1014; v., brings about, results in, 1020; **reprouable**, a., blameworthy, damnable, 537.

reseywyste, v. 2 sg. pr. [*OFr recoivre* f. L *recipere*] receive of God: to take (the soul) into his care, with the implication of taking possession of one's fief, 320.

resythe; see **reysyst**.

reson(e), **resun(e)**, **reasun**, n. [*OFr reisun*, *reson* f. L *rationem*] cognitive faculty (divided into higher and lower parts), 141, 145, 298, 1130; good sense, wisdom, 227, 523; "~ of," explanation of, 2; "by ~," in a way dictated by reason = OFr par raison, (according to reason), reasonably, 10; "of ~," with good cause, 113; "~ veray," true reason, spiritual truth, 155; "by hys ~ wythin," through the faculty of reason which God has instilled in us, 160; "haue ~," are right, 445; "wyth ~," with rational argumentation, 482; **resons**, pl., reasons, 448*, 480; see **know(e)**; **ne(y)ther**; **sensualyte**.

resort(e), v. [*OFr resortir*, *rebound*] resort, return, 800; go to for aid, 207, 938, 940, 991.

resorte, n. [*OFr* _res(s)ort_, *resource, aid, spring f.* _resortir_; *see* **resort(e)**, *v.*] retinue, group of associates, 692.

rest, v./n. [*OE* _ræstan/ræst(e)_, _rest(e)_] y., rest, 380; ꞑ., rest, quiet, 59; "at ~," in a state of repose, 742; **restynge**, prp. a., "~ place," abode 132, 176; see **tyght(e)**.

restore, v. tr. [*OFr* _restorer_ f. L _restaurare_] restore to original condition, 239; re-establish, 327.

resun(e); see **reson(e)**.

resurreccyon, n. [*OFr* _resurrecciun_, ult. f. L _resurgere_, *resurge, rise again*] resurrection, 940; "haue a new ~," be newly reborn, 1071; see **lyff**.

retenance, n. [*OFr* _retenance_ f. _retenir_, *retain*] retinue, 686.

retorne, v. [*OFr* _retorner_] return, 912sd, 943; **retornys**, n. pl., writ returns, reporting extent to which writ has been carried out, 791.

reuell, n. [*OFr* _revel_, *tumult f.* L _rebellare_, _rebel_] riotous merry-making, 505.

reuerens, n. [*OFr* _reverence_ f. L _reventia_] deep respect for sacred character of God. 1147; "for my ~," out of respect for my revered or sacred status as God, 1038.

revylyde, v. pp. [*OFr* _reviler_ + _-yde_] be degraded, debased, 985.

rewlyde, v. pp. [*OFr* _r(e)uler_ + _-yde_ f. L _regulare_, *regulate*] rule, "be not ~ ordynatly." do not submit to orderly guidance or authority, do not listen to reason, 138.

reyall, **ryall**, a. [*OFr* _roial_ f. L _regalem_] royal, high-born, belonging to the king, 0sd*, 585; see **hood(e)**.

ryche, a./n. [*ComTeut OE* _rice_; *Goth* _reiks_ *represents an eTeut adoption of Celtic* _rix_ = L _rex_, *king*] a., splendid, royal, 0sd, 16sd; powerful, exalted in society, wealthy, 503, 585, 866; ꞑ., those prosperous or wealthy, those possessing riches, 601; **rycher**, adv., richer; "be seen ~," project an image of greater wealth and position, 818.

ryches n. [*OFr* _richeise_, *wealth, opulence; in E pl. form construed as a sg. noun*] wealth (spiritual), 37; (worldly), 458, 474, 582, 587.

ryght, a./adv./n. [*ComTeut OE rihf*] a., right hand side, 0sd, 36; true, whole, upright, 993; adv., by right, 121; quite, 486; "~ nought/non," absolutely nothing, of no worth, 201, 234, 628, 676; n., equity, justice, 668, 738; "þe ~," justice. 722; **ryghtusnes**, n., divine justice, 1157; **tak(e)**.

ryse, v.[*ComTeut OE risan, (rare)* f. *arisan, arise; not found outside Teuf*] recover from a spiritual fall, 202.

ryve, v. tr.[*ON rifan*] tear out, 175. NOTE: Could be an *aphetic variation (14-15c) of OFr ariver ult. f. L adriba, "to shore"; once assimilated in E = "to land"*, meaning to attain or achieve as a result of continuous effort; hence, without emendation the line would read: "Ye Godys ymage euer xall ~," shall always achieve the image of God, 175.

roddys, n. pl. [*OE rodd*] rods, sticks, 1017.

rore, v. [*OE rarian*] roar, 325.

rose, n. [*OE rose* f. *L rosa; in ME reinforced by OFr rose*] rose (considered of surpassing beauty, fragrance, and color), 388.

rought, pp. a. [*OE ruh*] rough, covered with wounds. 1051; rought as an early variation of rough does not conform to rhyme scheme.

row, v. [*OE rowan*] row (used figuratively), 491.

rowte, v. [*OFr router* f. *route, band or troop*] behave riotously in a raucous group, 505.

rubbyt, v. 3 sg. pr. [*ME/LG rubben; ety. obscure*] clean by rubbing, 964.

ruthe, n. [*eME reuðe* f. *rewen, v. + ON hryggð*] the pity of God. 316; mischief, 720*.

ry-, listed as if ri-.

S

sacramentys; **sakyrment**.

sage, a. [*OFr sage (11c) ult. f. L sapere, be wise; ME term "the sage" often followed proper name; instance in* **Wisdom** = *collective "we"*] gravely wise, dignified, as tempered by age and experience. 892.

say; see **sey**.

sakyrment, n. [*OFr sacrement, ult. f. L sacrare, consencrate*] sacrament, 1111; **sacramentys**, pl., the seven Catholic sacraments, 124, 125; see **penance**.

saluacyon, n. [*OFr sauvacion, salvatiun ult. f. L salvare, save*] salvation, 450, 465.

same, pron. [*ComTeut-lost in OE; ME same, sama; retained only in E & Scand*] the same, 0sd.

satysfye, v. tr. [*OFr satysfier f. L satisfacere, do enough*] atone for, (theo.) used of Christ's sacrifice, 1080; **satysfaccyon**, n. (theo.), atonement for sins (associated with Wyll); 3rd and final step leading to penitence (the others being **confessyon** and **contricyon**; "yeldynge du ~," making full restitution for sin, 975; see **confes**; **contricyon**; **trespas**.

sauyde; see **save**.

sauour; see **sawowre**.

sauowr, n. [*OFr saueour*] saviour, God, 208.

save, v. [*OFr sauver f. L salvare, save*] deliver from sin, "Gode me ~," God save me, (ironic oath), 834; **sauyde**, 2 sg. pa., saved, 311.

sawowre, **sauour**, n./v. [*OFr savour, savourer ult. f. L sapere, taste*] n., fragrance, 388; **sauour**, v., savor, take pleasure in, 87; see **cunnynge**.

say; see **sey**.

schadow, n. [*OE scead(u)we*] shadow; "dyrke ~. . . of humanyte," shadow of sin and death, 166.

schame, n. [*ComTeut OE sc(e)amu*] shame, consciousness of guilt, 597, 608.

schappe, n. [*OE 3esceap*] image, represented form, 20.

scharpe, a. [*ComTeut OE scearp*] prickly, 1050, 1060.

sche, pron. 3rd sg. nom. [*Origin uncertain, probably f. OE seo*] she, 816, 835.

schendeschyppe, n. [*OE (3e)scendan, shame + OE -scype*] disgraceful behavior, 634.

scheptur, n. [*OFr sceptre*] royal scepter, 0sd.

schere, n. [*OE scir*] shire-court (county court), 851.

schew, v. [*ComWG OE sceawian, look at (shift in meaning circa 1200 difficult to account for)*] illlustrate through logical "proof," "Sen I xall ~ hym perfyghtnes . . . ," I shall show him perfection [to be] sin, 377; display, show, 726; **sew**, show, reveal, 929; **schewyde**, pp., 746; **schewynge**, **schewenge**, prp., revealing, 540, 992.

schylyngys, n. pl. [*ComTeut OE scilling*] shillings, 830.

schrew, v. tr. [*OE screawa; not elsewhere in Teut*] curse; "~ I,"/"I ~," I curse, 759, 777.

schrewde, a. [*ME schrewed prob. f. shrew; n. formation coincided w. pp. of schrew, v. f. which some meaning may derive*] cunning, artful, 864; **shrewed**, a., shrewish, loud and boisterous, naughty, 550sd* (M = **screwde**).

schulde; see **xall**.

sckyppe, v. [*MSwed skoppa; history of vowel unclear*] skip, 561.

scolys, n. pl. [*OE scol, anglicized form of scholium f. L schola*] doctrines, 86.

se, n. [*ComTeut sæ*] sea, 1010.

secunde, a. [*OFr second utl. f. L sequi, follow*] second, 1005.

se(e), v. [*ComTeut OE seon*] understand, perceive, take note of, 185, 266, 927; make certain, 298; see, look (at), 501, 503, 650, 725, 747, 880, 1097; imp., 432, 454, 464, 707, 875, 901; inf., 583, 691, 693, 815; **sene**, 3 sg. pr., find, come to know, 59; pp., seen, 1044; **seen**, pp., regarded as, 818; **seyn**, pp., judged, 853; see **let(t)**; **mynde**; **ryche**; **þa(e)t**.

see, n. [*OFr se(d) ult. f. L sedere, sit*] seat, throne, dwelling place of a ruler, (understood theologically as the see of Wysdom), 132.

seyntys; see **sent**.

seke, a. [*ComTeut OE seoc*] corrupted by sin, 947; sick, 1030.

sek(e), v. tr. [*OE secan*] seek, look for, 205, 931, 970; **sowght**, **sowte**, pp., sought, 18, 21.

seker, **sekyr**, a. [*OE sicor (rare); eTeut adoption f. L securus*] certain, sure, 368, 534, 971; secure, 886; **sekyrnes**, n., security; "in ~," in the safety of, 60.

seme, v. [ON *soma*, *beseem*, *befil*] intr. inf., seem, appear, 52, 590; impers., "me ~/(**semyt**)," it seems to me, 445, 485, 554, 567; tr., think, 608, 743; **semyth**, intr., 3 sg. pr., seems, 480, 573; impers., 597; see **dysgysynge**.

sen, see **synne**. ; see **schew**.

send, v. [ComTeut OE *sendan*] absol., send (means), 824; **sent**, set, ordered to go, 1023; pp., 879.

sene; see **se(e)**.

sensyble, a. [OFr *sensible* ult. f. L *sentire*, perceive, *feel*] corporal, bodily, endowed with the faculty of sensation as well as cognition, 96.

sensualyte, n. [OFr *sensualité* f. L *sensualis*] the part of humanity concerned with the senses (as opposed to **reson(e)**), 135, 139, 154, 296, 1070; **sensualite**, n., a name for Wyll, 478.

sent, 2 sg. pa.; see **send**.

sent, a. [OFr *saint/seinf*] saint, a title associated with proper noun,   "~ Audre of Ely," Audrey of Ely, 832; "~ Powle," Paul, 487 903, 1149; **se(y)ntys**, n. pl., 255, 1056.

sepulkyr, n. [OFr *sepulcre* ult. f. L *sepelire*, *bury*] sepulchre, 1024.

ser, sb. [Reduced form of *sire* f. OFr *sire* ult. f. L *senior*] Sir, a title of address: ordinarily used before name of a knight, a gentleman, or an ordinary priest; in the play used by Lucyfer without name as a term of respect or mock respect, 397, 399, 463, 487, 500; "~ Wyly," ironic epithet, poss. referring to Lucyfer himself, 604.

serue, v. tr. [OFr *servir* f. L *servire*, *be a servant or slave*] serve, 630; **serwyt**, 3 sg. pr., is a servant (of God), 144; **serwynge**, prp., "be ~," are servants of, 137; **serwantys**, n. pl., servants, 406.

set(t), v. [ComTeut OE *settan; confusion between **set** & **sit** arose in early 14c*] 1 pl. pr., establish, 786; 1 sg. pr., lay out, 819; fix, set the course of, 492; pp., fixed, set firmly, established, 0sd, 219, 229, 233; remain fixed in one position, 742; value; "~ befor," valued more highly, 417; "~ þe at nought," consider worthless, 764; "~ full of," filled with, 1060; "moche . . . ~ bye," highly valued, 600*; **settys**, intr., 2 sg. pr., set, place value (on); "by myn ~ lyght," place little value on my counsel, 923; see **perfyghte**; **pynne**; **tyght(e)**; **wertu**.

seth, conj.; see **sythe**.

seth(e), v.; see **sey**.

sethe, n. [*Aphetic variation of assethe, caused by mistaking phrase "make assethe" for "make a seth"; see asythe*] atonement, 122.

sevyn, a. [*OE seofon*] seven, 124; **vii**[ie], ellip. a. as sb., seventh, 696, 1045.

sew; see **schew**.

sew(e), v. [*AFr suer/suir = OFr sivre ult. f. L sequi, follow*] tr., seek, 665; follow, carry out, adopt, 383, 429, 431, 1163; intr., "~ of," result in, 369; "~ to," seek, make suit to, 633; absol., "hathe for to ~," must seek, sue for position, favor, 664.

sey, v. [*OE secgan*] say, 485, 885, 899; inf., 161, 750, 752, 864, 884, 1141, 1149; **say**, 208, 430* (M = say); **seth(e)**, 3 sg. pr., 997, 1005, 1013, 1021, 1029, 1037, 1045, 1053, 1057; **seyst**, 2 sg. pr., 888; **seyth** 3 sg. pr., 478; **seyde**, pp., said, 966; mentioned, 237; **seyenge, seyng(e)**, prp., 0sd, 16sd, 324sd; **seyer**, n., spokesman, professional speaker, 864; see **how(e)**; **wene**.

shrewed; see **schrewde**.

syde, a. [*OE side*] reaching or hanging far down (on the person), 16sd, 510; see **aray**; **tasselys**.

syde, n. [*OE side; perhaps related to side, a., denoting the long part or aspect of a thing*] side 36, 37; 1064sd; "on ~," = aside, (slip) aside, 565.

syght(e), n. [*OE sihð (rare), usually 3esihð*] sight, thing seen, 573; poss., sight, power of vision, 68; power of perception, insight, 992, 1097; "Godys ~," sight of God, 118, 335; **syghtys**, pl., sights, powers of vision (internal and external), 1086; see **ey**.

sygnyficacyon, syngnyfycacyon, n. [*OFr signification ult. f. L significare, signify*] signification, symbolical meaning, 13; contrasted to **propertye**, 182; **sygnyfye**, v. 3 pl pr., represent, symbolize, 149.

sylence, n. [*OFr silence ult. f. L silere, be silent*] silence; "kepe ~," observe monastic silence, 435.

symylytude, n. [*OFr similitude ult. f. L similis, like*] likeness, symbolic representation of, 284, 350.

symony(e), n. [*OFr symonie f. medL simonia f. the name of Simon Magus, in allusion to his offer of money to the Apostles, Acts 8.18-19*] simony, 602, 639.

symple, n. [*OFr simple f. L simplus*] common people, simple things, 457.

syn(e); see **synne**.

syne, n. [*OFr si(g)ne f. L signum, mark, token*] sign, a signifying characteristic, 471.

syne, v. [*OE syngian*] engage in sin, 941; **synnyde**, 1 sg. pr. sinned, 315; for related form, see **synne**.

synge, v. [*ComTeut OE singan*] sing, tr., 164sd, 324sd, 751; intr., 613; **syngyth**, 996sd; **syngynge**, prp., singing, 1064sd; **songyn**, pp., sung, 996sd; **songe**, n., song, 324sd.

syngler, a. [*OFr s(e)inguler ult. f. L singularis; Fr form w. -er used until 17c*] solitary, private (and by implication lonely), 441, 452; sole, 574.

syngnyfycacyon; see **sygnyficacyon**.

synne, **syn(e)**, n. [*OE syn(n), poss. related to L sons, guilty*] sin, 53, 91, 111, 117, 125, 126, 140, 153, 158, 224, 235, 304, 311, 332, 362, 473, 474, 528, 545, 951, 962, 974, 978, 980, 1090, 1123; **sen**, 377; **synnys**, pl., 466, 530, 540, 715, 896, 909, 926, 958, 960, 1012, 1070, 1110, 1112, 1137; **synfull**, a., sinful, 930; **synfullnes**, n., sinfulness, 198; **synners**, n. pl., sinners, 425; see **actuall**; **dey**; **fele**; **olde**; **orygynall**; **schew**.

Sypres, n. [*OFr Cypre, island of Cyprus; after the Crusades, place from which various fabrics were brought*] a cloth of gold or other valuable material imported f. Cyprus; "berde of golde of ~ curlyde," curled beard made f. Cyprian cloth of gold, 0sd*.

syster, n. [*ComTeut OE sweoster; modern spelling of Scan derivation*] sister, 1085.

sythe, conj. [*Reduced f. OE siððan*] since, 107, 952; **seth**, 680.

[six], **vi**, a. [*Com Teut OE si(e)x*] six, 692sd, 724sd, 752sd. 912sd; **vi**[ᵗᵉ], ellip. a. used as sb., sixth, 1037.

skyn, n. [*ON skinn*] skin, 168, 490.

slandyr, n. [*OFr eschandle f. ecclL scandalum, cause of offense or stumbling; in Hellenistic lit = snare for an enemy*] slander, 1020.

sleyght, n. [*eMe sleþ/ON sloe3 f. sloeg-r, sly; orig. = "able to strike"*] trickery (personified), 725; **sleyghtys**, **sleyttys**, pl., tricks, 674, 865.

slepers, n. pl. [*OE slæp* + *-ers*] sleepers, idle persons (personified), 753.

slyppe, v. [*Prob. f. MLG slippen*] slip, 565.

slumber, v. [*ME slumerenn perh. f. ME slumen, doze or ME sluma, gentle sleep*] slumber, 894; **slumberyde**, pa., slept, 978.

smale, **small**, a. [*ComTeut OE smæl*] small, 912sd, 1061.

smerte, a. [*OE smeart; not in cogn. langs.*] sharp, 1101.

smylynge, vbl. sb. [*ME smilen*] smile, 596.

snowte, n. [*ME snute; origin obscure, prob. f. LG*] contemptuous expression for the nose, especially when mishapen, 506.

so, adv./a./conj. [*ComTeut OE swa*] adv., so (much, great, many), 49, 67, 85, 331, 360, 390, 567, 607, 641, 655, 658, 671, 673, 675, 679, 729, 842, 862, 905, 907, 942, 982, 1004, 1091, 1139; a. phrase, "~ many," so many, 910; conj., thus, 526, 531, 542, 662, 683, 834; "~ þat," so that, 367, 856, 1061; "& ~," and thus, 376, 484, 912sd, 1162; see **neuer**; **moche**; **þa(e)t**; **vse**.

solace, n. [*OFr solas ult. f. L solari, comfort, console*] solace, comfort, 574.

soleyn, a. [*Prob. f. AFr !solein f. OFr sol, sole*] alone (because of one's superiority over others), aloof, 577.

some; see **sum(m)/(e)**.

son, adv. [*OE sona*] soon, quickly, 595.

son(e), **sune**, n. [*ComTeut OE sunu*] son; "þe/the (. . .) ~," son of God, Christ, 10, 13, 280, 1067, 1157.

songe; see **synge**.

soper, n. [*OFr soper, super*] supper, 817.

sor(r)e, adv. [*OE sare*] severely, 331; vigorously, 790.

sorow(e), n. [*ComTeut OE sorh, sorȝ*] sorrow caused by recognition of sin, (a key to achieving penitence) 196, 967, 977; "~ veray," true sorrow of heart, 963.

sothe, n. [*OE soð*] truth, 750; see **wene**, adv..

souere(y)n, a./n. [*OFr soverain* ult. f. L *super*, *above*] a., sovereign, royal, designates attributes of Wysdom, 39, 77, 1145; of God as creator, 69; "~ joy," sovereign joy (addressed to Christ) 83; "~ auctoure," sovereign author, 99; "~ lorde," sovereign lord, 309; "~ remedy," sovereign remedy, 1011; "vertu ~," sovereign virtue, 1036; "~ person," sovereign person, (Ihesus), 1142; **souereyn**, n., "lowyde ~," beloved sovereign, a term used to imply the relationship of a ruler or feudal sovereign to a subject, 261; **souereyngys**, n. pl., social superiors, 588; **souerenly**, adv., royally, as a sovereign, 259, 1057; to a supreme degree, 254; see **fayer(e)**; **gouernyde**.

soule, soull, sowle, sowll, n. [*ComTeut OE sawol*] the soul, used frequently in the modern sense, often personified as a central character; 16, 55, 92, 96, 101 . . . 1160; **sowlys**, pl., 45, 107, 171; **soullys**, 260; see **clene**; **euery**; **pynne**; **w(h)at**.

sowght, sowte; see **sek(e)**.

sowle, sowll; see **soule**.

space, n. [*OFr espace* ult. f. L *spatiari, walk, extend*] place, 719; distance, 1018.

spar(e), v. [*ComTeut OE sparian*] tr., save from harm, 295; save money, 584, 709, 736; intr., refrain, hold back, 508, 614, 769, 771; **sparyth**, 3 sg. pr., tr., spares, 76.

speche, n. [*OE spræc, sprec; -r- obs. by mid-12c*] saying, utterance, 275; speech, 719, 1038; see **fayer**.

specyall, n./a. [*OFr especial* f. L *specialis, individual. particular* f. *specere, look, behold*] n., particular intimate, 131, 1113; a., "~ grace," the redemptive grace of God, 203, 946: **specyally**, adv., above all, particularly, 11, 19, 58, 390, 1008. 1139: see **Cryst**.

specyfye, v. tr. [*OFr specifier* f. medL *specificare, descrbe*] descrbe in detail, 65, 407.

spede, v./n. [*OE spedan/OE spowan, prosper*] v. intr., succeed, 800; tr. imp., assist, aid; "þe/the dewyll/deuell:me/hym ~," the devil help me/him, 508, 620; refl. imp., "yll ~ þe," bad luck to you. 769; n. aid. help, 636.

speke, v. [*OE sprecan*] talk, 40, 41; **spekynge**, prp. saying. speaking, 591; **spoke**, pp., declared, 64.

spellys, v. 3 sg. pr. [*OFr espeller; of Germanic origin*] comprehends, especially through careful study or observation. 275.

spende, v. [*OE* *spendan f. *L expendire*, pay, weigh out; *ME spende* possibly an aphetic variation of *OFr despendre*, dispense] spend, 646, 709, 736, 820, 828; **spendys**, spends, gives out money rather than taking it in, 801.

spyll, v. [*OE spillan*] tr., destroy, 713; defile (the soul), 526; intr., perish, be damned, 215, 292.

spoyll, v., imp. refl. [*OFr espoillier* f. *L spoliare*] strip (yourself), 1137.

spoke; see **speke**.

spows(e), n. [*OFr sp(o)us*] spouse, 15, 19, 57, 69, 1085; see **haue**; **tak(e)**.

spousebreche, n. [*OFr sp(o)us*, spouse + *OE bryce*, breach; after *OE æwbryce*, adultery] adulterer (personified), 755.

sprede, v. [*OE sprædan*] spread; "abrode . . . ~"/"~ abrode," stretch forth, stretch out, 453, 1102.

sprynge, v./n. [*ComTeut OE (a)springan* f. *OFr espringuer*, dance/*OE spryng*] v., grow, 92, 1159; originate, 288, 1028; jump quickly, 561, 615; n., dance; "~ of Lechery," a dance led by lechery, (personified), 747; **spronge**, pp. a., sprang, derived, descended (from), 124.

stable, adv. [*OFr stable* ult. f. *L stare*, stand] steadfastly, 944.

stande; see **stonde**.

starre, v. [*OE starian*] stare; "swere & ~," swear and stare (phrase denoting rage), 739.

stat, n. [*Aphetic variation of OFr estat* ult. f. *L stastare*, stand] spiritual condition, 880.

stedfast, adv. [*OE stedefasf*] firmly fixed; " haue ~," firmly place, 48.

stenche, n. [*OE stenc*] stench, 1099.

stepe, n. [*OE stæpe, stepe*] step, 1044.

ster(r)e, v. [*OE stieran* f. *ComTeut !steuro*, rudder; *OE* sense "to rebuke" may be related to *OE !stere*, strong, severe] induce by suggestive means, 527, 1046; **sterynge**, prp. sb., inward prompting, suggestion, 153; **steryngys**, pl., 304.

sterrys, n. pl. [*OE steorra*] stars, 29; see **dysposicyon**.

stew(y)s, n. poss./pl. [*OFr estuve* f. *vulgar L stup(h)a*; *related to Teut root !stud*; *in OE stuf-bæþ, hot air bath*] n. poss., brothel, so-called because of frequent use of hot-air baths as brothels, 749; pl., section of city occupied by brothels, 800; see **clene**.

stynke, v. [*ComWG OE stincan*] stink, 896.

stodyes, n. pl. [*OFr estudie* f. *L studium, zeal, affection*] meditations, 470.

stonde, **stande**, v. [*ComTeut OE standan*] flourish, 678; 1 sg. pa., remained stedfast, 317; **stondyt**, 3 sg. pr., exists, 220; **stondyth**, 3 sg. pr., stands erect, 289; **stondynge**, prp., standing firmly, 172.

stonys, n. pl. [*ComTeut OE stan*] precious gems, 0sd.

stoppyt, v., 3 sg. pr. [*OE !stoppian*] hinder or prevent a legal action from taking place or legal judgment from being rendered, 862.

store, n. [*Aphetic variation of OFr astore* f. *estorer, build*] "in ~," adv. phrase, in abundance, 1003.

streytt, a. [*Adjectival use of pp. of strecchen, stretch; ComWG OE streccan*] narrow, stretched out, 729; **streytly**, adv., strictly, 1033; **streightly**, adv., rigidly, 584* (M = **strenght**); see **as**.

strengtheth, v. 3 sg. pr. [*OE !strengan*] strengthen morally, 55.

stryve,v. [*OFr estriver, quarrel, contend*] fight, strive, 661; **stryvande**, prp., fighting, quarrelling, 779.

sturdynes, n. [*OFr estourdi, violent + -nes*] fierceness (personified), 693.

substance, n. [*OFr substance* ult. f. *L substare, stand under*] essence, essential nature, 80; goods, wealth, 762.

suche, demon. a. [*OE swelc*] such, of the same kind as, 304. 305, 441, 848.

sue; see **sew(e)**.

suffer, **suffyr**, v. tr./intr. [*OFr soffrir* ult. f. *L sufferire, to bear*] tr., endure, undergo, 1063; intr., hold out, endure (patiently) 1013; **suffyryth**, 3 sg. pr., suffers, 1019.

suffycyent, a. [*OFr sufficient* ult. f. *L sufficere*] sufficient; as a legal term, implies a document adequate to achieve a legal result; as a theological term, usually assoc. w. grace, as a term implying "adequate," often assoc. w. efficient, as sufficient and efficient grace; can also refer to a person adequate or equal to his task or position; in this instance, the position of the term is ambiguous; it may modify **asythe** or **fadyr**: a) "**make asythe** . . . ~,**"** make a sufficient penance for atonement for sinfulness or b: "**fadyr** ~," God as a father capable of granting sufficient grace, 1096; **suffysyt(h)**, v., 3 sg. pr., "~ to," suffices for, 147, 465.

suggestyon, **suggestyun**, n. [*OFr suggestioun* ult. f. *L suggerere, suggest*] prompting or incitement to evil the first of three steps to sin; associated with Mynde, 301, 365, 400, 497; see **delectacyon**; **co(n)sent**.

sum(m)/(e), demon. pron./a. [*ComTeut OE sum*] **pron.**, some, 439, 519, 866; **some**, 743; **sum**, **a.**, some, 483, 766.

sumtyme, adv., [*ComTeut OE sum* + *OE tima*] and then, occasionally, 425, 426, 802; formerly, 516, 588; "~ . . . ~," at certain times . . . at other times, 427, 647.

sune; see **son(e)**.

support(e), v./n. [*OFr supporter* f. *L supportare, carry*] **v. tr.**, maintain, support financially, provide social position, 635; see **to-support**.

suppos, v. [*OFr sup(p)oser* f. *L supponere*] suppose, guess, 422.

sure, adv./a. [*OFr sure* f. *L securus, without care*] **adv.**, sure, certain, 50, 216; **a.**, secure, safe, 264; see **as**.

surfet, n. [*OFr surfet, excess, surplus*] surfeit, excess (personified), 754; **surphettys**, pl., 435.

sut(e), n. [*OFr sieute, ult. f. L !sequere, follow*] livery; "in . . . ~," wearing the livery of a patron, 324sd, 692sd, 724 sd, 752sd.

swere, v. [*ComTeut OE swerian*] swear, 642, 739; **swore**, pp. tr., 699; see **starre**.

swet(e) a. [*ComTeut OE swete*] beloved, 70, 1066; fragrant, 92, pleasing to the ear, 758; "~ herte," beloved one, dear heart, 1103; **swetter**, comp., sweeter, 388.

swyn, n. [*ComTeut OE swin*] swine, 831.

swyre, n. [*OE sweora*] neck, 1102.

swore; see **swere**.

sy-; listed as if **si-**.

T

(including *þ/th* as if *th-*)

tabernacull, n. [*OFr* *tabernacle* *ult. f. L* *taberna, hut*] in Jewish history, the tent housing the Ark; in Christian theology, the box containing the Host; "~ of Cedar," the Temple of Solomon, 167.

tak(e), v. [*IOE* *tacan* *(circa 1100) f. ON* *taka, grasp, seize; in ME it replaced OE* *niman, possess*] take, 221, 228, 240, 457, 476, 624, 640, 646, 660, 676, 765, 802, 1025; pp., taken, paid, 676; imp., 900; "~ to me," keep for myself, 807; "~ not drede," keep in mind, hold no fear, 895; "mynde ~," keep in mind, 957; "~ Vndyrstondynge," understand, 1125; **taketh**, 3 sg. pr., 483; **takyt**, 3 sg. pr., 550sd; "~ . . . to spowse," marries, devotes oneself to, 57; **takynge**, prp., inheriting, 111; **toke**, 2 sg. pa., "~ to yowr mercy," show me your mercy, 1079; see **amende**; **cure**; **entent**; **hede**; **thought**; **vengeaunce**.

tarythe, v. tr. 3 sg. pr. [*Origin uncertain; possibly linked to OE* *ter3an, vex or OFr* *tarier, tease*] delay, 872.

tasselys, n. pl. [*OFr* *tas(s)el*] a pendant ornament prob. made of cords or a large fringe; "knottys of golde & syde ~," tassles hanging from two knots or buttons of gold, 16sd.

tastyt, v. 3 sg. pr. [*OFr* *taster* *ult. f. L* *taxare, touch, feel, taste (13-14c)*] tastes, 50; **tastyde**, 1 sg. pa., 1100.

teche, v. [*OE* *tæcan*] teach, 86; **tawt**, 2 sg. pa., taught, 314.

tell, v. [*OE* *tellan*] tr., describe, 626; tell, 879; count, 583; intr., tell, say, describe, 62, 776; **telles**, implied pl., 270* (M = **tell**); **tolde**, pp., told, 64; see **howe**, a.

temple, tempull, n. [*OE* *temp(e)l; reinforced by OFr* *temple* *f. L* *templum*] temple, dwelling place of God, 264, 1108; see **as**.

tempte, v. [*OFr* *tempter* *f. L* *temptare, try*] tempt, 331, 345. 361, 373.

tende, vbl. sb. [*Aphetic variation of OFr* *adtendre* *f. L* *adtendere, stretch*] listen to, 355.

tender, v. [*OFr* *tendrir; see* ***tender***, a.] receive favorably, 461.

tender, a. [*OFr tendre, soft, delicate; linked w. tender, v. meaning highly value*] tender, delicate; " ~ of age," young, 890; **tendyrly**, adv., tenderly, 67; **tenderschyppe**, n., esteem; "in grett ~," (held) in great esteem, 631.

tenker, n. [*Origin uncertain; echoic term poss. onomotopaeic*], in a clumsy and inefficient manner, i.e., like a tinker, a craftsman who mends things (often thought to be a bungler), 752.

tenowr, n. [*OFr tenor ult. f. L tenere, hold*] a tenor voice in music, 617.

tere, n. [*OE tear*] tear, 963, 1006.

terme, n. [*OFr terme, (Ch de Rol) f. L terminum, limit, boundary*] term appointed for courts of law, especially the King's Bench, Common Pleas, and Chancery, which all sat at Westminster, 790.

þan, than, then, conj./adv./dem. pron. [*OE þanne, þænne, used as comparative conjunctive particle and as adv. of time; originally same word*] conj., than, 33, 606, 646, 904, 1009, 1016, 1023, 1032, 1041, 1049, 1056, 1059, 1063; adv., then, used frequently in the modern sense, 113, 119, 139, 140. 207 . . . 1141; **then**, dem. adv., then, as a result of this understanding, 785; **than**, rare variant of **that**, deriving from þaem,the dative singular of OE þaet, that, 493; see **fowll(e)**; **þa(e)t**.

than, þan, dem. pron. [*ME repr. OE þam, dat. sing of þæt, that*] that, 1040, 1048; see **þat**.

þa(e)t, that, dem. pron./rel. pron./a./conj. [*OE þaet*] that, used frequently in the modern sense, (most common form, **þat**), 3, 21, 34, 40, 66* . . . 141* (M = **the**) . . . 340* . . . 416* (M = **þis**) . . . 430* . . . 1164; "or ~," before, 226; imp.,"se ~," see that, 298; "so ~," so that, in order that, 367; equivalent to **what**, 713, 807, 922, 924; **þat**, rare variant of **þan**, following a comp., than, 1001; see **care**; **lyff**; **mynde**; **nede**; **þan**; **wer**; **wyche**; **worde**.

þe, the, def. art./adv. [*OE se(o); later þe, þeo þaeþ*] def. art., the, used frequently in the modern sense, 0sd(*), 1, 2, 7, 10 . . . 380*. 388* . . . 1157; adv., "~ more verely," the more truly, 98; "~ . . . ~." by how much . . . by so much, 797; see **abowt(e)**; **actuall**; **all**; **at**; **blake**; **bon**; **dysposicion**; **fende**; **go**; **in**; **jug(e)ment(e)**; **last**; **lengthe**; **lewe**; **merowre**; **more**; **natur**; **n[e]ther**; **passyon**. **pyttys**; **place**; **rechace**; **ryght**; **son(e)**; **spede**; **ver(r)ay**; **wey**. **wyrry**; **wys(e)**; **worlde**.

the, pron. 2 sg. pl.; see **thou**.

the, v. [*OE þion, þeon*] prosper, 866, 867.

thedyr, adv. [*OE þæder; later OE ðider, þider* under infl. of *hider*] thither, 199, 732; see **hedyr**.

þey, they, pron., 3 pl. nom. [*eME þei* f. *ON þeir*] they, used frequently in the modern sense, 46, 52, 53, 138, 146 . . . 996sd; **thay**, 878; **thei**, 254* (M = **þe**), 256* (M = **þer**), 305* (M = **the**); **þer, poss.**, 48, 438, 746, 895, 896; **pron.**, an obs. variation of **þey**, 298; **them**, obj., 68, 664, 810, 811, 939; see **all**; **hem**; **her**.

þer, ther, adv. [*OE þaer, þar, þer*] there, 107, 223, 346, 438, 463, 490, 572, 649, 650, 659, 661, 667, 679, 774, 800, 801, 837, 859, 861, 1027, 1093; **þer**, conj. adv., where, 805, 806; **þerby**, adv., because of that, 845; **therfor, þerfor**, adv., therefore, 13, 222, 225, 469, 632, 705, 938, 983; **þerin(ne)**, adv., in that (place, condition, fact) 302, 308, 345, 498, 911; **þerof**, adv., of that, 50; **þeron**, adv., thereon, 889; **þerto**, adv., to that, 299, 499; **therto**, 689; **þerwp(p)on**, adv., thereupon, 0sd, 450; **þerwppeon**, 16sd; **þervpon**, 724sd; **thore**, adv., in that way, 329, 413; see **go**; **lende**.

þer, pron.; see **þey**.

þi/thi; see **thou**.

thynge, n. [*ComTeut OE þing*] thing, 1026; "no ~," nothing, 297; imp. pl., things, 465; "all ~," everything, 58, 291, 379, 401* (M = **thnge**), 475, 1047; **thyngys**, pl., 133, 146, 442, 607.

thynke, v. [*OE þenc(e)an*] think, reflect, 889; imp., 450; **thynkynge**, prp., 195.

thys, þis, dem. pron./a. [*OE þes, þeos, þis; orig. nom. neuter sg., now sole sg. form of OE dem. þes*] this, used frequently in the modern sense, 13, 18, 38, *66, 73 . . . 258* . . . 371* (M = **hys**) . . . 732* (M = **þe**) . . . 1121; **þis**, pl., these, 721, 760; **thes**, pl., these, 149, 277, 288, 402, 574, 607, 612, 613, 709, 715, 767, 883, 960. 1064; see **aboue**; **damesellys**; **dyspute**; **feer**; **how(e)**; **in**; **lande**; **maner(e) of(f)**; **place**; **thus**; **wys(e)**.

thore; see **ther**.

thornys, n. pl. [*OE þorn*] thorns, 1050.

thorow, prep. [*OE þurh*] through, 1049; by means of, 311. 1150; throughout, 760.

þ(o)u, thou, thow, pron. 2 sg. (familiar) [*ComTeut OE þu*] used frequently in the modern sense, 163, 310, 311, 312, 313 . . . 1061; **tho**, 1076; **the/þe**, obj. cases, 309, 772, 867, 869, 873, 917, 1002, 1071, 1073; **thy**, poss.,

107, 999, 1002, 1038, 1039, 1042, 1069; thi, þi poss., 80, 81, 94, 324*
(M = þu), 770 . . . 1104; see dysposicyon; forth(e); how(e);
passyon; remembyr; turne.

though, see thow, conj..

thought, n. [OE *þoht*] thought, what one thinks, 218; the thinking faculty, the
    mind, 236; the process of thinking, 661; "take no ~," refuse to think
    about the consequences of action, 624, 660; thowte, thought, 955.

thow, though, conj. [OE *þe(a)h*; *-o-* forms f. ON *þoh* infl. spelling, replacing
    native form in lit by 15c] although, 75, 362, 602, 668, 670, 808, 809,
    957; even though, 740* (M = thouht).

thow, þow, dem. pron. [OE *þa*] those, 163, 470, 686, 690, 1074.

thowsende, a. [OE *þusend* ult. f. Indo-Eur *tus*, multitude, force] thousand, 1049.

thowte; see thought.

thre, iii, a./n. [OE *þri*] a., three (the most frequently used number), 177, 277, 283,
    288, 293, 357, 715, 759, 828, 1033; w. pron. in reference to Mynde,
    Wyll, and Wndyrstondynge, 180, 181, 288, 324sd, 495, 683, 685, 752sd,
    813, 949, 1141; n., 8, 179, 646, 658, 794; threys, adv., thrice, 646;
    iii^de, a., third, 245; ellip. a. as sb., 1013; see myght.

threttys, n. pl. [OE *þreat*] threats, 712.

thryve, v. [ON *þrifask*] thrive, prosper, 662, 788; thryvande, prp., increasing,
    thriving, 778; thryfte, n., prosperity, 644.

thus, adv. [OE *þe(o)s, dem. stem of *þis*;= OSax *thus*] used frequently in the
    modern sense; thus, in this way, 0sd, 16, 16sd, 157, 161 . . . 1149;
    thys, thus, 289, 812, 817, 839.

tyde, n. [OE *tid*] time, 317.

tyght(e), adv. [altered form of *thight* (1375) f. ON *þetir, close in texture, solid*]
    densely as a wood, firmly, closely, securely; "at rest sett als ~," remain
    comfortably fixed as securely as in dense woods (waiting for a victim),
    742; "as ~," as firmly, 855.

tyll, conj./prep. [ON *til*] conj., until, to the time that, 380, 1043, 1051; so that, 847;
    prep., to, 997, 1053.

tyme, n. [*OE tima*] (specific) time, 106; allotted time (for a particular activity), 403; "many a ~," over and over again, 724; **tymys**, pl., times, 1049; **tymes**, "dew ~," allotted time, 401.

to, **ii**, a. [*OE twa*] two, 16sd, 718, 794, 870.

to, adv. [*Stressed form of OE to, prep. (see above); spelled too f 16c*] too, 87, 482; also, 796; see **cunnynge**; **moche**.

to, prep. [*OE to*] to, used frequently in the modern sense, 4, 10, 11, 35, 44 . . . 190* . . . 676* . . . 1152; w. inf. constructions, 41, 91, 194, 204, 223 . . . 1162; as, 19, 57; for, 408; in, 404; w. gerund, 226, 252; see **affynyte**; **aplye**; **arest**; **attende**; **avowe**; **cunnynge**; **dysgysynge**; **fall**; **for**; **haue**; **iug(e)ment(e)**; **last**; **law**; **lyke**; **lyknes**; **loweday**; **nought**; **plenerly**; **ples**; **sew(e)**; **spowse**; **suffycyent**; **tak(e)**; **wyll**, n.

togedyr, adv. [*OE togædere*] together, at one time, 8, 197; in agreement, of one will, 495; **togydyr**, 728; see **acorde**.

toke; see **take**.

tolde; see **tell**.

tomorow, adv. [*ME to + morȝen; written as 2 words until 15c*] tomorrow, 811.

tonge, n. [*OE tunge*] tongue, 1039.

torne; see **turne**.

to-supporte, n. [*To + support; see support*] maintenance of a person by a supply of funds (personified), 796.

towchynge, vbl. sb. [*OFr toucher*] the sense of touch: "by ~," through the sense of touch, 1101.

trace, n. [*OFr trace, f. tracier, sketch*] dance, (steps), 746. **traces**, pl., dances, 717.

tramposyde, v. pp. [*Poss. scribal error for transposyde f OFr transposer, transform, convert*] transformed, 1001.

tranqwyllyte, n. [*OFr tranquillité*] tranquillity, 59.

tre, n. [*OE treow*] wood, 1059; see **pyler**.

trebull,n. [*OFr treble* f. *popL triplus*] treble part, highest part in harmonic music, 619.

tremble, v. [*OFr trembler ult.* f. *L tremere*] tremble, shake with the fear of God, 903; **trymbull**, 898.

trespas, n. [*OFr trespas, passing across; legal application of the word restricted to E*] sin, transgression; "dyde ~," committed sin, 1095; "satysfye my ~," atone for my sin, 1080.

trew; **trewthe**; see **tru**.

tribulacyon, n. [*OFr tribulacion ult.* f. *L tribulare, oppress, persecute*] vexation, tribulation, 427.

try; see **tru**.

trye, v. tr. [*OFr trier origin unknown*] try, attempt, 861.

trynyte, n. [*OFr trinite* f. *L trinus, threefold; Christian use* f. *Tertullian*] Trinity, 7, 178.

trymbull; see **tremble**.

trost; see **trust**.

trow, v. [*OE treowan*] believe; "~ ye," do you suppose, 621, 645; "I ~," I trust, 752.

trowthe; see **tru**.

tru, a. [*OE treowe*] honest, reliable, 736; true, genuine, 1157; **trewe**, true, accurate, 430* (M = **trew**); **try**, true, accurate, 641; **trew**, sb., the true God, 385; **trowth(e)**, **truthe**, n., truth, honesty, 565, 654, 676, 724; true doctrine, 314; "by my ~," by my troth, an oath, 493; **trewþe**, "in ~," truly, 869.

truly, adv. [*OE treowlic*] faithfully, 409; truly, actually, 445, 498.

trumpes, **trumpys**, n. pl. [*OFr trompette (14c)* f. *trompe*] trumpets, 692sd, 702.

trust, v. [*ON treysta*] trust, have faith in, 488; **trost**, believe, 824; **trustynge**, prp., believing, having faith, 985.

truthe; see **tru**.

turne, torne, v. [OE _tyrnan, turnian_ f. L _tornare_] change, 1047; imp.,"~ þi weys," change your ways, return to the spiritual grace of God, 874; **turnyt, 3 sg. pr.**, transforms, 281.

tweyn, n./a./v. [OE _twe3en, nom./acc. masc. of numeral twa_] n., two, 149, 863; a., two, twin, paired, 135, 1073, 1077, 1086; "I ~," I too, 821; v., separate; "on & ~,"(move) on and get out, (colloq.), 776; see **ey; myght**.

twelve, [xii], a. [ComTeut OE _twelf_ f. _twa_, two + _lif_-, leave] twelve, 1023.

thy-, þy-; listed as if **thi, þi**.

V

(includes consonantal v- words and words in which v- = mod.
English u-)

varyance, n. [OFr _variance_ f. L _variantia_] changeableness, variation; "wythowt ~," without change, just as usual, 789.

veyn, a. [OFr _veyn_ f. L _vanus, empty_] worthless, 195.

vengeaunce, n. [OFr _vengeance_] vengeance, retribution, 972, 1098; "tak ~," seek revenge, (spoken by Mynde as a vulgar gesture), 765; spoken by Christ with reference to his death, 1025.

ver(a)y, a. [OF _verai_ f. L _verus_] true, 30, 134, 155, 184, 244, 835, 844, 933, 961, 963, 971, 973, 996, 1108, 1132; **verray**, 127; **wery**, 15; **veryly, adv.**, truly, verily, 57, 64, 98, 232, 902, 1118; **verely(e), vereyly,** 151, 544, 985, 1091, 1134; **veraly,** 389; **werely,** 546. see **feyth(e); know(e); reson(e); sorow(e)**.

vertu, n. [Fr _vertu_ f. L _virtus, manliness_] power of God, 924; a particular moral quality, 1036; see **souere(y)n**.

victoryall, a. [OFr _victorial_ f. L _victorialis_] signifying victory, 1115.

vycys, n. pl. [OFr _vice_ f. L _vitium, fault_] vices (personified), 766, immoral habits, 1161.

vyolence, n. [*OFr violence* f. *L violentia* ult. f. *violare, violate*] perversion, distortion of nature (poss. infl. by **vyolacyon**, violation, f. *L violare*, violate, ult. f. **vis**, power)], violence, 108; **vyolens**, violence, injurious treatment; "for peyn & ~," because of (self-inflicted) pain and violence, 1043; **vyolent**, a., passionately angry, 1097.

vyrgyne, n. [*OFr virgine* ult. f. *L virgo, maiden*] prop. n., "~ Marye," Virgin Mary, 1067; **vyrgyn(e)s**, pl., virgins, maidens; "v . . . ~," five virgins, i.e., five inner senses linked with the daughters of Jerusalem, 162, 164sd; see **prudent**.

vysurs, n. pl. [*AFr viser* f. *OFr vis, face*] masks, 752sd; **vyseryde**, pp. a., masked, 724sd; see **conregent**; **dyuersly**.

vnablythe, v. tr. 3 sg. pr. refl. [*OFr inhabile* or *L. inhabilis*] renders (himself/themselves) unfit, 893.

vndyrstondynge; see **wndyrstondynge**.

vnstabylnesse, n. [*OFr (e)stable* f. *L stare, stand*] instability, 199* (M = **sustabullnes**).

vnto; see **onto**.

vp(e); see **wp**.

vs; see **ws**.

vse, v. [*OFr user* ult. f. *L uti, use*] use, make use of, 442, 637; **wse**, pursue or follow as customary, 434; **vsyde**, pp., used, practiced, 146, 684, 909; **wsyde**, pp., that which is or has been made use of, 409; **vsande**, prp., "~ off," practiced by, 681-2; **vsance**, n., enjoyment from wide use; "in so grett ~," in such favor from habitual use, 655; "wyth goode ~," with good practice, i.e. when practiced responsibly, 1027.

vy-; listed as if **vi-**.

W

way; see **wey**.

wake, v. [*Originally 2 words: OE wacen, wake up + !wacian, stay awake*] be aroused, awaken, 223; watch, remain awake for a devotional vigil, 433, 1021; **wakynge**, prp. as sb., keeping vigil as an act of devotion, 1026.

walke, v. [*OE wealcan*] walk, 799.

wan, conj.; see **wen**.

wan, v. [*OE wanian*] to become weak, diminish in capacity (to reason) as a result of temptation, 346.

warder, n. [*ME warderer; poss. f. AFr !warderere, look out behind*] staff symbolizing office, authority or command in office (historically used to signal the beginning and end of hostile engagement in a battle or tournament), 692sd.

ware, v.¹; see **was**.

ware, v.² [*OE warian; in ME infl. by wær, a., vigilant; both f. OTeut !war(o), observe, take care of*] tr., take heed of, guard against, 604; imp., (used mainly in hunting and as a warning cry), watch out, 773; see **beware**.

was, v. 1/3 sg. pa. of verb be [*see be*] 21, 110, 121, 310, 312, 314, 316, 333, 421, 423, 428, 516, 928; 2 sg. pa., 831; as aux., 24, 123, 187, 352, 419, 680, 681, 781, 907, 941; **wer(e)**, 2/3 pl. pa., were, 107, 588, 679, 987, 1091, 1109, 1123; subj. 3 sg., 40, 484, 520, 521, 688, 811, 1044, 1051; pl., 1050; **ware**, 2 pl. (formal), were, 105; **wore**, 3 pl., subj., were, 330, 489, 1001; see **ber(e)**.

wasche, v. tr. [*ComTeut OE wæscan, wascan*] cleanse from the stain of sin; "~ awey," cleanse, 125; **waschyt**, 3 sg. pr., 964; **waschede**, pp., cleansed, 1069.

wastyde, v. pp. [*OFr wast f. L vastus, desert, waste; replaced OE weste*] lost strength, been weakened, 437.

water, n. [*ComTeut OE wæter*] water, 1010, 1034.

we, pron., 1 pl. nom. [*Com Teut OE we*] used frequently in the modern sense, 75, 107, 108, 180, 234, . . . 600*, . . . 1163.

wede, n. [*OE wæd(e)*] apparel, clothing, 454.

wedys, n. pl. [*OE weod*] weeds; figuaratively used in respect to sin, 91.

weell; see **well**.

wey, n. [*ComTeut OE weȝ*] way, road, path, 644, 741, 885; "go(th) yowr/hys (. . .) ~," depart, 509, 550sd, 958; **way**, "comun as þe ~," as familiar as the (public) road, 652; **weys**, pl., paths, streets, 799; ways (used figuratively), 883; habits, 874; see **all**; **forth(e)**; **turne**.

weke; see **wyke**.

wel(l)fare, n. [*Derived f. vbl. phrase wel fare, to do well*] prosperity, well-being, 625, 735.

well, adv. [*ComTeut OE wel(l); v. stem identical w. wyll*] well, clearly, 359, 399, 440, **wele**, well, with good food, 459* (M = **werkys**); in a friendly way, 829; morally well, 877; **weell**, 222; **wyll**, properly, firmly, 225.

wen, wan, conj./adv. [*OE hwanne*] when, used frequently in the modern sense, 115, 138, 185, 197, 231 . . . 1004; **whan**, 345; **when**, 969; see **ay**; **mynde**.

wenche, n. [*Shortened form of eME wenchel f. OE wence*] wench, girl, 815.

wende, v. [*ComTeut OE wendan*] turn, 531; **went**, 2 sg. pa., "~ wpon," climbed up, 1059.

wene, v. [*ComTeut OE wenan*] expect, suppose, 57; think; "~ sey sothe," think they tell the truth, 750* (M = **veyn**).

wepe, v. [*ComTeut OE wepan*] weep, cry penitently, 435, 977, 1006; **wepte**, 2 sg. pa., mourned, 1009; **wepynge**, prp. a., weeping, 990.

were, v. [*OE werian, with implication of both defending and preventing*] defends or supports a cause; "yff nede ~," if necessity requires (it), 811.

wer(e), v.; see **was**.

wer, conj. [*OE hwær*] conj., where, wherever, 305, 586. 766. "~ þat," wherever, 46; **werfor**, adv., for which reason, 323, 336; **werof**. adv., the means with which, 194; **werto**, adv., to which, 344.

werely; **wery**, a.; see **ver(a)y**.

wery, v. inf. [*OE wer(i)ȝian*] grow weary or despise, 843.

werkys, n. pl. [*OE weorc*] works, actions (of God), 250, 257, 306.

werkyst, v. [OE _wyrcan_] do, perform, 923; **wrought**, created, fashioned, 953;
　　　"all (. . .) ~, created everything, 251, 768; performed, 965; pp.,
　　　created, 266, 352, 922; **wrowte**, pp., created, 20; see **yll**.

werof; **werto**; see **wer(e)**.

wers, comp. adv. [OE _wyrsa, wiersa_] worse, 809; see **n[e]ther**.

wertu, n. [OFr _vertu_ ult. f. L _vir, man_] moral excellence, goodness in conformity
　　　with the Divine Will, 378, 382, 1047; **wertus**, pl., particular moral
　　　attributes (faith, hope, charity), 288; **wertuus**, a., powerful in effect, 92;
　　　wertuusly, adv., virtuously; "~ sett," endowed with natural virtue, 219.

wet(e), v. [ME _wete_ related to _wit_ f. ComTeut _witan_ v. form obs. by 16c] know,
　　　understand, discover, 1, 440, 852; **wott**, 3 sg. pr., knows; "Gode ~,"
　　　God knows, used to emphasize the truth of a statement, 560.

wethyr, rel. adv. [OE _hwider_, rarely OE _hwæder_] whithersoever, to whatever
　　　place, 525.

whan; see **wen**; **w(h)o**.

w(h)at, (inter.) pron./a. [OE _hwæt_] inter. pron., what, 73, 78, 102, 120, 147, 148,
　　　246, 457, 478, 645, 875, 884, 911, 913, 954, 1117; **watt**, 133; a., what
　　　kind of, 66*, 96, 190, 420, 455, 473, 474, 880, 900; "~ soule," that soule
　　　which, 217; "~ &," what if, 857; see **lyff**.

when; see **wen**.

white; see **wyght**.

w(h)y, inter. adv.[OE _hwi, hwy_] why, for what reason, 108, 905, 913, 914, 921,
　　　922, 923, 924, 950; adv., "cause ~," the reason why, 432; see **wyppe**.

w(h)o, inter. pron./rel. pron. [OE _hwa_] who, whoever 50, 57, 71, 444, 665, 666,
　　　677, 710, 711, 738, 863, 872, 961, 1019; **woo**, 271; **w(h)om**, whom,
　　　264, 723, 763, 852, 918, 937, 1079; **whan**, obs. form of **whom**, 338;
　　　woso, whosoever, 412.

whoo; see **wo**, adv.

whow(e), interj. [OE _hu, !hwo_] variant of **how**, how is that, why, 891.

wy, inter. adv.; see **why**.

wy, interj. [*Onomatopoeic*] why, expression used to introduce an anxious question or statement for emphasis or a means of demanding attention, 517; see **wyppe**.

wyche, rel. a./rel. pron. [*OE hwelc, hwilc, hwylc*] rel. a., 5, 124, 125, 154, 741, 1077; rel. pron., 134, 136, 178, 241, 244, 269, 281, 353, 529, 930, 932, 936, 942, 994, 1030, 1131; "~ þat," how, 1158; see **fele**.

wyde, adv. [*ComTeut OE wide*] far abroad, 549.

wyff(e), n. [*OE wif*] wife, 16, 406; possibly mistress, 476; married woman, 816; **wyve**, v., marry, 663; **wywande**, prp., wiving; "yll ~," unhappily married, 783.

wyght, n./a. [*OE hwit*] n., white clothing, 151, 155; a., white, 16sd, 324sd; **white**, 164sd* (for D in white, M = **wyth**).

wyke, n. [*ComTeut OE wice*] week, 751, 996sd; **weke**, 1033; see **passyon**.

wykkydnes, n. [*ME wikked, wyked f. OE wicca*, wizard/*OE wicce*, witch + -*nes*] wickedness, sinful behavior, 378.

wylde, adv. [*ComTeut OE wilde*] wildly, like a beast, 616.

wyly, a. [*eMe wil -y; origin obscure poss. f. ON vel, artifice, craft*] guileful, 341; used as proper name, possibly for Lucyfer, 604; see **ser**.

wyll, conj. [*Abbrev. f. OE phrase þa hwile þe, during the time that*] while, 543, 660.

wyll, v. [*OE !willan, to will, wish--often indistinguishable f. OE willian, direct by one's will, to intend; also used as the future tense aux.*] wish to, 1, 217, 666; will, be willing to, 102, 711; direct by my will, 525; strongly desire (that), 887; fut. aux., (often implies a strong intention), 353, 361, 371, 375, 395 . . . 991; will go, (w. inf. understood) 741; **woll**, 491, 492, 765, 832; fut. aux., 511; **wolde**, would, 40, 374, 451, 452, 699, 713, 840, 919.

wyll, n. [*OE willa*] will, power of choice in regard to action, frequently personified as a faculty of the soul, 88, 180, 213 . . . 1055; linked with the Holy Ghost as the 3rd member of the Trinity, 287; "go(o)de ~," will as the faculty of human choice, (fixed on God) 215, 216, 231, 237, 999; (used ironically by Lucyfer), 468; "free ~," power of human choice of good or evil, 290; **wylfully**, with the power of the will, "to do ~," to perform through the power of the will, 230* (M = **wysly**).

wyll, adv.[1]; see **well**.

wyll, adv.^{2} [*ON villr, bewildered, erring, astray*] astray, 319.

wyn(e), n. [*OE win ult. f. L vinum*] wine, alcoholic beverages, 473, 825, 868.

wynke, v. [*OE wincian*] close the eyes, 894.

wynn, v. [*ComTeut OE winnan*] win, 548; **wynnande**, prp., winning, gaining profit, 677.

wyppe, vbl. imp. as inter. [*Origin uncertain; eTeut form of MLG wippen, leap about, dance*] sudden leap about for joy; alliterative phrase: "wy ~," why (or, colloquially, whee), whip!, 517; "~ wyrre," whip, whirr, 552.

wyrre, vbl. imp. as interj. [*Prob. f. Danish hvirre*] rush, hurl (oneself) noisely, 552; see **wyppe**.

wyrry, n. [*Unattested development f. OE wyr3an; n. not recorded in OE; apparently derived f. verb, to kill (a person or animal) by strangling*] a killing grasp, "in þe ~," in a stranglehold, 840.

wys(e), n. [*OE wise*] manner, fashion; "in no ~," in no way, 116, 299; "on thys/þis ~," in this way, 324sd, 1037; "in þe most . . . ~," in the most (horrible or lamentable) way, 902sd, 996 sd.

wysdom(e), **wsydam**, n. [*OE wisdom*] wisdom — an attribute of God, grounded in love, fear of the divine, and self-knowledge; associated with Christ, frequently personified as Christ, 0sd, 4, 7, 8, 9, 14, 16, 16sd, 22, 33, 39, 56, 77, 89, 93, 121, 259, 306, 879, 1145, 1163; "in ~," through my relationship with wisdom, 24; wisdom defined as falsehood (used ironically), 604.

wyse, a. [*OE wis*] wise, 743; **wysly(e)**, adv., wisely, 493, 509.

wyse, n. [*OE wise, manner, mode, cause*] manner, mode, fashion, 324sd, 902sd.

wyth, prep. [*OE wið*] with, used frequently in the modern sense, 0sd(*), 16sd, 23, 42 . . . 1162; against, 339; by, 224, 348, 1062; through, by means of, 542, 639, 858, 974, 1016, 1097; **wyt**, 215, 975; **wythin**, **wythin(n)e**, adv., lined on the inside, 0sd; costume underneath, 324sd; within the soul, internally, 160, 163, 168, 544, 964; prep., 980; **wythowt(e)**, prep., without, not having, 28, 139, 191, 203, 216, 247, 248, 761, 789, 907, 937, 967; adv., on the outside (opposite to **wythin(e)**), 167, 324sd; **wythowtyn**, 47, 1116; see **ende**; **lesynge**; **loweday**; **mengylde**; **reson(e)**; **varyance**; **vse**.

wyttys, n. pl. [*OE wit*] senses, faculties of perception, 438; "owt(e)warde ~," sensory faculties of the body, 137, 1075; "inwarde ~," inner wits, faculties of the spirit, 1074; "v/fyue/fywe ~," five senses (usually personified), 163, 295, 324sd, 453, 479, 1064sd, 1076, 1093, 1095; "~ fyve," 173.

wyve; **wywande**; see **wyff(e)**.

wnclosyde, v. pp. [*un-* + *ME closen* f. *OFr clore, close*] opened, 227.

wndyr, prep. [*ComTeut OE under*] under the cover of, concealed under, 379, 912sd.

wndyrstondyng(e), **vndyrstondynge**, prp. as sb. [*OE understondan*] the power of discursive reason, frequently personified as a faculty of the Soul (linked with Christ as the second member of the Trinity), 180, 245, 246, 273, 278 . . . 1125; see **tak(e)**.

wndyrtake, v. [*OE under-* + *lOE tacan; modelled after OE underniman, interrupt*] affirm, 976.

wo, pron.; see **w(h)o**.

wo, **whoo**, adv. [*OE wa, wæ; Common IndoEur interj., used as an expression of lament; OE wa*] full of woe; "~ ys hym," woeful is he, 347, 784.

wolde, **woldyst**, **woll**; see **wyll**, (v.).

wolffe, n. [*ComTeut OE wulf*] wolf, 490.

wom; see **w(h)o**.

woman, n. [*OE wifmann = wif, woman + mann, human being; formation peculiar to E*] woman, 573; **women**, pl., women, 752sd.

wondyde, v., 2 pl. pa. [*OE wundian*] wounded, injured with a lover's wounds, emotionally touched, 1085.

wondyr, n./adv./v. [*OE wundor/wundrian*] n., wonder, "haue ~ of," be amazed at, 865; adv., extremely, 616; v., gaze in amazement, 734; **wondyrly**, adv., marvellously, 257; **wondyrfull**, a., very fine, 752sd; see **conregent**.

woo; see **w(h)o**.

woode, a. [*OE wod*] mad, without benefit of reason, insane, 330, 484, 489.

woode, n. [*OE widu, later wudu*] woods, 741.

worde, n. [*OE word*] word, 1014; "on þat ~," for that insult, 765; **wordys**, pl., words, 591.

wordly; see **worlde**.

wore; see **was**.

worlde, n. [*ComTeut weorold*] secular life, made up of those concerned only with temporal affairs, 464, 625, 657; earthly life, 660; "all þe/the ~," all the world, i.e., all those that give their lives to worldly pleasure, 670, 734; "be/go in þe ~," live a worldly life, leave cloistered contemplation, 442, 486, 501; one of three temptors of humanity (along with the Devil and the Flesh), 294; **worldys**, worldly, 578; **worldly**, worldly, 33, 51, 1009; **wordly**, worldly, 405; see **abowt(e)**; **fende**.

worschyp(p)e, n. [*OE weorðscipe f. weorð, value + scip; formation peculiar to E*] worldly renown, esteem, glory, 455, 578, 629; **worschyppys**, pl., honors belonging to a high social position, 513, 514.

worthy, a. [*OE weorð(e) + -y*] honorable, morally estimable, 69; appropriate, 935; **worthynes**, n., worthiness, high value, 38, 186; "hye ~," of extraordinary high value, 61.

woso; see **w(h)o**.

wott; see **wet(e)**.

wow, n. [*OFr vo(we) f. L vovere, solemnly promise*] vow. an oath (sworn to the devils of hell), 372.

wp(pe), **vp(e)**, adv. [*OE upp, up*] in high repute, 518; upheld, 669; uphold, 699; gather up, collect, 804; "hurde ~," hoard up, 582; lefte ~," raise morally, 939; see **ber(e)**, **engose**.

wpon, prep. [*eME upon f. OE up(p), adv. + OE on, distinct f. eME uppon--variation of up, prep.*] on, 0sd, 1042, 1059. see **wende**.

wrathe, n. [*OE wræððu*] wrath (personified), 716.

wrechydnes, n. [*Irregular variation f. OE wrecca*] misery, 235

wreche, n. [*OE wræc*] vengeance (personified), 695; **wre[c]h**, wretch, wretched person, 66** (D **wreth** a prob. error for wreche).

wrye, v. [*OE wrion*] conceal, hide, 858.

wrynge, v., 3 sg. pr. subj. [*Variant of* _ring_ f. *OE* _hringan_] squeeze dry or press painfully, 614.

wronge, n. [*Substantive use of a.* f. *IOE* _wrang_] wrong, injustice, 669, 738, (personified), 725; **wrongys**, pl., 857.

wrought; **wrowte**; see **werkyst**.

ws, **vs**, pron., 1 pl. obj. [*ComTeut OE* _us_] us, 231, 382, 386, 390, 613, 625, 657, 662, 734, 744, 763, 779, 813, 827, 872, 938, 995, 1151.

wse; **wsyde**; see **vse**.

wy-; listed as if **wi-**.

X

xall, v. [*ComTeut OE* _sceal_] sg./pl. pr., shall, used frequently in the modern sense; 51, 52, 59, 98, 109 . . . 1159; **xulde**, (in modal functions w. infin.), primarily expressing obligation, meaning should, ought, 251, 297, 340, 429, 484, 522, 702, 1004; **schulde**, pl. pa., should, 891; see **schew**.

Y

(includes *y-* words = Mod. English *y-* and *g-*;
for *y-* = *i-*, see *I/Y*)

ya, **ye**, inter. [*Affirmative particle ult.* f. *primitive Teut*] yes, yea, 414, 487*, 491, 506, 684, 710, 736, 778, 813, 891.

yche; see **eche**.

ydyll; see **i**.

ye, pron. 2 sg./pl. [*OE* _ȝe_] you, used frequently in the modern sense, 175, 279,t 280, 293, 393 . . . 430* . . . 496* . . . 1160; **ȝe**, 1, 58, 95, 98, 102, 104, 105, 113, 115, 116, 117, 174, 181, 290, 295, 302, 307, 395, 445, 485, 566, 645; see **laddys**; **reforme**; **ryve**; **trow**.

ye, inter.; see **ya**.

yeff; see **yeue**.

yeftys, n. pl. [*ComTeut OE 3iff*] gifts, 640.

yelde, v. [*OE 3ieldan*] pay, render, repay, 194, imp., 1147; **yeldynge**, prp., offering, paying, 391; restoring, making restitution, 975; see **satysfye**.

yer, n. [*OE 3ear*] year, 823; **imp**. pl., 1032; **yerys**, pl., years, as a figurative expression of time, 36, 198; see **day**; **lengthe**.

yet; see **yit**.

yeue, v. [*ComTeut OE 3iefan; forms w. initial guttural first recorded circa 1200, prob. reflecting Scandinavian infl.; palatal forms disappeared circa 1500; frequently different forms appear in same text*] give, grant; **yeue**, 73, 78, 82, 504; **yewe**, 226, 411; **yeff**, 647, 1148; **gyff**, 479, 550, 999; **geve**, 689; **yewyst**, gives, 922; **gaff**, gave, 410; **yewyn**, pp., given, 576; **yowe**, pp. a., given (to), committed (to), eager, 941; given, 1078; **yevynge**, prp., 704.

yff; see **I/Y**.

ygnorans; see **I/Y**.

yiffte, n. [*ComTeut OE 3ift; recorded meaning restricted to "payment for a wife" (sg.)/"wedding" (pl.)*] gift (of the spirit), 946; **yeftys**, pl., gifts, bribes, 640.

yis, v.; see **I/Y**.

yis, adv. [*OE 3ese prob. f. yea + si, 3 sg. pr. of beon, to be*] yes, 399* (M = **thys**), 802.

yit, yet, adv. [*OE 3iet(a)*] still, even so, nevertheless, 107, 415, 483, 714, 890, 899, 960, 1080; still, even now, 342; see **can**.

yll; see **I/Y**.

ymage; see **i/Y**.

yn; see **I/Y**.

ynowe; see **inow(e)**.

yomandrye, n. [*ME 3oman (14c) poss. f. OE 3ingra, vassal + -drye*] a company of young vassals, 698.

yougthe, n. [*OE ʒeoguþ*] youth, 18* (M = **thowte**).

yow, pron. pers. [*OE eow*] you, used frequently in the modern sense; 73, 84, 174, 288, 296 . . . 1147; **your**, **yowr**, poss., used frequently in the modern sense, 20, 25, 71, 74, 76 . . . 1137; **yowrselff**, **yowrsylff**, refl. pron., yourself, 95, 97, 902; see **bethynke**; **dylygens**; **ey**; **kepe**; **know(e)**; **passyble**; **ples**; **wey**.

yowe; see **yeue**.

ys; see **I/Y**.

yt; see **I/Y**.

SELECTED BIBLIOGRAPHY

ABBREVIATIONS FOR NOTES AND BIBLIOGRAPHY:

abbr. = abbreviation
Addit. = Additional (a British Library Manuscript series)
Bodl. = The Bodleian Library at Oxford University
Brit. Lib. = British Library
ctd. = cited
CUL = Cambridge University Library
D = The Digby Manuscript
EDAM = Early Drama, Art, and Music
EETS = Early English Text Society
es (following EETS) = extra series
fol. = folio
M = The Macro Manuscript
MED = Middle English Dictionary
Ms. = Manuscript
OED = Oxford English Dictionary
os (following EETS) = original series
REED = Records of Early English Drama: 1540 - 1642
rpt. = reprinted
ss (following EETS) = supplementary series
qtd. = quoted
SUNY = State University of New York
Unpub. diss. = Unpublished dissertation

MANUSCRIPTS CITED:

A. Source documents

CHARTERS OF PARDON, ETC. (anonymous):
    Brit. Lib. Addit. Ms. 37049, fol. 23r
    CUL Ms. Ff.5.45 contains a *charter of heaven*
    Brit. Lib. Ms. Addit. 24343 contains a similar charter entitled
        Carta Redempcionis humanae
    Brit. Lib. Ms. Addit. 5960 contains a *Carta [Jesu Christi] de*
        liberatibus mundi
    CUL Ms. Ff.5.45
    Brit. Lib. Ms. Addit. 37049 fol. 23
    Brit. Lib.. Ms. Addit. 24343 fol. 6
    Brit. Lib. Addit.Ch. 5960
    Brit. Lib. Ms. Harley 6840 fol 239b
Hilton, Walter. *Scale of Perfection* and *Vita Mixta* ; for a full listing of
    British manuscripts of the *Scale of Perfection*, see Sargent 1983.
    Brit. Lib. Ms. C.21.b.15: 343ff; also contains Walter Bond's
        Consolatory
    Brit. Lib. Ms. Royal 17C. xviii; *VM*
    Brit. Lib. Ms. Harley 2397; *Scala II*; *VM*
    Brit. Lib. Ms. Harley 2254; *VM*
    Bodl. Ms. Laud misc. 685
    Bodl. Ms. Rawlinson C.894; *Scala I*; *VM*
    Bodl. Ms. Rawlinson A.355; *VM*
    Bodl. Ms. Rawlinson a.356; *VM*
    Bodl. Ms. Royal 17 C.xviii; *VM*
NINE POINTS OF VIRTUE (anonymous):
    Bodl.lat.liturg.e17
    CUL Ms. Ff.vi.33,
    CUL Ms. Dd.11.89
    CUL Ms. Dd.xiv.26 III
    CUL Ms. Dd.xi.89
    CUL Ms Ii.iv.9, fol. 64
    Bodl. Ms. Douce 141
    Brit. Lib. Ms. Harley 1704
    Brit. Lib. Ms. Harley 2409
    Trinity College Cambridge Ms. O.2.53

Seuses, Heinrich (Heinrich Suso). *Heinrich Susos (seuses) Buch genannt der Süse (Süsse) mit voraufgehendem Register.* Codex Guelf, 78.5, Aug. fols 97r-122v, c. 1473, in the Herzog-August-Bibliothek, Wolffenbüttel. *Die Handschriften der Herzoglichen Bibliothek zu Wolfenbüttel.* Ed. Otto von Heinemann. Wolfenbüttel: Verlag von Julius Zwissler, 1900. For a full listing of Suso's German manuscripts, see Künzle.

Suso, Heinrich. *Orologium Sapientiae,* or *The Seven Poynts of Trewe Love* :

Corpus Christi College, Cambridge, Ms 268 (complete)

Bodl. Ms. Douce 114 (complete)

Bodl. Ms. Ms. e. Museo 111 (complete)

Ms. Tanner 398 (complete)

Brit. Lib. Addit. Ms. 37049 (points 4 & 5; the only illustrated English Suso manuscript; see Hogg in primary materials below).

CUL Ms. Ff.v.45 (point 5 only, on knowing how to die)

Bodl. Douce 522 (point 5 only)

Brit. Lib. Ms. Harley 1706 (point 5 only)

CUL Ms. Hh.1.11 (point 6)

CUL Ms. Ii.iv.9 (excerpts)

B. Other manuscripts:

Boethius. *De Consolatione Philosophiae;.* Trans. John Walton. Ms. 615 Martin Schoyen Collection Checklist, 1992. A commentary note with the ownership incription of Thomas Hyngham, monk of Bury St. Edmunds Benedictine Abbey, which establishes both the name and location in Bury St. Edmunds of the scribe of the Macro Manuscript.

Herradis of Landsberg, *Hortus Deliciarum,* Strasbourg: Lib. Bibliothek de la Villa, fol 225r.

A Sentence to them that be in Temptation, Bodl. Ms. Harley 1706, fol. 127.

Brit. Lib. Ms. Royal 18, B. 23, fol. 142. Ctd. by Owst.

CUL Ms. Dd.14.26; includes a dialogue between Augustine & St. Bernard.

EDITIONS OF EARLY PLAYS:

Wisdom:

The Digby Text:
Baker, Donald C. and J. L. Murphy, eds. *The Digby Plays: Facsimiles of the Plays in the Bodley MSS Digby 133 and E Museo 160.* Leeds: University of Leeds, 1979.
Baker, D.C., J. L. Murphy, and L. B. Hall, Jr., eds. *The Late Medieval Religious Plays of Bodleian MSS Digby 133 and E. Museo 160.* Oxford: Oxford University Press, 1982.
Furnivall, Frederick J. *The Digby Plays, with an incomplete 'Morality' of Wisdom Who is Christ.* EETS es 70. 1896. Rpt. Oxford: Clarendon Press, 1930.
---. *The Digby Mysteries.* London: New Shakespeare Society, 1882.
Sharp, Thomas. *Ancient Mysteries from the Digby Manuscript.* Edinburgh: Abbotsford Club, 1835.

The Macro Text:
Bevington, David, ed. *the Macro Plays. The Castle of Perseverance, Wisdom, Mankind: A Facsimile Edition with Facing Transcription.* New York: 1972.
Eccles, Mark, ed. *The Macro Plays.* EETS os 262. London: Oxford University Press, 1969.
Farmer, John S., ed. *Wisdom or Mind, Will, and Understanding: The Macro Plays No. 2.* The Tudor Facsimile Texts. London and Edinburgh: T. C. & E. C. Jack, 1907.
Furnivall, F. J. and Alfred W. Pollard, ed. *The Macro Plays.* EETS os 91. London: Kegan Paul, Trench, Trübner, and Co., 1904.
Turnbull, W. B. D. D., ed. *Mind, Will, and Understanding: A Morality.* Edinburgh: The Abbotsford Club, 1837.

Other plays:

Beadle, Richard, ed. *The York Plays*. London, Edward Arnold, 1982.
Block, K. S., ed. *Ludus Coventriae, or the Plaie called Corpus Christi* . EETS es 120. 1917. Rpt. London: Oxford University Press, 1961.
Chester cycle. See Lumiansky and Mills.
Croxton Play of the Sacrament. See Davis, Norman.
Davis, Norman, ed. *Croxton Play of the Sacrament. Non-Cycle Plays and Fragments*. EETS ss 1. London and New York: Oxford University Press, 1970. 58-89.
England, George, and Alfred W. Pollard, eds. *The Towneley Plays*. EETS es 71. London: Kegan Paul, Trench, Trübner, and Co., 1897.
Hick Scorner, see Lancashire.
Jonson, Ben. *Bartholomew Fair*. Ed. Eugene M. Waith. New Haven, CT: Yale University Press, 1963.
---. *The Complete Plays*. London: J. M. Dent & Sons, and New York: E. P. Dutton, 1910.
---. *Works*. Eds. C. H. Herford and Percy and Evelyn Simpson. 11 vols. Oxford: Clarendon Press, 1938. Vol. 6.
Lancashire, Ian, ed. *Two Tudor Interludes: The Interlude of Youth, Hick Scorner*. Manchester: Manchester University Press, 1980.
Lester, G. A., ed. *Three Late Medieval Morality Plays: Mankind, Everyman, and Mundus et Infans*. Ed. G. A. Lester. London: A. & C. Black, 1981 and New York: Norton, 1990.
Lumiansky, R. M. and David Mills, eds. 2 vols. *The Chester Mystery Cycle* EETS ss 3 and 9. London & New York: Oxford University Press, 1974, 1986.
Medwall, Henry. *Nature*. New York: AMS Press, 1970.
---. *The Plays of Henry Medwall*. Ed. Alan Nelson. London: D. S. Brewer and Totowa, NJ: Rowman and Littlefield, 1980.
Mundus et Infans. See Lester.
N-Town Cycle. See Spector.
Skelton, John. *The Complete English Poems*. Ed. John Scattergood. New Haven and London: Yale University Press, 1983.
---. *Magnificence*. Ed. Paula Neuss. Manchester: Manchester University Press, and Baltimore, Johns Hopkins Press, 1980.
---. *Magnificence*. Ed. Robert Lee Ramsay. EETS. London: Oxford University Press, 1906.
Smith, Lucy Toulman. *York Plays*. Oxford: Clarendon Press, 1885.

Spector, Stephen, ed. *The N-Town Play.* EETS ss 11 and 12. New York and Oxford: Oxford University Press, 1991.

Stevens, Martin and A. C. Cawley. *The Towneley Plays.* EETS ss 13 and 14. London and New York: Oxford University Press, 1994.

Towneley Cycle. See Stevens and Cawley; see also England and Pollard.

Udall, Nicholas. *Ralph Roister Doister: A Comedy.* Shakespeare Society Publication 34. 1970. Rpt. London: The Shakespeare Society, 1977.

York Cycle. See Beadle; see also Smith.

PRIMARY NON-DRAMATIC SOURCES (INCLUDING RECORDS):

An Alphabet of Tales. See Banks.

Anderson, J. J., ed. *Records of Early English Drama: Newcastle upon Tyne.* Toronto, Buffalo, and London: University of Toronto Press, 1982.

Alfred, King. *Proverbs of King Alfred. Reliquiae Antiquae: Scraps from Ancient Manuscripts illustrating chiefly Early English Literature of the English Language.* Eds. Thomas Wright and James Orchard Halliwell. 2 vols. London: J. R. Smith, 1845. See esp. Vol. 1.174.

Banks, Mary Macleod, ed. *An Alphabet of Tales: an English 15th Century Translation of the Alphabetum Narrationem of Etienne de Besancon from [Brit. Lib.] Addit. Ms. 25719.* EETS es 126-127. London: Kegan Paul, Trench, Trübner, and Co., 1904-1905.

Berners, John Bouchier. *The Boke of duke Huon of Burdeux.* EETS os 122 London: Kegan Paul, Trench, Trübner, and Co., 1882-83.

Biblia Sacra: Juxta Vulgatam Clementinam Divisionibus, Summariis et Concordantiis Ornata. Rome: Society of St. John the Evangelist, 1947.

Brie, Friedrich W. D. *The Brut, or the Chronicles of England, ed. from Ms Rawl. B171, Bodleian Library.* EETS os 131, 136. London: Kegan Paul, Trench, Trübner, and Co., 1906-1908.

Brown, Carleton, ed. *Religious Lyrics of the Fifteenth Century.* Oxford: Clarendon Press, 1939.

Brown, Carleton, ed. *Religious Lyrics of the Fourteenth Century.* 1924. 2nd ed. rev. by G. V. Smithers 1952. Rpt. Oxford: Clarendon Press, 1957.

Brut, or the Chronicles of England. See Brie.

Chaucer, Geoffrey. "The Parson's Tale." *The Canterbury Tales. The Complete Works.* Ed. Walter W. Skeat. 7 vols. 1894. 2nd ed. 1900. Rpt. Oxford: Clarendon Press, 1972. Vol. 4: 570-644.

Churchyard, Thomas. *A Discourse of the Queenes Maiesties entertainment in Suffolk and Norffolk. Records of Early English Drama: Norwich—1540-1642.* Ed. David Galloway. Toronto: U of Toronto Press, 1984.

Clopper, Lawrence M., ed. *Records of Early English Drama: Chester.* Toronto, Buffalo, and London: University of Toronto Press, 1979.

Crosse, Henry. *Vertues Common-wealth, or the Highway to Honour. . . .* London, 1603. Rpt. A. B. Grosart. Occasional Series of Rare Books 18. Manchester, C. E. Simms, 1878.

Cursor Mundi. Ed. R. Morris. 7 parts in 4 vols. EETS os 57, 99, and 101 (vol. 1); os 59 and 62 (vol. 2); and os 66 and 68 (vols. 3 & 4). Oxford: Clarendon Press, 1874-93.

The Dance of Death. Eds. Florency Warren and Beatrice White. EETS os 181. London and New York: Oxford University Press, 1931.

Dawson, Giles E., ed. *Records of Plays and Players in Kent, 1450-1642.* Malone Society Collections 7. Oxford: Oxford University Press, 1965.

Douglas, Audrey and Peter Greenfield, eds. *Records of Early English Drama: Cumberland, Westmorland, Gloucestshire.* Toronto, Buffalo, and London, 1986.

Doyle, Ian. *A Survey of the Origins and Circulation of Theological Writings in English in the Fourteenth, Fifteenth, and Early Sixteenth Centuries with Special Consideration of the Part of the Clergy Therein.* Unpub. diss. Cambridge University: 1950.

---. ed. *The Vernon Manuscript: A Facsimile of Bodleian LIbrary Oxford Ms. Eng. Poet. A.1.* Cambridge: D. S. Brewer, 1987.

Dugdale, William. *Monasticun Anglicanum.* London: James Bohn, 1846.

Fisher, John. "A mornynge Remembraunce." *English Works of John Fisher,* ed. J.E.B. Mayor. EETS es 27. London: Kegan Paul, Trench, Trübner, and Co., 1876.

Furnivall, Frederick J. ed., *Political, Religious, and Love Poems .* EETS os 15. London and Oxford: Clarendon Press, 1903.

---. *Hymns to the Virgin and Christ, The Parliament of Devils, and Other Religious Poems, Chiefly from the Archbishop of Canterbury's Lambeth Ms. no. 853.* EETS os 24. Oxford: Clarendon Press, 1867.

Galloway, David ed. *Records of Early English Drama: Norwich.* Toronto, Buffalo, and London: University of Toronto Press, 1984.

Galloway, David and John M. Wasson, eds. *Records of Plays and Players in Norfolk and Suffolk: 1330-1642.* Malone Society Collections 11. London and New York: Oxford University Press, 1980-1981.

George, David, ed. *Records of Early English Drama: Lancashire.* Toronto, Buffalo, and London, University of Toronto Press, 1991.

Gibbs, Hannah Hucks, ed. *The Life and Martyrdom of St. Katherine of Alexandria.* Roxburghe Club. London: Nichols, 1884.

Gower, Edmund. *Confessio Amantis.* Ed. Russell A. Peck. New York: Holt, Rinehart and Winston, 1968.

Grants, etc., from the Crown during the Reign of King Edward the Fifth, Taken from the Original Docket-Book Ms. Harley 433. Ed. J. G. Nichols. Camden Society Publications 60. London: The Camden Society, 1854.

Greene, Richard Leighton, ed. *Early English Carols.* Oxford: Clarendon Press, 1977.

Harrad of Landsberg. *Hortus Deliciarum.* Ed. Rosalie B. Green. London: Warburg Institute, 1979.

Harris, Mary Dormer ed. *Coventry Leet Book.* EETS os 134, 135, 138, 146. London: Kegan Paul, Trench, Trübner & Co., 1907-13.

Harvey, R., ed. *R. Misyn's Fire of Love, and Mending of Life.* EETS os 106. Oxford: Clarendon Press, 1896.

Heller, Nicholas. See Suso.

Henry the Minstrel, *The actis and dreidis of the illusteire . . . Schir William Wallace* c. 1470. London: W. Blackwood and Sons, 1889.

Hilton, Walter. [Hylton, Walter]. *Scala Perfectionis.* Westminster: Wynkyn de Worde, 1494. Commissioned by Margaret Beaufort; contains the *Vita Mixta* as Part III of the *Scale of Perfection.* There is a copy in the Pierpoint Morgan Library.

---. *The Scale of Perfection.* Trans. Evelyn Underhill. London: John Watkins, 1923.

Hoccleve, Thomas. *Hoccleve's Works: The Minor Poems.* Eds. F. J. Furnivall and I. Gollancz. 3 vols. EETS es 61, 72, and 73. Oxford: Oxford University Press, 1892-1925. Rev. by J. Mitchell and A. I. Doyle. 1 vol. EETS es 61 and 73. Oxford: Oxford University Press, 1970.

Hodnett, Edward. *English Woodcuts.* 1935 (for 1934). Rpt. with additions and corrections. London: Oxford University Press, 1973.

Hogg, James, ed. *An Illustrated Yorkshire Carthusian Religious Miscellany: British Library London Additional Ms. 37049. Analecta Cartusiana.* Salzburg: Institut für Anglistik und Amerikanistik at the University of Salzburg, 1981. Vol. 3: Illustrations (this is the only volume published in a projected edition of the entire manuscript, which contains the only known English illustrations of the work of Henry Suso.)

Horstmann, K. tr. *Orologium Sapientiae or The Seven Poyntes of Trewe Wisdom. Anglia* X (1988): 323-89. Also see Suso in Manuscripts Cited and below.

Ingram, R.W., ed. *Records of Early English Drama: Coventry.* Toronto: University of Toronto Press, 1981.

James, Montague Rhodes *The Apocryphal New Testament.* 1924. Rpt. London and Oxford: Oxford University Press, 1980.

---. "Bury St. Edmunds Manuscripts." *English Historical Review* 41 (1926): 251-260.

---. *A Descriptive Catalogue of the Manuscripts in the Library of Corpus Christi College, Cambridge.* Cambridge, ENG: Cambridge University Press, 1912.

Jeaffreson, John Cordy and A. T. Watson. *Middlesex County Records.* 4 vols. London: Middlesex County Records Society, 1886-1892.

Johnston, Alexandra F. and Margaret Rogerson, eds., *Records of Early English Drama: York.* 2 vols. Toronto, Buffalo, and London: University of Toronto Press, 1979.

Kahrl, Stanley J. *Records of Plays and Players in Lincolnshire, 1300-1585.* Malone Society Collections 8. Oxford and New York: Oxford University Press, 1969.

Ker, N. R. *Medieval Libraries of Great Britain: A List of Surviving Books.* 2nd ed. London: Offices of the Royal Historical Society, 1964.

Klausner, David N., ed. *Records of Early English Drama: Herefordshire Worcestershire.* Toronto, Buffalo, and London: University of Toronto Press, 1990.

Langland, William. *Piers the Plowman* ed. David C Fowler. Binghamton, New York: Medieval Renaissance Texts and Studies, 1992.

Layamon. *Brut.* Ed. Rosamund Allen. New York: St. Martin's Press, 1992.

Legg, Leopold G. Wickham. *English Coronation Records.* London: Archibald Constable & Co. and New York: E. P. Dutton, 1901. See esp. *Liber Regalis*, p. 122; and "Little Device for the Coronation of Henry VII (20.10.1485)," pp. 223-224.

---. *The Sarum Missal.* Oxford: Clarendon, 1969.

Leland, John. *Joannis Lelandi Antiquarii de Rebus Britannicis Collectanea*, 6 vols., quoted by William Pickering. *The Privy Purse Expenses of York . . .* 1830. Facsimile Rpt. London: Frederick Muller, 1972. See esp. Vol. 4.216.

Liber Usalis Missae et Oficii pro Dominicis et Festis I vel II, classis cum cantu gregoriano expeditione Vaticana adamussim excerptis et rhythmicis signis in subsidium cantorum a solesminsibus monachis diligenter ornato. Paris: Society of St. John the Evangelist, 1931.

Lydgate, John. *Reason and Sensuality: The assembly of Gods.* Ed. E. Sieper. EETS es 84 and 89. London and Oxford: K. Paul, Trench, Trübner & Co., 1896, 1901-03.

---. *Lydgate's Fall of Princes*, tr. from Premeirfait's 2nd amplified French version (*Des cas de nobles hommes et femmes*) of Giovanni Boccaccio. *De Casibus Virorum Illustrium.* 1430-40. Ed. Henry Bergen. Washington, D.C.: The Carnegie Institution, 1923; Reissued as EETS es 121-124. London: Oxford University Press, 1924-27.

Meditationes Piissiimae de Cognitione Humanae Concitionis. Patrologia Cursus Completus, Series Latina. Ed. Jacques-Paul Migne. Paris, n.p., 1856. Vol. 194: 485-488.

Meredith, Peter and John E. Tailby, eds. *The Staging of Religious Drama in Europe in the Later Middle Ages: Texts and Documents in English Translation.* EDAM Monograph Series 4. Kalamazoo, MI: The Medieval Institute, 1983.

Minor Poems of the Vernon Ms. 2 vols. Vol 1: ed. Carl Horstmann. EETS os 98. London: Paul Kegan, Trübner and Trench, 1892; Vol. 2: ed. F. J. Furnivall. EETS os 117. London: Paul Kegan, Trübner and Trench, 1901. See also Doyle for a recent edition of the Vernon Manuscript.

Muther, Richard. *German Book Illustration of the Gothic Period and the Early Renaissance, 1460-1530.* 1884. Trans. Ralph R. Shaw. Metuchen: Scarecrow Press, 1972. Plate 70: Suso woodcut.

Myroure of oure Ladye. Ed. J. H. Blunt. EETS es 19. Oxford: Clarendon Press, 1873.

Nelson, Alan H., ed. *Records of Early English Drama: Cambridge.* 2 vols. Toronto, Buffalo, and London: University of Toronto Press, 1989.

New Oxford Annotated Bible with the Apocrypha, Revised Standard Version. Eds. Herbert G. May and Bruce M. Metzger. 1973. Rpt. New York: Oxford University Press, 1977.

Northbrooke, John. *A Treatise Against Dicing, Dancing, Plays and Interludes with other Idle Pastimes.* c. 1577. Shakespeare Society Publications 14. London: Shakespeare Society, 1843.

Peter Lombard. *Quatuor libri sententiarum* in *P. Lombardi Magistri Sententiarum Parisiensis Episcopi Opera Omnia.* 2 vols. *Patrologia Cursus Completus, Series Latina.* Ed. J. P. Migne. vols. 191-192. Paris, 1854-1855. Rpt. 1980. Book 4.16.

REED. See Anderson (Newcastle upon Tyne), Clopper (Chester), Douglas and Greenfield (Cumberland, Westmorland, and Gloucestershire), Galloway (Norwich), George (Lancashire), Ingram (Coventry), Johnston and Rogerson (York), Klausner (Herefordshire and Worcestershire), Nelson (Cambridge), and Wasson (Devon).

Riley, Henry Thomas, ed. *Liber Albus: The White Book of the City of London.* London, R. Griffin, 1861.

Robertson, J. and D. J. Gordon, eds. *A Calendar of Dramatic Records in the Books of the Livery Companies of London: 1485-1640.* Malone Society Collections 3 and 5. London and New York: Oxford University Press, 1954, 1959.

Rolle, Richard. *Contemplations of the Dread and Love of God.* Ed. Margaret Connolly. EETS es 303. London and New York: Oxford University Press, 1993.

---. *The Psalter or Psalms of David and Certain Canticles.* Ed. Rev. H.R. Bramley. Oxford: Clarendon Press, 1884.

Ross, Woodburn O. *Middle Endligh Sermons: Edited from British Museum MS. Royal 18 B.23.* EETS os 209. Oxford: Oxford University Press, 1940.

Schramm, Percy Ernest. *A History of the English Coronation.* London: Oxford, 1937.

Stow, John. *A Survey of London.* 1603. Rpt. with notes and introduction by Charles L. Kingsford. Oxford: Clarendon Press, 1908. The 1603 edition also rpt. with additional notes London: J. M. Dent, 1980.

Strutt, Joseph, ed. *the Regal and Ecclesiastical Antiquities of England.* London: H. G. Bohn, 1842. Esp. 81-91 and related plates.

Stubbes, Phillip. *Anatomy of the Abuses in England in Shakespeare's Youth, A.D. 1583*. Ed. Friedrich J. Furnivall. New Shakespeare Society series 6, nos. 4, 6, 12. London: N. Trübner & Co., 1877, 1879, 1882.

---. *The Anatomie of Abuses: contayning a discoverie or briefe summarie of such notable vices and imprefections, as now raign in many christian contreyes of the world . . . .* London: R. Jones, 1583. Rpt. New York: DaCapo Press, 1972.

Suso, Heinrich. "Das Horologium und das Buchlein der Ewigen Weisheit." *Heinrich Seuses Horolgium Sapientiae*. Ed. Fr. Pius Kunzle. Frieburg: Universitatsverlag, 1977. 28-54. This is the definitive edition, but see also Bihlmeyer, ed., below for an excellent earlier edition.

---. *Heinrich Seuss, Deutsche Schriften*. Ed. Karl Bihlmeyer. Stuttgart: 1907.

---. *Das Buch Genannt Der Seuse*. Augsburg: Anton Sorg, 1482. A copy of this volume in the Pierpoint Morgan Library, New York, has handpainted woodcuts; a copy with unpainted woodcuts is in the Spencer collection of the New York Public Library.

---. *Das Buch Gennant Der Seuse*. Augsburg: Anton Sorg, 1501. Copy in the Spencer Collection of the New York Public Library.

---. *Diss buch das da gedicht hat der erleücht vater Amandus, genañt Seüss Begreift in jm vil guter gaistlicher leeren*. Augsburg, H. Otmar for J. Rynmann, 1512; in the special collection of the Van Pelt Library, University of Pennsylvania.

---. *The Exemplar*. Trans. from *Des Mystikers Heinrich Suso* by Nicholas Heller. Dubuque, Iowa: Priory Press, 1962.

---. *Horologium Aeternae Sapientiae*. Cologne: Conrad Winters de Hamborch, c. 1480. Latin text. Pierpoint Morgan Library.

---. *L'Orloge de Sapience*. Paris: Antoine Verard: March 1493/94. A beautiful edition printed on vellum. Pierpoint Morgan Library.

---. *VII poyntes of true loue & euerlastyng wysdom drawen of the boke that is wryten in laten named Orologium Sapiencie. A boke of Divers fruytful ghoostly matters*. Westminster: William Caxton, 1491. There are five known copies, the only perfect one being in Cambridge University Library. Pierpoint Morgan Library has one incomplete copy, both examined for this edition.

---. *Wisdom, Orologium Sapientiae or The Seven Poyntes of Trewe Aus Ms. Douce 114*. Trans. K. Horstmann. *Anglia*. X (1888): 323-89. See also Manuscripts Cited.

---. See Hogg above.

Thoresby, John. *The Lay Folks Catechism, or, The English and Latin Versions of Archbishop Thoresby's Instruction for the People*. Eds. Thomas Frederick Simmons and Henry Edward Nolloth. EETS os 118. London: Kegan Paul, Trench, & Trübner, 1901.

Wasson, John M., ed. *Records of Early English Drama: Devon*. Toronto, Buffalo, and London: University of Toronto Press, 1986.

Whiting, Bartlett J. *Proverbs in the Earlier English Drama*. Cambridge, MA: Harvard University Press, 1938.

---. *Proverbs, Sentences, and Proverbial Phrases for English Writings Mainly before 1500*. Cambridge, MA: Harvard Univeristy Press, 1968.

William of Shoreham. *Poems*. Ed. Matthias Konrath. EETS es 86. London: Kegan Paul, Trench, Trübner, and Co., 1902.

Wilson, F. P. Ed. *The Oxford Dictionary of English Proverbs*. 3rd ed. Oxford: Clarendon Press, 1982.

Wright, Thomas, ed. *Political Poems and Songs Relating to English History*. Rolls Series 1. (1859-61). Esp. pp. 258-259.

Wyclif, John. Selection in *Political Poems and Songs Relating to English History*. Ed. T. Wright. Rolls Series 1. London, 1859-61. 258-259.

---. *An Apology for Lollard Doctrines*. Ed. J. H. Todd. Camden Society Publications. London: J. B. Nichols, 1842.

Year Books of Henry VI: I Henry VI, A.D., 1422. Ed. C. H. Williams. London: The Selden Society, 1933.

SECONDARY STUDIES:

Bibliographies:

Berger, Sidney. *Medieval English Drama: An Annotated Bibliography of Recent Criticism*. New York: Garland, 1990.

Cawley, A. C., Marion Jones, Peter F. McDonald, and David Mills. *The Revels History of Drama in English*. Vol. 1: *Medieval Drama*. London and New York: Methuen, 1983. 303-336.

Emmerson, Richard. "Dramatic Development: Some Recent Scholarship on Medieval Drama." *Envoi* 1.1 (1988): 23-40.

Ferguson, Carole, ed. "Bibliography of Medieval Drama 1977-1980." *Emporia State Research Studies*. 37.2 (Fall 1988): 5-53.

Houle, Peter J. *The English Morality and Related Drama: A Bibliographical Survey*. Hamden, CT: Archon, 1972.

Hunter, G. K. in *The English Drama 1485-1585*. Ed. F. P. Wilson. Oxford: Clarendon Press, 1969. 202-237.

Lancashire,Ian,ed. *Dramatic Texts and Records of Britain: A Chronological Topography*. Toronto: University of Toronto Press, 1984.

Leyerle,John. "Medieval Drama." *English Drama (Excluding Shakespeare): Select Bibliographical Guides*. Ed. Stanley Wells. London: Oxford University Press, 1975. 17-44.

Murphy, Maria Spaeth and James Hoy, eds. "Bibliography of Medieval Drama 1969-1972." *Emporia State Research Studies*. 34.4 (Spring 1986): 1-41.

Murphy, Maria Spaeth, Carole Ferguson, and James Hoy, eds. "Bibliography of Medieval Drama 1973-1976." *Emporia State Research Studies*. 35.1 (Summer 1986): 1-41.

Stratman, C. J. *Bibliography of Medieval Drama*. 2 vols. 2nd ed. New York: Frederick Ungar, 1972.

Historical, Critical, and Linguistic Studies:

Adamson, J. W. "The Extent of Literacy in England in the Fifteenth and Sixteenth Centuries: Notes and Conjectures." *The Library* Fourth series 10 (1930): 163-193.

Artaud, Antonin. *Le Théâtre et son Double*. 1938. Paris: Gallimard, 1964.

Alexander, Michael Van Clive. *The First of the Tudors: A Study of Henry VII and His Reign.* Totowa, NJ: Roman & Littlefield, 1980.

Anglo, Sydney. *Spectacle, Pageantry, and Early Tudor Policy.* London: Oxford University Press, 1969.

Armstrong, C. A. J. "The Piety of Cicely, Duckess of York." *England, France, and Burgundy in the Fifteenth Century.* London: Hambledon Press, 1983.

Aston, Margaret. "Iconoclasm in England: Official and Clandestine." *Iconoclasm vs. Art and Drama.* Eds. Clifford Davidson and Ann Eljenholm Nichols. EDAM Monograph Series 11. Kalamazoo, MI: Medieval Institute, 1989. 47-91.

---. *Lollards and Reformers: Images and Literacy in Late Medieval Religion.* London: The Hambledon Press, 1984.

Baldwin, Frances Elizabeth. *Sumptuary Legislation and Personal Regulation in England.* Baltimore: Johns Hopkins University Press, 1926.

Bates, Katherine Lee. *The English Religious Drama.* 1893. New York and London: Macmilla & Co., rpt. 1926.

Bäuml, Franz H. "Varieties and Consequences of Medieval Literacy and Illiteracy." *Speculum* 55.2 (1980): 237-265.

Beadle, Richard, ed. *The Cambridge Companion to Medieval English Theatre.* Cambridge, ENG: Cambridge University Press, 1994.

---. "Prologomena to a Literary Geography of Later Medieval Norfolk." *Regionalism in Late Medieval Manuscripts and Texts: Essays Celebrating the Publication of A Linguistic Atlas of Late Mediaeval English.* Ed. Felicity Riddy. London: D. S. Brewer, 1991. 89-108.

---. "The Scribal Problem in the Macro Manuscript." *English Language Notes* 21.4 (1984): 1-13.

Beckerman, Bernard. *Dynamics of Drama: Theory and Method of Analysis.* New York: Albert A Knopf, 1970.

Benskin, Michael and Margaret Laing. "Translations and *Mischsprachen* in Middle English Manuscripts." *So meny people longages and tonges: Philological Essays in Scots and Mediaeval English presented to Angus McIntosh.* Eds. Michael Benskin and M. L. Samuels. Edinburgh: Middle English Dialect Project, 1981. 55-106.

Bennet, H. S. *The Pastons and their England.* Cambridge, ENG: Cambridge University Press, 1951.

Bennett, Josephine W. "The Mediaeval Loveday." *Speculum* 33 (1958): 351-370.

Bergeron, David. "Medieval Drama and Tudor-Stuart Civic Pageantry." *The Journal of Medieval and Renaissance Studies* 2.2 (Fall 1972): 279-293.

Bevington, David "'Blake and wyght, fowll and fayer': Stage Picture in *Wisdom Who is Christ*." *Comparative Drama* 19.2 (1985): 136-150. Rpt. in *The Wisdom Symposium*. Ed. Milla C. Riggio. New York: AMS Press, 1986. 18-38.

---. "*Castles* in the air: the morality plays." *The Theatre of Medieval Europe*, ed. Eckehard Simon. Cambridge, ENG: Cambridge University Press, 1991. 97-116.

---. "Political Satire in the Morality *Wisdom Who is Christ*." *Renaissance Papers* (1964 for 1963): 41-51.

---. *Tudor Drama and Politics*. Cambridge, MA: Harvard University Press, 1968.

Briscoe, Marianne G. and John C. Coldewey, eds. *Contexts for Early English Drama*. Bloomington, IN: Indiana University Press, 1989.

Bristol, Michael. *Carnival and Theater: Plebeian Culture and the Structure of Authority in Renaissance England*. New York and London: Routledge, 1989.

Brown, E. Martin. "The Medieval Play Revival." *Contemporary Review* 219 (1971): 132-137.

Bynum, Caroline Walker. *Fragmentation & Redemption: Essays on Gender and the Human Body in Medieval Religion*. New York: Zone Books, 1991.

---. *Holy Feast and Holy Famine: The Religious Significance of Food to Medieval Women*. Berkeley: University of California Press, 1987.

---. *Jesus as Mother: Studies in the Spirituality of the High Middle Ages*. Berkeley: University of California Press, 1982.

Carpenter, Christine. "Law, Justice, and Landowners in Late Medieval England." *Law and History Review* 1.2 (Fall, 1983), 205-237.

Carpenter, Sarah. "Masks and Mirrors: Questions of Identity in Medieval Morality Drama." *Medieval English Theatre* 13.1 (1991): 7-17.

Carruthers, Mary. *The Book of Memory: A Study of Memory in Medieval Culture*. New York and Cambridge, ENG: Cambridge University Press, 1990.

Chambers, E. K. *English Literature at the Close of the Middle Ages*, Oxford: Clarendon Press, 1945.

---. *The Mediaeval Stage*. 2 vols. Oxford: Clarendon Press, 1903.

Chrimes, S. B., C. D. Ross and R. A. Griffiths, eds. *Fifteenth-century England 1399-1509*. Manchester: Manchester University Press and New York: Barnes and Noble, 1972.

Coldeway, John. "The Non-cycle Plays and the East Anglian Tradition." *The Cambridge Companion to Medieval English Theatre.*Ed. Richard Beadle. Cambridge, ENG: Cambridge University Press, 1994. 189-210.

Coletti, Theresa. "Reading REED: History and the Records of Early English Drama." *Literary Practice and Social Change in Britain 1380-1530.* Ed. Lee Patterson. Berkeley and Los Angeles: University of California Press, 1990. 248-284.

---. "'Ther be But Women': Gender Conflict and Gender Identity in the Middle English Innocents Plays." Martin Stevens and Milla C. Riggio, eds., *Medieval and Early Renaissance Drama: Reconsiderations* special edition of *Mediaevalia* 18 (1995 for 1993): 245-261.

Colledge, Edmund and J. C. Marler. "'Mystical' Pictures in the Suso 'Exemplar'."*Archivum Fratrum Praedicatorum* 54 (1984): 293-354.

Compston, H. F. B. "The Thirty-Seven Conclusions of the Lollards." *English Historical Review* 26 (1911): 738-749.

Craig, Hardin. *English Religious Drama of the Middle Ages*. Oxford: Clarendon Press, 1955.

Craik, T. W. "The Tudor Interlude and Later Elizabethan Drama." *Elizabethan Drama*. Ed. John Russell. Stratford-upon-Avon Studies 9. London: Brown & Bernard Harris, 1966.

Crow, Bria. "Lydgate's 1445 Pageant for Margaret of Anjou." *English Language Notes* 18.3 (March 1981): 170-174.

D'Amico, John F. *Theory and Practice in Renaissance Textual Criticism*. Berkeley and Los Angeles: University of California Press, 1988.

Davenport, W. A. *Fifteenth-Century English Drama: The Early Moral Plays and Their Literary Relations*. Cambridge, ENG: D. S. Brewer and Totowa, NJ: Rowman and Littlefield, 1982.

---, Tony. "'Lusty Fresch Galaunts.'" *Aspects of Early English Drama*. Ed. Paula Neuss. Totowa: Barnes and Noble, 1983. 111-128.

Davidson, Audrey Ekdahl, ed. *The Ordo Virtutem of Hildegard of Bingen: Critical Studies*. EDAM Monograph Series 18. Kalamazoo, MI: The Medieval Institute, 1992.

Davidson, Clifford, C. J. Gianakaris, and John Stroupe, eds. *Drama in the Middle Agies: Comparative and Critical Essays*. New York: AMS Press, 1982.

Davidson, Clifford and John Stroupe, eds. *Drama in the Middle Ages: Comparative and Critical Essays—Second Series*. New York: AMS Press, 1991.

Davidson, Clifford. *Drama and Art: An Introduction to the Use of Evidence from the Visual Arts for the Study of Early Drama*. EDAM Monograph Series 1. Kalamazoo, MI: The Medieval Institute, 1977.

---. *Visualizing the Moral Life: Medieval Iconography and the Macro Moralities*. New York: AMS Press, 1990.

Davis, Natalie Zemon. "Women on Top." *Society and Culture in Early Modern France*. Stanford, CA: Stanford University Press, 1975. Rpt in *The Reversible World: Symbolic Inversion in Art and Society*. Eds. Barbara Babcock and Victor Turner. Cambridge, ENG: Cambridge University Press, 1978. 147-90.

Davis, Norman. *The Language of the Pastons*. Proceedings of the British Academy 40. London: 1955.

Denny, Neville, ed. *Medieval Drama*. Stratford-upon-Avon Studies 16. London: Edward Arnold, 1973.

Dictionnaire de Spiritualitè ascetique et mystique, doctrine et histoire. Paris: G. Beauchesne, 1932.

Dixon, Mimi. "'Thys Body of Mary': 'Femynyte' and 'Inward Mythe' in the Digby *Mary Magdalene*." Martin Stevens and Milla Riggio, eds. *Medieval and Early Renaissance Drama: Reconsiderations*, special edition of *Mediaevalia* 18 (1995 for 1993): 221-244.

Dobson, E. J. "Early Modern Standard English." *Transactions of the Philological Society* (1955): 25-54.

---. "The Etymology and Meaning of Boy." *Medium Aevum* IX.3 (October 1940): 121-154.

Douglas, D. C. *The Social Structure of East Anglia*. London: Oxford University Press, 1927.

DuBoulay, F. R. H. *An Age of Ambition: English Society in the Late Middle Ages*. London: Thomas Nelson and Sons, 1970.

Eccles, Mark. "The Macro Plays." *Notes and Queries* 31.229.1 (March 1984): 27-29.

Elam, Keir. *The Semiotics of Theatre and Drama*. New Accents Series. London and New York: Metheun, 1980.

Elton, G. R. *The Tudor Revolution in Government*. Cambridge, ENG: Cambridge University Press, 1953.

Emmerson, Richard K., ed. *Approaches to Teaching Medieval Drama*. New York: The Modern Languages Association of America, 1990.

---. "The Morality Character as Sign: A Semiotic Approach to the *Castle of Perseverance.*" Martin Stevens and Milla C. Riggio, eds., *Medieval and Early Renaissance Drama: Reconsiderations,* special edition of *Mediaevalia* 18 (1995 for 1993): 245-61.

Fifield, Merle. "The Assault on the *Castle of Perseverance—The Tradition and the Figure.*" *Ball State Univesity Forum* 16.4 (Autumn 1975): 16-26.

---. *The Rhetoric of Free Will: The Five-action Structure of the English Morality Play.* Leeds Texts and Monographs no. 5 (Leeds, 1974).

---. "The Use of Doubling and 'Extras' in *Wisdom, Who is Christ.*" *Ball State University Forum* 6 (Autumn 1965): 65-68.

Flew, R. Newton. *The Idea of Perfection in Christian Theology.* Oxford: Oxford University Press, 1934.

Flanigan, Clifford. "Liminality, Carnival, and Social Structure: The Case of Late Medieval Biblical Drama." *Victor Turner and the Construction of Cultural Criticism.* Ed. Kathleen Ashley. Bloomington, IN: Indiana University Press, 1990. 42-63.

Florovsky, G. *Vizantiiskie otssy V-VIII.* Paris: n.p., 1933.

Forsyth, Ilene H. *The Throne of Wisdom: Wood Sculptures of the Madonna in Romanesque France.* Princeton, NJ: Princeton University Press, 1972.

Gatch, Milton McC. "Mysticism and Satire in *Wisdom.*" *Philological Quarterly* 53.1 (Jan., 1974): 342-362.

Gibson, Gail McMurray. "The Play of *Wisdom* and the Abbey of St. Edmund." *Comparative Drama.* 19.2 (1985): 117-135. Rpt. in *The Wisdom Symposium.* Ed. Milla C. Riggio. New York: AMS Press, 1986. 39-66.

---. *The Theater of Devotion.* Chicago: the University of Chicago Press, 1989.

Gierke, Otto. *Political Theories of the Middle Ages.* Trans. F. M. Maitland. Cambridge, ENG: Cambridge University Press, 1913.

Gilman, Donald. *Everyman and Company: Essays on the Theme and Structure of the European Moral Play.* New York: AMS Press, 1989.

Gombrich, E. H. *Art and Illusion: A Study in the Psychology of Pictorial Representation.* New York: Pantheon Books, 1960.

Goodwin, A. *The Abbey of St. Edmundsbury.* Oxford: Basil Blackwell, 1931.

Gellrich, Jesse M. *The Idea of the Book in the Middle Ages: Language, Theory, Mythology, and Fiction.* Ithaca: Cornell University Press, 1985.

Guéranter, Abbot *The Liturgical Year: Passiontide and Holy Week.* Trans. Laurence Shepherd. Westminster, MD: The Newman Press, 1949.

Happé, Peter. "A Guide to Criticism of Medieval English Theatre." *The Cambridge Companion to Medieval English Theatre: Origin and Early History of Modern Drama.* Cambridge, ENG: Cambridge University Press, 1994. 312-343.

---. Review of *Wisdom* production, staged by John Marshall at Winchester Cathedral, 1981. *Research Opportunities in Renaissance Drama* 24 (1981): 196-197.

Hardison, O. B., Jr. *Christian Rite and Christian Drama in the Middle Ages.* Baltimore: The Johns Hopkins University Press, 1965.

Harrington, Gary. "The Dialogism of the Digby Mystery Play." Martin Stevens and Milla C. Riggio, eds. *Medieval and Early Renaissance Drama: Reconsiderations,* special edition of *Mediaevalia* 18 (1995 for 1993): 67-80.

Harris, John Wesley. *Medieval Theatre in Context: An Introduction.* London and New York: Routledge, 1992.

Hassel, R. Chris, Jr. *Renaissance Drama and the English Church Year.* Lincoln, NEB and London: University of Nebraska Press, 1979.

Hill, Eugene. "The Trinitarian Allegory of *Wisdom.*" *Modern Philology* 73.2 (1975): 121-135.

Homo, Memento Finis: The Iconography of Just Judgment in Medieval Art and Drama. EDAM Monograph Series 6. Kalamazoo, MI: The Medieval Institute, 1985.

Holdsworth, W. S. *A History of English Law.* 12 vols. 4th ed. London: Methuen and Co., Vol. 3, 1935 and Vol. 4, 1937.

Howard, Donald. *The Three Temptations: Medieval Man in Search of the World.* Princeton: Princeton University Press, 1966.

Hozeski, Bruce. *Ordo Virtutum: Hildegard of Bingen's Liturgical Morality Play.* Unpub. diss.: Michigan State University, 1969.

Jeffrey, David. *Franciscan Spirituality and the Rise of Early English Drama. Mosaic* 8.4 (summer 1975): 17-46.

Jones, Marion. "Early Moral Plays and the Earliest Secular Drama." Eds. A. C. Cawley et al. *The Revels History of Drama in English.* Vol. 1: *Medieval Drama.* London & New York: Methuen, 1983. 263-291.

Jones, Michael K. *The King's Mother: Lady Margaret Beaufort, Countess of Richmond and Derby.* Cambridge, ENG & New York: Cambridge University Press, 1992.

Jones, Nicholas R. "Medieval Plays for Modern Audiences." *Gamut* 4 (Fall 1981): 47-58.

Johnston, Alexandra F. "The Audience of the English Moral Play." *Fifteenth Century Studies* 13.213 (1988): 291-297.

---, ed. *Editing Early English Drama, Special Problems and New Directions: Papers Given at the Nineteenth Annual Conference on Editorial Problems, University of Toronto, 4-5 Nov., 1983.* New York: AMS Press, 1987.

---. "*Wisdom* and the Records: Is there a Moral?" *The Wisdom Symposium.* Ed. Milla C. Riggio. New York: AMS Press, 1986. 87-101.

Kahrl, Stanley. *Traditions of Medieval English Drama.* London: Hutchinson's University Library, 1974.

Kelley, Michael R. *Flamboyant Drama: A Study of The Castle of Perseverance, Mankind, and Wisdom.* Carbondale and Edwardsville, ILL: Southern Illinois University Press, 1979.

Kendall, Paul Murray. *Richard the Third.* New York: W. W. Norton, 1956.

---. *The Yorkist Age: Daily Life during the Wars of the Roses.* London: George Allen & Unwin, Ltd., 1962.

Kernodle, George R. *From Art to Theatre: Form and Convention in the Renaissance.* Chicago: University of Chicago Press, 1944.

Kihlbom, Asta. *A Contribution to the Study of Fifteenth Century English.* Uppsala: A. B. Lundequistske Bokhandeln, 1926.

King, Pamela. "Morality Plays." *The Cambridge Companion to Medieval English Theatre.* Ed. Richard Beadle. Cambridge, ENG: Cambridge University Press, 1994. 240-264.

Kitzinger. Ernst. *The Art of Byzantium and the Medieval West: Selected Studies.* Ed. W. Eugene Kleinbauer. Bloomington and London: Indiana University Press, 1976.

---. "The Cult of Icons." *Dumbarton Oaks Papers.* Cambridge, MA: Harvard University Press, 1954. 83-150.

Knight, Alan. "The Condemnation of Pleasure in Late Medieval French Morality Plays." *The French Review* 57.1 (1983): 1-9.

Knowles, David. *The English Mystical Tradition.* New York: Harper, 1961.

Kobialka, Michael. "Historic Time, Mythical Time, and Mimetic Time: The Impact of the Humanistic Philosophy of St. Anselm on Early

Medieval Drama." *Medieval Perspectives* 3.1 (spring 1988): 172-190.

Kolve, V. A. *The Play Called Corpus Christi.* Stanford, CA: Stanford University Press, 1966.

Koontz, Christian. "The Duality of Styles in the Morality Play *Wisdom Who is Christ: A Classical-Rhetorical Analysis.*" *Style* 7 (1973): 251-270.

---. *A Stylistic Analysis of the Morality Play Wisdom Who is Christ.* Unpub. diss.: Catholic University of America, 1971.

---. *Hickscorner.* Manchester: Manchester University Press, 1980.

Lander, J. R. *Conflict and Stability in Fifteenth-Century England.* London: Hutchinson, 1969.

---. *Government and Community, England, 1450-1509.* Cambridge, MA: Harvard University Press, 1980.

---. *Crown and Nobility, 1450-1509.* Montreal: McGill-Queen's University Press, 1976.

Langlois, Ernest. *Recueil D'Arts de Seconde Rhétorique.* Paris, 1902. Rpt Genieva: Slatkine Reprints, 1974.

Leff, Gordon. "The Condemnation of 1277." Eds. Arthur Hyman and James J. Walsh, *Philosophy in the Middle Ages.* New York: Harper and Row, 1967.

---. *Medieval Thought: St. Augustine to Ockham.* Baltimore: Penguin Books, 1958 and London: Merlin Press, 1959.

Lobel, M. D. *The Borough of Bury St. Edmund's: A Study in the Government and Development of a Monastic Town.* Oxford: Clarendon Press, 1935.

Lockrie, Karma. *Margery Kempe and Translations of the Flesh.* Philadelphia: University of Pennsylvania Press, 1991.

Lompris, Linda and Sarah Stanbury, eds. *Feminist Approaches to the Body in Medieval Literature.* Philadelphia: University of Pennsylvania Press, 1993.

Lossky, Vladimir. *Mystical Theology of the Eastern Church.* 1957. 1968. Rpt. London: James Clarke, 1991. First published as *Essai sur la Theologie Mystique de l'Eglise d'Orient.* Paris, 1944.

Lovatt, Roger. "Henry Suso and the Medieval Mystical Tradition in England." *The Medieval Mystical Tradition in England.* Ed. Marion Glasscoe. Exeter: University of Exeter Press, 1982. 47-62.

MacKenzie, W. Roy. *The English Moralities from the Point of View of Allegory.* Boston: Ginn, 1914. Rpt. New York: Gordian, 1966.

---. "The Origin of the English Morality." *Washington University Studies*
    Series 4, vol. 2 (1915): 141-164.

Maas, Paul. *Textual Criticism*. Trans. Barbara Flower. Oxford: Clarendon
    Press, 1958.

Marshall, John. "Modern Productions of Medieval English Plays." *The
    Cambridge Companion to Medieval English Theatre*. Ed. Richard
    Beadle. Cambridge, ENG: Cambridge University Press, 1994.
    290-311.

Marx. William George. *Medieval Religious Drama in Modern Production:
    An Application of Selected Stanislavski Techniques to the
    Interpretation and Staging of Cycle and Morality Plays from the
    English Middle Ages*. Unpub. diss. Michigan State University,
    1991.

Mastriani, Ralph. *Wisdom, Who is Christ and its Relationship to the
    Medieval Sermon*. Unpub. diss. St. Louis University, 1977.

Mellinkoff, Ruth. "Judas's Red Hair and the Jews." *Journal of Jewish Art*
    9 (1982): 31-46.

---. *Outcasts: Signs of Otherness in Northern European Art of the Late
    Middle Ages*. Berkeley, CA: University of California Press, 1993.

Mertes, Kate. *The English Noble Household, 1250-1600:   Good
    Governance and Politic Rule*. Oxford and New York: Basil
    Blackwell, 1988.

Miles, Margaret. *Carnal Knowing: Female Nakedness and Religious
    Meaning in the Christian West*. Boston: Beacon Press, 1989.

---. *Image as Insight: Visual Understanding in Western Christianity and
    Secular Culture*. Boston: Beacon Press, 1985.

Mills. David. "Modern Editions of Medieval English Plays." *The Theatre of
    Medieval Europe*. Simon Eckehard. ed. Cambridge, ENG:
    Cambridge University Press, 1991. 65-79.

Molloy, J. J. *A Theological Interpretation of the Moral Play, "Wisdom, Who
    is Christ"* Washington, D.C.: The Catholic University of America
    Press, 1952.

Moorman, Charles. *Editing the Middle English Manuscript*. Jackson:
    University of Mississippi Press, 1975.

Myers, J. H. *England in the Late Middle Ages*. 1952; rpt. Middlesex:
    Pelican Books, 1966.

Neuss, Paula, ed. *Aspects of Early English Drama*. London: D. S.
    Brewer, 1983.

Orgel, Stephen. *The Illusion of Power*. Berkeley and Los Angeles:
    University of California. Press, 1975. 1-36.

---. "The Spectacles of State." *Persons in Groups: Social Behavior or Identity Formation in Medieval and Renaissance Europe.* Ed. Richard Trexler. Medieval and Renaissance Texts and Studies (MRTS) 36. Binghamton, New York: SUNY Press, 1985. 101-121.

Owst, G. R. *Preaching in Medieval England,* Cambridge, ENG: Cambridge University Press, 1926.

Ozment, Steven E. *Mysticism and Dissent: Religious Ideology and Social Protest in the Sixteenth Century.* New Haven: Yale University Press, 1973.

Parry, David. "Masks and Other Devices in *Wisdom.*" Unpublished Essay presented at the Trinity *Wisdom* Symposium, 1984.

Petroff, Elizabeth. *Medieval Women's Visionary Literature.* New York: Oxford University Press, 1986.

Petronella,Vincent. "Royal Duality and *Everyman*: Dante to Shakespeare." *Humanities Association Review* 30 (1979): 131-146.

Petti, Anthony G. *English Literary Hands from Chaucer to Dryden.* Cambridge, MA: Harvard University Press, 1977.

Pettitt, Thomas. "Tudor Interludes and the Winter's Revels." *Medieval English Theatre* 6.1 (July 1984): 16-27.

Piersall,Derek,ed. *Manuscripts and Readers in Fifteenth-Century England: The Literary Implications of Manuscript Study.* London: D. S. Brewer, 1983.

Piltch, Ziva S. "From Cosmology to Psychology: The Transformation of Acidia in the Medieval Morality Play." *Centerpoint* 1.1 (1974): 17-23.

Pollard, Graham. "The *Pecia* System in the Medieval Universities." *Medieval Scribes, Manuscripts, and Libraries: Essays Presented to N. R. Ker.* Eds. M. B. Parkes and Andrew Watson. London: Scolar Press, 1978.

Potter, Robert. "Escaping from English Literature: Dramatic Appproaches to Medieval Drama." Ed. Richard Emmerson. *Approaches to Medieval Drama.* New York: Modern Languages Association, 1990.

---. *The English Morality Play: Origins, History and Influence of a Dramatic Tradition* , London: Routledge and Kegan Paul, 1975.

---. "The *Ordo Virtutum*: Ancestor of the English Moralities?" *Comparative Drama* 20.3 (Fall 1986): 201-210.

---. "The Unity of Medieval Drama: European Contexts for Early English Dramatic Traditions." *Contexts for Early English Drama*. Eds. Marianne Briscoe and John Coldeway. Bloomington, IN: Indiana University Press, 1989.

Preston. Michael. *A Concordance to Four "Moral" Plays: The Castle of Perseverance, Wisdom, Mankind, and Everyman*. Boulder, CO: University of Colorado Press, 1975.

Prosser, Eleanor. *Drama and Religion in the English Mystery Plays: a Re-evaluation*. Stanford, CA: Stanford University Press, 1961.

Quinn, Esther C. *The Quest of Seth for the Oil of Life*. Chicago, IL: University of Chicago Press, 1962.

Raftery, M. M. "Dangerous Names: Devils and Vices in the Medieval English Drama." *Nomina Africana* 5.1 (April 1991): 45-64.

Ramsey, Robert Lee, ed. "Introduction." *Magnificence* by John Skelton. EETS. London: Kegan Paul, Trench, Trübner, and Co., 1906.

Rastell, Richard. "'Alle hefne makyth melody.'" *Aspects of Early English Drama*. Ed. Paula Neuss. London: D. S. Brewer, 1983. 1-12.

---. "Music in the Cycle Plays." *Contexts for Early English Drama*. Eds. M. Briscoe and J. Coldeway. Bloomington, IN: Indiana University Press, 1989. 192-218.

Reau, Louis. *Iconographie de l'art Chrétien*. 3 vols. Paris: Presses Universitaires de France, 1955-59. Esp. Vol. 2.

Rice, Eugene F., Jr. *The Renaissance Idea of Wisdom*. Cambridge, MA: Harvard University Press, 1958.

Riehle, Wolfgang. "English Mysticism and the Morality Play *Wisdom, Who is Christ*." *The Medieval Mystical Tradition in England*. Ed. Marion Glasscoe. Exeter: University of Exeter, 1980. 202-215.

---. *The Middle English Mystics*. London: Routledge and Kegan Paul, 1981.

Riesenberg, Peter N. *Inalienability of Sovereignty in Medieval Political Thought*. New York: Columbia University Press, 1956.

Riggio, Milla C. "The Allegory of Feudal Acquisition in *The Castle of Perseverance*." *Allegory, Myth, and Symbol*. Ed. Morton W. Bloomfield. Cambridge, MA: Harvard University Press, 1981. 187-208.

---. "Festival and Drama." *Approaches to Teaching Medieval English Drama*. Ed. Richard K. Emmerson. New York: The Modern Languages Association of America, 1990.

---. "The Staging of *Wisdom.*" *Research Opportunities in Renaissance Drama* 27 (1984): 167-177. Rpt. in *The Wisdom Symposium.* Ed. Milla C. Riggio. New York: AMS Press, 1986. 1-17.

---. "*Wisdom* Enthroned: Iconic Stage Portraits." *Comparative Drama* 23.3 (1989): 228-254.

---, ed. *The Wisdom Symposium.* New York: AMS Press, 1986.

Ringbom, Sixten. *Icon to Narrative: The Rise of the Dramatic Close-up in Fifteenth-Century Devotional Painting.* Abo [Turku, Finland]: Abo Akademi, 1965.

Roach, Joseph R. "Power's Body: The Inscription of Morality as Style." Eds. Thomas Postlethwait and Bruce A. McConachie. *Interpreting the Theatrical Past: Essays in the Historiography of Performance.* Iowa City: University of Iowa Press, 1989.

Robinson, J.W. *Studies in Fifteenth-Century Stagecraft.* EDAM Monograph Series 14. Kalamazoo, MI: The Medieval Institute, 1991.

Ross,Lawrence. "Art and the Study of Early English Drama." *Renaissance Drama* 6 (1963): 35-46.

Rossiter, Arthur Percival. *English Drama from Early Times to the Elizabethans.* London: Hutchinson's University Library, 1950.

Routh, Enid M. G. *Lady Margaret.* London: Oxford University Press, 1924.

Salet, Francis. *Le Madeleine de Vezelay* with iconographic study by Jean Adhémar. Melun: Librairie d'Argences, 1948. Esp. 122, 181-182.

Samuels, M. L. *Linguistic Evolution with Special Reference to English.* Cambridge, ENG: Cambridge University Press, 1972.

---. "Spelling and Dialect in the Late and Post-Middle English Periods." *So meny people longages and tonges: Philological Essays in Scots and Mediaeval English presented to Angus McIntosh.* Eds. Michael Benskin and M. L. Samuels. Edinburgh: Middle English Dialect Project, 1981. 43-54.

Sargent, Michael G. "James Grenehalgh as Textual Critic." Ed. James Hogg. *Analecta Cartusiana* 1 (Salzburg: 1984): 214-223.

---. "Three Notes on Middle English Poetry and Drama." *A Salzburg Miscellany: English and American Studies 1964-1984* Salzburg, Austria: University of Salzburg, 1984. 131-180.

---. "The Transmission by the English Carthusians of some Late Medieval Spiritual Writings." *The Journal of Ecclesiastical History* 27.3 (July 1976): 225-240.

---. "Walter Hilton's *Scale of Perfection*: The London Manuscript Group Reconsidered." *Medium Aevum* 52.2 (1983): 189-216.

Scally, William A. "Modern Return to Medieval Drama." *The Many Forms of Drama.* Ed. Karelisa Hartigan. Lanham, MD: University Press of America, 1985. 107-114.

Scattergood, V. J. *Politics and Poetry in the Fifteenth Century.* London: Blandford Press, 1971.

Schiller, Gertrud. *Ikonographie der christlichen Kunst.* 5 vols. Gütersloh: G. Mohn, 1966-76. The first two volumes are available in English: *Iconography of Christian Art.* Trans. Janet Seligman. Greenwich, CT: New York Graphic Society, 1971-1972. See esp. Vol. I: "Throne of Wisdom" and Vol. IV.

Schirmer, Walter F. *John Lydgate: A Study in the Culture of the XVth Century.* Trans. Ann E. Keep. Berkeley and Los Angeles, CA: University of California Press, 1961.

Schmitt, Natalie Cronn. "The Idea of a Person in Medieval Morality Plays." *Comparative Drama* 12 (1978): 23-34. Rpt. in *The Drama of the Middle Ages.* Eds. Clifford Davidson, C. J. Gianakaris, and John Stroupe. New York: Ams Press, 1982. 302-315.

Sheingorn, Pamela. "On Using Medieval Art in the Study of Medieval Drama: An Introduction to Methodology." *Research Opportunities in Renaissance Drama* 22 (1979): 101-09.

---. "The Visual Language of Drama: Principles of Composition." *Contexts of Early English Drama.* Eds. Marianne G. Briscoe and John C. Coldeway. Bloomington, IND: Indiana University Press, 1989. 173-191.

Sheingorn, Pamela and Theresa Colletti. "Playing *Wisdom* at Trinity College." *Research Opportunities in Renaissance Drama* 27 (1984): 179-184.

Sigmund, Paul E. *Nicholas of Cusa and Medieval Political Thought.* Cambridge, MA: Harvard University Press, 1956.

Simon, Eckehard. *The Theatre of Medieval Europe: New Research in Early Drama.* Cambridge, ENG: Cambridge University Press, 1991.

Sisson, Charles. "Marks as Signatures." *The Library* Fourth Series 9.1 (June 1928): 1-47.

Smart, William. *Some English and Latin Sources and Parallels for the Morality of Wisdom.* Menasha, WIS: George Banta, 1912.

Smith, Sister Mary F. *Wisdom and Personification of Wisdom Occuring in Middle English Literature before 1500.* Washington D.C.: The Catholic University of America, 1935.

Solway, Susan. "A Numismatic Source of the Madonna of Mercy." *The Art Bulletin* 67.3 (Sept. 1985): 359-368.

Spalding, Mary Caroline. *The Middle English Charters of Christ.* Baltimore: J. Furst Co., 1914. Also published as Bryn Mawr Monographs 15.

Spector, Stephen. "Paper Evidence and the Genesis of the Macro Plays." *Mediaevalia* 5 (1979): 217-232.

Spekkens, Hubert J. "Three Models of Staging the Mediaeval Play." *Fifteenth-Century Studies* 13.213 (1988): 615-619.

Spencer, Theodore. *Shakespeare and the Nature of Man.* Cambridge, ENG: Cambridge University Press, 1942; 2nd ed. New York: MacMillan, 1949.

Stevens, Martin. *Four English Mystery Cycles.* Princeton, NJ: Princeton University Press, 1987.

---. "Illusion and Reality in the Medieval Drama." *College English* 32 (1971): 448-464.

---. "Medieval Drama: Genres, Misconceptions and Approaches." *Approaches to Teaching Medieval English Drama.* Ed. Richard K. Emmerson. New York: Modern Languages Association of America, 1990. 36-49.

---. "The Performing Self in 12th Century Culture." *Viator* 9 (1978): 193-212.

---. "The Reshaping of Everyman: Hofmannsthal at Salzberg." *Germanic Review* 48 (1973): 117-131.

---. "The Theatre of the World: A Study in Medieval Dramatic Form." *The Chaucer Review* 7 (1973): 234-249.

--- and Milla C. Riggio, eds. *Medieval and Early Renaissance Drama: Reconsiderations,* special edition of *Mediaevalia* 18 (1995 for 1993).

Stone, Charles V. *Dramas of Christian Time: Temporal Assumptions and Dramatic Form in the Medieval Mystery Cycle, the Morality Play, and Shakespeare's Second Tetralogy.* Unpub. Diss. University of Minnesota, 1971.

Stone, Lawrence. *The Crisis of the Aristocracy, 1588-1641.* Oxford University Press, 1965.

Stubbs, William. "The Clergy, the King, and the Pope." *Constitutional History of England.* 5th ed. London: Oxford University Press, 1903. Vol. 3; chapter 19: 697-729.

Taylor, Jerome and Alan H. Nelson, eds. *Medieval English Drama: Essays Critical and Contextual.* Chicago: University Of Chicago Press, 1972.

Todd, James H., ed. *An Apology for Lollard Doctrines*. London: Camden
    Society Publications, 1842.
Thompson, E. Margaret. *The Carthusian Order in England*. London:
    MacMillan, 1930.
Traver, Hope. *The Four Daughters of God*. Bryn Mawr Monographs 6.
    Bryn Mawr, PA: Bryn Mawr College, 1907.
Travis, Peter. "The Social Body of the Dramatic Christ in Medieval
    England." *Early Drama to 1600*. Ed. Albert H. Tricomi. Center for
    Medieval and Early Renaissance Studies. Binghamton, New York:
    SUNY Press, 1987. 17-36.
Trinkaus, Charles and Heiko A. Oberman, eds. *The Pursuit of Holiness in
    Late Medieval and Renaissance Religion*. Leiden: E. J. Brill, 1974.
Twycross, Meg. "'Apparel Comlye.'" *Aspects of Early English
    Drama: Coventry*. Ed. Paula Neuss. Cambridge, ENG: D.S.
    Brewer, 1983. 30-49.
---. "The Theatricality of Medieval English Plays." *The Cambridge
    Companion to Medieval English Theatre*. Ed. Richard
    Beadle. Cambridge, ENG: Cambridge University Press,
    1994. 37-84.
Tydeman, William. *Medieval English Drama*. London: Routledge and
    Kegan Paul, 1986.
---. *The Theatre in the Middle Ages: Western European Stage Conditions
    c. 800-1576*. Cambridge, ENG: Cambridge University Press, 1978.
Ullman, Walter. *The Individual and Society in the Middle Ages*.
    Baltimore, MD: Johns Hopkins University Press, 1966.
Van Dyke, Carolyn. *The Fiction of Truth: Structures of Meaning in
    Narrative and Dramatic Allegory*. Ithaca, NY: Cornell University
    Press, 1985.
Visser, F. Th. *Part One: Syntactical Units with one Verb. An Historical
    Syntax of the English Language*. Leiden: E. J. Brill, 1963. 245-
    247; 270-272.
Wasson, John. "The Morality Play: Ancestor of Elizabethan Drama?"
    Comparative Drama 13 (1979): 210-221. Rpt. *The Drama in the
    Middle Ages*. Eds. Clifford Davidson, C. J. Gianakaris, and John
    Stroupe. New York: AMS Press, 1982. 316-327.
Westfall, Suzanne R. *Patrons and Performance: Early Tudor Household
    Revels*. Oxford: Clarendon Press, 1990.
Wickham, Glynne. *Early English Stages, 1300 to 1600*. 3 vols. London:
    Routledge and Kegan Paul, 1959-1981. 2nd ed. Oxford: Phaidon
    Books, 1992.

Wilken, Robert L. *Aspects of Wisdom in Judaism and Early Christianity.* Notre Dame and London: University of Notre Dame Press, 1975.

Williams, Arnold. *The Characterization of Pilate in the Towneley Plays.* East Lansing: Michigan State University Press, 1950.

---. *The Drama of Medieval England.* East Lansing: Michigan State University Press, 1961.

Williams, E. *Early Holborn and the Legal Quarter of London.* London: Sweet & Maxwell, 1927.

Winfield, Percy Henry. *The History of Conspiracy and Abuse of Legal Procedure.* Cambridge, ENG: Cambridge University Press, 1921.

Woehlk, Heinz D. *The Staging of Wisdom.* Unpub. Diss.: University of Colorado at Boulder, 1978.

Word, Picture, and Spectacle. EDAM Monograph Series 5. Kalamazoo, MI: The Medieval Institute, 1984.

Wormald, Francis "Some Popular Miniatures and their Rich Relations," *Miscellanea Pro Arte: Festschrift fur Hermann Schnitzler.* Dusseldorf: Schwann, 1965. 279-285; figure 1.

---. "The Throne of Solomon and St. Edward's Chair." *Essays in Honor of Erwin Panofsky.* Ed. Millard Meiss. De Artibus Opuscula 40. Vol. 1. New York: New York University Press, 1961.532-539.